Counseling with Confidence:
From Pre-Service to Professional Practice

Nicholas D. Young, Ph.D., Ed.D.
Christine N. Michael, Ph.D.

Published by:
The Synthesis Center Inc.
274 North Pleasant Street
Amherst, Massachusetts 01002
USA
www.synthesiscenter.org

ISBN # 978-096785705-3

Type set in Adobe® Jensen Pro on a Macintosh® computer
Technical editor/layout : Ted Slawski

Printed by:
Lightning Source Printing
www.lightningsource.com

First Printing: 12/2009

Preface

A review of national counseling board licensure requirements will con-firm that counselors are not required to take courses in their pre-service or ongoing in-service programs to prepare them for the personal and professional journey that accompanies the different career stages in the helping field. A recent survey of counseling student graduates, referenced in the final article in this book, further indicates that counselors themselves recognize the inherent struggles that accompany those early days in the field—struggles that are common and emotionally taxing and frequently correspond to periods of professional uncertainty.

Our purpose in collaborating on this book is not to highlight per se the challenges in the different counselor career junctures, but rather to provide pertinent information, as food for thought, to help guide the practitioner during those times, especially in early stages of professional practice, when it is not always clear what step to take or knowledge to consider when tackling the next obstacle to success. We recognize that no book can cover all of the details of the counseling profession; thus it was not our intent to consider all possible subjects or topics in this one. We did, however, see merit in offering insights into major issues that can serve to guide the counselor with further reflection, information gathering, or in-service development. Becoming an experienced counselor takes considerable time and effort and requires ongoing study, mentorship, and supervision, at least peer supervision, for many years. One might argue that even our most seasoned counselors are "counselors-in-training," which is a reminder that we all need to remain vigilant about staying current with advances in assessment, intervention and the human side of our profession, namely how best to connect and work with our deserving clients, throughout what we hope will be long and productive careers.

Career Stages in the Helping Profession

In order to communicate confidence in a client's ability to grow and be transformed through the therapeutic process, the counselor must possess self-confidence. This simple statement belies the fact that practitioners at all stages of their counseling careers are human beings, attempting to provide the best service possible to those for whom they advocate, while addressing their own needs, questions, and doubts. This is particularly true for novice practitioners—those entering professional practice for the first time or shifting the emphasis of their practice.

Fessler and Christensen (1992), in their work on the "teacher career cycle," describe the various challenges to teaching professionals in the early stages of their career. They begin by speaking to the needs of "pre-service" individuals, who are studying to enter a profession or a new niche within a profession. In the pre-service period, a great emphasis is placed on learning the research, theories, past schools of thought, and contemporary thinking about their field and their specific population of interest. Through formal academic study, mentoring, and field placements, the pre-service teacher absorbs a large body of information and the "tools of the trade" that will allow entrance into the actual practice. This stage, and its attendant developmental tasks, is equally applicable to the novice counselor.

Leaving pre-service, new teachers, or counselors transitions to what Fessler and Christensen term the "induction" stage. In the first few years of practice, the new professional is both socialized into the profession and simultaneously expected to function as a member. Inductees can serve with some level of confidence only when they have reached a certain degree of comfort in dealing with the day-to-day issues and stressors of their work with students or clients. Newcomers also must come to terms with the harsh necessity of reckoning with the disparity between their strongly held ideals and beliefs and the realities of actual practice. Theories and strategies from textbooks may not actually work smoothly in "real life." Questions of professional self-identity frequently rear their heads.

As new practitioners survive their first few years in the field, they will progress to the "competency-building" stage. In this stage, certain skills have been mastered well enough to allow counselors to function on a level of "automatic pilot" so that they can attend to finer details and nuances of the counseling relationship. Having established a tentative professional identity, new counselors are more comfortable leaving the textbooks behind and venturing into some initial theory building that has "goodness of fit." They can also can be more open to new, and sometimes conflicting or challenging, ways of thinking about practice. Greater self and professional confidence permits more porous boundaries, allowing practitioners to accept critique and suggestions, as well as being more comfortable with self-scrutiny and sharing with others.

How This Book is Organized

This book is a collaborative attempt to provide those moving from pre-service into actual practice, or those moving from one professional role to the other, an opportunity to hear what their colleagues have to say. It is divided into various thematic sections that address topics important to the formation of a confident counseling identity. In Section One—"Finding One's Fit"—the authors suggest ways that new practitioners can go about identifying and solidifying a professional identity that is consonant with their personal styles, beliefs, and values. This section also explores research on qualities of effective counselors.

The second section is entitled "The Nuts and Bolts of Practice" and exposes the novice to pragmatic information intended to help in considering some of the more practical aspects of the professional. Such topics as "navigating the mental health system," setting up a practice, and considering the legal and ethical intricacies of one's work form the basis for these entries.

The third section focuses on providing concrete counseling strategies and techniques that may be useful. While "An Overview of Counseling Theories and Interventions" is intended to summarize major thinking in the field, other writers hone in on specific strategies such as using group counseling or expressive arts therapy with clients.

Next, attention is given to the developmental implications of counseling. In covering issues of children, adolescents, and geriatric clients, the authors remind us of the unique needs of individuals at various stages of the life cycle. The inextricable link between counseling psychology and developmental psychology are emphasized in these writings. Further, the authors demonstrate how a working knowledge of lifespan development can increase a practitioner's confidence in dealing with a wide range of clients. While most novice practitioners enter the pre-service stage with a preference for working with certain populations and ages, in reality, it is rare the new counselors will not be required to work with a much more varied clientele.

Finally, the last section, called "Crisis and Self Care," reminds us that counselors cannot grow and thrive, let alone withstand the stresses of the helping profession, without attending to their own health and well being. Building personal and professional resilience are themes echoed in this set of essays. It is the authors' hope that the combination of these writings will bolster new counselors and encourage them to find a confident professional identity to bring to this crucial and challenging work.

Request to Counselors

We want this book to work for you. Should you have comments on this book that you wish to share to help us improve, by all means share those with us. What did you find useful? What other issues or topics do you think should be considered in future such books? What was confusing or unclear? What do you think are the biggest challenges and/or struggles for counselors at the different career stages?

Please send your reactions and suggests to Nicholas Young or Christine Michael at Union Institute & University, The Brattleboro Center, 3 University Way, Brattleboro, VT 01075. Or you may opt to email us at Nicholas.Young@myunion.edu or Christine.Michael@myunion.edu.

About the Co-Editors and Chapter Contributors

We invite you, the reader, to review the biographies of all who contributed to this book in the final section. As you will see, several highly experienced practitioners made a contribution to this book. While most are seasoned counselors, there are a few who also offered their insights from either a higher education or the legal profession perspective. All have a passion for the helping profession, recognizing that working with counselors provides a tremendous opportunity to positively impact the lives of so many clients in the years ahead.

Acknowledgements

This book is dedicated to our students, who inspire us every day. It is also a product of a collaboration with colleagues, who over the years have helped us expand our knowledge and refine our practice. Finally, it is a tribute to the mentors—academic and professional—who have helped to mold, encourage, and support us in this important work. We also wish to acknowledge and thank Didi Firman and Ted Slawski for their invaluable publishing insights, copy editing, and layout support and assistance. Together, their efforts made this project possible and manageable.

Table of Contents

Section One

The Personal in the Professional

Counselor and Character:
Essential Elements
By: Richard D. Judah, D.Ed. & Walter Stephaniv, Ph.D.

Rather than continuing to ignore the philosophical underpinnings of research and clinical work, I urge my colleagues to "return to the roots" of psychology and consider the importance of philosophical thought in understanding the complexity of psychotherapy (as well as all other aspects of human experience). Attempting to answer the good-therapy question without such reflection seems an oddly unscholarly and unpsychological way to proceed. We continue the uninformed and unreflective push toward answering this question "once and for all" at the peril of psychology and psychotherapy. (Walsh, 2004, p. 464)

Research and pedagogy of counseling for mental health is rich with information about the effectiveness of different ways of helping people change or enhance their lives. However, what appears to have received less emphasis in recent years is a focus on qualitative features that have traditionally been regarded as fundamental to the process of helping people develop and change. Perhaps the pursuit of professional excellence and reliance on operational definitions of what constitutes effective methodology has led to a myopic perspective on the nature of the profession, as well as a loss of reliance on some of the historically honored perspectives. In this regard, one observant psychiatrist has chronicled: "Explosive progress in the neurosciences and psychopharmacology during the past 25 years—and the rise of managed care during the past decade—have been accompanied by decreased access to highly qualified psychotherapists and decreased emphasis on psychotherapy during psychiatric training" (Barret, 2006, p. 117).

Another explanation may be that the things of this nature function in a wave-like fashion, and putting it most simply; some things need to be periodically reiterated, lest they be forgotten.

In discussing these "lost" or near-forgotten components of effective mental health counseling, Rheid (2007) cites conditions imposed by managed care as well as stipulations imposed by universities and professional credentialing as promoting the "manualization" or trivialization of counseling, resulting in emphatic encouragement of the kind of interactions between counselors and clients that are more technical than personal. Some might argue that this is the way it should be. Conversely, others will agree that there is often something missing in the how the process of counseling is both understood and taught.

If the above statements are to be supported, then there must be means of identifying what tends to be missing or what has been lost or forgotten in the contemporary approaches to counseling. What are the essential and elusive qualities that provide a basis for a truly helping professional relationship? The premise here is that what really makes a difference in the counseling process is not just the method but what the "messenger" contributes. This narrative is an attempt to economically identify and discuss qualitative variables that, at this point in the process of developing models of contemporary counseling, warrant reiteration and recognition.

Type of Therapy versus Type of Counselor

Efforts to measure outcomes on the basis of types of counseling to determine if one model of counseling is more effective than another present an array of results and the crux is ambiguity: No one type of counseling is obvious in terms of overall effectiveness. This is not intended to contraindicate the general findings that counseling has been established as effective for a wide range of problems in mental health and person adaptation. But, if the aggregate effect of different types of counseling is positive, and if there is no evidence to support a specific type of counseling that is generally effective, then what are the critical factors that provide for the effectiveness of counseling? The answer must be the counselor. In this vein, Krause, Lutz, and Saunders (2007) state:

> It is therapists not treatment forms that actually treat clients. Therefore, what should primarily be given preference in practice is not treatments empirically certified on the basis of their results in randomized clinical trials but psychotherapists empirically certified to practice on the basis of their results in actual practice. (p. 347)

In support of this, Schwarz (2007) states that good counseling is an interpersonal and moral endeavor requiring as much value judgment and practical thinking as it does reliance on theoretical and technical phenomenon:

> We talk a lot about types of counseling from Psychoanalysis to Cognitive Behavioral and Dialectical Behavioral and then to EMDR and about the advantages and disadvantages of each. However, one of the things I have

learned over the years of my practice is that regardless of the type of therapy that is practiced, it is the relationship between therapist and patient that is the most important ingredient towards regaining mental health. (Schwarz, 2007, ¶ 2)

Schwartz (2007) goes on to describe eight essential features that characterize a truly therapeutic counselor. These are:

+ The ability to carefully listen to what the client is presenting;
+ Capacity for conveying understanding;
+ The counselor should be able to comment and interact as well as listen;
+ Caring without emotional involvement;
+ Memory for what client presents;
+ A non-judgmental perspective/position;
+ Provides a trusting, safe environment;
+ Provides a warm and pleasant setting for the client.

These characteristics seem entirely consistent with those postulated by one of the founding fathers of counseling, Carl Rogers (1961; 1995), whose concepts of genuiness/congruence, unconditional positive regard, and empathic understanding are core elements in counseling. Even though some approaches do not consider such characteristics as either essential or necessary, their presence is more apt to enhance than hinder the quality of counseling. In other words, these features are not bound by a specific therapeutic framework or typology and can be applied effectively within the framework of any approach.

Some might argue that emphasis on such qualitative conditions renders counseling more art than science. Unfortunately, approaching counseling and mental health counseling as an art form is not apt to work well either. The nature of interpersonal interaction and the variability of human nature render this representation very risky. Buying a ticket to hear a bad musician or paying admission to view a bad painting or play is not apt to have the far-reaching consequences as paying to see a bad counselor. Regulation, control, and accountability are indeed necessary to reduce the incidence of human rights violations and incompetence in the field of mental health. One of the concerns here, however, is that emphasis on professional certification and accountability, although critically important, should not overshadow the importance of qualitative counselor attributes.

Challenges

In discussing the necessary conditions for effective counseling, Millin and Roll (1986) identify common impediments or challenges to the process of counseling. These major barriers that all counselors have to deal with include: (a) The status and character of counseling as a professional endeavor; (b) maintaining an equilibrium between thought and emotion during counseling; (c) resolving transferential rage without counterproductive counter-transference; and (d) the counselor's tendency to control or manipulate.

These impediments are not mutually exclusive. They collectively imply the importance for counselors to be individuals with ability to manage their own dynamic psychological worlds. Counseling involves a complex set of problems requiring a complex set of skills. In this regard, three principal criteria or major areas of competency should be met: (a) Proper training and credentialing; (b) Personal stability; and (c) Integrity. These are discussed below.

Credentials versus Credibility

In the second half of the twentieth century clinical psychology and counseling became popular as graduate offerings. Programs accredited by the American Psychological Association (APA) exposed students to an array of multiple and confusing approaches to counseling. According to Rodgers (2000), this anarchy gave rise to a somewhat eclectic mix of guru-led models that combined techniques such as Client Centered active listening with direct inquiry, systematic relaxation, and behavioral contracts. "Therapies ranged from the most conservative to encouragement of open marriages, LSD, and free love. And it was all called counseling" (Rodgers, 2000, ¶ 6).

Recognition for statutory regulation of the practice of counseling became more evident in the 1970s. This resulted from public pressure for conventionality and predictability as well as insurance regulations relating to third party payments. Later on managed care gave rise to the demise of the widespread idiosyncrasies and applied the final layers of constraint, consistency, and conformity to professional standards of practice relating to the interaction between the mental health counselor and client.

In the last twenty years, there has been a growing effort to "narrow the gates", so to speak, and adopt widespread procedures and mandates that assure counseling as professional endeavor. In keeping with the comments of Dr. Brian S. Canfield (2008), current President of the American Counseling Association (ACS), there was a period in history when anyone who wanted to could adopt the title "counselor" or "psychotherapist". Changes have occurred in recent years that make this no longer the case, even though, as Canfield (2008) states, "these criteria are not yet universal" (¶ 2). Also, in recent decades there is an increasing array of diversity and specialization in the area of counseling. In this regard, Canfield (2007) reports that in the past 50 years the American Counseling Association has grown from an amalgamation of four organizations to a confederation involving 19 divisions with in excess of 100,000 Licensed Professional Counselors in the Continental United States.

It seems important to emphasize that certification and credentialing provide tiers of standards and protection starting at the institutional level and culminating at the level of the individual practitioner via: (a) Certification of programs of training and education through such bodies as the American Psychological Association (APS) and Counsel for Accreditation of Counseling and Related Educational Programs (CACREP); and (b) Credentialing of the individual or practitioner, where the aspiring professional counselor must meet government regulated standards and requirements to practice counseling that are established by collaboration between state licensing boards and national bodies such as the National Board for Certified Counselors (NBCC). However, looking at the distinction between what is currently necessary and sufficient offers little in determining efficacy in counseling. In other words, what is necessary to be identified and perform as a professional counselor is not, in most cases, sufficient to ensure that counseling is either efficacious or "good". Dawes (1994) controversial position, expressed in *House of Cards: Psychology and Counseling Built on Myth*, cites evidence to suggest that neither training nor credentialing result in more efficacious outcomes in counseling. In a similar sense, Schaler (1994) writing in the *Washington Post*, astutely yet somewhat provocatively, points out: "Psychotherapists claim that licensure protects clients from bad therapists. That's fiction. The fact is that psychotherapists not their clients, are protected by licensure" (¶ 11).

Schaler (1994) goes on to state that licensing of counselors basically facilitates third party payments and is actually a violation of confidentiality. Also, licensure is no guarantee of accuracy of diagnosis and treatment. Shaler (1994) states, "The fact is that psychotherapists are not medical doctors," and mental illness," does not meet the nosological criteria for disease classification by pathologists" (¶ 13).

Comments made earlier by Friedman (1982) tend to support the points made above:

> In the arguments that seek to persuade legislatures to enact such licensure provisions, the justification is always said to be the necessity of protecting the public interest. However, the pressure on the legislature to license an occupation rarely comes from the members of the public who have been mulcted or in other ways abused by members of the occupation. On the contrary, the pressure invariably comes from members of the occupation itself. Of course, they are more aware than others of how much they exploit the customer and so perhaps they can lay claim to expert knowledge. (p. 140)

There is an interface between the training an individual receives and the individual's characteristics or attributes. These attributes can be positive and negative. While training can enhance the skill level of a potential counselor, the individual's characteristics can shape that person's eventual capacity for entering into a helping relationship. The synergy between positive characteristics and training is obvious.

However, training imposed on certain negative characteristics can have devastating effects on the potential clients of a counselor whose constitution is ill suited for functioning in a helping relationship. These negative characteristics are often associated with a predatory mentality either in a passive or active form. Active predatory behaviors often lie in the form of overt exploitation while passive ones are usually nested in less overt agendas. Nonetheless, these passive attributes can be just as harmful. Use of counseling for furthering issues of narcissistic need or pursuit of personal agendas often creates iatrogenic problems that compound the client's initial presenting problem. Often recognition of potential sources of such agendas is an important growth process reserved for individuals of character, integrity, and maturity.

It is unfortunate that the kinds of positions cited above have often been interpreted to suggest that neither training nor credentialing is necessary. Although there is some merit and logic to the position that training and credentialing do not ensure good counseling, requirements for minimal training and credentialing do serve a critical purpose of protecting consumers from persons who do not meet minimal competencies. So, even though these minimal competencies do not ensure that clients will be safe from bad counselors, there is fairly good assurance that clients will be protected from untrained and uninformed counselors.

The Character of the Counselor

In this regard, possession of a graduate degree, passing a professional examination, and licensure may be sufficient to qualify as a counselor but they are not sufficient to define a good counselor. Beyond the usual criteria, great emphasis should be on encouraging counselors and counselors-to-be to have their lives in order so that their personal problems and personal motives do not interfere with their ability to do effective counseling. Also, it seems reasonable to encourage counselors to have at least a general understanding of what it means to be a client.

The notion that having the experience of counseling is necessary for those who are training to become counselors can be traced to Freud, who said, "Every analyst ought periodically...to enter analysis once more, at intervals of, say five years, and without any feeling of shame in doing so" (Freud, 1963, pp. 267-268). Needless to say, the implication here is that counselors should undergo counseling as part of their required training.

Although the research on focusing on counseling for counselors has been somewhat of a rarity and, at times, inconclusive, much of what has been conducted is suggestive. Shapiro (1976), Kasow (1984), and Pope and Tabchnick (1994) found that the majority graduates of programs that involved counseling as part of a training in counseling reported that their experience increased self-awareness or self-knowledge, improved their skills as counselors, and allowed them to learn what it is like to be a clients and what sorts of interventions are helpful and useless. Also,

Greenberg and Staller (1981) cite Strupp's (1973) work which yields evidence that counselors who have had personal counseling are more active, cognizant and responsive to the needs of their clients.

In relation to these ideas and findings, the work of Bandura (1997), although not aimed at suggesting counseling for counselors-to-be, points out that development of certain personal characteristics consistent with personal stability, specifically self-efficacy, are likely to be as important as the development of reliable skills in determining counselor competence. Extensive work by Larson and Daniels (1998) provides very strong support for the premise that effectiveness in dealing with clients involves more than just certain behaviors or knowing what to do. Citing Bandura (1982, p. 122), Larson and Daniels (1998) state: "It involves a generative capability in which component, cognitive, social, and behavioral skills must be organized and integrated courses of action to serve innumerable purposes" (p. 179). The very important implications of the rather exhaustive work of Larson and Daniels (1998) are: Counselor Self Efficacy (CSE) is positively related to personal variables such as self-concept, self-reflective variables, self-awareness, and self-confidence. In this regard, there is a strong need for programs that provide training for counselors to adopt models for both helping counselors-to-be to develop positive Self-Efficacy (SE) as well as measure potential effectiveness of training and counselor readiness based on paradigms of counselor character.

Therapeutic Integrity

A discussion of what constitutes and encourages good counseling may fall somewhat short of its purpose without some reference to what constitutes bad counseling. In this regard, Barret (2006) seems to cover considerable ground in citing those characteristics that make for a bad counselor:

+ Hugging or repeatedly touching the client
+ Non-therapeutic contact away from the place of counseling
+ Employing or using the client as a volunteer
+ Discussing other clients
+ Disclosure of personal problems or personal details, such as sexual experience
+ Accepting or giving gifts or loans
+ Using a pet name to address the client
+ Dressing inappropriately or seductively
+ Disregarding unpaid client bills
+ Not charging or reducing fees, even when the client can afford the cost
+ Using information from counseling for personal gain
+ Counselor talking about personal problems
+ Promoting the counselor's religious belief system or a social or political cause

+ Sharing in an investment of financial venture
+ Encouraging clients to regard the counselor as a guru
+ Attributing the client's problems to a simplistic cause, like seeing most or all clients as suffering from some sort of repression related to sexual abuse
+ Engaging in sexual behavior with a client

Murphy and Steele Verme (1997) offer four sensible principles for good counseling

+ Treat the client respectfully, regardless of their gender or gender preference, marital status, ethnic group, and age.
+ Actively interact with the client by careful listening, appropriate inquiry, and response to the individual's own needs, concerns, and circumstances.
+ When providing information, give enough that the client can make informed decisions but not so much that the client is overwhelmed.
+ Tailor and personalize information by giving clients specific information they need and want and assisting them in processing that information.

Other general conditions associated with positive outcomes in counseling include:

+ The span of time between asking for and receiving counseling is related to undesirable outcome (Luborksy, 1994).
+ The counselor assumes a collaborative approach versus an authoritarian style (Bisese, 1990).
+ Encouraging the client to assume a problem-solving attitude (Luborsky, 1994; Suh, Strupp, H, & O'Malley, 1986).
+ Active engagement in experiences that help client's master problematic situations (Luborsky, 1994).
+ Collaboratively structures sessions where mutual roles are clearly identified and the client is prepared ahead of time tend to have more successful outcomes (Jessness, 2005).

Finally, in relation to counselor integrity, no narrative would be complete without reference to the importance, dissemination, and adherence to the primary guidelines that provide the foundation for professional behavior. Although the presence of these regulations cannot ensure professional integrity and appropriate counselor behavior and practices, the Code of Ethics created by the American Counseling Association (2005) and the Ethical Principles of Psychologists and Code of Conduct prepared by the American Psychology Association (2002), certainly provide a framework detailing very sensible and reasonable conditions that should apply to all professional practitioners. Even though, strict adherence to the conditions and practices inherent in these documents may not be a prime factor that determines positive outcome in a counselor-client relationship, adherence to the conditions is likely to provide significant assurance that less harm will befall that client than when these minimal requirements and conditions are not adhered to.

Counselor Training

Though much of what makes a counselor is intrinsic to that individual's personality, poor training can aggravate deficiencies in being effective in a helping relationship in an individual of good character. Good training can help identify weakness in both character and skills and provide appropriate response to remedy the deficit(s). There should be no options; effective training of counselors must rest on the solid foundation of an individual with character and integrity. Since the mid 1970's there have been dramatic strides in the endorsement and formalization of standards of training by such organizations as the Association for Counselor Education and Supervisors (ACES) and the Council for Accreditation of Counseling and Related Educational Programs (CACREP), as well as The National Board for Certified Counselors (NBCC) which have been effective in providing broad national standards that govern coursework and experience provided by Universities and Colleges. These organizations have been impressive in providing comprehensive guidelines for educating learners and providing meaningful experiences and frameworks for learning. However, it appears that national and institutional guidelines for assessing and ensuring emotional stability of the learners are minimal or non-existent. Credentialing both institutions and individuals to provide professional service is an ongoing, progressive, and non-static significant step in truly ensuring professional service and should involve accrediting bodies and institutions working cooperatively to develop standards and means for assessing and encouraging personal stability for the learner. Although this may prove a difficult and controversial endeavor, the potential outcomes may outweigh the challenge.

So, What is a Good Counselor?

At this point, it is summarily postulated that "good" counseling depends on a variety of counselor based conditions or traits that include:
- Emotional stability and credibility of the counselor
- Effective communication and interpersonal skills
- Appreciation of diversity
- Training and Education
- Integrity/Ethics

Conclusion

It is important to recognize that the traits or conditions delineated above are not mutually exclusive of one another. Ensuring these conditions should involve an ongoing effort with primary emphasis on ensuring that counselors are empirically qualified to practice and promote empirically verified treatments. The task of ensuring qualified counselors in the field is certainly not static process; it is one that requires ongoing qualitative and quantitative research, professional debate, and professional dialogue. Also, as educational models or training advanced, innovative training models using the Internet are likely to proliferate, internet based training programs can make this assessment of potential counselors more difficult in that the contact between student and trainee becomes that much further separated by distance and an intervening medium. This is apt to foster more emotional and personal anonymity. Beyond this is an even more challenging endeavor as the meaning of interpersonal communication and professional relationships are redefined by information technology giving rise to phenomenon such as the availability of counseling to diverse populations and online education as a vehicle for counselor training, and online counseling.

References

Bandura, A. 1982. Self-efficacy mechanism in human agency. *American Psychologist*, 37, 122-147.

Bandura, A. (1997). Self-efficacy: The exercise of control. New York: W. H. Freeman.

Barrett, Stephen. 2006. Mismanagement of counseling. In S. Barrett, W. London, R. Baratz, & Kroger, (2007) *Consumer health: A guide to living healthy* (pp. 117-119). Columbus, OH: McGraw-Hill.

Bisese, V. (1990). Therapist specific communication styles and patient resistance: An analogue study. *Counseling Psychology Quarterly*, 3, 2, 171 – 182.

Canfield, B. (2008). President's message: From the president—Who are we? Retrieved 02/06/2008 from American Counseling Association website on the Word Wide Web: www.counseling.org/Publications/PresidentsMessage. aspx?AGuid=07a6c3d7-21a2-4187-8857-766297880084

Dawes, R. (1994). *House of cards: Psychology and counseling built on myth.* Glencoe, IL: Free Press

Friedman, M. (1982). *Capitalism and freedom.* Chicago: University of Chicago Press.

Freud, S. (1963). Analysis terminable and interminable. In P. Rieff (Ed), *Sigmund Freud: Counseling and technique* (pp. 233-271). New York: Collier.

Greenberg, R. P. & Staller, J. (1981). Personal counseling for counselors. *American Journal of Psychiatry.* 138, 11, 1467-1471.

Jesness, B. (2005). How you can tell of psychological treatments are good (usually). Retrieived 02/28/2008 from The Core Psychology Website on the World Wide Web: http://www.cyberper.cnc.net/FAQ.html.

Joyce, A. & Piper, W. (1998). Expectancy, the therapeutic alliance, and treatment outcome in short-term individual counseling. *Journal of Counseling Practice,* 7, 236-248.

Kaslow, F. W. (1984). *Psychotherapy with psychotherapists.* New York: Haworth.

Krause, M., Lutz, W., & Saunders, S. (2007). Empirically certified treatments or counselors: The issue of separability. *Counseling: Theory, Research, Practice, Training* 44, 3, 347-353.

Larson, L. & Daniels, J. (1998). Review of the counseling self-efficacy literature. *The Counseling Psychologist.* 26, 2. 179-218.

Luborsky, L. (1994). Therapeutic alliances as predictors of psychotherapy outcomes: Factors explaining the predictive success. In O. Horvath & L. S. Greenberg (Eds). *The working alliance: Theory, research, and practice.* Hoboken, NJ: John Wiley & Sons.

Millon, L. and Roll, S. (1965). Common impediments to good counseling —or hell is other people. *Journal of Contemporary Counseling.* 16, 2, 115-120.

Murphy, E. and Steele Verme, C. (1996). Client-provider interactions in family planning services: Guidance from research and program experience. In: Technical Guidance/Competence Working Group. Recommendations for Updating Selected Practices in Contraceptive Use. Vol. 2. Chapel Hill, NC: INTRAH.

Pope, K. & Tabachnick, B. The counselor as clients. Retrieved January 19, 2008 from Articles, Research, & Resources in Psychology web site on the World Wide Web: http://www.kspope.com/therapistas/research9.php

Rheid, J. C. (2007). Dangers inherent in the trivialization of therapy. Retrieved from Blogging on good therapy on GoodTherapy.org website on World Wide Web: http://www.goodtherapy.org/custom/blog/?s=.++Dangers+inherent+in+the+trivialization+of+therapy.

Rogers, C. (1961). *On becoming a person.* Boston: Houghton Mifflin.

Rogers, C. & Kramer, P. (1995). *On becoming a person: A counselor's view of counseling.* New York: University of Chicago Press.

Rodgers, D. A. (2000). A view of counseling in the last half century. *The National Psychologist,* 9, 1. Retrieved March 12, 2008 from http://www.national-psychologist.com/articles/art_v9n1_1.htm.

Schaler, J. (1995, August 2). Good therapy. *Washington Post,* p. nval.

Schwartz, A. (2007). Home again, what makes for good counseling? Retrieved January 18, 2008, from MentalHelp.net. Website: http://www.mentalhelp.net/poc/view_doc.php?type=weblog&id=235&wlid=5&cn=145.

Shapiro, D. (1976). The analyst's own analysis. *Journal of the American Psychoanalytic Association,* 24, 5-42.

Strupp, H. (1973). The therapist's performance, A: Psychiatrists in psycho-therapy. In H. Strupp (Ed.), *Clinical research and theoretical issues* (pp. 541-543). New York: Jason Aronson.

Suh, C., Strupp, H., & O'Malley, S. (1986). The Vanderbilt Process Measures: The Psychotherapy Process Scale (VPPS) and the Negative Indicators Scale. In L. Greenbert & W. Pinsof (Eds.), *The psychotherapeutic process: A research handbook* (285-323). New York: Guilford.

Walsh, R. (2004). What is good psychotherapy. *Journal of Humanistic Psychology,* 44, 4, 455-467.

Stepping up:
Strategies for the New Counselor
By: Dorothy Firman, Ed.D.

Coming to the field of counseling is a process of evolution based in an individual's own experience of purpose, meaning and values. It is not a field people enter to become rich or famous. It is not a field they enter for an easy way to get by. The human services are filled with people who want to help. A career choice to work so closely with other people is inevitably guided by an inner calling for deep and meaningful work. However, by the time a counselor has finished college, graduate school, internships, licensure tests and getting a job, the connection to "why" may have become lost. The "how" may exact a high toll that sets the new counselor on an early career path disconnected from that which is most important to the quality of work and well being as a helping professional. The early days in the field are the ground upon which each counselor builds a professional identity. When consciousness is brought to bear in creating a new identity (in any endeavor) that identity will likely be a closer reflection of what is deeply true for that person. A good actor is not just a skilled technician. A good parent is not one who has read all the books. A good counselor is not just one who has been well trained. One of the gifts of the profession of counseling is that it is, in fact, an invitation for the counselor to be true to his or her own values and beliefs. In fact, the invitation is even more expansive, as being a counselor really does offer the practitioner a place to be authentic, to be the person s/he is, to do work that is a fit, both at the level of skill and training and at the level of purpose, meaning and values. Counseling can, and in the right circumstances is, a path of right livelihood.

Remembering Why

As the dust settles from years of training, and even during those years, the counselor (or counselor to be) is constantly choosing. Given training in myriad theories of psychology and styles of counseling, some will appeal more than others. How does one become a Rogerian, another a psychodynamic counselor, and others advocates of as many theories as exist, and then some? Why does one person end up specializing in work with children, another does animal-assisted therapy, a third works with the expressive arts? Straight out of graduate school, the counselor may have strong leanings and plans for continued training or the new counselor may come out well rounded, but without a strong sense of identity. In these early years of training and beginning work, it is important to ask (and begin to answer) the questions that will help define a unique and appropriate professional identity. The building of a new identity, like any building, requires a blue print of sorts.

A first consideration will wisely be a reconnection to purpose. Sometimes it is a well-known connection. It is not infrequent that a counselor can remember, back as far as childhood, the threads that moved him or her towards this field. It may be a thread traced back to one's own experience of being helped in counseling. For some, it is more casual, that natural unfolding of things such that one ends up in this place rather than another. For many, it is a second career, a conscious choice to find work that has more meaning and is a better fit. Checking in for that connection is worth doing as a beginner and often, along the way of maturation in the field.

It is an easy exercise to trace the *counseling inclination*, if you will, to the affairs of childhood. Were you the child who talked to everyone? The one who wondered about the world? The rescuer of small animals? Did you notice kids in need? Chafe at perceived unfair treatment? Were you the puzzle solver? The thinker? The one who got hurt yourself? There's no formula, of course, but it is worth taking the time to find out a bit about how you got where you are today. Think back to books you loved, heroes you had, games you played. What was the role you played in the family, in the school community, with grandparents, siblings, friends? Where, in your young life, did you experience resonance, that sense that we all have from time to time, of being meaningfully connected—to what you are doing, to the environment, to yourself, to another person?

Purpose, meaning and values define a life, not as predictable outcomes (Frankl, 1959; May, 1975; Assagioli, 2000), but as woven threads of unique ways of knowing, threads that begin young, and continue to be woven throughout life: A tapestry, that, at its best, is a deep reflection of the call of Self.

>...The deeper invitations of Self are potential to every person at all times. ...this deeper direction may be assumed to be present implicitly in every moment of every day, and in every phase of life, even when we do not recognize this. Whether within our private inner life of feelings and thoughts or within our relationships with other people and the wider world, the call of Self may be discerned and answered. (Firman & Gila, 2002, p.39)

To help connect to the purpose that has moved you to become a counselor, you might just ask:

+ What attracted me to counseling in the first place?
+ What is the meaning it has for me?
+ What is my vision for myself as a Counselor?

The answer to these questions assures a deep will alignment as the new counselor steps into a professional identity that will be both difficult and rewarding. There is nothing more crucial than staying connected to purpose. From this source derives our very will to be the best we can be. "The chief characteristic of the volitional act is the existence of a *purpose* to be achieved; the clear vision of an aim, or goal, to be reached" (Assagioli, 1973, p.138). In the early stages of training, the purpose is to gain the skills to fill up the toolkit that will be with us throughout our careers. But by the time we sit face to face with another human being, the purpose will have changed. We will be there to help, to serve, to offer support, to challenge, to care. We will also be there to have a profession, to earn a paycheck, to be a contributing member of our society. But really each purpose will be different.

As these answers connect the counselor to a sense of purpose, they will strengthen the move into an identity that is new in form, but feels like home, because in fact, the new professional identity will be a set of clothes that fits you perfectly. After all you've been shopping for quite awhile.

Challenges to Staying Connected

Staying connected to deeper meaning and purpose while stepping into the counselor role, into that new set of clothes, invites the counselor to know him or herself—in a profound way. Gaining those skills and training and filling that toolkit defined purpose earlier, but is now replaced by a purpose that includes being present, being there, being authentic. And yet that simple purpose, which really asks only that we know who we are, is much harder to achieve than one would wish.

> In the process called growing up, most of us have been taught to forget this innate presence. The remembering of such an inner radiance is radical. Establishing contact with such aliveness will do nothing less than turn our lives inside out. (Santorelli, 1999, p. 14)

The risk is that we buy the clothes that don't fit, whether that happens under duress in a job, in internships, in training or whether it happened long ago, in family and culture. Santorelli's "innate presence" in childhood is clothed, early on, in what has been called a survival personality (Firman & Gila, 1997). Language and concepts that describe early wounding in the family of origin are as vast as the theories that make up the field of psychology, but it is clear, from almost any theoretical orientation, that the early years condition us, for better and for worse. Conditioning, as defined by the American Psychological Association is "The process by which certain kinds of experience make particular actions more or less likely" (APA, p 214). The work each counselor needs to do is about peeling away any conditioning that limits the ability to be true to oneself. Conditioning that makes authenticity less likely needs to be challenged. Conditioning that makes defensiveness more likely needs to be challenged. And the list goes on. For in the conditioning of the child, everything limiting or wounding in the family, the peer group, the educational system and the culture will potentially bury some of what it really means to be me...or you.

Subpersonality theory (Brown, 2004; Firman, in Young & Michael (eds), 2007; Rowan, 1990) among others, elaborates the ways each individual splits, creating an inner world of partial selves conditioned by our environment. The ways we learn to be, the messages we get, the subpersonalities and scripts (James & Jongeward, 1976) that are created in childhood are unconsciously invited to live in our heads forever. The loudest and most limiting of these typically come from our family of origin, the place we first split, the place we first took in an internalized "critical parent" voice (James & Jongeward). This is work we will do with our clients. No one comes away from a life of conditioning with out this cast of characters, noted most frequently by the never reticent inner judge or critical parent or top dog (Passons, 1975) and the oft-wounded inner child. "Our varying models of the universe color our perception and influence our way of being. And for each of them we develop a corresponding self-image and set of body postures and gestures, feelings, behaviors, words, habits and beliefs" (Ferrucci, 1982 p. 47).

Everyone has different ways of being—some that serve, some that don't. In many ways, the counselor sits in the same condition that the client does—part unique self, part conditioned by-product of a life. Building a new identity requires some work.

Our own unique inner saboteurs, well known to us, may rear up to throw us just when we need to step fully into this new identity. Any shifting identification is met with pulls from old ways of knowing, old defensive structures, old beliefs. Once a person has created safety in any identity, moving to a larger or different identity will create at least some threat to the system. "As human beings, we seek homeostasis. We like things to remain the same. There is an element of survivability and safety in keeping things as they are." (Belair, 2005, pp. 15-16) Normal developmental processes are at work. A child does not become an adolescent overnight...or with ease. A student does not step into a professional identity, whatever it is, with any less difficulty.

How does one optimize that move from student to professional? Good training, skilled teachers and mentors, successful internships and getting a job all help! Many people have those things as they step into the work world. Most people have some of those things, but not all. And yet even with that, the inner voices that may have plagued the student, the intern, even the child, adolescent and adult, will still be there to offer a challenge. These voices will become blocks to a healthy professional identity.

> Blocking beliefs are the thoughts, sometimes conscious, sometimes not, that stop us before we get started. They're the mental naysayers that hinder our momentum in making changes. (Seixas, 2006, p. 41)

We come to the field with a call, a longing, a belief, a fair amount of faith and a lot of not knowing. Each positive experience helps us build an identity that is stronger and more comfortable. Each setback feeds our own voices of doubt. "Can I do this?" "Am I good enough?" "Will I hurt someone when I want to help them?" These "mental naysayers" are blocks to developing a strong and authentic professional identity, a deep sense of "I". Thus, they need to be challenged, understood and healed. And at the same time, the deeper knowing of who we are needs to be freed from the grasp of those limiting subpersonalities.

> In my experience as a psychotherapist I am frequently witness to the way in which the "I" is subsumed or *usurped* by the *sub*-personalities it is its function to experience, observe, direct, and guide. This usurpation in effect disables the most basic activity of the "I" and may even serve to clarify what many consider Freud's most lasting insight: namely that those who do not analyze their self-experience are destined to *enact (repeat) what happened to them.* (Klugman, 2007, p 173)

It is a mandate to counselors to do the work that they will ask their clients to do. It is the work of self-discovery. In claiming the right and the deep need to know ourselves, in this professional identity, we must face our own limiting conditions, blocking beliefs, old messages and personal demons. In the end, what we don't want is for the inner judge and scared child to be running the show: not in our personal lives and not in our professional lives. But be sure that the pull of this dynamic is strong. Even the seasoned veteran will come away from work on a bad day, full of the voice of self-criticism. And surprise of surprises, that voice will be very much the same as it was when that now-adult counselor was a young child. And on another, not so good day, that mature individual, well trained, highly acclaimed, grey hair and all, will *feel* like a child. This is to be expected and we would set ourselves up for a fall if we thought otherwise. What will serve us throughout our career, though, is having such a strong professional identity (Kottler, 1987; 2004), anchored into the best of who we are, that it is *this* self that shows up for work, sees clients, gets supervision and monitors the shenanigans of our old, deeply embedded, still wounded subs.

The good counselor has plenty of bad days and hears old inner voices, feels young inner feelings, and visits self-doubt regularly. The danger (and it is dangerous for both counselor and client) is that these experiences are unconscious, unmonitored, taken as the whole truth, repressed or projected or otherwise included in dysfunctional and dangerous ways: Thus the importance of creating, early on, that professional identity whose foundation is built on purpose, meaning, values, skills, unique attributes of the counselor-to-be and a deep sense of Self that is more than our conditioning.

+ What are the limiting beliefs that hinder me professionally?
+ What subpersonality steps in when there are challenges in the work?
+ Am I still trying to be something to someone from my past?
+ Who am I beyond any limiting conditioning from my life?

As you work to uncover the wounds and reclaim the essence of who you are, you will be able to build a professional identity that is truthful, authentic and unique to you. And you will become, then, an honest and available model for your clients.

Finding Self

More than half a century ago, Abraham Maslow (1968) brought the field of counseling to a new consideration of what human beings are, essentially. The work of humanistic and transpersonal psychology paved the way for seeing humans beyond conditioning. The very basics that most counselors so often take for granted, now, about those that sit facing them, are basics that tell us about ourselves, as people and as professionals. Maslow's advice about human nature bears repeating.

Among other things, he mentions that human nature, "inner nature," is either good or neutral, but not bad. And thus his advice is to bring out that inner nature and encourage it to grow. "If this essential core of the person is denied or suppressed he [sic] gets sick, sometimes in obvious ways, sometimes in subtle ways, sometimes immediately, sometimes later" (p.4). Inner nature, though, as Maslow points out, is not a strong instinct. It is "delicate and subtle and easily overcome by habit, cultural pressure, and wrong attitudes towards it." (p. 4).

Inner nature, essential core, innate presence, self, I, center are among the many phrases used to describe the *who* that each of us is, before or beyond or in spite of our conditioning. And it is our job to bring it out, nurture it and finally become it. Become our Selves.

Without trying to answer the biggest questions about these lofty ideas, it is clear enough that we can become more authentic people and professionals through our own work and through our own commitment to being true to ourselves. Another early voice in the field, Moustakis (1956), offers a broad description of this process of becoming self. "True being is self and other, individual and universal, personal and cultural. It cannot be understood by comparison, evaluation, diagnosis, or analysis." (p. 4)

What then are we looking for? In a very simple way we are always looking and listening for cues, insights, felt-senses and intuitions to guide us. In the theory of psychosynthesis (Assagioli, 2000) this is referred to as an internal unifying center: That is the experience of self that is steady and timeless, around which we can build or refine our personalities, make choices, honor values and move in the world through deeper relationship to who we are. More simply stated we are talking about the who that I am. This sense of *I* is a balance of how we have always known ourselves, what makes each of us unique, the still calm center that we sometimes find inside and the ways we are part of a larger whole.

> *The self can also be defined as the only part of us which remains forever the same.* It is the sameness which, once found and fully experienced, acts as an ever-present pivot point for the rest of the personality, an inner stronghold to which we can always refer in order to regain a sense of poise and self-consistency. Then we can see that self remains the same in ecstasy and despair, in peace and turmoil, in pain and pleasure, in victory and defeat. (Ferrucci, 1982 p. 61)

The fields of psychology, philosophy, and religion are full of thoughts and theories about this concept. Definitions are not, in the end, needed. People who are self-reflective will know, intrinsically, when they are operating from center, being true to themselves, and living authentically. They will know when they are not. Anchoring back into that knowing of self will stand the counselor in good stead, for the journey is not easy. It will take us through all of the feelings that humans can have. It will feed every old wound that we have. It will make us feel great and lousy. And yet, if we are not at the mercy of every passing experience, but know ourselves in that "inner stronghold" we will not be tossed about on the waves so easily.

It is assumed that counselors will be self-reflective and so this work is a given as we train in, step into and live through the field we have chosen to be in.

+ Who am I?
+ How do I know my own inner nature?
+ How will I support myself in being true to myself?

A seasoned counselor offers us a frame of reference for the asking of these questions.

> Perhaps the notion of *becoming*, then, is a better road to walk; that is, instead of seeking a static, formulaic answer to the puzzle of "Who Am I?" we might view the questions as demanding more of us than that. Certainly it is closer to our experience that being a person is a *process* of some sort, regardless of how we respond to the anxiety that this process involves us in from time to time. (Klugman, 2007, pp 163-4)

And anxiety is inevitable. How we respond to it and other tumultuous experiences is the key. And how we know ourselves will give us the stance from which to encounter everything that comes our way.

No one does well as a round peg in a square hole, but unless we know a fair amount about who we are, we will truly not know where we fit. It is a worthwhile reminder for the beginning counselor that the work will unfold more seamlessly if it is work that is right for you. And you will better know what work is right for you, when you know more about who you are. A professional identity can be bought off the rack at your first job. It will look, more or less, like everyone else's who works in that agency. If you're not careful the identity you assume will look like a favorite teacher's or an old role model's, though it won't fit you nearly as well as it fitted them. You want a designer outfit. It will be made just for you. And it will fit perfectly. This new identity will just be you, dressed for work.

The Unique Counselor

> Professional identity formation and development are individual maturation processes that begin during one's training for the profession, evolve during entry into the profession, and continue to develop as the practitioner identifies with the profession. These processes can be viewed as the experiences that help the practitioner wed theory with reality in the direction of greater flexibility and openness. (Brott &Kajs, para.7)

In order to move towards an identification that is a good fit, the beginning counselor will need to know a lot about him or herself. Doing some work on meaning and purpose and checking into those old, family-of-origin issues that are the bread and butter of our field begin this process in a healthy fashion. At the same time, the new counselor will want to assess personal realities.

+ What's in that toolkit that I have?
+ What styles, skills, strategies am I really comfortable with?
+ What am I missing?
+ What do I deeply believe that is important to my work?
+ Where do I want to head now that I'm in the field?

Staying in touch with one's strengths and weaknesses, preferences, skills, and best practices is a lifelong task. This is a good thing and allows the new counselor to enter the field fully equipped to work with the people who come to the door. Not only training, but personality and style, have some bearing on who each of us can and should work with and how we will work. New counselors will be more ready to work with that first round of people who come into the office if they have taken stock. If I have easily available qualities of humor and compassion, then I will have solid strengths to start out with. If I am uncomfortable with certain techniques I've been taught, I will be in better shape, knowing this and taking it easy as I start out. If I have sensitivities or my own wounding, preferences or judgments, I want to know them. The more I know, the more I can choose, appropriately, how to work with each person who comes to me. Our first clients are our rite of passage, and even now, looking back thirty years, I can remember them fondly and with appreciation for how I worked with them, as new as I was to the field. At the same time, any counselor who has been in the field is likely to look back on his or her early days with a note of wonder, asking: "How did I do that?" Of course, each helping professional will learn more, become more skilled, be more comfortable and ultimately find more and more out about the field and about his or her own uniqueness in the field, as the years progress. But one doesn't wait for yet more training, more books read, more theories understood, to step up and do the work.

> …learning the art of helping is a journey. It is described as a journey with a beginning but no real endpoint. Those who embark on this course find it to be a lifelong process of discovery rather than a destination. (Young, 2001, p. v)

Walking in to that first day on the job and every one of those early days in the early years is an opportunity to anchor into the strengths and gifts that are immediately available. And first and foremost is the gift of Self. Young notes: "A client will have a relationship with you, not a set of skills." (Young, 2001, p.18). What an essential reminder this is. As you come forth into the field, you are the helper. You are not a set of theories or skills. These will be in your toolkit and they will serve you well. But also in that toolkit will be a lifetime of experience in the world, your own struggles and hard won successes and the very core of your purpose for being in the helping professions, however you may know that. And **you** will be the helper sitting in the seat opposite your client. Whoever you are, with strengths and weaknesses alike, is who will be in the chair. And that is a great start.

"Genuine helpers are non-defensive. They know their own strengths and deficits and are presumably trying to live mature, meaningful lives" (Egan, 1998, p. 50). Being in this field is part of the meaningful life you are carving out for yourself. Training, study, self-reflection and on-going work are the tools that mature people use to be good at what they do. This is what stepping up as a counselor is all about. And each counselor is unique. For this we can be grateful. As every client is unique and should be seen that way, so are we.

To honor that which is unique about you promises the ability to be genuine, to show up with skills and authenticity and to be that counselor who knows how to do this work over many years, without illusion or pretense, knowing the ups and downs and coming to work, with all of who you are.

There is not a right set of skills or theories. There is no assumption that counselors need to be a certain way. We all know the guidelines, ethical mandates, legal requirements and basic training that are the foundation of our work. Beyond those, it's just a single person, bringing whatever he or she has to offer, in service of a personal, meaningful and clear purpose to help other human beings. The authenticity that you bring to bear on your work will make all the difference in the world…to you, to your clients, to your family and community and to the field itself. You are the counselor.

Bouncing Back

"It was difficult to embrace a professional identity that had been in place only 48 hours. I reacted with an acute bout of indigestion" (Bender & Messner, 2003, p. 9).

No matter how well we build a professional identity, it will be challenged, both in the beginning of our careers and from time to time throughout. Early on the voices of doubt will make every minor challenge into a big deal and counselors who are paying attention will notice how often they stretch too far to accommodate a client or hold boundaries too tightly in order to feel "professional" or stick too closely to the rules in order to be safe or some such unconscious strategy to help transition into this new world. That's all fine. Having some safety mechanisms, some healthy defense structures in place is a good idea. What we want, though, is not to get stuck in rigid roles or ideas about who we should be. And in that opening to more authentic ways of being, defenses are lessened. That's good and bad news. Truly authentic people—open, caring people—are relatively undefended. This allows deeper empathy, clearer access to intuition and the profound possibility of the I-Thou relationship. The bad news is that letting go of defensiveness creates vulnerability in ways that may leave us open to wounding. Tough choice. But the really good news is that over time and with practice, in life and in the profession, each of us can become both more "defenseless" and "safer". True safety lies not in a good shield, but in an openness that needs no defense. And then, from this ideal model of a place we'd like to be, comes the invitation to let it be okay to make mistakes. Because, okay or not, we will.

> Everyone makes mistakes. No matter how "together" we are, how "with it," how well-prepared for any particular moment, at times we all stumble, blunder, unwillingly expose our uncertainties, imperfections, and shortcomings. There are times for all of us when, unpleasantly taken by surprise, we are exposed as momentarily unable to cope. All it takes to feel overwhelmed is a situation that has become too much to handle. It is then that we feel helplessly foolish and embarrassed. If we have been exposed to excessive shaming as children, we may also experience the needless pain of feeling deeply ashamed. At such moments, it is hard to remember that this happens to everyone, that the awful sense of ineptness and confusion will soon pass. Most of us do not understand how to go about making new space for ourselves. We can be needlessly hard on ourselves, slower to forgive than we would be with another. (Kopp, 1976, p. vii)

The new counselor need only pay attention to the title of the book quoted above to take heart in the face of the inevitable falls that will be encountered on the journey of being a counselor: *The Naked Therapist: A Canterbury Tales Collection of Embarrassing Moments from More than a Dozen Eminent Psychotherapists!*

Bouncing back is a skill to be learned and one that will be strengthened by the very nature of our professional identity. If the counselor defines him or herself with the undertones of childhood wounding, unrealistic cultural expectations or any other perfectionist, "should" based, defensively-driven mandates, that counselor will fall harder and bounce back less easily than the one whose professional identity is defined from within a deeper core truth and a lot of self-understanding. The less-defended counselor will bounce back more easily, knowing, both cognitively and emotionally, that to be human is perfectly acceptable. It is one of the gifts of this field. Our very humanness, in its very real imperfection, is part and parcel of who we *should* be. Or else how could we ever relate to the other in front of us?

There are some guidelines to help. Note the risk for the beginner of being performance driven or, even more basically, of thinking that there is a right way (and then of course a wrong way) to do counseling.

> The first stage is the dualistic or absolutist position that can also be called the "right/wrong" stage. It is characterized by the belief that a helper's responses to a client are either right or wrong. …This black/white, success/failure way of thinking increases internal pressure and makes the helpers overly concerned with their own performance. (Young, 2001, p. 6)

Of course there are some basic rights and wrongs but these aren't the ones that are likely to trip us up. What will trip us up are the things that already lurk inside as doubts and fears, old messages, too high expectations and the like. Better to go in knowing you will trip…and fall…and get up again. We all do.

> No matter how much craft a therapist learns, he is lost if he suppresses his power to feel ruffled, distressed, helpless, or to feel exhilarated, or even loved by a patient. The ability to react internally and at the same time to control outward behavior, is a requisite for the therapist; the good therapist has reason to be proud of his ability to feel and to know what he's feeling. (Weinberg, 1996, p. 4)

This is the key. We will have many experiences, some good, some bad. So much will transpire in our offices. Some of it will help another human being. Some of it will not. But we will live in this world and feel the feelings that are in us and some of those that come at us. Our job is to be aware and to know how to behave. That's why we have done our own personal work. That's why we've been well trained in the profession. We'll get mad, but will likely never scream. We'll get sad and we'll have to choose whether to let our sadness show. We'll get scared and we'll keep right on working.

+ What's likely to trip me up?
+ What do I know that will help me bounce back?
+ Am I willing to be human?

Going Forward

The U.S. Department of Labor tells us that counseling jobs are increasing every year with an expectation that the number of jobs for counselors will rise by 30% over the next few years. Counselors were employed in approximately 635,000 jobs in 2006. (Occupational Outlook Handbook, 2008) The field is open and continues to grow. New counselors will carry the field forward and will become the wise elders of the future. There is opportunity and responsibility in this role.

When we know ourselves deeply, even as we step into new and unknown worlds, we step in on solid footing. Any illusion we have that we will know enough, have the answers, solve the problems, cure the client, will drag us down. Knowing who we are and why we are doing this work, will enter us into a powerful world of transformation and of mystery.

One of our oldest and wisest voices in the field, James Bugental (1985), reminds us of this. He invites us *To Seek a Wild God.*

> The wild god is the god of mystery. And mystery is a word too seldom found in psychological writing or psychotherapeutic discourses. We deny mystery; we pretend it exists only in the minds of children, authors, and mystics. And we fool ourselves and blind ourselves when we do so. Mystery enfolds knowledge, contains knowledge. Mystery is infinite, knowledge finite. As knowledge grows, mystery grows even more. Mystery is the latent meaning always awaiting our discovery and always more than our knowing. (p.273)

Welcome to the new professional identity that you are claiming. It is a gift, a challenge, a responsibility, and a long learning curve. It is your home away from home, your job, your calling. It is a mystery and it is a chance to be alive and to live in your own deep truth.

References
American Psychological Association. (2007). *APA dictionary of psychology.* Washington,DC: Author.

Assagioli, R. (1973). *The act of will.* NY: The Viking Press.

Assagioli, R. (2000). *Psychosynthesis: A collection of basic writings.* Amherst, MA: The Synthesis Center Press.

Belair, L. (2005). *Walk on water: How to make change easier.* VT: Change Agent Press.

Bender, S & Messner, E. (2003). *Becoming a therapist: What do I say, and why?* NY: The Guilford Press. Brott, P & Kajs, L. (ND) *Developing the professional identity of first-year teachers through a working alliance.* retrieved Feb. 20 from www.alt-teachercert.org/Working%20Alliance.html.

Brown, M. (2004). *Unfolding Self: The practice of psychosynthesis.* NY: Helios Press.

Bugental, J. (1987). *The Art of the Psychotherapist.* NY: WW Norton & Co.

Egan, G. (1998) *The skilled helper: A problem management approach to helping.* Pacific Grove, CA: Brooks/Cole Publishing Co.

Ferrucci, P. (1982). *What we may be: Techniques for psychological and spiritual growth through psychosynthesis.* Putnam: NY

Firman, D. (2007). A transpersonal orientation: Psychosynthesis in the counselor's office. In N.Young & C. Michael (eds.) *Counseling in a complex society: Contemporary challenges to professional practice.* Amherst, MA: The Synthesis Center Press.

Firman, J & Gila, A. (1997). *The Primal Wound: A transpersonal approach to trauma, addiction and growth.* NY: SUNY Press.

Firman, J & Gila, A. (2002). *Psychosynthesis: A psychology of the spirit.* NY: SUNY Press.

Frankl, V. (1959). *Man's search for meaning: An introduction to Logotherapy.* NY: Washington Square Press.

James, M. & Jongeward, D. (1976). *Born to win: Transactional analysis with gestalt exercises.* Reading, A: Addison-Wesley Publishing Company.

Klugman, D. (2007). *The feeling life: Reclaiming your emotional vitality and purpose.* NY: Feeling First Publications.

Kopp, S. (1976). *The naked therapist: A Canterbury Tales collection of embarrassing moments from more than a dozen eminent psychotherapists.* San Diego, CA: EdITS Publishers

Kottler, J. (1987). *On being a therapist.* San Francisco: Jossey-Bass Publishers.

Kottler, J. (2004). *Introduction to therapeutic counseling: Voices from the field.* CA: Brooks/Cole-Thomson Learning.

Maslow, A. (1968). *Toward a psychology pf being.* NY: Van Nostrand Reinhold Company.

May, R. (1953). *Man's search for himself.* NY: Dell Publishing Company.

Moustakas, C. ed. (1956). *The self: Explorations in personal growth.* San Francisco: Harper & Row.

Occupational Outlook Handbook. (2008). Retrieved Feb. 10, 2008 from http://www.bls.gov/oco/ocos067.htm.

Passons, W. (1975). *Gestalt approaches in counseling.* NY: Holt, Rinehart and Winston.

Rowan, J. (1990). *Subpersonalities: The people inside us.* NY: Routledge

Santorelli, S. (1999) *Heal thyself: Lessons on mindfulness in medicine.* NY: Random House.

Seixas, A. (2006) *Finding the Deep River Within: A Woman's guide to recovering meaning and balance in everyday life.* CA: Jossey-Bass.

Weinberg, G. (1996). *The heart of psychotherapy.* NY: St. Martin's Griffin

Young, M. (2001) *Learning the art of helping: Building blocks and techniques.* 2nd ed.Upper Saddle River, NJ: Merrill Prentice Hall.

Temperament, Personality and Goodness of Fit in the Counseling Relationship
By: Emily Davis, Psy.D.

One of the primary functions of a professional counselor is to get to know the unique essence of who each client is and how he/she operates in the world—to know the client's "personality." Seeking this knowledge, the counselor approaches and engages the client in a therapeutic process within the consultation room which the client internalizes, is transformed by, and carries within him or herself to interactions with the "outside" world. Client retention is perhaps the first sign of a successful approach by the counselor; the client moves through any immediate resistance to the therapeutic alliance to engage in an ongoing process. Beyond initial retention is the active treatment phase, during which the counselor applies therapeutic strategies to precipitate positive growth and change.

Researchers have derived effective techniques from decades of research on effective therapist characteristics and style, while less attention has been given to qualitative factors influencing the *goodness of fit* between counselor and client. Contemporary professional counseling, by the postmodern assumption of inter-subjectivity, assumes that both the counselor and the client approach the therapeutic engagement with a complex historical repertoire of values, thoughts, feelings, assumptions, and beliefs. These respective contributions traditionally belong to the realm of transference/countertransference phenomena, but that venue is limiting in that it can foster the pathologizing of individual differences related to normal temperament or personality type. If the counselor does not carefully attune him or herself to these characteristics, the asynchrony between two different drummers may be misunderstood and an opportunity for meaningful therapeutic exchange may be missed.

Researchers have derived various systems for categorizing individuals that are helpful to understanding the temperamental and personality characteristics the client brings to the treatment setting. As "taxonomies are very useful tools in explaining and predicting given phenomena" (Strelau, 1998, p. 57), they appeal to the student of human psychology and behavior—the professional counselor.

Therapist Qualities of Style

More than a decade ago, Lazarus (1993) suggested that "the fact that it is essential for therapists to tailor their interpersonal styles and stimulus values to different clients has not been given much (if any) attention in most…training programs" (p. 405). Further, he stated that "a flexible repertoire of relationship styles, plus a wide range of pertinent techniques, seem to enhance treatment outcome…[and] if the therapist's style differs markedly from the patient's expectations, positive results are unlikely" (p. 404).

Lazarus was accurate to acknowledge the role of an individual therapist's style in obtaining desired treatment outcome. Bernstein states "therapeutic style refers to the way a therapist does therapy, as distinguished from their theoretical orientation, which refers to the way they explain therapy" (2001, p. 183). Nevertheless, it is difficult to conceptualize the multiple, ill-defined variables that factor into professional style, and there is no consensus in the counseling field about just what constitutes "the therapist's style." Dualistic constructions emerge: directive vs. non-directive, supportive vs. confrontational, client-centered vs. goal-directed, and so on.

While such frameworks are useful, they are nonetheless limiting as they focus primarily on *conscious techniques* at the expense of various other *qualitative predispositions* a therapist contributes to the dyad through his/her own personality. Research demonstrates a link between interpersonal variables characteristic of the therapist and treatment efficacy/outcome. Clients' appraisals of "perspective convergence" and ability "harmoniously to follow each other" within the psychotherapeutic dyad have been found to affect rates of premature treatment dropout (Reis & Brown, 1999). Administration of a personality type indicator found that "the greater the overall similarity [between clients and their counselors], the greater the length of counseling" (Mendelsohn & Geller, 1963, p. 71).

Clients, and people in general, are most likely to prefer a type or style of making sense of the world that is either similar or closely compatible, or a *good fit* with, one's own type or style. A relationship of *fitness* in the counselor-client dyad requires sensitivity to each individual's qualitative predispositions of temperament, personality type, and personal lexicon as manifested in the counseling experience.

Temperament

One such qualitative predisposition clients and counselors alike present in the therapeutic environment is individual temperament. The notion of temperament, historically touted by philosophers and physicians alike, has enjoyed a relatively recent renewal in the field of psychology since Thomas and Chess' (1977) *Temperament and Development.* While "there are a number of specific definitions of temperament...there is overall agreement that temperament is biologically based, is evident early in life and has some stability over time and situations" (Keogh, 2003, p. 1).

Most psychologists regard this term as "referring to stable profiles of mood and behavior with a biological foundation that emerge early in development..." (Kagan, 2003, p. 8) and have a genetic origin. This notion suggests that individuals are born with a biologically based, constitutional quality of behavioral reactivity to stress and subsequent capacity to be soothed. Nature, and not nurture, primarily contributes these temperamental underpinnings upon which physical, emotional, psychological and social development will find their footing.

Over the past century, psychologists and theorists alike have defined temperament differentially, depending on the relative emphasis placed on genetically predisposed biology versus systemic contexts and environmental factors. G.W. Allport, the founder of trait-oriented personality psychology, presented an *emotion*-oriented definition of temperament. Allport (1937) delineates two aspects of temperament that can be characterized by quantitative dimensions: "broad emotions—narrow emotions, which refers to the range of objects and situations to which an individual reacts emotionally; and strong emotions—weak emotions...which pertains to the intensity of feeling evoked by objects and situations" (Strelau, 1998, p. 29). Further, Allport suggests that temperament should be regarded as psychobiological, dependent on one's biochemical constitution:

> Temperament refers to the characteristic phenomena of an individual's emotional nature, including his susceptibility to emotional stimulation, his customary strength and speed of response, the quality of his prevailing mood, and all peculiarities of fluctuation and intensity in mood; these phenomena being regarded as dependent upon constitutional make-up, and therefore largely hereditary in origin. (1937, p. 54)

Thomas and Chess (1977) describe temperament as a *behavioral* style with nine dimensions: activity level, rhythmicity, approach/withdrawal, adaptability, threshold of responsiveness, intensity of reaction, quality of mood, distractibility, and attention span/persistence. They further describe three main types of temperament in children, an idea captured nearly thirty years later by Keogh (2003):

> "Easy" children are characteristically adaptable, positive in mood and moderate in the intensity of their reactions. They are interested and approaching to novelty and are sociable and friendly. "Difficult" children, in contrast, tend to be negative in mood, intense, low in adaptability and withdrawing in new situations. They are sometimes described as "prickly." A third group, those considered "slow-to-warm-up,"...while initially shy and withdrawing

in new situations…are moderate in the intensity of their reactions, but given time they adapt well and when comfortable, they are positive in mood, responsive and sociable. (p. 3)

Rothbart (1989) expanded upon the behavioral construction of temperament to emphasize the integration of biological *and* behavioral components. She referred to temperament in infants as constitutionally based differences in *reactivity and self-regulation*. Rothbart's definition of temperament states that:

'Constitution' refers to relatively enduring biological processes influenced in part by heredity and in part by experience. 'Reactivity' refers to the ease of arousal of motor, affective, autonomic, and endocrine responses. 'Self-regulation' refers to the processes that modulate reactivity, including attention, approach, withdrawal, attack, inhibition and self-soothing. (Kagan, 2003, p. 8)

Perhaps the greatest pioneer of temperament theory and research has been developmental psychologist Jerome Kagan. He found (Kagan, 1989) that at age four months, two infant temperament profiles emerge in response to unfamiliar stimuli: high-reactive and low-reactive. By age two, these profiles can be correlated with temperamental categories: excessive shyness/sociability and timidity/boldness as observed in response to unfamiliar events. Further, "one third of the high-reactive infants become very fearful and are called inhibited…[and] one third of the low-reactive infants become minimally fearful and are called uninhibited" (Kagan, 2003, p. 9). In reference to children who were extreme on measures of inhibited and uninhibited behavior, Kagan (1989) stated that "some investigators believe that these qualities form a continuum; hence, it is important to determine whether these two groups of children lie on a continuum of sociability, or whether they represent two qualitative types" (p. 671).

Temperament as Deterministic

If one considers that early temperamental qualities are more or less stable across settings throughout the lifespan of development, then they can be assumed to transfer into the therapeutic environment as individual qualities of both the client and counselor. However, Kagan (2003) also articulates factors that raise doubt about infant determinism, "the popular assumption that early experiences create psychological structures that persist for an indefinite time" (p. 11). He identifies two underlying beliefs to such a conception: "that the dispositions established in early childhood persist and, second, that they will be actualized in different contexts because, like skin color, they are stable features that belong to the child" (Kagan, 2003, p. 11). He asks: "Why have many social scientists been persuaded of the permanent power of the early years, especially when evolutionary biologists have demonstrated that the persistence of a feature over generations depends on its adaptive value in a particular ecological niche?" (p. 11).

Kagan (2003) suggests that in order for the psychological products (including temperamental presentations) of the first two years of life to be maintained, one's environment must sustain them. Further, other factors including "the child's birth order, profile of identifications, cultural context, and historical era also critically influence development, but these factors are not operative during the infant years" (p. 13). Certain aspects of development are affected by identifications with class and ethnic categories, gender, and the historical era in which one's adolescent years are spent. All of these factors can influence adult values beyond those biologically determined factors observable in infancy and early childhood. Finally, Kagan highlights the faulty assumption made by infant determinists that "a particular behavior, or biological reaction, maintains the same meaning across different incentives and contexts" (2003, p. 15) throughout the lifespan.

> Other theorists also have questioned the limits of the deterministic qualities of infant temperament. Super and Harkness (1982), upon discovery of cultural differences in the expression and function of temperament, presented the concept of *developmental niche* to include the importance of the organization of environments. "The niche consists of the physical and social setting children are found in; the culturally regulated customs for child care, socialization, and behavior management; and the psychology of the caretakers, including beliefs and values about the nature of development" (Super & Harkness, 1986, p. 133). "Temperament is important for several reasons. It describes individual behavioral styles that contribute to personal/social interactions, it evokes responses from others in the child's life, and it affects the range and nature of children's experiences...Developmental psychologists stress that adult-child interactions are reciprocal—that is, that adults influence children's behavior, but that children also influence adults' behavior (Keogh, 2003, p. 3).

Goodness of Fit

In subsequent parenting literature, the concept of "fit" represents the symbiotic, reciprocal interactions characteristic of the infant-parent developmental relationship and suggests that optimal parenting is characterized by the caretaker's ability to adapt his/her personal predispositions and tendencies of preferred modes of interaction to accommodate the infant's alternating needs for stimulation and soothing. Talwar, Nitz and Lerner (1991) assert that"

> This perspective involves the ideal that development occurs through reciprocal relations, or dynamic interactions between organisms and their contexts...The goodness of fit concept derives from the view that the person-context interactions depicted within developmental contextualism involve

'circular functions'...that is, person-context relations predicated on others' reactions to a person's characteristics of individuality." (p. 30)

Other researchers, as well, emphasize the relationship between two sets of characteristics: an individual's and some environmental factor(s):

+ "Goodness of fit refers to the match between a child's characteristics and the characteristics of the environment—including the values, expectations, demands and temperaments of adults" (Keogh, 2003, p. 3).

+ "The construct of *goodness of fit*...implies that the adequacy of the individual's functioning is dependent on the degree to which environmental demands are in accord with the individual's own characteristics...[Further], poorness of fit between the child's temperament and parental (caretaker's) practices or other environmental demands enhances the risk that difficult temperament could lead to behavior disturbances" (Strelau, 1998, p. 340).

+ "From the perspective of the goodness of fit model, adaptive psychological and social functioning do not derive from either the nature of the person's characteristics of individuality per se or the nature of the demands of the contexts within which the person functions...Rather, to the extent that a person's characteristics of individuality meet (or exceed) the demands of a particular setting, adaptive outcomes in that setting will accrue. In turn, people whose characteristics do not fit (or fall short of) the context's demands should show evidence of non-adaptive outcomes" (Lerner, 1986, p. 101).

J. V. and R. M. Lerner later applied their efforts to the task of operationalizing the concept of goodness of fit as related to studies on temperament. They, among others, assume that a variety of demands other than their temperament are placed on children and adolescents "by the social and physical environment, such as (1) attitudes, values, or stereotypes held by others, especially parents and other caregivers (expectational demands), (2) demands imposed by the temperaments of significant others, and (3) demands on temperament imposed by physical settings. In children whose temperament characteristics are incongruent with one or more of the demands mentioned (mismatched children), risk of maladaptive behavioral and cognitive development occurs" (Strelau, 1998, p. 342).

To the extent that infant determinism holds true, clients and counselors alike approach their experiences with certain unconscious, qualitative characteristics that predispose them to react and respond in somewhat predictable, or at least understandable, ways given their respective places in the taxonomies of temperament. Inevitably, there is some degree of *goodness of fit* between any two individuals, and this stands for the counselor-client dyad as well. The accommodating counselor will be sensitive to such issues of fit, and can be empowered to adapt the environmental demands of the therapeutic experience to meet the temperamental predispositions of the client.

From Temperament to Personality

Another construct beyond that of basic temperament to which researchers apply taxonomies is *personality*. There has long been a tendency to differentiate temperament from personality. Goldsmith and Campos (1990) view temperament "as individual differences in tendencies to express the primary emotions" (p. 1945); as such, these dimensions of temperament "form the emotional substrate of some later personality characteristics" (Goldsmith et al., 1987, as cited in Strelau, 1998, p. 31).

Strelau (1998) warns "when we consider temperament to be equivalent to personality we are unable to grasp the specificity of temperament mechanisms or traits as compared with other personality characteristics, namely those for which the variance is primarily determined by social factors" (p. 43). He suggests that whereas temperament results mainly from biological evolution, personality is the product of the social environment; "however, this product emerged on the basis of the biological endowment regarded as a component of personality" (p. 47).

G. W. Allport regards temperament as a component of personality. As "one of the founders of the individual-differences approach to personality, [he] treats the concept of personality as a very general one, comprising such phenomena as habits, specific and general attitudes, sentiments and dispositions; the last two are described in terms of traits which also include temperamental characteristics. For Allport, individual differences constitute a definitional component of personality" (Strelau, 1998, p. 39).

Taxonomies of Personality

Just as clients and counselors transfer their temperamental qualities into the therapeutic relationship and environment, so do they present with certain personality types or styles that have developed over the course of time in response to myriad environmental demands. Use of a sort of shorthand for conceptualizing a client's normal personality functioning enables and empowers the counselor to tailor his or her approach and engagement with the client so as to optimize the probability of a good fit and therapeutic facilitation. Professional counselors can use any of numerous typologies and taxonomies to size up their clients; many are empirically derived and some are more accessible than others.

The Big Five Factors of Personality

Norman (1963), through analysis of different personality scales, classifies personality characteristics into five factors, which came to be known as the Big Five.

These factors have been found to hold up across various research and therefore have become popular in the literature on the human personality.

Norman labels them as:
+ Factor I: Extroversion or Surgency;
+ Factor II: Agreeableness;
+ Factor III: Conscientiousness;
+ Factor IV: Emotional Stability; and
+ Factor V: Culture.

Various authors have since speculated on the role of temperament in each of the Big Five personality characteristics. Developmentalists have concluded that an infant's temperament characteristics function as precursors to these characteristics as they appear in adolescence and adulthood.

Personality Types

The early foundations of personality typologies can be traced back to Hippocrates' and Plato's work on the four "temperaments" or "humours": sanguine, choleric, phlegmatic, and melancholic. The characters of Greek gods and goddesses embody these qualitative characteristics in the dramas of mythology, and to an extent set the stage for contemporary taxonomies with which to organize personality profiles.

Jung's psychological types

Carl Jung, the highly influential personality theorist, published his book *Psychological types* in 1921. He follows the Greeks in his division of human psychological qualities into opposite categories or "general attitude types," the first of which is the popular Introversion-Extraversion type. These general attitude types, which Jung asserts must be due to some unconscious, instinctive cause, can be distinguished by the direction of a person's general interest and energy as directed inward or outward (the Latin "extra" means outside, "intra" means inward, and "vertere" to turn): "The introvert's attitude is an abstracting one; at bottom he is always intent on withdrawing libido [interest and energy] from the object...The extravert, on the contrary, has a positive relation to the object. The object [other] can never have enough value for him, and its importance must always be increased" (Jung, as cited in Campbell, 1971, p. 179).

Jung goes on to suggest that the two major categories, introversion and extraversion, will "self-balance" within one individual through conscious and unconscious processes. One could say that

Extraverts tend to focus on the outer world of people, things and activities, and are energized by others. They love to talk, participate, organize, and socialize...

Introverts are energized by the inner world of reflection, thought, and contemplation. They direct their energy and attention inward and receive energy from reflecting on their thoughts, memories and feelings. They can be sociable but need space and time alone to recharge their batteries. (Hilliard, 2001)

In his personality typology, Jung further articulates four "functional types" beyond the initial introversion-extraversion distinction; each of these four functions may serve a superior or dominant role in the personality. They include the "Rational" functions of *thinking* and *feeling*, and the "Irrational" functions of *sensation* and *intuition*. While the first two functions enable us to judge and decide, the second two allow us to gather information and perceive. Jung insists that both of these abilities, information gathering and deciding, are necessary to survive and have normal functioning behavior.

Finally, Jung constructs eight major "Psychological Types" by adding a "general attitude type" (introversion or extraversion) to each of the four superior functions listed above. Each type does not make up the whole of a personality, but rather represents the primary, or dominant, way of engaging with the world around oneself. Jung's original intent for his psychological theory of personality type was for use in the clinical setting, to understand where the client is coming from on a cognitive level. However, his theories today are widely used as the basis for psychometrics and personality testing, and personality theorists continue to expand upon Jung's initial work.

Myers Briggs

The Meyers Briggs Type Indicator (MBTI) (1962) brought visibility to the personality types by placing greater consideration on the auxiliary, or less prominent, functions of one's personality. In doing so, it defined another preference not considered by Jung: Judging and Perceiving. Today's theory asserts that every individual has a primary mode of operation within four categories, that two preferences are available within each category, and that one's personality type is defined by the combination of the four preferences:

Primary Mode of Operation	Preference
1.) our flow of energy	Extraverted or Introverted
2.) how we take in information	Sensing or Intuitive
3.) how we prefer to make decisions	Thinking or Feeling
4.) the basic day-to-day lifestyle that we prefer	Judging or Perceiving
(BSM Consulting, n.d.)	

One's "flow of energy" refers to how the essential part of one's stimulation is received—from within oneself or from outside, external sources (Extraverted-Introverted). How one "takes in information" has to do with the primary method of trusting the five senses, versus relying on instincts (Sensing-Intuitive). The preference for "making decisions" can be based on logic and objective consideration, or on personal subjective value systems (Thinking-Feeling). And finally, how one "deals with the external world" refers to being organized and purposeful with a preference for scheduled, structured environments; or flexible and diverse, with a penchant for open, casual environments (Judging-Perceiving). (BSM Consulting, n.d.)

Sensing-Intuitive: *Sensing* people rely primarily on the five senses, taking in information that is real and tangible. They are most interested in what is really and actually happening, and observe the specifics of what goes on around them. They tend to be practical and realistic, perhaps so focused on details that they may miss the big picture. Finally, Sensing types tend to use words literally, and prefer to "do" rather than "think" (Hilliard, 2001).

In contrast, *Intuitive* people tend to trust their hunches and seek out the big picture. With an interest in patterns and relationships between facts, they are conceptual and thereby may ignore certain details. They are future-oriented and seek new possibilities; they would rather "think" than "do" (Hilliard, 2001).

Thinking-Feeling: *Thinking* people prefer to make decisions on the basis of analysis, logic and reason. They analyze a choice or action based on the logical consequences, and identify what is wrong with something so that they can problem-solve. Thinking people may at times seem tactless and uncaring about feelings. They follow their head over their heart, and value truth and fairness (Hilliard, 2001).

In contrast, *Feeling* people tend to consider what is important to themselves and others when making decisions, and their personal likes and dislikes. Supporting and praising others energize them, which serves to treat them as unique individuals. Feeling people tend to value interpersonal harmony and kindness, and want to be liked by others (Hilliard, 2001).

Judging-Perceiving: *Judging* people regulate and manage their own lives in a planned and orderly way. They tend to be organized and structured, and prefer to make decisions and gain closure. They are focused on only the essentials of completing the task at hand, and are energized by "getting things done." (Hilliard, 2001)

In contrast, *Perceiving* people are spontaneous and averse to deadlines or plans. They tend to gather more information before making decisions and feel confined by finality, preferring to be open to new last-minute options. Perceiving people are flexible and like to multi-task. (Hilliard, 2001)

These very different ways of engaging with the world and people around oneself are quite normal given one's personality type. The sensitive counselor must be savvy to these differences in the therapeutic relationship so as not to misunderstand, pathologize, or miscommunicate with his/her clients. Such characteristics should not be thought of as "wrong" or "unhealthy" in any way. Rather, the personality type shorthand of individual similarities and differences is most effectively applied with consideration for its neutral and universal qualities.

The MBTI has been applied widely to the studies of personality type and marriage, learning styles, occupation, and motivation (Briggs Myers & Myers, 1980). These applications assume that there is relevance to considerations of fit between the personality types of individuals and others in relationship, the engagement and accomplishment of certain types of tasks, and effectiveness in particular role assignments within social groups.

Kiersey's Pygmalion Project

Keirsey and Bates (1978) and Keirsey (1998) presented the *Please Understand Me: Character and Temperament Types* books to the helping professions and lay public. Keirsey posits "there are two sides to personality, one of which is temperament and the other character. Temperament is a configuration of inclinations, while character is a configuration of habits. Character is disposition, temperament predisposition" (1998, p. 20).

This system, rife with metaphor, promotes a stance of acknowledgement and understanding of individual differences between the various personality or character types. The usefulness of Keirsey's typology lies in its application of easily referenced "characters" to each of the different types, and the detailed and comprehensive description offered for each. In capturing the range of characters, he warns that acceptance of natural differences is key to any relationship. Referring to the Greek myth of Pygmalion he writes "the task of sculpting others into our own likeness fails before it begins. Ask people to change their character, and you ask the impossible" (Keirsey, 1998, p. 2).

The Keirsey Temperament Sorter is perhaps the most widely used inventory of personality type. Like the Myers-Briggs, the Keirsey scales yield sixteen different profiles of four components each: these are the sixteen personality subtypes. Keirsey divides all individual personality types into four general styles: *Rational, Idealist, Guardian* and *Artisan*. These four styles correlate with the Greek humors and are derived from Jung and Myers Briggs personality types, with some theoretical distinctions.

Kiersey's types have certain dimensional elements, and can be said to differ in the way they use words (abstract vs. concrete) and the way they use tools (as a cooperator or a utilitarian). Thus, a concrete communicator with utilitarian tool use is the Artisan, while a concrete communicator with cooperative implementation is the Guardian type. Amongst those who use words abstractly are the cooperative (tool use) Idealist and the utilitarian Rational (Keirsey, 1998).

The four major personality types, or characters, can further be identified by their unique core values across different dimensions. The self-image of these types, as well, differs based on the normal preferences and inclinations of the Artisan, Guardian, Idealist and Rational. Given that a large part of an individual's well-being relates to core personal values and self-image, it behooves the professional counselor to become familiar with these factors as they may inform effective therapeutic interventions with clients of various types. The characteristic values and self-images of Keirsey's four types are summarized below for easy reference:

Value	Rationals	Artisans	Guardians	Idealists
Being	Calm	Excited	Concerned	Enthusiastic
Trusting	Reason	Impulse	Authority	Intuition
Yearning	Achievement	Impact	Belonging	Romance
Seeking	Knowledge	Stimulation	Security	Identity
Prizing	Deference	Generosity	Gratitude	Recognition
Aspiring	Wizard	Virtuoso	Executive	Sage

(Keirsey, 1998)

Self-Image	Rationals	Artisans	Guardians	Idealists
Self-Esteem	Ingenious	Artistic	Dependable	Empathic
Self-Respect	Autonomous	Audacious	Beneficent	Benevolent
Self-Confidence	Resolute	Adaptable	Respectable	Authentic

(Keirsey, 1998)

As discussed earlier, both the counselor and the client bring certain qualitative predispositions into the treatment setting; temperament and personality types are two such examples. Each individual presents with a unique set of characteristics: flow of energy, how one takes in information, how one prefers to make decisions, one's day-to-day lifestyle preferences, how one uses words and tools, and one's core personal values and self-image.

Counselor Type

According to Keirsey, the Idealist role variants (Teacher, Counselor, Champion, and Healer) are most prominently represented within the counseling profession. Their intellect, interests, self-image and values are conducive to the social roles and tasks of the helping professional. While highly compatible with most other types, however, even Idealist counselors at times face difficulties with rapport, therapeutic roadblocks, or treatment plateaus. By understanding and respecting the personality patterns of clients, the counselor can adapt his or her stance to forge the most effective connection possible within the therapeutic environment.

Some researchers have searched for a relationship between therapist personality type and preferred therapeutic interventions. McCann (1998) found, consistent with prior studies, that more Intuitive than Sensing types can be found within the therapist population. She concluded, however, that there was no significant relationship between therapists' temperament (as measured by the MBTI-G) and their selected therapeutic mechanisms of change. Regardless of therapist type (and experience level), the "preferred mechanisms of change were respectively acceptance, insight and interaction" (McCann, 1998, p. 6240).

Varlami and Bayne (2007), however, did find that the psychological type of counselor trainees influences their choice of counseling orientation. Their study found that Sensing-Judging types were more likely to choose the CBT model, Intuition-Feeling-Judging types preferred the Psychodynamic model, and Intuition-Feeling-Perceiving types chose the Person-Centered model.

Psycho-Education About Type

Regardless of theoretical or therapeutic orientation, awareness of and sensitivity to the respective differences in values, emotional experiencing, cognition, and communication styles of the various character and personality types enhances interactions between and among the types. The concepts of personality types and styles can be tools for clients to develop insight, both within the session and generalized to outside relationships and dilemmas. An understanding of general temperament and personality type increases one's ability to work with an individual to promote self-awareness.

"When a person becomes self-aware, he is in a position to acknowledge responsibility for that which he does including that which he does to himself, to acknowledge that he is the cause of his actions and thus to take ownership of his life… self-responsibility grows out of self-awareness" (Kocinski, 1984, p. 171).

> Jung suggests that the more aware one is of the four functions within oneself (whether they be conscious or unconscious, rational or irrational), the more balanced a life he or she could live. "Man's increased understanding of himself and his world has long been a major ingredient in the history of human society. The chief intellectual characteristic of this history has been man's ability to increasingly remove himself from the concrete experience of the phenomenological 'here and now' and place himself in an abstracted world of concepts and logic" (Thomas & Chess, 1977, p. vii).

Interpersonal sensitivity and responsiveness to the client's temperament and personality type can take various forms in the counseling environment. Professional counselors can provide psycho-education to clients about normal differences in individual temperaments and personality types in structured or unstructured ways. A structured approach might include distributing reading materials about personality type, assigning "observe and report" homework, or even having a client complete a formal measure (such as the Keirsey Temperament Sorter II, 1998) to identify his/ her own type.

Unstructured approaches are more opportunistic and rely on the emergence of issues during sessions. At the right time, the counselor can reflect and validate verbally any of the various dimensions of temperament and personality as relevant to the client's narrative. Consider the following counselor statements:

> "Given that you prefer working to a deadline, it makes sense that you would feel frustrated with the open-ended timeline of the project." (Judging dimension)

> "Since you are the type of person who needs quiet time to yourself, it is important to set limits as you have done." (Introvert)

> "I'm not surprised that you need more time, given that you're slow-to-warm up to new people and situations." (Thomas & Chess, temperament)

> "As important as it is for you to help others, a part of you is missing now that your daughter no longer lives at home." (Idealist)

Highlighting normal individual qualities and characteristics not only allows for validation of the client's experience, but it also can serve to facilitate increased awareness and sensitivity to others' experiences. Recognition of natural type differences can precipitate a de-centering from one's own, often limited, point of view. Insight can foster developmental growth through movement from being embedded in one's own subjective experiential style to a more objective, flexible position.

From the more objective position, a client can acknowledge multiple, and potentially equally valid, styles. This often results in decreased subjective distress by improving interpersonal observation and analysis skills, promoting effective communication skills, and relieving rigidity of negative thought patterns. These elements provide the impetus for a client to expand his or her behavioral repertoire and dynamics so as to interact more effectively with the world around him or her.

Personal Lexicons

Another way the professional counselor can apply knowledge of temperament and personality types is in the language, or lexicon, used to communicate within the therapeutic dialogue. A personal lexicon represents a lifetime's accumulation of experience within oneself, with others, and in the contexts of larger social systems and institutions. When client and counselor both contribute their personal lexicons to the therapeutic dyad, they co-construct a dialogue on the common ground between them. This common ground is established through the identification of shared or compatible lexicons that *fit* together to allow for the client's "personality" to be understood, reflected, and reflected *upon* by the counselor.

Clients' temperaments and personality types influence the way they use words and tools to communicate and interact with the world around them. They use words to convey their inner experiences and their reactions to events (be they interpersonal or behavioral). In order to be a *good fit* with their clients, counselors should become familiar and comfortable with tailoring and implementing different lexicons.

First level of lexical fitness

The first level of lexical fitness between counselor and client lies in the use of abstract versus concrete words. Rational and Idealist types tend to use words abstractly, while Guardians and Artists prefer concrete communication.

Keirsey (1998) proposes looking at the words one uses to orient him or herself to reality. He states: "Abstract words can be used in slightly different but related ways—analogical, categorical, fictional, figurative, general, schematic, symbolic, and theoretical. Likewise, concrete words can be used in slightly different but related ways—detailed, factual, elemental, empirical, indicative, literal, signal, and specific" (p. 27).

Consider the following examples of client communication:

> "When we have to do the timed math tests, it's like I'm a bomb just waiting to explode. As soon as I can't do one, the fuse is lit and it's all over with." (Abstract)

> "The teacher told us to take out our pencils and get ready for timed math. When I messed up on a problem, I threw my pencil at the desk." (Concrete)

> "I feel like an astronaut or an alien looking down at my children from above. If only I could find a way to be more down to earth with them, or even just on the same planet, I might not feel as guilty about working such long hours." (Abstract)

> "If I get home late, after dinner, and ask about their homework, they act like I'm not even there. They don't even need me to check in with them anymore." (Concrete)

Just as a client's use of words can be abstract or concrete, so can the counselor's. In order to promote a sense of good fit within the dyad, counselors should be able to accommodate either lexical style. It is often advised that counselors master the art of the "neutral," open-ended question, such as "What do you think about that?" or "How does that make you feel?" but even such benign statements can be a roadblock in mismatched communication styles.

Second level of Lexical Fitness

Not only does an individual's personal lexicon tend toward abstract or concrete word usage, but it also represents the way one experiences oneself, others, and the world around oneself. The second level of lexical fitness between counselor and client is in the preferred functions of their primary modes of operation: Introvert-Extravert, Sensing-Intuition, Thinking-Feeling, and Judging-Perceiving. Consider the following client responses, and the therapist's reflection:

What will it be like for you to go back to work on Monday after disability leave?

> "I just hope to heaven no one has wormed his way into my locker—I need my personal space in that crazy place." (Introvert)

"You're worried about your territory..."

> "I can't wait to see the guys. We have such a blast on the floor" (Extravert)

"You like being with people at work..."

> "Just thinking about it makes my boots heavy on my feet; I can already smell the burning rubber and my eyes squint up just thinking about it. I can't wait for that paycheck come Friday though, so I can get those new wheel rims from my brother." (Sensing)

"Hard work always pays off..."

> "My sixth sense tells me that it should go pretty well. It seems like they've kept up with things while I've been out, so my guess is we're not ready to go under or anything like that." (Intuition)

"Your hunch is 'no major disasters'..."

> "I've been thinking about keeping up the pace, what with my shoulder and all...I don't even want to think about being the guy who keeps us from making our numbers. I need the money, though, to get brakes for the car and to give to my mother since the porch collapsed." (Thinking)

"It's hard to think about not making your numbers..."

> "Somewhat sad, leaving the kids behind again after being home with them for so long; Jackie will miss me the most. I'm not looking forward to the same old grind, second shift, it's just not who I really want to be as a person." (Feeling)

"You're happiest when you're with your loved ones..."

> "I think I'll get up early to miss the bridge at rush hour. If I have Jack load the truck with me the night before, then I can finish the schedule and get back on the road in time to check on the kids before bed. Maybe I'll design

the new balusters for the porch." (Judging)

"You've planned accordingly…"
   "Well, we'll see how it goes. You never know what the day may bring. Not sure how quickly I'll be ready to get down to business." (Perceiving)

"Who knows? Anything could happen…"

In responding to the client with the same functional mode, the counselor stays more closely aligned with the client's subjective experience. Such a strategy demands, however, that the counselor adopts an unconditionally accepting, non-judgmental stance toward the client's communication, and maintains awareness of the natural, normal differences of personality types. Employing such a lexical matching strategy consistently early on in the developing relationship is likely to improve the goodness of fit within the dyad, and to optimize client retention in treatment.

Summary

For nearly a century, helping professionals have sought the hallmark theories and techniques of effective therapeutic intervention. While researchers have studied the possible influence of theoretical models and therapist orientations, little attention has been paid to other qualitative characteristics of goodness of fit between the counselor and client.

The various taxonomies and typologies of human temperament and personality are rich sources of information that offer counselors a sort of conceptual shorthand for understanding a presenting client. The astute and skillful practitioner will become familiar with such systems, and through psycho-education will empower clients to develop their own insights and understanding of self and others. Further, one can employ informed strategies to promote a goodness of fit in the therapeutic dyad and thereby recognize the equally valid and normal temperament, personality and lexical characteristics of each unique individual in the treatment setting.

References

Allport, G.W. (1937). Personality: A Psychological interpretation. NY: Henry Holt.

Bernstein, A. (2001). Psychotherapy as a performing art: The Role of therapeutic style. *Modern psychoanalysis, 26*(2):183-190.

Briggs Myers, I. & Myers, P. B. (1980). Gifts differing: Understanding personality type. Mountain View, CA: Davies-Black Publishing.

BSM Consulting, n.d.. Retrieved from http://personalitypage.com/info/html on April 14, 2008.

Campbell, J. (Ed.) (1971). The Portable Jung. New York: Viking Penguin Group.

Hilliard, D. (2001). Learning styles and personality types. Retrieved from www.wnc.edu on April 14, 2008.

Kagan, J. (1989). Temperamental contributions to social behavior. *American Psychologist, 44* (4): 668-674.

Kagan, J. (2003). Biology, context, and developmental inquiry. *Annual Review of Psychology, 54*: 1-23.

Keirsey, D. & Bates, M. (1978). Please understand me: Character & temperament types. Del Mar, CA: Prometheus Nemesis Book Company.

Keirsey, D. (1998). Please understand me II: Temperament, character, intelligence. Del Mar, CA: Prometheus Nemesis Book Company.

Keogh, B. K. (2003). Understanding child temperament can have far-reaching impact on behavior and quality of life. *The Brown University Child and Adolescent Behavior Letter*, Oct. 2003: 1-4.

Kocinski, R. R. (1984). *The effect of knowledge of one's learning style by freshman nursing students on student achievement.* Unpublished doctoral dissertation, Rutgers University, New Jersey.

Lazarus, A. (1993). Tailoring the therapeutic relationship, or being an authentic chameleon. *Psychotherapy, 30*(3), Fall 1993: 404-407.

McCann, G. S. (1998). The Selection of therapeutic mechanisms of change in relation to therapist temperament. *Dissertation abstracts international: Section B: The Sciences and engineering, 58*(11-B), May 1998: 6240.

Reis, B.F. & Brown, L.G. (1999). Reducing psychotherapy dropouts: Maximizing perspective convergence in the psychotherapeutic dyad. *Psychotherapy: Theory, Research, Practice, Training, 36*(2), Summer 1999: 123-136.

Rothbart, M. K. (1989). Temperament in childhood. In *Temperament in childhood,*

Strelau, J. (1998). Temperament: A Psychological perspective. Hingham, MA: Kluwer Academic Publishers.

Thomas, A., Chess, S. (1977). *Temperament and development.* NY: Brunner-Mazel.

Varlami, E., & Bayne, R. (2007). Psychological type and counseling psychology trainees' choice of counseling orientation. *Counseling psychology quarterly, 20*(4), Dec 2007: 361-373.

Section Two:

The Nuts and Bolts of Practice

Navigating the Mental Health System
By: Sandra Valente, Ph.D., LADC, LPC

Mental health and addiction counselors who enter the field as novices frequently discover that they lack practical advice and training in the area of navigating the system. They may face obstacles and waste time in their attempts to obtain needed services for their clients. Some of the difficulties faced include finding and getting clients into inpatient treatment, collaborating with agencies such as the courts, insurance companies, medical doctors, Departments of Children and Family Services (DCF), and finding psychiatrists for medication support and referrals. Newcomers to private practice are often faced with this issue once they have already started their work with a client, and may waste time in obtaining these needed services.

The purpose of this chapter will be to provide practical advice to help novice clinicians throughout the treatment process and to address issues that often come up through the counseling process including collaborating with other professionals, handling crises and identifying and connecting with resources. The chapter will progress through the intake, screening, treatment planning, counseling and discharge process and identify at each step, potential challenges that may arise as it relates to "navigating the system." Recommendations are offered throughout to assist novice counselors with challenges that often present when working as a counselor in private practice.

Obtaining Referral Sources

One task of counselors is to help clients become self sufficient, and productive. This may involve connecting a client to an outside agency or individual to provide assistance with specific skills areas. Developing a list of referral sources will help reduce the time it takes once clients start coming through the door. Development of a referral network involves an investment of time and energy on the part of the counselor. The counselor's referral network should include names of other counselors with various specialties (i.e. domestic violence, working with children, adolescents, adults or the elderly, special populations, special areas of expertise such as sexual abuse, grief counseling, etc.). Other individuals may include a psychiatrist, social service agencies, credit counseling services, and local attorneys who specialize in mental health practice or family law. A comprehensive list of referral sources may include the following:

- Case managements services
- Children and family departments (local case workers, 24 hour hotline phone number)
- Churches and charitable organizations
- Court/probation services
- Domestic violence groups/programs
- Employment Services
- Employee assistance programs (EAP)
- Insurance companies contacts
- Mental health evaluations (licensed psychologists, social workers, etc)
- Rehabilitation Services
- Respite Care
- Support groups (Alcoholic Anonymous, Narcotics Anonymous, Al-Anon, Sexual Abuse Survivors Group, Divorce, Grief and Loss, etc)
- Social Service programs who assist those people with serious mental illness who are homeless to secure housing and financial resources
- Supportive housing or other housing assistance programs
- Substance abuse evaluations (Licensed Substance Abuse Counselors)
- Transportation
- Twenty-Four Hour Crisis services (phone numbers and addresses of facilities in the vicinity of your practice.
- Veterans Administration hospitals
- Vocational Rehabilitation Program

One practical way to build a referral network includes asking other professionals in your community about their referral sources and services that local community mental health centers provide. Call the local hospital to obtain numbers and names of individuals who provide crisis counseling. Obtain numbers and locations of local Women's shelters, homeless shelters, and hospital crisis centers. It is also helpful to establish rapport with professionals in your area by meeting with them, and sending out copies of your brochure and business cards.

How Do You Refer?

The need to refer may occur for a variety of reasons, such as when a client demonstrates difficulty beyond your abilities. When you have to make a referral to your client, explain the reason for making the referral and obtain consent for the referral particularly in the case when you need to speak directly with that person to share information about the client. When explaining the need to refer to your client, it may be helpful to state, "I need to refer you to "so and so" because I am not qualified for the type of counseling you need, or "so and so" can provide you with ___." Let your client know you are concerned about their welfare but that the problem is beyond your scope of expertise. The purpose of making a referral is to ensure that the client gets the best possible care. When managed appropriately, referrals can be viewed as a reflection of the counselors concern for the client.

Intake and Screening

The intake and screening process involves the gathering of information about the problems for which the client is seeking treatment. At this point of the process, it may be determined that the client may need inpatient hospitalization, for a psychiatric emergency, suicidal ideation, etc. or detoxification from drugs or alcohol before they can benefit from outpatient counseling in a private practice setting. This section will provide specific ideas on how to identify problems utilizing a biopsychosocial perspective. Ideas about assisting clients in reducing their fears, or addressing denial that a problem exists and potential problems associated with getting a client into inpatient treatment will be discussed.

Seven to ten million people in the United States have at least one mental disorder in addition to an alcohol or drug abuse disorder (SAMHSA, 2002; Watkins et al, 2001). Too often, these individuals are treated for only one of the two disorders, resulting in an increase in mental health problems or addiction issues or both. Historically, patients with psychiatric conditions were rarely asked about the presence of a substance use disorder or whether they used drugs or alcohol at all. There has been a lack of attention paid to the potential effects of illicit substance use on the existing progression of mental health disorders.

When working with clients, attempt to utilize a biopsychosocial perspective with every client encounter. As counselors accept the philosophy that quality health care and public health require integrating psychological and physical care, it becomes incongruent to practice in old, fragmented ways (Levant & Heldring, 2007). The biopsychosocial model emphasizes collaboration between social, medical and behavioral health providers. It is also pertinent that screening for both mental health as well as addiction disorders is accomplished to ensure that adequate treatment and service planning occurs. Incorporating a substance abuse screening instrument, as a component of the intake process will help identify potential issues with addiction disorders. Such simple screening instruments include the MAST, CAGE, AUDIT or SASSI screening instruments. Use of a form, such as a comprehensive biopsychosocial, which touches upon all areas of functioning, will help in identifying other potential areas that require assistance (i.e. financial, family, housing, education, social services etc). Though practitioners are trained to provide mental health services alone, the likelihood of a mental health condition exacerbating will occur if other areas of the client's life are not addressed as well. The ability to identify needed services or supports during the intake assessment will help promote the overall health and well being of the client.

In the next section, topic headings of a common biopsychosocial are utilized to identify potential areas of need that might be incorporated into the treatment plan for direct service or referral.

Family and Significant Relationships

Family members have the power to reinforce or undermine a client's success in treatment. Considering the needs of primary family members should also be considered as they relate to the ongoing stress of the identified client. Are family members supportive, enabling, or enmeshed with the primary client and/or their presenting problem? Incorporating the family into treatment planning including educating them about the mental illness, progression of addiction and the treatment process will help both the client and family members. Family members need encouragement and support as much as the client. When assessing the client, identify specific problems, recent changes, and stressors that may be contributing to the problem. Resources that may be beneficial in this area include Marriage and Family Counselors, and Family Service agencies.

Working with Families

Collaboration with families will help promote reinforcement of treatment goals, and help endorse clear communication, encouragement and support. Working with family members, and/or spouse is also important, as they may be enabling behavior that contributes to relapse behaviors. Developing contracts and establishing specific rules and consequences for future behavior is helpful. If the primary client has a long history of abusing drugs or alcohol and has other family members that may also be suffering from an addiction, these factors will also need to be taken into consideration. When developing the treatment plan with the client, discuss the possibility of including the family in on a "future session." Educating the client about the impact of the addiction or mental illness on the family may help them understand the need to include the family and/or spouse in treatment planning. Ask the client how they feel about having their spouse or family members participate in a "family session." Presenting the need to educate family members about what the mental illness is, and how the mental illness or addiction disorder is treated, and what to expect from counseling may be a way to reassure the client.

Financial

If the client is having financial problems such as difficulty with paying bills, significant debt, or loss of income, suggest possible resources that may be of service. Many states have Credit Counseling Service agencies that help with debt consolidation, contacting creditors and assisting clients with paying down their debt. Provide phone numbers and ask the client in the next session how they did with getting in contact with the agency. It is important to let your clients know that you will be asking them in the next scheduled session whether they followed through with phone calls, scheduling outside appointments, etc. This is helpful with keeping them on task.

Spiritual/Religious

In this area, some clients may describe a history of involvement with a church, synagogue, or religious practice, and may have difficulty reconnecting. Often, providing support with contacting the pastor or priest may be all the encouragement needed. Incorporating a client's spirituality into the treatment plan allows for additional support and individualization.

Legal

When clients indicate during the intake assessment that they have legal involvement it is important to identify whether there are upcoming court dates, probation requirements, or other obligations. Have clients sign releases so that contact can be made with lawyers, court or probation personnel and call them to let them know of your involvement with the client and desire to collaborate. Often, if the client is court mandated (such as for anger management training, domestic violence classes, or evaluation for substance abuse or mental illness), there will be a need to write a summary of the treatment plan, progress in treatment and discharge plan. Counselors may be faced with clients who are confused about why they were arrested in the first place (such as in domestic violence, breach of peace cases). Counseling may need to include educating clients about the legal charges—what they mean, what will happen in court and the long term implications of their legal charges. Counselors who have their name listed with the local courts as a resource for mental health and substance abuse evaluations and services, will need to ensure that they have an understanding of their states laws, and processes involved with "court referrals."

Medical

Identification of existing medical issues will alert the counselor to potential difficulties that may need to be addressed such as the need for a physical (ask your client, "when was the last time you had a physical?"), and identification of medical symptoms that have not been addressed, such as problems with sleep. Educate clients about caring for their wellbeing and encourage them to maintain adequate health practices such as keeping up to date on physical exams, and specialized yearly exams. For individuals without insurance, referral to a social service agency that will assist with connecting the client with needed medical services may need to occur. Often during the intake the client may talk about having a medical condition that they are having difficulty adjusting to. This may need to be incorporated into treatment planning.

Substance Abuse Issues

The intake and assessment process should include identification of licit and illicit substance use in the past and present. Use of a substance abuse screening instrument will support the data gathered through the biopsychosocial form at the initial intake session. For individuals who are actively using licit or illicit drugs or alcohol, determination of need for inpatient detoxification and a subsequent referral for inpatient treatment will need to occur. For those practitioners who solely provide mental health counseling, a referral to a Licensed Alcohol and Drug Counselor may need to occur to address the presence of substance abuse-specific disorders. Later in this chapter, suggestions for getting clients into inpatient facilities are presented.

Mental Health Issues

Mental health issues are often the primary reason a client is referred to counselors. Initial contact with the client may reveal a stressor within the home or family, but further investigation and questioning may suggest the need for evaluation by a psychiatrist, medication, or need for stabilization in an inpatient setting. Sometimes a client may come into the first session in crisis in which case obtaining immediate services and ensuring safety take precedence. These issues are addressed later in this chapter.

Treatment Planning

Treatment planning should encompass all potential areas of need identified through the biopsychosocial assessment process though the counselor may only provide treatment for one particular identified problem. Individualized treatment plans should promote resiliency and recovery. Too little support can result in poor functioning and exacerbation of symptoms (Barry, et al., 2007). Treatment planning is a process in which the strengths of the client are identified, self-efficacy is encouraged, connections with supports are made and attention is focused on capabilities and options rather than perceived dead ends. Treatment planning can be particularly challenging such as addressing financial hardship, legal issues and incorporating the family into treatment. This section will discuss collaboration in treatment planning, and provide specific suggestions about establishing a connection with and working with the courts, police, working with clients with dual diagnosis, psychiatrists, and getting clients into inpatient treatment facilities

Integration and Collaboration in Treatment Planning

The goal of treatment is to enable alcohol and drug users as well as those with mental illness to access a range of treatment options to achieve better health, sobrieties, reduce criminal activity, and develop skills necessary to return to mainstream lifestyles (Davis, 2001).

The President's New Freedom Commission on Mental Health called for integrated care as one solution to the fragmented U.S. mental health care system. Specifically, it called for better coordination between mental health care and primary health care (Mental Health Commission, 2003). The commission also believed that a shift was needed, in which "mental health is viewed as essential to overall health and that mental illness be treated with the same urgency as physical illnesses" (Mental Health Commission, 2003, p. 7). Collaborative treatment planning is a process through which the counselor and client develop desired treatment outcomes and identify the strategies for achieving them. At a minimum the treatment plan should address the identified substance use disorder(s), and/or mental illness as well as issues related to treatment progress, including relationships with family and significant others, employment, education, spirituality, health concerns, and legal needs. Collaboration should also incorporate other already existing systems of care such as the schools, community and other agencies involved with the identified client (Greenberg et al., 1999). The more common types of providers which should be collaborated with include psychiatric treatment, case management, court mandated counseling, psychological testing, department of children and family contact, and family counseling. To collaborate with other treatment providers, obtain a release of information and inform the client about the purpose of speaking with the other providers. Collaborating through phone contact is easiest and more efficient. When speaking with other providers, discuss what your role is, and how you would like to work together with them in helping the client. This process is also helpful in identifying other issues or missing data that your client did not share during the intake and initial sessions.

Working with the Courts/Criminal Justice System

In the U.S., approximately 1.3 million people are in State and Federal prisons, and 4.6 million are under correctional supervision in the community (Beck, Karsberg, Harrison & Bureau of Justice Statistics, 2002; Beck, 2000). The rate of serious mental illness is 15 to 20 percent of the correctional population and three to four times that of the general U.S. population (Teplin, 1990). Offenders who return to the community need support in such areas as employment, housing, education, and social support.

Counselors working with clients referred by the court system handle such matters as domestic violence education, mental health and substance abuse evaluations and treatment, and anger management counseling. When setting the first appointment for court-referred clients, ask them to bring any court documents that they received. These documents will often provide specific information as to what type of evaluation is needed, and what specific type of counseling services are needed, such as domestic violence, anger management, couples or individual counseling.

When working with clients who have been referred by the court, it is important during the intake process to get a signed Release of Information for the Family Court Division (or other Court Division), so evaluations and other written correspondence can be exchanged. Often it may be necessary to contact a specific Court Division to obtain further supporting/accurate information about your client, particularly if they present with difficulty in sharing information, appearing to be dishonest, or there is a feeling that not all information is being shared.

Disclosing to your client that you will contact the Court Division related to their case is important. To dispel concerns or revocation of the release, assurance that this is an essential component of the evaluation and ensuring there is complete information for the report, etc. may help in reducing the fears of your client.

Education/Feelings About Legal Involvement

When clients are court referred this may be the first time that they have ever been involved with being arrested, having to go to court, obtaining a lawyer, and learning about the "legal process." Feelings of fear, embarrassment, and confusion about state laws, shame and depression may be present. Counselors may need to address these feelings and help the client learn about their state laws, and how the court process will go, as the first step towards helping the client.

Working with the Police

There are several issues that counselors may face when working in private practice resulting in the need to contact police. The potential for clients to show up under the influence of drugs or alcohol is a possibility as well as working with clients who are depressed, suicidal, or indicate homicidal ideation. On rare occasions, a client may demonstrate hostility, or threaten the counselor. Having an established plan as to how these issues will be handled is important, prior to taking in the first client.

Having the phone numbers of the local police, or contacting them initially to orient them to your presence in the community and practice will be helpful. Having a cell phone next to your chair/desk with a speed dial to 911 can expedite getting police there quickly in cases where there is an emergency.

When there is a need to call the police, or emergency personnel, it is important to always discuss your actions with your client first. Let them know what you are doing, i.e. calling the police because they refuse to let you have the keys or get a friend to drive them (if under the influence of alcohol). Give them a choice. Indicate that there are only two options; get a friend to pick you up, or drive you to the emergency room, or 911 will be called. Explain why there are only two options and let them decide. Describe the behaviors that you are observing rather than personality characteristics. In an emergency be clear in disseminating information to the police or emergency personnel. You may need to assist your client in remaining calm and providing reassurance.

Case Example # 1

A client who was falling asleep in the waiting room appeared to be extremely lethargic. It was known that he had to take many different types of meds for his mental health condition and had days earlier had a girlfriend break up with him. Though he indicated he was "fine," he clinically was depressed, and had suggested that his life was over. It was discussed with him that I could not work with him clinically given his condition, and that he had to be evaluated by the hospital because of his behavioral presentation. (I described how he was asleep when I came to get him and that I had difficulty waking him or getting him to respond. I also described that when he talked, his speech was extremely thick and difficult to understand). In spite of his denial, and statements of "I'm fine," I only spoke about his behavioral presentation and indicated the two choices. He finally allowed me to have his father drive him to the ER, and I called ahead to the hospital to provide clinical information. In this case, collaboration with the client by sharing of information and options, being very specific about what I was going to do and say, speaking with the family, and the hospital provided accurate communication, and sped up the time it took him to be seen. When he was discharged, the physician provided discharge information directly back to me, promoting further collaboration and continuity of care. (Personal communication 1, 2007)

Police Contact with Mentally Ill Clients in the Community

Mentally ill persons have been forced to leave locked institutions as a result of federal and state legislation. Many of these individuals do not receive ongoing services and as a result, when their behavior becomes bizarre, they get into trouble with the law. Police are authority figures and do not take orders-rather they give them. When responding to calls in the community for individuals who possesses a mental health condition, in crisis, many police officers go into these situations not knowing there is a mental illness present. The individual may overreact to the authority of the police officers and the police officer may use restraint, such as hand-cuffing to handle the client because of the resistance of the client. This presents a no win situation. The patient is challenging the authority.

How Can Counselors Help a Client with a History of Police Involvement?

When working with clients with whom there is a known possibility of getting into trouble (clients with bipolar disorder who are not medication compliant, schizophrenia, conduct disorders, etc.), teach them to present themselves to police in a non-threatening stance. Acknowledge that having one or several police officers arrive may be upsetting but that the situation can be handled in an appropriate manner as long as they stay calm. Teach clients to request an officer who is Crisis Intervention trained (CIT). Existing research shows that CIT training is a promising practice for changing officer attitudes and diverting people with mental illnesses to treatment (Compton, Watson & Oliva, 2008; Dupont & Cochran, 2000). Clients may believe that police presence is not warranted, but they have to realize that if a call is made, they have to respond. Encourage clients to ask police whether they are being taken into custody or to the hospital and that they will go voluntarily. Inform clients that their behavior at the time that police arrive is an indication of their ability to discuss the situation rationally. Inform clients that if they are brought to the hospital against their will, they need to remain calm, and explain the same things that you shared with the police in a calm manner. Educate clients about their right to request an advocate or lawyer if they feel that their rights were violated.

Allow them to use counseling sessions to role-play potential involvement with the police, allowing them to try these skills before they actually have a crisis. In cases where the client has a history of needing police interaction, there is a need to incorporate into treatment planning education about handling police encounters. Plan and conduct a "team meeting in which family members, the client and local police (those who might be involved in responding to the client), are present. Discuss who should be contacted in the case of a crisis, where the client should go, if hospitalization is needed, and methods that have been effective in helping the client to remain calm. Write up the plan, and distribute this to all parties involved in the planning process.

Case Example # 2

In one case, an individual with bipolar disorder often became manic, which caused him to leave home, and at times engage in behavior that often warranted police intervention (driving on yard, creating public disturbance, etc). When police responded, he often became resistant (because he was in a manic state) and stated, "I just need my medication." He would speak in a very loud voice and appear to be combative. Because this individual was very tall, he presented as a potential danger and police had to handle it accordingly. He was often brought to the hospital against his will, and given medications to "calm him down" that resulted in further exacerbation of his symptoms. This in turn resulted in him having to be admitted to the hospital for an extended period of time. A crisis plan was developed for this client with family members, psychiatrist, police, and counselor present which identified who should be called, what hospital to take him to, and assuring that the hospital was called with his history and current medications to prevent the use of medications which would make his symptoms worse and promote a quick connection with the counselor and psychiatrist to stabilize his behavior. (Personal communication 2, 2007)

Working with Community Psychiatrists

When working with clients who have psychiatric diagnosis or dual diagnosis (i.e. addiction and a mental health disorder) the screening process should identify behaviors that warrant immediate intervention or hospitalization. It is important to remember that when addiction is present addicts are at high risk for suicide, self-harm and potential harm of others. Once safety and ability to communicate is assured, psychiatric management should be incorporated into the treatment plan. If the individual is already under psychiatric care having a release signed by the client is beneficial so that communication and coordination can occur. In the case where there is no psychiatrist, providing a phone number, business card or brochure of local psychiatrists will be helpful. When referring a client to a psychiatrist for the fist time there may be feelings of denial that medication is needed or denial of the psychiatric condition. Clearly establishing a plan and time limit to call and make an appointment and support, encouragement and reassurance will help the client in obtaining needed psychiatric care.

Education about the psychiatric condition, how medications work and brochures with this information and handouts are also useful. Psychiatric involvement should be symptom-dependent and may start off conservatively with a meeting and initial consult with the psychiatrist. More highly structured involvement should occur to ensure control of incapacitating symptoms.

When a Psychiatric Diagnosis is Present

Case notes should document the presence of impairment, or dysfunction that persists, and is a result of a mental illness consistent with specific symptoms and criteria found within the DSM-IV TR (American Psychiatric Association, 2000). It has been found that psychotherapy in combination with pharmacotherapy, increases adherence to prescribed medications and enhances symptom resolution (Ellison, 2005). In private practice, it is beneficial to have a psychiatrist that the counselor can refer to on a regular basis. Efficacious treatment often involves the use of medication. In many cases practitioners may need the expertise of a psychiatrist to conduct evaluations when significant symptomology is present.

Monitoring of Medication

When a client has been started on medication the counselor may be the first person to know whether medication is working and managing symptoms. It is important to follow up with clients about whether they are noticing any changes in behavior or side effects. Encouraging a client to contact their psychiatrist may need to occur particularly in cases where clients are resistant to use of medications initially. Education about the time period it takes for medications to start working is important. There are many charts and brochures about different types of medications that can be distributed to your clients to support this process. If concerns are raised about cognitive or sexual functioning problems, encourage the client to talk and share these issues with their psychiatrist and review whether other meds may be helpful.

Working with Addictions

When working with clients who present with substance use or dependence disorders, counselors may have clients who are in active crisis, clients who experiment with substance use, or clients who are in recovery. Counselors will need to collaborate with doctors, family members, police, and psychiatrists to determine the client's condition and situation. They may need to send clients to other support services such as social or employment services, a food pantry for meals, or homeless shelter for housing. In the case of unemployment, the need for job retraining or employment services warrants a referral to employment or Temp Agencies. Counselors who work with clients with substance use issues would benefit from having the following available resources to support recovery:
+ Alcoholics Anonymous Meeting books
+ Narcotics Anonymous Meeting books
+ Al Anon Brochures
+ **Alcoholics Anonymous**
  International fellowship for men and women with a desire to stop drinking.www.alcoholics-anonymous.org
+ **Al-Anon**
  Help for families and friends of alcoholics. www.alanon.org
+ **Alateen**
  Recovery fellowship for teenagers who want to stop drinking._www.al-anon.alateen.org
+ **National Alliance of Advocates for Buprenorphine Treatment**

Naabt.org
+ **National Council on Alcoholism and Drug Dependence**
   Advocates for treatment. http://ncadd.org
+ **Narcotics Anonymous**
   International fellowship for men and women with a desire to stop using drugs. www.na.org
+ **NarAnon**
   Help for families and friends of drug addicts. www.nar-anon.org

It will also be important to have a listing and phone numbers of inpatient rehabilitation facilities. To obtain these, conduct a search online and/or in local phone books. Contacting local mental health agencies and behavioral health departments of local hospitals will help identify the names and contact information of treatment facilities with a reputation for effective treatment.

Working with Inpatient Facilities (Drug Detoxification, Mental Health)

In the mental health and addictions field, clients may need to be referred to an inpatient facility for detoxification, treatment for depression, suicidality, or other mental health condition which cannot be managed on an outpatient basis. The use of American Society of Addiction Medicine Patient Placement Criteria ASAM Criteria (1996) will be helpful to identify when to refer clients to inpatient settings using indicators across several psychosocial dimensions. Clients with behavioral or emotional disorders who are at risk of hurting themselves or others, and those with a high risk for relapse, or a poor recovery environment may benefit from inpatient treatment. Having these criteria at the intake session with the biopsychosocial is a helpful reference. Detoxification is often considered a precursor of treatment, because it is designed to treat the acute physiological effects of stopping drug use. Medications are available for detoxification from opiates, nicotine, benzodiazepines, alcohol, barbiturates, and other sedatives. In some cases, detoxification may be a medical necessity, as untreated withdrawal may be medically dangerous or even fatal.

Often clients who are attending counseling on an outpatient basis will insist that they can detox, cut down and/or stop their drug or alcohol use on their own. In cases when a client is attempting to reduce their use of benzodiazepines or alcohol, when consumption is at daily/high doses there is a need for immediate placement in a hospital or inpatient facility to provide medical supervision as these cases can result in death. A counselor may recognize the need for inpatient treatment and suggest this to the client. If the client refuses, suggesting that they cut down on their use can be a start (in the case of benzodiazepine or alcohol use, this may be judgment call—and the need for consultation with a clinical supervisor or colleague, medical professional who specializes in addictions is warranted). It is important to remember that empowering the client and encouraging them to take responsibility for their behavior is crucial. Establish specific criteria for how much the client will decrease their usage and document it in a contract form and have the client sign. Discuss consequences if there is no follow through. Referral to Alcoholics Anonymous, Cocaine Anonymous, and Narcotics Anonymous are options to get the client involved in a support group. In many cases, allowing the client to attempt to reduce their use, results in self-realization that they cannot do it on their own. At this point they will often ask for the counselor's assistance to get into an inpatient program Reassurance that they tried, and continual support and assistance with connecting them to a facility at this stage will be the focus of treatment.

Tips on Getting Clients Inpatient

When working with a client who has indicated their willingness to go inpatient, discuss with them the possible facilities you are recommending. Educate the client about the process involved in getting admitted to the facility, insurance or self pay options and the types of treatment they will receive. The client may need assistance with calling the facility. Encourage the client to make the call or have them make the call while they are in the office with the counselor present. The facility will ask for information about the client, amount of substance being used, and other information. They will also ask to interview the client to determine their willingness to get inpatient. At times clients are put on waiting lists and asked to call each day to ask for bed availability. If this is the case, they do need to call everyday or they will be removed from the list. Calling every day is an indication that they are serious about wanting treatment. Families may need support during this time as the substance abuser may still be home, they may be in withdrawal, and family members need to be educated about what the client is experiencing, the potential health risks, symptoms that they are observing and when they need to call for emergency assistance. Give phone numbers of the facility to the client and family members if there is a need to wait until a bed opens. Usually the inpatient facility will ask for insurance information up front to pre-certify clients prior to coming in. When contacting a facility to get a client services offer your name and contact information. Upon discharge, clients are often encouraged to call their individual counselors for follow up, or discharge summaries are sent to the counselor describing the treatment received and discharge status of the client. These discharge summaries provide helpful information that may need to be incorporated into treatment planning if they return back to the individual counselor.

Hospitals

Individuals with mental illness who seek treatment at hospitals are often faced with a level of force and possible coercion not shared by other patients seeking treatment. This treatment is largely due to hospitals personnel's responsibility to detain and examine patients who are believed to be dangerous to themselves or others. Those who voluntarily seek help are often detained against their will because of having to wait for a psychiatrist or mental health professional to conduct the evaluation. Policies for those seeking mental health services may include removal of clothing, shoelaces, detainment in isolation rooms etc, which make the individual feel overwhelmed and traumatized. Counselors who send their patients to the hospital for emergencies, assessment or crisis intervention can help reduce trauma, by calling ahead with information about the client, history, medication and indicated lack or presence of dangerousness to themselves or others. Counselors can also educate clients about how they present when walking into an Emergency Room for services. A client's behavior may suggest a need for restraint or seclusion if there is a presence of raised voices, impatience, etc. Utilization of police officers who are CIT trained will help in communicating to hospital personnel the nature of the mental illness and level of dangerousness. The ability of an officer to communicate level of impulse control, dangerousness, will promote reduction of restraint, isolation and help to de-escalate the patient.

Issues Associated with Counseling

Practitioners, by the very job they do, have the ability to promote positive life outcomes and prevent further problems, by providing mental health counseling, collaborating with family members, doctors, community agencies, and ensuring that clients have established a healthy life style prior to discharge. The efforts involved in ensuring that these services are in place prior will reduce the potential for relapse and recidivism. Monitor the quality of services and follow through of clients with obtaining support services. Encourage self-management and ability of the client to exert control over their day-to-day and long-term decision making. Promote access to health care. Encourage contact with and development of support systems outside the counseling setting. The more supports present the less stress associated with the mental illness. In this section, discussion will focus on the challenges which may arise with clients possessing addiction and co-occurring disorders during the treatment phase such as those who chronically relapse, working with insurance and managed care companies, use of EAP, helping clients with housing issues, and handling crises.

The Chronic Relapser

Relapse is best described as a regression in one's medical or psychiatric condition after a period of recovery from a particular illness. In the world of drug addiction treatment, or alcoholism treatment, relapse is defined as returning to a specific behavior after a period of abstinence from that behavior. Relapse is **not** an indication that the client has failed, nor does the client lose all the recovery "tools and information" they learned and practiced over the years. The relapsing client will always have that knowledge and history. Chronic relapsers are those clients that may have been in multiple treatments, they have had long periods of recovery, they know the lingo, the tools and the "Program", but they can't seem to stay clean and sober.

When working with a client who relapses frequently, focus on identifying underlying core issues that may not have been addressed earlier. Often times these issues continue to plague and sabotage a client's recovery despite their best efforts. Lingering issues of low self-esteem, self-doubt and self-hatred are often the result of unresolved childhood trauma. Counseling may involve teaching the client new techniques and coping mechanisms. When establishing a treatment plan, work with family, coworkers, close friends, medical doctor, psychiatrist and any other community services that may provide support to the client. Ask the client to hold a "team" meeting in which planning will occur with all possible stakeholders. Review the diagnosis, history of relapse, identify behaviors which others see which indicate relapse and develop coping strategies and plans to address each of the "precursors." Utilize the following questions in developing the treatment plan for the chronic relapser:

+ What behaviors does the person engage in?
+ What hospitals are usually the one's they attend?
+ Who needs to be contacted if person leaves, becomes manic?
+ Which hospital is preferable?
+ Who will contact the hospital to provide client history, medication and treatment information?
+ Who is the primary therapist- to be discharged to?
+ Who are the emergency contacts (person to be called for assistance)?
+ What is a "safe place" for person to go to
+ What medications is the client on?

When working with chronic relapsers, the goal of treatment is to decrease the number of relapses over time as well as the intensity, and frequency of behaviors associated with the relapse. In counseling sessions, what new behaviors can be taught to decrease relapse potential? (Examples might include: carrying medication on their person, in car, getting to a "safe place" as soon as behavior increases or excesses are noted). The following recommendations may help reduce the possibility of relapse:

+ Advocate for a complete detoxification
+ Establish daily structure and routine (develop a written document with the client that they can post at home)
+ Establish employment
+ Exercise
+ Self help group participation
+ It is also essential that the client have a strong support network in friends,

family members and co-workers
* Addicts who are chronic relapsers need to cut all ties with their old lifestyle

When your client comes back after a relapse, or inpatient placement it will be important to reevaluate the treatment plan and revise it. Questions that may be asked include, what is different this time? What did you learn inpatient about yourself, your addiction or mental health condition that you did not know before? What steps do you need to take this time that you have not done in the past? Specific objectives relating to the answers to these questions should be included in the treatment plan. Support systems need to be reevaluated again. Who exists in the person's life currently that can be used for support? What new supports need to be incorporated into your life? Identify triggers that led to relapse and develop specific coping strategies for each trigger. Recommendations that were not followed through previously, such as keeping medication on self, calling a sponsor, staying away from peer who uses, needs to be looked at and discussed in sessions.

Obtaining Insurance and Practicing Under Managed Care

Counselors often practice under managed care direction that necessitates creativity, and working within established limitations in the time period allowed for treatment. The purpose of managed care is to make sure that services provided to patients are necessary and that monies are used appropriately. In the area of addictions treatment, length of treatment stays have been shortened due to limited funding. This has resulted in a need for brief therapy and assisting clients in accessing community supports. Limited interventions are preferable to most insurance companies.

During the screening process when clients first call for services, it will be determined whether the client has insurance or not. A client's ability to pay may be limited or non-existent. Financial policies and a signed contract should be handled at the beginning of the first session so that all questions and payment is clearly understood. Provide phone numbers and addresses of local social service agencies for those clients who do not have insurance and provide ongoing support in their attempts to get assistance. Agencies that may be helpful in connecting clients with insurance include; Department of Social Services, Medicaid, and Husky programs. Keep several copies of applications on hand to give to your clients to help expedite the process. Educating clients about how to access health insurance may become a discussion during part of a counseling session. Insurance is generally available through employers or as an individual plan. If a client had insurance through their employer and lost their job, educating them about COBRA will be beneficial. Consolidated Omnibus Budget Reconciliation Act (COBRA) of 1985 requires a continuation privilege meaning that you can keep group insurance coverage by

Americans age 65 or older and people with certain disabilities can be covered under Medicare. Clients may need to be educated about paying the premiums themselves if they leave the group for a specified time period.

When discussing payment for services, be committed to the client by providing as much information about the cost of counseling, your ability to use a sliding scale, describe what their insurance coverage is and co-pay costs, and ensure that they are very clear about costs associated with missed appointments, insurance not paying, and collections. Utilize available resources, and "advocate for the greatest good for the greatest number," (Miller, 2005, p.5).

It is important to educate your clients about managed care and how the insurance companies warrant or do not warrant treatment. What conditions need to be present to obtain treatment? What will they pay or not pay for and why? What happens after the allotted number of sessions has been used up? Relate to the client that their ability to show improvement in the goals and objectives established in the treatment plan relates to whether an insurance company will allow more sessions.

Counselors often see the impact that poor, inadequate or a total lack of funding does with clients in need of services. Clients receiving substance abuse treatment are often discharged soon after admission for detoxification and sent back home to the same environment that they were using in. Evidenced based practice indicates that longer treatment stays promote longer periods of abstinence. It is also known that funding for services through insurance, Medicare, and other programs are inconsistent, complex to understand and fragmented. Counselors may need to provide support and explanations to clients who get discharged earlier than they expected.

Using Employee Assistance Programs (EAP)

The primary goal of an Employee Assistance Program (EAP) is to ensure the mental health of individual employees so that they can contribute to their company or facilities growth. EAP referrals encompass stress related issues, family issues, mental health issues, substance use, marital and or family issues. They may pay for three to six sessions with the goal of reducing the amount of time employees have to take away from work and improve and maintain productivity, increase morale, and reduce absenteeism. The rationale behind this is that when an individual is suffering from mental illness, substance use issues, or personal crisis at home or with the marriage, work productivity suffers. EAP's also have an advantage in their ability to connect employees with the appropriate service according to their needs. Encourage clients to check with their Human Resources person, or policy to determine if their company provides EAP services. Another resource is to look for local or statewide behavioral health networks that provide a broad range of services including independent EAP providers.

Housing

Social support is important for all groups. Those without social support are more at risk for detrimental mental health. Effective service delivery for persons with severe mental illness requires supported housing and supported employment. (Illovsky, 2003,). One of the most mentioned concerns among individuals who receive mental health services is related to housing. Many individuals coming out of jail, recuperating from mental illness, or struggling with addiction live at or near poverty level and available housing options are substandard. If dealing with a client who needs housing, connect them with social services agencies that can provide them with the information. Supportive housing programs can assist with reintegrating persons with mental illness, chemical dependency, and chronic health problems by providing basic needs for housing. Supportive housing programs also provide case management services so that individuals can also receive help in obtaining community based employment services, and support in independent living.

Handling Crises

Counselors may handle crises which include clients who present with suicidality, homicidality, abuse and neglect of children, sexual trauma, domestic violence and significant others in crisis. In an emergency, it is important to act rather than hesitate. In situations involving potential danger or a medical emergency, calmly get on the phone, and call 911. In psychological or emotional crisis there may be a need to sit with the client and talk with them about their options, and help them to calm down before any contact is made with outside assistance. "Can your parent (spouse, friend) get you to the hospital, or should I call for emergency services?" It is important to allow the client to make choices. In the case that a client has to go to the hospital, call ahead to make arrangements and provide information to support the care such as medications, name, address, emergency contacts, and the estimated time they may arrive at the facility.

Discharge Planning

Addiction and many co-occurring disorders are chronic, meaning the counselor may be working with the same client on and off over several years. Mental illness is often episodic and people who suffer mental illness should be able to flexibly enter and exit mental health services as needed just as others seek out medical care for health conditions only as needed. It is recognized that at times, community and other service providers have unrealistic expectations of public mental health services, such as an expectation that anyone with a chronic mental illness will remain under the care and treatment of a counselor, psychiatrist or other treatment provider. When clients are discharged it should be emphasized that they may always return to counseling should it be clinically indicated. Counselors should also educate their client about how to go about this process. Effective discharge plans should be written, and include appropriate referrals to community based providers or services. Prior to discharge, follow up with the client to ensure that contact has been made with service agencies so that there is no interruption in needed care and treatment.

Client Networking.

One of the advantages of reaching out to others is that it puts an end to much of the isolation and sense of being alone that clients experience. Clients not only have a chance to be heard, but to make new and valuable contacts with others while learning that they are not the only ones who have addictions or mental illness. Networking as a component of client treatment may include recommending participation in support groups such as women's support groups, Alcoholics Anonymous, Al-Anon, Narcotics Anonymous, Grief Support groups, Divorce Support, etc. When considering starting a private practice, contact local support groups and ask for brochures and handouts that can be given to clients. Hospitals and larger agencies may hold various types of support groups meetings including anger management groups, parent education, domestic violence groups, and groups with a focus on chronic health conditions. Follow up with clients when they come for counseling and ask about whether they are attending/not attending and whether they are deriving benefit from these groups.

Future Trends and Issues

Advocacy

Advocacy is an element of private practice not always addressed in graduate education programs and is a component of ethical practice. There are many areas of need with regards to dissemination of education/knowledge to the police, court systems, and social service agencies that provide services for those with addictions and mental illness.

Stigma

According to the President's New Freedom Commission on Mental Health (Mental Health Commission, 2003) mental illness continues to hold a stigma. Though a person may recognize that they are experiencing difficulty with some type of mental illness they may fail to seek treatment as a result of stigma by society or within their own cultures. Individuals in the military continue to face this dilemma currently as they fight for our country in Iraq, yet come home with serious post-traumatic stress disorder. The general public continues to hold on to antiquated notions about mental illness and chemical dependency. Counselors should continue to dispel these myths and educate communities, professionals, and the court systems, about the strengths, and capabilities that people with mental illness and addictions possess. Collaboration with members of the treatment team, family, and community providers, and contacts made at discharge, should focus on the assets, and progress that the client has made as well as their abilities, and successes. Encourage clients who have been successful in their treatment, who go on to become successful community members, to become a part of the education process through their own example.

Educating the Community

As mental health practitioners, we need to continue to work at reducing the stigma associated with mental illness and addiction and get involved in educating others about the efficacy of obtaining and funding treatment. Counselors can do this by offering targeted workshops and help educate their local communities about mental health, and the connection between good mental health and overall quality of one's personal health.

Counselors can also advocate for those with mental illness and addiction issues by joining national and state groups, which advocate against the negative impact of managed care. Contacting state counseling associations may provide a place to connect with others who are involved with advocacy initiatives.

CABLE and CIT Training

One example of a training initiative to help police work with clients with mental illness is called CABLE. CABLE is a program established to provide training and support to police who work with clients in the community. One focus of CABLE is the provision of safe and effective law enforcement and community response to those individuals who are in psychiatric crisis. This group has instituted Crisis Intervention training (CIT) for police personnel who tend to be first responders. CIT training is being offered across the United States but more education and training is needed.

Use of Medication Assisted Treatment for Addictions

Another area that has been receiving empirical support is in the use of medication to help prevent substance use as an adjunct to psychotherapy. Agents such as methadone, naltrexone, antabuse, LAAM, buprenorphine and acamprosate have been found to be effective in reducing withdrawal, and helping addicts maintain sobriety.

Summary

Counseling individuals with mental health and addiction problems can be very rewarding. When starting up a private practice, planning and identification of resources and referral sources is an important first step in ensuring timely and effective treatment. When gathering information during the intake session, it may be determined that the client needs further services, or placement into inpatient settings. This chapter discussed how the biopsychosocial can be utilized to identify areas of need and suggestions were made to assist counselors with connecting their clients to needed services, inpatient detoxification and community based agencies. One focus of this chapter was to promote collaborative treatment planning and counseling services across the mental health continuum. Strategies were presented in collaborating with the criminal justice system, police, psychiatrists, hospitals and other mental agencies. Specific challenges such as dealing with chronic relapse, managed care and insurance companies and handling crises were discussed as well as the need to advocate for the clients we serve. It is hoped that this chapter provides some direction to those who are new to the field who may not know the "ins and outs' of navigating the mental health system. Below is a list of suggested resources that relate to the topics covered in this chapter.

Suggested Resources

Advocacy Unlimited- site provides websites/links to various resources for individuals with mental illness (http://www.mindlink.org/index.html)

Bazelon Center for Mental Health Law
http://www.bazelon.org/

Better but not well: Mental health policy in the United States since 1950 by Richard G. Frank and Sherry A. Glied (2006). Journal of Mental Health Policy and Economics. 2007 Sep Vol 10(3) 153-154

Emergency Department Treatment of the Psychiatric patient: Policy Issues and Legal requirements, Susan Stefan, J.D.(2006) Oxford University Press

Health Care Coverage Options Database This website provides information about all of the major federal and state programs providing coverage for persons age 65 and younger. It provides contact information for each state for Medicaid, State Children's Health Insurance program, Federal health Care Tax credit program, and other state, federal and national health care assistance programs. (http://www.nahu.org/consumer/healthcare/topic.cfm?catID=3)

Lord, Vivian B. (2004). "Suicide by cop" inducing officers to shoot. Looseleaf Law Publications, Inc.

National Alliance of Advocates for Buprenorphine treatment (Naabt.org)

National Alliance on Mental Illness
Website for national health organization which promotes improvement in lives of persons with mental illness. Advocacy, education and leadership opportunities. Provides links to public education and individuals and families (http://www.nami.org/)

National Low Income Housing Coalition (NLIHC)
727 15th Street NW, 6th Floor
Washington, D.C. 20005
202/662-1530 | Fax 202/393-197393-1973

Prescription Drug Assistance program-web site dedicated to providing assistance for obtaining medications to low income individuals or families. (http://www.mindlink.org/prescription_help.html)

Resource Center to Address Discrimination and Stigma
ORC Macro
11420 Rockville Pike
Rockville, MD 20852
Phone: 1-800-540-0320
Fax: 240-747-5470
Web: http://stopstigma.samhsa.gov/
Director: Michelle Hicks
Email: stopstigma@samhsa.hhs.gov

Substance Abuse and Mental Health Services Administration (SAMHSA) (http://www.samhsa.gov/)

References

American Psychiatric Association (2000) Text Revision. *Diagnostic and statistical manual of mental disorders.* Washington, DC: Author.

American Society of Addiction medicine (ASAM). 1996. Patient placement criteria for the treatment of psychoactive substance use disorders. Washington, D.C.: ASAM.

Barry, James, R., Lambert, Daniel, R. Vinter, Patricia, Fenby, Barbara, L. (2007) Evaluating Risk and Functioning in Persons with Serious and persistent mental illness. *Psychological Services*, Vol. 4, No. 3. pp. 181-192

Beck, A. J. (2002). Jail population growth: National trends and predictors of future growth. *American Jails*, 9-12.

Beck, A. J., Karsberg, J. C., Harrison, P. M., & Bureau of Justice Statistics. (2002). Prison and Jail Inmates at Midyear 2001 (Rep. No. NCJ 191702). Washington, DC: U.S. Department of Justice, Bureau of Justice Statistics.

Compton, B., Watson, O. (2008). A comprehensive review of extant research on crisis intervention team (CIT) programs. *Journal of the American Academy of Psychiatry and the Law online.* 36:1:47-55.

Davis, S.R. & Meier. (2001). The elements of managed care.

Dupont R, Cochran S: Police response to mental health emergencies: barriers to change. *Journal American Academy of Psychiatry Law* 28:338–44, 2000[Medline]

Ellison, J., M. (2005). Teaching Collaboration between pharmacotherapist and psychotherapist. *Academic Psychiatry*, 29-2, May-June 2005.

Greenberg, M. T., Domitrovich, C., & Bumbarger, B. (1999). *Preventing mental disorders in school-age children: A review of the effectiveness of prevention programs.* Rockville, MD: Center for Mental Health Services, U.S. Department of Health and Human Services.

Illovsky, M., E. (2003) *Mental health professionals, minorities, and the poor.* Bruner-Routledge. New York and Hove.

Levant, R, F. and Heldring, Margaret. Commentary: Health care for the whole person. (2007) Professional Psychology: Research and Practice June 2007 Vol. 38, No. 3, 276–277

Mental Health Commission (2003). *President's New Freedom Commission on Mental Health.* Retrieved December 28, 2007, from http://www.mentalhealth-commission.gov/reports/FinalReport/FullReport-02.htm

Miller, G. (2005). *Learning the language of addiction counseling.* John Wiley & sons, Inc., Hoboken, New Jersey.

Substance Abuse and Mental Health Services Administration (2002). Report to Congress on the Prevention and Treatment of Co-occurring Substance Abuse Disorders and Mental Disorders. Bethesda, MD: Substance Abuse and Mental Health Services Administration.

Teplin, L. A. (1990). Policing the mentally ill: Styles, strategies and implications. In H.J. Steadman (Ed.), Jail Diversion for the Mentally Ill: Breaking through the Barriers (pp. 10-34). U.S. Department of Corrections, National Institute of Corrections.

Watkins, K. E., Burnam, A., Kung, F. Y., & Paddock, S. (2001). A national survey of care for persons with co-occurring mental and substance use disorders. *Psychiatric Services*, 52, 1062-1068.

Considerations for Designing and Opening a Private Mental Health Practice
By: Warren Corson III, PhD, NCC, LPC, ACS

Many clinicians enter the field with the goal of one day opening their own private practice or a program that follows their particular vision. While graduate programming prepares individuals for practice in the field, few programs offer information pertaining to starting a private practice. Therefore, many clinicians either abandon their goal of private practice or begin their exploration full of fear and trepidation. While there is no magic wand that can ensure that your endeavor will be a success, with proper planning and research you can make this transition as smoothly as possible. On the other hand, you may learn that private practice is not for you. (You also may learn from your exploration that you prefer the relative safety of working as part of a larger practice or program.) Either way, this chapter seeks to help the exploration begin so that you can make an educated decision into your future clinical practices.

Credentials-Are You Qualified to Practice in Your State?

Every state has requirements pertaining to setting up a private practice. While some practitioners use these requirements to circumvent the law such as using terms and titles that are not regulated, this discussion will focus on those who legitimately want to open a qualified practice. Some well meaning practitioners have decided to practice using unregulated titles, in the hopes of establishing a practice while seeking to become licensed. This is not recommended nor is it ever a good idea; it weakens the counseling profession and may also serve to taint your reputation once you secure the required credentials. You only get one chance to make a first impression and there is only one chance to make a solid name for yourself in the profession. Do it the ethical and legal way and you will see your name and practice grow, do it on the fringe and you may find yourself always seen as a fringe practitioner regardless of how many credentials you secure in the future.

Certification or licensure in the field is required to practice as a private practitioner. The exact type of credential required will depend on the state you intend to practice in and the types of services to be offered. In general you need a minimum of a master's degree in counseling or a related discipline, post graduate experience, and a passing score on a certification or licensure exam that is recognized by your state. For more information on requirements for your state contact the division of professional licensure (board of health department) in your state.

Identifying the Type of Practice You Want to Open

Planning your future career is analogous to constructing a building. The foundation type will depend on the typography of the lot, the type and size of the structure, etc. The foundation of your future practice will also be affected by similar issues: what type of population do you want to serve, in what kind of environment, what is your niche, what size practice do you desire, what are your funding sources, etc? How you answer these questions will directly relate to the foundation of the practice as well as the location, focus, and path you will take to reach your goals. For this chapter we will assume that you are seeking to open either a private (solo) practice or a small group practice that will be under your direction.

Selecting a Space

Selecting a space for a practice can be a daunting task, a task made more or less difficult depending on many variables. The type of space you select will depend a great deal on the population you wish to serve, availability of transportation, central location to the chosen population and unique factors in the area you are practicing in.

Cost will likely be a factor in selecting a location. Be sure to find a location that allows for ample room, has restroom access, a waiting area, area for files and billing, as well as an area for the receptionists You may choose a one person office where the clinician also performs all office related tasks. This set up, though not uncommon often puts undue strain on the clinician and can hinder positive growth due to the time consuming tasks such as answering phone calls, scheduling appointments, billing, filing etc. In the beginning some clinicians decide to share space in an existing practice. This can often be done on a per-session, per day, weekly, monthly or on a leased basis. Rates for this type of set up differ greatly as do services included. If exploring this type of situation ask the following questions:

1. What exactly is included in this agreement?
2. Is it renewable?
3. What are the parameters of termination of this agreement?
4. Does this agreement cover space only or will it include support staff, phone access, etc.?

5. Will the office refer clients to me?
6. Am I expected to refer only to members of the group?
7. Will the office handle billing?
8. Will the office billing department add me to the insurance panels?
9. Does this agreement include bookkeeping and tax related services?
10. Does this agreement include maintenance services and supplies?
11. Does this agreement include advertising?
12. Will I be listed as part of the group or am I just allowed access to a vacant office as needed?
13. Will I have access to the groups' clinical documentation and file storage or will I need to store my own files and develop my own documentation?

When first attempting a limited private practice many clinicians will often attempt to rent space from an existing office. This can be a positive experience providing one finds an office that is both a good fit physically and mentally- that is to say, are you comfortable in the space or does it feel too out of sync with your personal style? Do you feel you mesh well with the other clinicians or is their style too different from yours to be a good fit? Do your philosophies and techniques mesh or clash? If your styles clash this could cause a great deal of difficulty and lead to a failed attempt. It is best to learn all you can about those you may be sharing space with before any commitment is made.

Some shared space situations include only the use of a vacant office and nothing more. You may not be given access to a phone line, a computer, a support staff or documentation, all of which can be very expensive to develop or to supply yourself. Be sure to learn exactly what is included before signing a contract. Details that are not included may result in far too many hidden costs. For instance, a local company offers office space for part time practitioners. They advertise the use of an office for a flat rate of $20.00 dollars per session. On face value, many new private practice clinicians jump at this as the company only charges if the session takes place (there is no charge if the session is cancelled or if the person does not show up). After carefully exploring this possibility it becomes clear that this could indeed prove to be a costly contract. When exploring the office space one learns that it does not offer access to a phone line, no scheduling, no advertising, no listing on the office directory, it offers no computer use, no billing, no chart storage and no access to documentation for charts. Clinicians are responsible to find their own clients, provide their own scheduling, have a cell phone or other means to communicate with clients and they are responsible for providing and storing their own charts off site. The going rate for services in this area is $65.00 per therapeutic hour. If you take $20.00 from each session to pay for your office space that would leave $45.00 to pay for taxes (which can take about 1/3 of your income), leaving the rest to pay for your time and for all of the services not covered by your agreement.

Another agency in a different town advertises shared office space in their practice. They do not offer a flat fee per session nor do they offer a flat rate per month. Instead they take a percentage of the gross fees you collect per month (many of these situations range from 30-60 percent) and in return for this fee they provide you with such amenities as:

+ Your own private office.
+ Full computer access.
+ A phone line.
+ Full secretarial services.
+ Full billing services.
+ Full book keeping services.
+ Advertising.
+ Referral network.
+ Maintenance staff/grounds keeper services.
+ Charts and related documentation and storage.
+ Listing on the office staff list.
+ Business cards and related materials.

For many individuals this can provide a ready-made practice as it provides the infrastructure for a set percentage of your income. Should your income fluctuate, so too would your billing.

Others feel that they do not want to become part of an established group practice, as they want the thrill of opening a practice and to be independent of others. While perhaps the most difficult choice, it has many rewards:

+ Independence to design and implement your own vision of a practice.
+ Ability to personally select any employees.
+ Ability to select the types of payment methods, insurance plans.
+ Ability to set work days, hours, dress code and atmosphere of the office.
+ Ability to select the client type and focus of the practice.

There are many negatives to opening a private practice as well:

+ *Getting established-* A private practice offers no team of professionals to divide the work of establishing a practice. All responsibilities fall upon the practitioner who is opening the practice. This process of starting from scratch and developing the program will fall on the private practitioner unless they can afford to hire support staff to handle some of the requirements.
+ *Costs-* All costs are your responsibility. You have no other clinicians to help bare the burdens of maintaining and operating a practice.
+ *Isolation-* Many private practices remain small and have a limited consultation network. It can be hard to stay current and to have sufficient op-

portunities to connect with other professionals.

- *Supervision-* Supervision is necessary regardless of license type. Small practices must find outside sources for clinical supervision (see below for more information regarding supervision).
- *Lack of back up/long hours-* A private practice has no built-in network for back up should a practitioner be sick or otherwise unable to meet the needs of their clients. A private practice practitioner will need to establish a relationship with another practice or practices in the event you are unable to provide care for a period of time. This provision is a must in order to become a provider for certain insurance panels. Lack of back up also often leads to long work hours, as the private practitioner may struggle to meet the demands of clients.
- *Referrals-* Large practices often have built in referral networks. Independent offices have to develop their own networks.

Financing a Private Practice

The type and extent of financing needed to open a private practice will differ based upon the specific needs and type of practice as well as geographic location. For instance, opening a practice in a small town with low rent and readily available office space will be far cheaper than opening a practice in a location with little available space or one in a very large city such as Los Angeles, New York City, Boston, etc. where any space will be very expensive. Some clinicians initiate a private practice well funded, while others will have little financial reserves. For the sake of this discussion we will focus on those who have a noble goal but less than ample financial supports.

The Minimal Suggested Requirements for Opening a Practice

Space: This has been discussed previously, but is usually one of the most expensive aspects of opening a practice. The location needs to be easily accessible to your clients, preferably relatively easy to find and must have sufficient space to allow for a private office, waiting/reception area, an area to store charts, billing, etc. securely, as well as to have access to a restroom.

Sign: An office needs to have a clear sign. Investigate zoning and building regulations prior to ordering. Violating city zoning or the rules of the building could cause removal of the sign and replacement by one that meets requirements. Signs may have (if permitted) the name of the practice, name(s) of clinicians, phone number, web address as well as phone number and office hours. If the office does not allow walk-ins then the sign or office door may decide to have "by appointment only" posted prominently. It should be noted that sign size as well as content may be regulated—it is recommended to adjust content of the sign accordingly. Some zoning regulations limit the size of signs to as little as one square foot. In this case it is best to keep the sign as simple as possible.

Liability insurance: Practitioners engaging in therapeutic services require liability insurance in order to help protect themselves from financial liability should they be sued. The minimal coverage is generally a one million dollar per occurrence and three million dollar aggregate coverage. This coverage typically covers financial liability including medical expenses, defendants' reimbursement, deposition fees and property damage. Deductibles are usually part of these plans and can be several thousand dollars. Liability insurance can be secured by a number of companies; professional associations offer discounted rates to members. Insurance can be secured for a few hundred dollars per year per practitioner, but rates may vary.

Registering with the Secretary of State: Businesses that open within one state usually have to register with their respective state and or local governments prior to opening. Fees vary but could run several hundred dollars. The process is often times not difficult with the necessary paperwork made available either on government web sites or through telephone or in person requests. They generally are straight-forward and may not require the guidance of a professional. This process cannot be accomplished until the practitioner decides on the type of incorporation (see types of incorporation below).

Staff: A new practice will likely start with minimal staff. There is a need for someone to take care of billing and scheduling as well as to handle ordering supplies, paying for services and other expenses, bookkeeping, etc. In many new practices the clinician handles many of these needs but this is only a short term solution. Once session times start to fill, there will be little time to take care of these needs. It is best to have a person or people to fill these needs prior to the practice becoming too busy. It may be better to work at a short-term financial loss than to be faced with too many tasks when business picks up. Many of these positions will be part time to reduce costs of wages and benefits. It is wise, however, to make sure the office needs are met with part time help. Part time positions may lead to higher turnover rates should the employee be seeking full-time employment but take this position as a stopgap measure. Here, semi-retired individuals may be a good option as they likely are looking for fewer hours and benefits may not be all too important.

Office equipment and supplies: Some of the basic requirements for a private practice will include, desks, secure locking cabinets for charts and other private documents such as billing and related materials, schedules etc., copier, fax and printer (all-in-one machines may be a good choice especially for a small office), a personal computer, business software (depending on your needs), and miscellaneous supplies such as pens, paper, post it notes, etc.

Phone system: What was once one of the very expensive components of equipping an office has become affordable with the advent of cheaper phone systems that offer features that once were found only in large expensive systems. Small offices often will have 1-2 phone lines. One line will be for incoming phone calls while the other will be reserved for fax use (and in some cases outgoing calls). Systems now can include hand held units, base units, message machines, etc. These systems often come with features such as call waiting, hold, conference and speaker capabilities. They also have features such as interoffice paging, which will allow you to call other offices within the office building without tying up the phone line. These systems can be purchased anywhere phone systems are sold for a few hundred dollars.

Billing equipment: Modern billing is 100% computer-based electronic billing. While some plans still require paper based billing, more and more companies are refusing to accept paper claims. Electronic billing is provided either through the use of a third party Internet-based system or through the individual insurance company web site billing software. In either case, the billing staff for your office will need a secure computer with Internet access as well as the ability to navigate these systems. They will also need access to postage, possibly a postal scale or combined scale/postage meter depending on the size of the office. The software for billing can be free from the insurance company or could cost up to one hundred dollars a month depending on the vendor and type of software. Some practices decide not to have a billing staff in house; they hire billing services (see below).

Furniture: Furniture needs will differ depending on the type and size of the office, but in general a practice will have the traditional office furniture you may expect to find in any office. You may also want to consider some "homey" touches such as a couch and a comfortable chair for the office and a comfortable couch or couches and chairs for the waiting room.

Fixtures: Proper lighting is one of the keys to a practice. There is little flexibility in lighting, as most office space will come with built in florescent fixtures which will meet most needs. The actual office where sessions are held may utilize floor and desk lamps. Other fixtures may include a water cooler, magazine rack, brochure rack, bulletin board etc.

Advertising: Advertising can be a very expensive item to factor into the budget of a new practice. It also can be one of the most worthwhile endeavors based on several factors: size of the office being opened, number of clinicians, rapidity of growth being planned, connections in the area, visibility of the office, and the number of insurance companies the practice belongs to. Advertising budgets for a new practice can range from hundreds of dollars for a small office to tens of thousands. It may be best to consult a business planner in your area for guidance. See below for more information on specific types of basic marketing that can be employed.

Documentation: A practice will need documentation for charts such as Screening, Insurance/client coversheet, Intake, HIPAA, Consent form, Releases, Assessment, Treatment/session notes, Initial treatment plan, Master treatment plan, Discharge. See below for more information.

Capital: Ideally, a practice should have between six months to one year worth of capital to call upon based on needs. This money will insure that all expenses will be covered while the practice is being established (the first 1-3 years of a practice are often the most lean). If no reserve is in place the practice may fail because it was not possible to meet its financial responsibilities while becoming established in the market.

Types of Financing

Business loan: Banks routinely loan money for business start-ups provided they are confident in the business plan and the ability of those seeking the loan to be able to guarantee payment. This process can be overwhelming for non-business orientated professionals and would likely require the assistance of a professional to help navigate the process.

Personal loan: Many private practices are financed through personal loans. These loans may come in the form of refinancing a property, taking out a personal non-secured loan or similar alternative. As with other types of loans, consulting a professional may be in your best interest.

Business partners/investors: Some practices will utilize business partners or investors for start-up capital. This choice may be beneficial as it lowers financial liability on any one party, but can become cumbersome. As with bank loans, this type of financing should utilize a trained professional.

Grants: Grants can be a source for funding if you are a recognized not-for-profit 501(c)(3) corporation. To qualify as a not-for-profit you will have to develop a mission statement that shows community support and involvement as well as other qualifications. This process can be difficult when taken on alone; it is advisable to utilize an attorney and an accountant for this process. For more information see "for-profit or not-for-profit" below. Many grants prefer agencies with a proven track record and community involvement so searching for grants to help start a nonprofit may prove to be a daunting task.

Types of Incorporation

A private or group practice should be incorporated in order to help protect against personal liability. When determining the type of incorporation, it is recommended that a tax specialist as well as an attorney that specializes in business law be consulted. The following is provided as an introduction only.

Budman (1997) discusses the basic types of incorporation. They are not for profit, limited liability corporations (LLC) and professional limited liability companies (PLLC). All incorporations protect the individuals involved from personal liability, with liability being limited to any funds that have been invested into the corporation. Limited liability corporations blend ownership with partnerships and allow limited parties to manage the corporation or if the corporation so desires, they can appoint a partner or designee to manage the corporation (see Younger, et al. 1996, for more information). Many states prevent members of licensed professions from establishing LLC's; in this instance the formation of a Professional Limited Liability Company (PLLC) may be indicated.

In addition to tax advantages and increased protection from personal liability, LLC's and PLLC's allow partners and the corporation to own the practice and to benefit directly from any and all profits, including any profits from subsequent sales of all or part of the corporation. LLC's and PLLC's are not able to benefit from tax deductible donations nor can they be exempted from paying taxes like a 501(c)(3) tax exempt, not for profit corporation.

501(c)(3) Not For Profits may be the choice for practices whose mission is to provide services for the public benefit. Examples of public benefit for clinical practice may include free or sliding scale services to those in need, offering public seminars, outreach or other types of support to the community. Practitioners who are interested in this type of corporation should note that a tax exempted not for profit is not owned by any one person, it is an entity that owns itself and is governed by a board of directors. Profits are not divided among partners nor can it be sold and have the proceeds divided by partners. This is not a good selection for those intending on building a practice for profit or future sale.

An advantage of 501(c)(3) not for profits is that they are tax exempted (as a corporation but any personal income of employees is subject to income and any other related taxes) and can receive grants and tax deductible financial contributions. Should a not for profit close operations, property and other assets are generally donated to another not for profit.

It should be noted that not all Not for Profit corporations will be exempted from tax liabilities. Consultation with a business lawyer as well as a Certified Public Accountant with knowledge specific to Not For Profit's is recommended.

Is a "Home-based Office" Ever a Good Idea?

A very popular idea that has its roots in such notable icons of the field as Freud and Ellis, the topic of home-based offices can be controversial and dangerous. A home-based office is defined as an office that utilizes space within the practitioner's home living space. In this situation a client will enter the home of the clinician and engage in a session either in a common area of the home or in a small room that is used as an office. In such a situation there are many inherent risks, most notably the enmeshment of work and home lives on the part of the clinician, the lack of clear boundaries as well as a perceived lack of storage space for confidential documents. Clearly allowing clients to have access to a clinician's personal space and loved ones is to be avoided, but there are ways that a practice in one's home can be effectively secured.

In the past several decades there has been a resurgence of homes that offer custom options during the design and building process. In other cases, homes that already exist can be retrofitted to serve two purposes, a home based business and a separate living area. These situations offer the lower cost of working at home but provide the privacy and separation that is needed and found in having an office separate from a home. An effective home-based practice will have separate office and living areas. Living areas will not be accessible to clients at any time. The office area will ideally have its own entrance, waiting area, bathroom and offices that are accessible to clients without having access to the living areas of a home. This is most often possible through either an addition to, or major modification to an existing home, or through careful design for a new construction.

There are many issues to be considered besides the expense of a major remodel. When selecting a potential property a practitioner will want to check with local zoning regulations to determine if such a use is permissible. They will also want to consider the location, traffic patterns, parking and overall flow of the property and office area. Considerations for potential expansion should be factored in at this time.

Multi family homes may be a good way to lower overall costs for the practice while maintaining separate living and working areas. The first floor of a multi fam-ily home may be well suited once the area has been converted. It should be noted however that in most cases converting a former living area into offices can be ex-pensive as the entire area will need to be made into viable office areas: this often requires the removal of the kitchen, the construction and removal of walls as well as the potential for large expenses in the future should that space no longer be desired for office space and it needs to be converted into living space once again.

Should the choice of renovating be made and costs are not beyond the means of the practice, this approach assists the owner/practitioner by lowering ongoing overhead as the costs of the office space can be assumed by the homeowner or the cost of the office space can be lowered by the availability of renting the other unit(s) which will provide income towards any mortgage or related expenses.

The practice will have clear signage directing clients to the proper entrance. The living areas of the home should be properly secured to insure no entrance is reasonably possible on the part of the client.

Personal Safety/Security

Personal safety should always be a consideration in private practice. Certain types of practices have more inherent risks than others. Forensic examiners who routinely work with people involved with the criminal justice system likely face more danger on a daily basis than would a general practitioner, but all need to be cognizant of the risks they take as well as of ways to limit the potential for harm.

One of the most basic safety measures is to limit being alone in an office space during business hours. At times the knowledge that there are people within earshot can influence a potentially violent person and reduce the risk of harmful behaviors. In this vein a practitioner would be well advised to have an office with at least one other person in close proximity or at the very least to rent space in an active office building where it is likely that there will always be people coming and going during business hours. An office building with security is always a plus, though not always possible.

Other safety considerations would include screening potential clients for violence prior to admission, implementing safety policies for all staff or utilizing body alarms or other signaling devices should there be a need for assistance. Limiting exposure to violence also includes limiting low visibility areas in and around the office and grounds, maintaining proper lighting and staggering entrance and exit times to the office as well as using various routes to and from the office.

Medication Management Related Issues

Traditional talk therapy is effective with a large percentage of clients who seek treatment on an outpatient basis, but there are a large percentage of individuals who seek treatment for mental health issues that will require medication maintenance for varying lengths of time (such as for depression, anxiety, bi-polar, etc.). For this reason many practices will have at least a part time psychiatrist or APRN on staff. For practices that elect not to have prescribers on staff, a strong referral network is recommended. This network for referrals should insure that clients referred from the practice are seen in a timely manner and regular contact between practitioners is maintained in order to provide seamless care.

Applying to Insurance Panels

For most practices becoming a provider to major insurance panels is vital to the success of the practice. While some practitioners choose to avoid third party payments, most individuals depend on these plans for access to health care as they lack the financial means to pay for services out of pocket. For new practitioners, the process of applying for panels can be daunting, but it does not have to be.

Applying to insurance panels can be time consuming as each plan has its unique paperwork and processes, but with practice this can become straightforward. Some practitioners however will hire consultants to negotiate with insurance panels on their behalf. These services can be billed on an hourly, per application, or package deal depending on the company hired. Some of these companies will also offer ongoing billing services once they secure placement on the panels. One advantage of hiring a consultant to handle this process is the amount of time and energy saved that can now be spent further developing the practice. This author opened a practice without the aid of a consultant; he did not know these services existed and lacked funds to outsource tasks. In hindsight, it would have been much easier to ship this aspect of establishing the practice to a trained professional as opposed to learning while applying.

For those who would like to apply to insurance panels independent of a consultant table one provides a list of Internet contacts for the major insurance panels.

Table 1
List of major insurance company contact information:

- **Aetna:** http://www.aetna.com/provider/join/index.htmlBCBS: http://www.anthem.com/forms/east/CTProviderApplicationRequest.html or www.anthem.com and search for provider information
- **Healthnet:** https://www.healthnet.com/portal/provider/content.do?mainResourceFile=/content/provider/unprotected/html/national/network_participation_request.html or www.healthnet.com and search for provider information
- **CIGNA:** http://www.cigna.com/customer_care/healthcare_professional/medical/credentialing.html or www.cigna.com and search for provider information
- **PCHS/Multiplan:** http://www.phcs.com/faq/faq_display.asp?val1=24&val2=Provider&val3=Application%20Requests/Status or www.phcs.com and search for provider information
- **Galaxy Health:** http://www.galaxyhealth.net/contact.html (click on email for Contracting)
- **First Health/Coventry:** Healthcare National Network: http://www.firsthealth.com/DoctorsHospitals/participate.html
- **CHN (Consumer Health Network):** http://www.chn.com/CredForms/CredForms.asp or www.chn.com and search for provider information
- **MNH (part of Healthnet, but apparently with separate credentialing):** https://www.mhn.com/provider/content.do?mainResource=pracJoin&category=JoinNetwork or www.mhn.com and search for provider information
- **TRIcare:** This is the military health insurance management company and it in turn is managed by different companies, depending on your region-Apply for credentialing to your particular region's HMO.
- **United Behavioral Health:** http://www.ubhonline.com/cred/credIndex.html

- **Magellan:** https://www.magellanprovider.com/MagellanProvider/do/LoadHome

Recently the desire to streamline the credentialing of providers and to eliminate the need for providers to remember and organize many different provider numbers (one for each insurance company they contract with) has brought about two national provider number services. They are CAQH and NPI. Information and web addresses follow.

CAQH *(Council for Affordable Quality Healthcare)*

The Universal Credentialing DataSource is a part of CAQH's credentialing application database project that seeks to make the provider credentialing process more efficient for providers as well as healthcare organizations. By creating an online database that collects all provider information necessary for credentialing, CAQH hopes to eliminate the paperwork and hassle that many providers face during the credentialing process. https://caqh.geoaccess.com/oas/

NPI *(NPPES Registry)*

The National Plan and Provider Enumeration System (NPPES) established an NPI Enumerator who is responsible for dealing with health plans and providers on issues relating to unique identification. A provider needs to contact the NPI enumerator to be added to the data base. The NPI Enumerator may be contacted as follows: By phone 1-800-465-3203 (NPI Toll-Free) 1-800-692-2326 (NPI TTY) by email: customerservice@npienumerator.com, by regular mail: NPI Enumerator PO Box 6059 Fargo, ND 58108-6059 or via their Web Site which can be found at https://nppes.cms.hhs.gov

Currently not all insurance companies utilize these systems resulting in the duplication of information and a time consuming and often frustrating process of providing information to these systems as well as to the panels ensues. As these systems become better known, more panels will adopt them and in theory the process of joining panels will become much easier and less time consuming.

There is no standard time that it takes for the processing of applications or subsequent joining of a panel. Some panels are very responsive and have been known to start a new provider in as little as several weeks. Others take six months or more to begin a review. It should be noted that having the proper credentials and experience (which differs from plan to plan) will not guarantee placement on any insurance panel. Every plan has its own system of determining need for providers in any given geographic area. This system of determination is not public knowledge, nor can a potential provider easily learn of openings in their area without beginning the process of applying. Though consumers in a geographic area may feel that they lack a proper selection of providers; only the insurance panel can decide if additional providers are necessary. This issue is often exacerbated by the fact that provider lists are often outdated and may not reflect the actual amount of available providers due to practices that have closed, providers who have died or have become closed to new clients.

It should be noted that though a provider is not on a panel, they may be able to see clients with a given insurance provided their plans allow for out of network benefits. In such a case, the provider should make sure that there are no hidden penalties for going outside the provider network. Penalties generally include increased co pay amounts, deductibles that can be in the thousands of dollars or other restrictions.

Billing Services

Some practices, especially smaller ones, will find that they lack the resources to perform all of the billing requirements for managed care but lack the volume to justify the expense of hiring a person to only do billing. In situations such as this, hiring a billing service may be a good alternative. Billing services can be found in any number of ways: yellow pages, Internet search, word of mouth or through professional associations. Costs will be based either on an hourly basis (if hiring a local private specialist) or more commonly on a percentage of the billing fees that are collected.

Getting Referrals/Basic Marketing

Many practitioners view psychotherapy as a basic human service; while this is true, it, like medicine, is also a business and as such, there is a need to find a sufficient customer (client) base in order to maintain and grow a practice. There is no way to guarantee a large successful practice but there are many things that can be done in order to increase the chances of success. An established practice normally will have no issues maintaining a client base whereas a new practice may find it difficult to attract new clients.

Some effective methods to help establish and maintain a practice follow:

- *Word of mouth:* As a practice gains clients; word of mouth from these clients, provided that they are happy with the services, can be one of the best ways to attract new clients. This author has gained as many as ten or more new clients based off of word of mouth from a single client. It should be noted however that word of mouth that is negative can also take away potential clients as well.
- *Professional associations and publications:* Many professional associations and publications offer referral lists for those seeking a therapist in their area. Fees to be listed on these lists vary as do the number of potential referrals generated from these lists. It is advisable to discuss with other practitioners in your area to learn what has worked for them. It may save

a lot of time and money.

- *Advertisements:* Ads in local papers may help generate some attention to a new practice. These however can often be costly and reviews on their efficacy have been mixed.

- *Provider lists:* Based on price alone (free for providers of insurance plans) this is definitely a solid place to secure referrals. These lists are maintained by the individual insurance companies and made available to members through publications, on line web sites and through calls to the insurance company. Members of insurance plans that are accepted by your practice can request names and numbers of practitioners in their area that accept their plans.

- *Yellow pages:* Commercial customers may elect to place an ad in the yellow pages to help increase business over simply electing a plain text listing. The success of these ads will depend to some degree on placement and the design of the ad. While fewer people are using print phone books for searches, online yellow page listings can be a great way to attract new clients.

- *Internet searches:* Practices with a web presence may find an increase in new clients depending on the ease of being located through Internet searches. More and more individuals are using such searches to find services, and trends suggest that this will increase for years to come. Web sites need not be very expensive or overly fancy to be effective.

- *Referrals:* One of the more effective ways to establish referrals is through working relationships with other professionals in the area. General practitioners, psychiatrists and related professionals are often in need of high quality referral sources. Networking in the area of the practice can help build the practitioner's referral lists as well as to keep a free source of continuing referrals as well.

- *Online maps etc.:* with the increased presence of the World Wide Web, practitioners can now find more and more avenues for free advertisements. Sites such as "Google maps" offer businesses free ads that are easily accessible by web users seeking services in their areas.

An Overview of Marketing Types

Web site: The World Wide Web is one of the fastest growing areas of marketing potential that exists today. As few as ten years ago only the largest and most profitable companies were exploring this area of marketing. In the nineties web sites were often crude by today's standards but companies found that they were able to attract business and establish themselves in an upcoming media. Web design was in its infancy and finding individuals who could design, build and maintain a web site was often difficult and very expensive. With the ever growing popularity of the

Internet and the profit potential for design companies to develop easy to program and build web site tools, web sites can often now be developed and maintained by novice designers. Now, not only do the large corporations own and maintain web sites, but so do medium and small businesses as well. Personal web sites are also common place.

Today's small practice can establish itself on the web for only a few hundred dollars, provided they are willing to put sweat equity into the project. Companies such as Network Solutions (www.networksolutions.com), offer web hosting packages that include the costs of registering a domain name (the web address for your business), Web hosting (space on an internet server where your web site is housed), as well as access to customer support services and use of computer programs that help you build and maintain your web site. These packages can vary between companies and based upon the size of the web site you desire as well as bandwidth (the amount of activity (i.e. visitors) your web site can process at a time, but many packages can be purchased for around two hundred dollars per year. Practices can also purchase ads for their web site as well as preferred placement on search engines for monthly fees. The typical practice will likely not need this service as they will not need the volume of visitors in order to sustain or build their client base.

Web sites should be user friendly, not overly complicated and provide visitors with an easy to read source of information pertaining to the services and practitioners employed. Add-ons to the site that could help alleviate some of the work of office staff would be the ability to have directions to the practice listed (MapQuest offers free plug-ins that allow the client to enter their address and then get free directions from their location to the office), or to offer easy payment via debit or credit cards.

When selecting a web address, much thought and effort should be employed to balance developing a web address that is easy to spell and remember while still identifying the practice. This author originally developed a web address for Community Counseling of Central CT Inc. that tested well with employees and associates, but lacked the ability to be easily remembered and subsequently failed in the eyes of clients and with referral sources who could not remember the address in order to pass this information on through word of mouth. It was felt that www.cccofcentralct.org would be relatively easy to remember and sounded professional. Unfortunately it proved complicated for many clients and was thus not effective. Here listening to a practitioner's client base can be one of the best assets a practitioner can have. The author noted that many clients who did not know one another were calling him "Doc Warren." They reported that that name just fit him and the practice. During a session a client was verbalizing her frustration over not being able to get the web address correct and stated "You're Doc Warren, why can't I just type that in and get your site?" www.docwarren.org was launched shortly after and has proved to be an effective marketing tool. It should be noted that both addresses are utilized, one for marketing and the other, the original address, is used for official publications (though both addresses go to the same physical site).

Magnets/Pens/Mugs/Apparel: Other low cost methods to market and gain referrals is through the use of such items as magnets, pens, coffee mugs or apparel. Magnets often come in business card size and may be a replica of the business card that is used by the practice. While more expensive than a regular business card, magnets are often stored in visible locations such as refrigerators, file cabinets or similar locations. This increased visibility may lead to contacts that would not otherwise have been made.

Pens can be a highly visual means of advertising provided they are distributed effectively. One common mistake practices make is to buy the cheapest quality pen available in order to lower expenses. This is not always the best choice as cheaper pens usually have much lower quality than that of moderately priced pens and will likely have a much shorter service life. Here a balance of price and quality should be found as a comfortable pen may have a service life of a year or more compared to a lower quality pen that will often be used a few times and discarded.

Practices sometimes turn to larger items for marketing. It is wise to remember the image that the practice is trying to establish and to keep such marketing tools as professional as practical. While contractors have found great success with tee shirts, hats and sweat shirts, clinical practices rarely utilize these items unless they are part of a special event. Coffee mugs can be a great way to market your practice and can be offered to referral sources along with pens, magnets, brochures or other marketing items. Calendars can also be utilized as they offer a yearlong source of advertising though many clients may be hesitant to advertise the services of a mental health professional at home or at work where they would likely be questioned about any association.

Marketing items can be found locally through most printing or office supply stores but can often be found cheaper on the Internet. A search for marketing items will result in pages of resources. Internet based companies often have a large selection of items but lack some of the quality and options that can be found in local companies, though due to the ability to customize your order costs may be higher.

Brochures

Brochures can be a simple and relatively straightforward way to market a practice. Brochures can be expensive at times while they can also be very cheap depending on the approach. Traditionally many practices have hired professionals to design, edit and print brochures. This approach while arguably the most professional looking has drawbacks. In addition to high costs, this process also can be very rigid in that revisions will often times come infrequently and the amount of brochures on hand can pose storage issues as well. Printers often have minimum printing

93

amounts that can result in many cases of brochures being printed at a time. In addition, should a program brochure need to be changed, there will be a considerable amount of waste to contend with. Because of this, many smaller practices have adopted to on demand printing.

On demand printing can come in many forms. The most common being that the brochure will be designed and written in house by a staff member or consultant. It will be typed into a word document and either printed in house on a laser printer or will be taken to the local copy center and copied there as needed. It should be noted that when copying from an original that some copy quality will be lost especially if photographs or shading is utilized. For this reason it is usually better to print straight from the file. Many copy centers now have this capability.

Some practices will spend a great deal of money hiring a designer to develop a logo for the brochure and other publications. This practice is strictly optional and some would argue is an unnecessary expense. Some practices that desire to have a logo will simply design one in house.

Table 2
Brochures
+ Use templates- Ready-made templates can serve as a good base that can be customized for the practice.
+ Simplicity- Make it simple and easy to read.
+ Print in house- On demand allows for rapid changes, lower costs and less storage needs.
+ Be informative- Make sure if covers everything you would want it to cover if you were the consumer but do not get too wordy.
+ Look at other brochures- Find elements you like and incorporate them into your design.
+ Capture what makes your office unique- Why should they see you instead of the other practitioners in the area? What makes your office better or more comfortable than the others?

Opening a Practice on a "Shoe String Budget"
One of the more common questions posed on discussion boards and raised during presentations based on opening a private practice is "how can I open a practice with very little start up costs?" While there is no way to answer or explore every possibility in this section, some of the more common ideas are presented here as well as a case study.

When establishing a practice with minimal capital, it is wise to explore the needs of the practice and to rate needs in order of importance. A practice is well served by spending financial resources on the most crucial items and delaying purchases of other items until the practice is able to afford them. For example, delay the purchase of a professional fax or copy machine and instead purchase a home style copy or fax machine until the practice could afford a professional model. A laser copier/fax machine will save money over the long term as the cost for operating the units and the cost of printing is less expensive then the ink jet types though the start up costs are much higher. In addition to fees due to government agencies, rent, and salaries, offices will need a physical space, a phone and in most cases Internet access as well as furniture. There is no way to avoid fees to government agencies or the cost of phones or Internet but there are many other ways to reduce start up costs.

Furniture for the office can often be purchased at used office furniture companies for pennies on the dollar. Most of these companies offer flat rates for delivery, meaning that you pay the same amount for one piece as you would for a truckload of pieces provided they are purchased and delivered at the same time. Developing a list of pieces needed prior to purchasing can help lower costs not only in delivery but also in time saved in the purchase process. This will lower labor costs and increase the chance of larger discounts for volume purchases. In some incidents, rented offices will come with furniture and fixtures that were left by the prior tenants. These items may serve the practice well, or at least until new items can be afforded.

Money can be saved in office space by shopping around and looking for low cost space. One common mistake by new practitioners is that they sometimes sign leases with one of the first opportunities they find as opposed to doing an in-depth analysis of the available offices in the area. Some practices will save money by leasing office space "as is" and remodeling the area to suit their needs rather than having the owner remodel it for their use.

Other options are to rent space from an existing practice until finances allow for the practice to expand and branch out on its own.

Case Study-Community Counseling of Central Connecticut, Inc.

Community Counseling of Central Connecticut Inc. (CCC) was founded in 2005 by this author. It had a very modest start-up budget of $7,000.00 that came in the form of a personal loan that the author took out in his name. The mission of CCC was to provide as many free or low cost sessions to those in need as possible, while being able to maintain itself and grow. Because of its mission CCC applied to the IRS and registered with the secretary of state as a 501(c)(3) not-for-profit. This process can take many months depending on the quality of the application submitted and the wait time the IRS has before it can review the documents. In the case of CCC, it took nine months before the documents were reviewed; they were approved on the first review.

While still in the planning stages, CCC looked at other agencies in town to help determine the competition that it would face as well as to learn the needs of the locale. Interviews with local people uncovered what CCC determined was a potential niche. Many people were not happy that the leading agency in town was a huge building complex. They reported they felt intimidated by the size of the building and by the corporate feel of the services provided. CCC would never attempt to out market or head-to-head compete with an agency that had a yearly budget in the hundreds of millions. Instead of taking on the competition, which would have been in vain, CCC's director sought to focus on what the competition could not offer due to the size of its corporation: personal service, a home like office, an anti-corporate feel. Searches for office space in traditional office settings were replaced for ones that had a home like feel and quality. CCC settled into an office that was a home in a non-commercial area; the nearest business being between one half to one mile away. The home was then converted into office space. The reception area had no sliding window separating the receptionist from the client, the offices were furnished not in industrial furniture but in chairs, couches and other pieces that can be found in nicer homes, and office equipment was present as needed but blended into the office space.

CCC, having no budget for advertising started a word of mouth campaign. It used its weaknesses as its strengths. Instead of being a small company with an uncertain future and no real finances, it was marketed as a small office that provided services, with a personal touch. Instead of being too small to be able to afford to advertise, CCC billed itself as an independent office that had chosen not to be listed in the phone book or to advertise in order to remain true to its mission of providing personalized service. The smaller office, the environment and the hand-selected people who work in the office helped to build a market in the town and soon without advertising or even being in the phone book, CCC was nearly at full capacity.

Instead of expensive ads, CCC utilized less expensive sources for advertisements. It gave out pens to clients and to potential referral sources, it developed a simple but effective brochure that was printed in house (and thus easily adaptable to reflect changes in the agency) and made it available to anyone with an interest. It also had business card magnets as well as other items that were cost effective to purchase but of enough quality to likely stay in use for some time.

Marketing was largely word of mouth and as referral sources were identified there were subtle changes in the way CCC supplied these sources with information. Utilizing a rapid response model, CCC supplied area referral sites with materials within hours or at most a day or two after the request. Instead of the usual methods of supplying these sites with minimal materials, CCC would supply these sites with a box of 250 business cards, brochures, pens, magnets etc. The rationale is that these supplies were relatively cheap and that referral sites are notorious for running out of materials and not calling to request more. CCC also established and maintains a web site that has helped attract clients.

When CCC opened for business it lacked some vital equipment such as a fax machine but it had secured the basic needs of the office through used equipment and office furniture retailers. As the business began to grow, profits were put back into the business to help furnish it. CCC's director has maintained a very fiscally conservative approach and has been able to grow and prosper without ever opening any additional lines of credit other than the first loan that helped open its doors.

Supervision and Other Ethical Responsibilities

Many clinicians wrongly assume that once they are licensed and in private practice that they no longer need a supervisor. This could not be further from the tenets of best practice and are incongruent with ethical guidelines. All practitioners, regardless of education, experience or credentials are required to meet all ethical guidelines including a requirement for competent supervisory experiences. These experiences can come in many forms, influenced greatly by the needs, experiences and credentials of the practitioner. An experienced clinical supervisor who provides in depth, structured supervision on a regular basis will best serve a new practitioner. More experienced practitioners may be well suited to less formal types of supervision such as group supervision, and or peer supervision.

Formal supervision consists of weekly (for a full time practitioner) supervision sessions where the supervisor will review treatment plans for current cases and provide in depth analysis and feedback to the practitioner to insure the highest quality of care. This is generally provided on an individual basis though practitioners with less need for supervision may choose to meet in groups. Groups offer the benefit of hearing others practitioners' experiences and how they have met the challenges posed to them in practice. However, groups will allow less time and focus for the individual practitioner.

More experienced and highly credentialed practitioners may elect to utilize peer supervision. Peer supervision can be a formal process where two or more practitioners meet to discuss cases or issues and to receive and provide feedback. This can be a formal process and part of a regularly scheduled meeting schedule or it can be far less formal and scheduled on an "as needed" basis.

Costs can differ a great deal for supervision depending on the type employed. Formal individual supervision will likely be the most expensive while peer supervision can often be secured free or at low cost.

Documentation Requirements

All practitioners, regardless of the size of the practice or type or funding, are required to maintain proper documentation. Some larger and well funded practices will utilize electronic forms that are programmed to collect the information and automatically place the information on the areas of the form where it is needed. When using computer-generated forms, this information can be placed on all forms simultaneously (i.e. DSM IV TR related information is automatically placed on all forms that require this information as soon as it is typed into the system). Some practices will have the funding or resources to have documents designed for their ready use, while many others will have to develop their own. All insurance companies have their own documentational guidelines that providers must adhere to, though many times these standards are similar from company to company.

Practitioners who would rather spend their time treating clients than "buried in paperwork" often view documentation requirements as cumbersome. Documentation serves as a legal record of treatment and client progress. This information is most important in the event that the treating clinician becomes unavailable for treatment and a new clinician needs to assume treatment. It can also be used in defense of any accusations of malpractice or to resolve billing issues.

The designing of documentational forms can be very expensive but is imperative that all major forms be utilized by practitioners regardless of practice size or funding.

Though beyond the scope of this chapter, downloadable sample documentation, rationale for and descriptions of individual forms and related information can be found at the following addresses: http://cccofcentralct.org/comcounselingreview.html or http://docwarren.org/comcounselingreview.html

Table 3
List of Practice Forms

+ Pre-Screening
+ Insurance
+ Client Coversheet
+ Intake
+ HIPAA
+ Consent to Treatment Form
+ Release of Information
+ Psychological Assessment Summary
+ Treatment/Session Notes
+ Initial Treatment Plan
+ Master Treatment Plan
+ Discharge Summary
+ Encounter Form (billing form)

References

Barry, P. (2006). Forming and belonging to a peer consultation group for your own mental health and creating a psychotherapy practice that addresses specific topics. *Perspectives in Psychiatric Care, 42(1),* 63-66.

Barry, P. (2006). Handling the finances: HMO versus private pay. *Perspectives in* Psychiatric Care, 42(2), 133-136.

Budman, S. H., & Steenbarger, B. N. (1997). The essential guide to group practice in mental health: clinical, legal, and financial fundamentals. New York: Guilford Press.

Kazanjian, V. (1982). Peer review: A private practice model. *Professional Psychology,* 13(1), 74-78.

McMahon, G., Palmer, S., & Palmer, C. (2005). The essential skills for setting up a counseling and psychotherapy practice. London: Routledge.

Meltzer, M. (1986). Community psychotherapy as a model for the new private practice of psychology.*Journal of Clinical Psychology, 42(2),* 392-398.

Pressman, R. M. (1979). Private practice: A handbook for the independent mental health practitioner. New York: Gardner Press.

Stout, C.E., & Grand, L. C. (2005). Getting started in private practice. The complete guide to building your mental health practice. Hoboken, NJ: Wiley.

U.S. Department of Health and Human Services. (n.d.). *Public law 104-191. August 21,1996. Health insurance portability and accountability act of 1996.* Retrieved February 15, 2008, from http://aspe.hhs.gov/admnsimp/pl104191.htm

A Frame of Reference for Ethics and Law for the Counseling Profession

By: Cynthia Rutledge, Ed.D. & Ann-Marie DeGraffenreidt, J.D.

Ethics codes were enacted to protect the clients and to offer guidance to the professional counselors who serve these clients. Various mental health organizations have developed their own codes of ethics, including the American Counseling Association (ACA), the National Board for Certified Counselors (NBCC), the American Association for Marriage and Family Therapy (AAMFT), the American Psychological Association (APA) and the National Association of Social Workers (NASW). Although each of these organizations has a different set of ethics codes that highlight different themes, each code of ethics accomplishes three common objectives: educate professionals about proper ethical conduct; promote accountability; and improve practice by offering answers to difficult questions and situations (Corey, Corey, & Callahan, 2003).

Ethics Framework for Counselors

Bersoff (as cited in Eddington & Shuman, 2005) identified ethical conduct as the result of knowledge and an understanding of the philosophical principles that underlie a code of ethics. Ethics are the ideal standards of performance set by the profession and are overseen by professional associations, national certification boards, and government boards, which regulate the mental health professions. Ethics for the counseling professional are standards of behavior imposed by the American Counseling Association (ACA) and the National Board for Certified Counselors (NBCC). Ethics are not governed by state or federally mandated laws, and there are no court imposed penalties for violations of the two codes of ethics espoused by these governing organizations. However, the law defines the minimum standards by which society as a whole will tolerate these standards and those laws are enforced by the government (Corey, Corey, & Callahan, 2003).

The original ACA Code of Ethics was instituted in 1961, has since undergone four revisions, and underscores the relevance and importance the association places on the welfare of each individual client. The current ACA Code of Ethics, which dates from 1995, establishes the principles that define ethical behavior for members of the association. The Code of Ethics is a concise, yet thorough document, that addresses the counseling relationship; confidentiality issues; professional responsibility; relationships with other professionals; evaluation, assessment and interpretation of those assessments; teaching, training, and supervision; research and publication; and resolving ethical issues. The Code of Ethics is the basis for processing ethical complaints lodged against association members. Members of the association can access the comprehensive code of ethics via the Internet (www. counseling.org).

The National Board for Certified Counselors (NBCC) publishes ethical standards for Nationally Certified Counselors (NCC) and those seeking national certification. The NBCC serves as the governing board and the basis for resolving all ethical matters, including mediation; ethics complaints and investigations; complaint resolution; ethics complaint hearings; hearing committee decisions and orders; and disciplinary actions. These standards are posted on the NBCC website (www.nbcc.org).

There are also individual state certification standards, and the professional counselor must conform to the professional standards of conduct of the state in which s/he practices, as well as the ethical standards of the ACA and the NBCC. Each state has a government website where a counselor can have direct access to the state standards and ethical considerations and practices.

Why Do People Choose to Become Counselors?

Exploring why one decides to enter the field of counseling helps us to understand that the first "ethical" step for the beginning counselor is to try to be as emotionally healthy as possible and to "know thyself." The beginning counselor needs to be able to objectively evaluate his or her own behavior and emotions and clearly examine his/her own goals for choosing the helping profession, as well as identify any personal issues that might adversely or ethically affect a client in therapy. Counselors need to be attuned to the client, and a counselor's own issues can interfere with this process. A client cannot advance beyond the level of emotional health of his or her own counselor, nor can the counselor ask the client to do what s/he is unwilling to do emotionally or psychologically. The counselor must protect the welfare and rights of the client and that cannot be accomplished if the counselor is not emotionally stable.

The beginning counselor must also be aware of the influence of his/her own personality and needs, and any unresolved personal conflicts. These might encompass the need to tell people what to do or to take away pain from clients. There also might be the need to have all the answers and to be the perfect person, or a deep desire to be recognized and appreciated as a caring person. Some counselors may have the strong egotistical need to assume too much responsibility for any positive changes in the client. The very last reasons one should become a counselor are to assuage the need to rescue clients, to improve a fragile self-esteem, and to reassure oneself about one's own attractiveness to others. It should be noted that many beginning counselors should assess the benefits that they might receive from participation in the counseling sessions themselves (Corey, Corey, & Callahan, 2003).

Why is the Counseling Profession so Concerned about Ethics?

Stein (as cited in Forester-Miller & Davis, 1996) opines that counselors are held to a higher code of ethics because they are entrusted to promote the goals of the client, protect the rights of the client and maximize the benefit of the counseling relationship, and minimize any potential harm that may befall the client during this professional relationship. The counselor, because of the nature of the client/counselor relationship, wields power, so it is imperative that s/he be aware that s/he can easily influence the decisions and choices that the client may make during this relationship, and that those choices may be life altering. The counselor, therefore, must ensure that s/he does not impose his/her own moral codes and ideals onto the client, and that the client's personal decisions must be respected, even though this may be difficult for the therapist to accept (Forester-Miller & Davis, 1996).

As a professional, it is the duty of each counselor to have a clear and distinct understanding of the codes of ethics for each organization of which one is a member and to be vigilant of any changes made to these ethical bylaws. Most counselors belong to professional organizations, either at the state or the national level. Through this involvement in state organizations, the counselor can become educated regarding new developments within the counseling profession, learn about new laws that may impact the counseling profession, maintain certification/licensure standards, and experience camaraderie within the profession. Dansby-Giles, Giles, Frazier, Crockett, and Clark (2006) propose that ethics circles for counselors are extremely important to help them learn and understand those ethical codes that all therapists must abide by, thereby allowing them to debate how to handle actual cases that have posed difficult ethical dilemmas. Mascari and Webber (as cited in Waltz & Yep, 2006) also recommend that counselors participate in such groups on a regular basis so that the understanding of the ethical codes is maintained and ethical decision making models are applied to these ethic circle cases across various counseling work settings.

Ethical Decision Making Using a Structured Decision Making Model

A graduate course in professional orientation and ethics and the ACA and NBCC Code of Ethics are only guidelines. As such, they cannot unequivocally answer all the ethical questions and dilemmas that will face the beginning counselor. Using these guidelines, one must develop the ability to make sound ethical decisions using logic, common sense, and good judgment. To enhance and hone these skills, the counselor has an obligation to continually read the latest literature on ethics, legal issues, and professional practice and to attend professional development activities regarding professional ethics and practices.

Ethical decision-making can be a complex and daunting process. While codes of ethics provide counselors with standards of behaviors, they do not provide them with an understanding of the process by which ethical decisions are examined and then made (Hill, 2004). An ethical dilemma requires careful study of the nature and breadth of the dilemma, as well as the consequences of any course of action taken to resolve the situation (Forester-Miller & Davis, 1996). Several authors have put forth models of ethical decision making that are designed to clarify the decision making process and provide counselors with a framework for evaluating and resolving ethical dilemmas (Cottone & Claus, 2000).

Principle ethics address the situation, and ask of the counselor, "is what I am doing ethical, according to the Code of Ethics standards and according to legal practices?" Aspirational ethics address whether the counselor is doing what is best for the client, is using the most effective treatment, and is experiencing the desired results through the use of that treatment. Professional orientation and ethics textbooks and the ACA espouse a variety of ethical decision-making models, but all concur that there are moral principles involved with such decision-making.

In a review of the literature, Cottone and Claus (2000) described three approaches to ethical decision-making. These approaches include theoretical based, practice based, and specialty relevant models. Kitchner (as cited in Forester-Miller & Davis, 1996) postulated the ethical decision making process around the theory of moral development. Practice based models provide an approach to ethical decision making that is less theory based and, instead, has functional steps that are the basis to be used during the decision making process (Cottone & Claus, 2000). Specialty relevant models describe steps to be taken during the ethical decision making process for a specific area of counseling for marriage and family therapy (Southern, Smith, & Oliver, 2005) and topics such as multicultural counseling (Frame & Williams, 2005).

The beginning counselor should use a structured ethical decision making model to guide this decision making process. This process begins by the counselor making a decision whether the ethical issue involves principle, or mandatory, ethics (that focus on ethical guidelines that are provided by ethics codes and standards with the goal of solving a particular situation), or aspirational ethics, which focus on the highest professional standards of conduct to which a counselor can aspire, as well as the moral fiber and character traits of the individual counselor.

Kitchner's Critical Evaluation Model of Ethical Decision Making is an example of a model based on the theory of moral development that can be applied to ethics issues and the virtues of making decisions (as cited in Forester-Miller & Davis, 2006). Kitchner's model is based on four basic moral principles: autonomy, beneficence, nonmalfeasance, and justice or fairness.

Autonomy is the promotion of self-determination or the freedom of clients to choose their own direction. It predisposes that independence is good. As a counselor, however, you must weigh the effects of autonomy for each individual client. Can the client make a sound and rational decision? If s/he can make such a decision, does s/he understand the impact of the decision upon others? If clients are incapable of making a competent choice, such as dependent children, then the counselor should not allow them to act upon any decisions that may be harmful to themselves or others.

Beneficence refers to promoting the personal growth and development of the client. What is the best interest for the client and who should determine the best interest? As a counselor, you must look at the values and morals that are involved. It is the responsibility as the counselor to ensure that harm to the client or others will be prevented, when at all possible.

Nonmalfeasance means that the counselor avoids risking harm to the client. It is frequently explained as "above all, do no harm" and is considered to be the most critical of all the principles. This would also include the counselor's changing a diagnosis or diagnostic label to benefit the client. Justice, or fairness, refers to providing equal treatment for all clients. If the counselor decides that an individual client must be treated differently than other clients, then the onus is on the counselor to explain the necessity of such a decision and the appropriateness of treating the client differently.

The American Psychological Association Ethics Code also includes fidelity, veracity, and self-interest to the ethical decision making process. Fidelity is the virtue of faithfulness, of the counselor being true to his/her commitments and obligations to his/her clients. Veracity implies that the counselor will be truthful and honest in all of his/her endeavors. Self-interest stresses the importance of adequate and appropriate attention being paid to the counselor's own self-care so that his/her competence and judgment do not become impaired.

When a counselor is faced with an ethical issue, the situation must be examined to see how all of these moral principles may have an impact on the issue facing the counselor. These moral principles have been set forth to assist in the resolution of ethical dilemmas, and they may make the decision an obvious choice once the issue is examined in light of these principles. However, in more complicated, convoluted ethical dilemmas, a practical approach using a structured model for decision-making may be more effective.

Most of the practiced based models have several key elements in common: identification of the ethical issue; application of the ethical codes; consideration of options and potential consequences; and the implementation of an action plan (Remley & Herlihy, 2005). The ethical decision making model outlined in *A Practitioner's Guide to Ethical Decision Making* by Forester-Miller and Davis (1996) is a seven step approach that is comprehensive, but very straightforward. The model is conceptually grounded in Kitchner's moral principles of autonomy, justice, beneficence, and non-malfeasance but is practical and easy to use.

The Seven Steps in Making Ethical Decisions

1. **Identify the problem**- this includes gathering relevant information, as well as reviewing the literature. The counselor needs to be aware of the different perspectives that may be used to identify the problem. The counselor needs to ask questions such as "is it an ethical, legal, professional, or clinical problem, or a combination of any of these issues?" If it is a legal issue, the counselor should seek the advice of legal counsel immediately. If the problem can be resolved based on agency or institution policies and procedures, s/he should use those guidelines to assist in the resolution of the issue.

2. **Apply the ACA Code of Ethics**- the code clarifies ethical responsibility, establishes principles that characterize professional behavior, and guides decision making. Consider autonomy, beneficence, nonmalfeasance, and justice. After applying these standards to the situation, if there is no resolution, then the counselor should proceed to the next step within the ethical decision making model.

3. **Determine the nature and dimensions of the dilemma**- ethical dilemmas exist when moral or ethical standards can be used to justify opposing actions, but neither action is more appropriate than the other. Consider both mandatory and aspirational ethics. The six moral principles that relate to professional functioning (autonomy, nonmalfeasance, beneficence, justice, fidelity, and veracity) may not apply to every situation.

4. **Generate potential courses of action**- following a comprehensive review of the ethical guidelines and reviewing the nature of the problem, all potential courses of action should be analyzed through a process of brainstorming, which would include the thoughts and ideas of colleagues as well. This would be considered the initial brainstorming or "what ifing" component of the decision making model.

5. **Consider the potential consequences of all options and determine a course of action**- after listing all possible courses of action, the next step in the decision making model is to evaluate the feasibility of the options and their consequences through consideration and application of information that has been collected during steps 1 through 4 of this model. The assessment should culminate in determining the course of action that will

lead to the most appropriate outcome without creating any new ethical or moral issues for the counselor.

6. **Evaluate the selected course of action**- after examining the potential consequences of the courses of action in step 5, a course of action must be selected. The professional counselor should assess his or her own sense of fairness by determining if s/he would treat a different client the same in this situation, if s/he would want his/her behavior reported to the press, and if s/he would recommend the same course of action to another counselor facing a similar ethical dilemma (Stadler, as cited in Schultz, 1990). If all three questions are reached satisfactorily, then the counselor should move to the final step of the decision making model.

7. **Conclusion**- the final step in ethical decision making is the implementation of the selected course of action, which should lead to the resolution of the ethical issue that confronted the counseling professional.

Following these seven steps of this ethical decision making model provides assistance to the counselor, but there is rarely a right answer to a complex ethical dilemma. The solution proposed does allow the counselor to reach an outcome that is based on an extensive analysis of the problem and is a decision based upon relevant ethical codes and literature (Forester-Miller & Davis, 1996).

Legal and Ethical Responsibilities of the Counselor

Protecting the Client's Rights

First and foremost, counselors have legal and ethical responsibilities toward the client. All clients bring certain enduring rights to every counseling session and the counseling relationship. Clients have the right to ensure that they receive sufficient information to make informed choices about entering and continuing the client-counselor relationship. Informed consent comprises the right of clients both to be informed of their rights concerning therapy, and to make an independent decision regarding the therapeutic process. The counselor must define and clarify the counseling relationship, which begins with the intake interview and continues until its termination. Four ethical codes specify the parameters of informed consent as follows:

1. The National Association of Social Workers (NASW) (1999) states that social workers should use clear and understandable language to inform clients of the purpose of the services, risks related to the services, limits to services because of the requirements of third party payer, relevant costs, reasonable alternatives, clients' rights to refuse or withdraw consent, and the timeframe covered by the consent.

2. The American Psychological Association (APA) (2002) states that when

psychologists conduct research or provide assessment, therapy, counseling, or consulting services in person or via electronic transmission, or other forms of communication, they obtain the informed consent of the individual or individuals using language that is reasonably understandable.

3. The American Association of Marriage and Family Therapy (AAMFT) (2001) states that marriage and family therapists obtain appropriate informed consent to therapy or related procedures and use language that is reasonably understandable to clients. The content of informed consent may vary depending upon client and treatment plan.

4. The American Counseling Association (ACA) (2005) states that when counseling is initiated, and throughout the counseling process as necessary, counselors inform clients of the purposes, goals, techniques, procedures, limitations, potential risks, and benefits of services to be performed, and other pertinent information. Counselors take steps to ensure that clients understand the implications of diagnosis, the intended use of tests and reports, fees, and billing arrangements. Clients have the right to expect confidentiality and to be provided with an explanation of its limitations, including supervision and/or treatment team professions, to obtain clear information about their case records, to participate in counseling plans, and to refuse any recommended services and be advised of the consequences of such refusal.

To protect these client rights, the first ethical concern is counselor competence. The counselor needs to undertake a critical self-analysis and review course work, seminars, certification exams, and professional supervision, and then examine his/her own personal strengths and weakness. The counselor must know the limitation of their training, as well as when to refer someone to another practitioner. Counselors must also keep current with the latest findings and techniques in the areas in which they are qualified. Knowing a number of counseling techniques is one sort of self-knowledge; knowing which techniques have been proven effective for conditions presented by clients is another level. Knowing the potential dangers of a technique, such as group therapy, is as important as knowing the benefits. Being able to objectively evaluate one's own behavior and emotions—another kind of self-knowledge—is critical in many ethical dimensions, especially in regard to handling transference, the process whereby clients project onto their counselor past feelings or attitudes they had toward significant people in their lives, and countertransference, the counselor's reaction to the client's transference response (being overprotective, rejecting the client, seeing oneself in the client, desiring a social relationship with the client). Koocher and Keith-Spiegel (1998) quote a list of red flag behaviors, which are warning signs of boundary crossing, and this list should be part of a regular self-review for any practitioner in the helping profession.

Questions the beginning counselor should ask regarding the ethics behind their services fall into the realm of considering whether the counselor is providing only services for which he or she is qualified. If a potential client wants services the counselor is not qualified for, what would be the ethical responsibility for the counselor? If the counselor has honestly reflected on personal competencies and has arrived at the decision that he or she is not qualified to provide the counseling services required for a specific client, then the ethical decision is to refer to someone who is qualified. If no such person exists, then it is up to the counselor to become competent enough to provide services in order to protect the client's rights. It is also required that the counselor strive for professional growth by recognizing that a degree does not mean the end of one's education, but quite the contrary, continued education is an absolute. The counselor must remain current in the field of practice and must learn new competencies as well.

Another aspect of self-knowledge as a core ethical principle is advocacy; every therapist should maintain regular contact with colleagues, either through peer-to-peer consultation and discussion, or by having his/her own therapist with whom s/he can discuss ethical issues or behavioral warning signs if and when they arise. A therapeutic relationship is not mandatory, but it should be considered as a strong ethical foundation for any therapist to have his or her own therapist, and certainly to have experienced more than a cursory amount of personal therapy.

Mascari and Webber (as cited in Waltz & Yep, 2006) encourage counselors to regularly participate in continuing education whereby ethical issues are presented and discussed so that counselors can learn the standard of care in comparison of their own professional behavior to those of their colleagues; further, they stress the importance of ethics circles for counselors, where counselors debate how to handle ethical dilemmas with their peers.

A counselor's responsibilities to retain membership in relevant professional organizations, comply with codes of ethics and regulations of those organizations, receive ongoing supervision and continuing education, and remain aware of professional limitations are important to any counselor's professional life. A marriage and family therapist (MFT) working with multiple clients must have an added sensitivity to and understanding of the structural context in which they are working (Mascari & Webber, as cited in Waltz & Yep, 2006).

Green, Shilts and Bacigalupe (2001) suggest that an MFT needs to examine his/her practice based on interaction, rather than linearly, since marriage and family counselors face clinical decisions about relational and contextual issues that individual counselors do not. In marriage and family therapy, there are multiple clients to take into consideration, even if there is only one client directly involved in the therapeutic relationship at a time (Koocher & Keith-Speigel, 1998). A marriage and family therapist must put the welfare of the family system ahead of that of an individual client. In individual counseling, the therapist has the client's best interest in mind when pursuing a course of treatment. Marriage and family therapy places equal importance on all members of the family, not necessarily the initiating client or the identified patient. This equal division of focus can create ethical dilemmas for the therapist in terms of balancing very different desires and client goals. Difficulties arise when the therapist's choice to promote the best interest of an individual interferes in the well being of the family unit. Corey, Corey, and Callahan (2003) suggest that the therapist must attempt to ensure that "the status of one partner or family member does not improve at the expense of the other partner or family members" (p. 400). The MFT who treats the entire family system as the client will avoid advocating for any individual and can assist in creating positive change within the family.

An effective informed consent procedure minimizes the client's misunderstanding and lowers the chances of suing the counselor on this basis. Somberg, Stone, and Claiborn (as cited in Eddington & Shuman, 2005) recommend a written, standardized consent form that includes: date of discussion about consent; name of the counselor and client; statement indicating that the client understood the information, statement of the client's right to withdraw from the counseling sessions; benefits and risks inherent in counseling; description of the type of treatment that will be administered during the counseling sessions; issues of confidentiality, privilege, and their limits; and the signature of the client. The counselor should also include the purpose of the counseling records and how they will be kept; fees; procedures for insurance reimbursement; and individual counselor or agency policies and procedures. Clients must also be aware that if they are participating in managed care that the HMO may influence the course of therapy, which would include the length of treatment, the number of sessions allowed, and the content of therapy. Clients have a right to know how their health care program will affect their case, and how confidentiality may be affected by the reimbursing agency's ability to access and review their records. (Smith & Fitzpatrick, as cited in Eddington & Shuman, 2005).

Privacy, Confidentiality, and Privileged Communication

Clients have the rights to privacy, confidentiality, and privileged communication. Beginning counselors are often confused regarding the difference among these three rights. Stadler (as cited in Schultz, 1990) opined that privacy means the clients have the right to choose what they reveal about themselves in a counseling relationship. Confidentiality refers to the *ethical* responsibility of the counselor to limit access to the personal information of the client based upon the clients' permission. Privilege refers to the *legal* responsibility of the counselor to protect client confidentiality. Confidentiality is the *ethical and legal* obligation that the counselor must give to the client, and privileged communication is the *legal* concept that prevents disclosure of the client's confidential information to others without the client's permission. Privilege prevents the counselor from answering questions in court and/

or refusing to produce records without fear of contempt of court. Gladding (2006) further espouses that confidentiality is the client's right to be able to speak to the therapist knowing, with confidence, that nothing said during a counseling session will be disclosed to others without implied or expressed authorization. Only two individuals know everything that happens in each counseling session: the client and the counselor. Whenever information gained through the counseling session is provided to third parties, it then becomes a legal matter.

State and Federal statutes govern when a counselor is either permitted or required to provide information to third parties. The Health Insurance Portability and Accountability Act (HIPAA) is the federal statute that governs access to health records, including mental health records. It also articulates the rights of individuals who participate in counseling.

The ethical issues regarding children are different from those in the adult counseling relationship. For dependent children, the parent or guardian is the only one who can authorize treatment and can obtain information regarding the overall treatment of the child, which includes diagnosis, prognosis, and treatment plan. The legal authority may be restricted to the parent/legal guardian, although individual state statutes vary. Counselors who work with children need to be aware of state and local statutes regarding parental rights.

Confidentiality is the primary right of the client, that disclosures during therapy sessions are protected within the professional relationship of the client-therapist. However, there are specific circumstances that confidentiality may be broken for ethical and legal reasons. Confidentiality may be breached to protect a client from suicide.

Confidentiality guidelines have been issued for these associations, and the beginning counselor needs to be knowledgeable with the all aspects of these guidelines:

1. **National Association of Social Workers**- social workers should protect the confidentiality of all information obtained in the course of professional service, except for compelling professional reasons. The general expectation that social workers will keep information confidential does not apply when disclosure is necessary to prevent serious, foreseeable, and imminent harm to a client or other identifiable person. In all instances, social workers should disclose the least amount of confidential information necessary to achieve the desired purpose; only information that is directly relevant to the purpose for which the disclosure is made should be revealed.

2. **American Association of Marriage and Family Therapists**- marriage and family therapists disclose to clients and other interested parties, as early as is feasible in their professional contacts, the nature of confidentiality and possible limitations of the clients' right to confidentiality. Therapists review with clients the circumstances where confidential information may be requested and where disclosure of confidential information may be le-

gally required. Circumstances may necessitate repeated disclosures.

3. **American Counseling Association**- the general requirement that counselors keep information confidential does not apply when disclosure is required to protect clients or identified others from foreseeable or serious harm or when legal requirements demand that confidential information must be revealed. Counselors consult with other professionals when in doubt to the validity of an exception.

4. **American Psychological Association**- psychologists disclose confidential information without the consent of the individual only as mandated by law, or where permitted by law for a valid purpose such as to (1) provide needed professional services; (2) obtain appropriate professional consultations; (3) protect the client/patient, psychologist, or others from harm; or (4) obtain payment for services from a client/patient, in which instance disclosure is limited to the minimum that is necessary to achieve the purpose.

Based on the tenets of each organization and legal requirements, there are times that confidentiality must be broken. It is sound practice for the counselor to inform the client that an issue has arisen during the therapeutic milieu that necessitates the breaching of confidentiality. If at all feasible, the therapist should engage the client in participating in the process, as this may negate a negative impact on the counseling relationship (Mappes, et al., as cited in Eddington & Shuman, 2005). Conditions under which confidentiality may be breached include these situations (Herlihy & Corey, 1996):

- when a client poses a danger to self or others
- when a client discloses an intention to commit a crime
- when the counselor suspects abuse or neglect of a child, or an elderly or disabled person
- when the court orders a counselor to make records available

Each client has the right to understand the exceptions to the right to confidentiality from the onset of the therapeutic relationship. If this has not been done, then the therapist has violated the right to informed consent. The important first step of having a signed consent form, which includes confidentiality and its exceptions, precludes the counselor from being confronted by ethical and legal situations, such as license revocation, expulsion for a professional organization, or a malpractice lawsuit. If the therapist breaches confidentiality, s/he may be liable under civil law for breaching confidentiality. The counselor may also risk the loss of his/her license to practice.

Confidentiality, Privilege, and Reporting Child Abuse

All states have reporting laws that require the counselor, who is a mandated reporter, to breach confidentiality and report child abuse suspicions to law enforcement officers or child protection agencies. All state laws require that the therapist put the child's best interest above the therapeutic relationship. State laws stipulate that the counselor is a mandated reporter and *must* submit a report based on suspicion. Since the implementation of these laws, the volume of reports being made to child protection agencies has increased dramatically; however, research studies have indicated that counseling professionals still fail to report such abuse for a variety of reasons (Pope & Bajt; Zellman, as cited in Eddington & Shuman, 2005).

If the client is the suspected victim, then there is no breach of confidentiality in reporting the abuser. However, if the evidence of abuse comes from the client, who is the suspected abuser, the counselor is faced with an ethical issue. Miller and Weinstock (as cited in Shultz, 1990) stated that this is difficult for those therapists who do therapy with sex offenders. The state laws are all created as the result of the federal child welfare laws (Child Abuse Prevention and Treatment Act, 2006).

There are civil and criminal liabilities when there is a failure to report child abuse by a mandated reporter. The child abuse reporting laws require that all known or suspected cases of child abuse be reported by those professionals who are mandated child abuse reporters, or those professionals risk liability by not filing a report (Besharov, as cited in Shultz, 1990). The counselor, as the mandated reporter, must notify the appropriate agencies, such as the police or child protective services, when child abuse is an absolute and is known to have occurred, as well as if child abuse is suspected by the counselor. Frequently, mandated reporters are required to submit a written report following the telephone call to the agency to which the initial report was made. In numerous states, the name of the reporter is also required to remain confidential. However, there are exceptions, such as if the mandated reporter's testimony is needed in court hearings related to the abuse or neglect. As such, state statutes include an expressed immunity from legal action for any counselor who breaches confidentiality to report child abuse, and attempts to comply with these statutes in good faith. In most state statutes there is a criminal penalty for failure to report, and not reporting is a misdemeanor that can be criminally prosecuted (Weinstock & Weinstock, as cited in Shultz, 1990).

Record Keeping and the Impact of State Statutes Governing Confidentiality

The professional counselor is required to maintain effective clinical notes to ensure that these comprehensive notes may protect the counselor from any disciplinary actions or legal actions (Schaffer, as cited in Eddington & Shuman, 2005). Each association has its own ethical codes regarding the keeping of confidential clinical notes. The American Association of Marriage and Family Therapists states that marriage and family therapist's store, safeguard, and dispose of client records in ways that maintain confidentiality and in accord with applicable laws and professional standards. The National Association of Social Workers states in its code of ethics that social workers should take reasonable steps to ensure that documentation in records is accurate and reflects the services provided. The American Psychological Association code of ethics requires psychologists to create, and to the extent the records are under their control, maintain, disseminate, store, retain, and dispose of records and data relating to their professional and scientific work in order to facilitate provision of services later by them or other professionals.

The code of ethics regarding records for the American Counseling Association is very descriptive and detailed. The ACA requires the counselor to ensure that records are kept in a secure location and that only authorized persons have access to these records; the counselor must obtain permission from clients before electronically recording a session; counselors must obtain permission prior to the client's being observed during a counseling session, or a supervisor's reviewing a transcript; counselors provide access to records when requested by competent clients. The counselor has a right to limit access to a client's records when there is compelling evidence that the records would cause harm to the client. When a client does receive his or her records, the counselor will provide consultation to interpret these records. Unless there is an exception to the confidentiality mandate, the counselor must obtain written permission from the client to disclose or transfer records to a third party.

Several statutes govern the confidentiality of client information, providing guidance on when a client's permission is required prior to the transmittal of information gained during the counselor client relationship to a third party and when release without a client's permission is required. Confidentiality statutes are designed to ensure that the client knows when, to whom, and for what purpose the information that s/he shared with the counselor is released to a third party. When the client is a child, there are two public agencies with whom a counselor is most likely to exchange information: the child welfare agency and the public school. A counselor may also exchange information with post secondary education institutions, when the client is an adult.

Both agencies' rules concerning the release of information are governed by federal law. The state child welfare laws concerning confidentiality and the release of information are designed to comply with the Child Abuse Prevention and Treatment Act (CAPTA) (2006) and Subchapter IV B of the Social Security Act (1974). Education records are governed by the Family Education Rights Privacy Act (FERPA) (1974).

All three statutes define the term "records" broadly. In the context of child welfare, the definition of record includes any and all information related to an allegation of child abuse. This includes information concerning treatment provided as a result of the abuse. Abuse is also defined broadly enough to include allegations of neglect. When child welfare information is in a client's record, it is essential for a counselor to remember that the counselor can release the child welfare information to another entity only if it is for purposes permitted under Title IV B or CAPTA. The simplest way to assure that this standard is met is to direct any entity requesting records from the counselor concerning information related to mandated reporting or treatment resulting from the intervention of the child welfare agency to the child welfare agency. This avoids the possibility of the counselor's releasing information that, though in the counselor's possession, the counselor does not have the authority to release.

Like CAPTA and Title IV B, FERPA prohibits the disclosure of most personally identifying education information without a release of information. Schools are permitted to release certain basic information without written consent if the school district annually tells parents and students what information will be released without written consent and provides an opportunity to opt out of this release. Education records under FERPA include those records that contain information directly related to a student and that are maintained by an educational agency or institution or by a person acting for such agency or institution.

When a client is an adolescent or older, other statutes governing the confidentiality of a client's records may be implicated in a counselor's request for information. These statutes govern records concerning alcohol, drug abuse, and mental health treatment records as per 42 U.S.C 290dd-2 (1994). Finally, the Health Insurance Portability and Accountability Act (HIPAA) governs a counselor's access to and dissemination of a client's confidential health information. It requires that healthcare providers give patients notice of their privacy practices and requires that specific information be provided to a patient in a release of information. When records are covered by FERPA, they are specifically excluded from HIPAA. A client's consent to release information is required even when all that is desired is to have a conversation, rather than securing a copy of the client's physical record. Therefore, a client's release of information should do the following in order to comply with HIPAA and the other confidentiality statutes discussed:

+ Identify the individual(s) who the information is about;
+ Identify the agency that is disclosing the information;
+ Identify the information that will be disclosed;
+ Identify the purpose of the disclosure;
+ Identify the agencies that will access or receive the information;
+ State the expiration date of the consent to release information or the circumstances upon which the consent automatically expires (for example, when a youth is successfully terminated from probation or court supervision);
+ Describe how consent can be revoked;
+ Identify who in the agency that is disclosing the information is respon-

sible for assuring that the agency complies with the laws concerning confidentiality;

+ State the date of consent with the youth's parent(s) or legal guardian's signature; and

+ State that the subject of the information has a right to a copy of the release.

School Records

There are several types of school records that are kept concerning a student. It is important to know what is available in order to ensure that, as a counselor, you know all sources of historical and current information concerning your client. Regardless of who has responsibility for keeping the physical record in the school, *all school records are governed by FERPA*. Frequently, different parts of a school record are the responsibility of different parts of a school system. When a copy of the entire school record is requested, it is essential that a clinician know who to contact if parts of the record are not received. A student's record can consist of the following parts: (a) the record maintained by the school nurse; (b) the academic record; (c) the special education record, including any progress notes made by any individual providing any type of therapeutic services to the student as a result of those services being determined necessary by either an IEP or a 504 team; (d) school based health clinic records; (e) discipline records; and (f) reports and other documents related to psychological and other testing conducted by the school or by a professional hired by the school, whether or not a child receives services determined necessary by a IEP team or a 504 team.

School Nurse's Records

The records kept by the school nurse are usually kept in the nurse's office. These consist of documentation of all of a child's trips to the nurse and documentation of any medication that is dispensed by the nurse. In addition, immunization records are kept by the school nurse and sometimes, depending on the school district, also the records concerning a plan created as required by Section 504 of the Rehabilitation Act of 1973 to assist a child having difficulty in school. Specifically, Section 504 of the Rehabilitation Act of 1973 requires that governmental entities make reasonable accommodations to address issues related to a disability that substantially limits one or more major life activities. These can be records and reports concerning the psychological makeup of the student and recommendations made to address any issues identified by completed evaluations of the student. Finally, a school nurse is also responsible for keeping the records of state mandated screenings, like those for scoliosis and hearing.

School Based Health Clinic Records

The records maintained by a school based health clinic are different from those maintained by the school nurse. A clinic's records are sometimes not considered part of a student's record under FERPA by the school district or the entity operating the clinic. Because the clinic is located in the school, whether or not a student is receiving services from the school is frequently unclear to the parent or guardian. Depending on the school district and the state, school based health clinics can be part of the municipal health department or a contracted service provided by one or more health providers within the municipality. The state laws governing the clinics can also be the responsibility of a state agency other than the one that governs public schools. Some schools will refer a student who does not otherwise qualify for services to the clinic to receive counseling. School based Health Clinics are governed solely by state statute.

Academic Records

When school personnel refer to a student's academic record, they usually mean report cards, standardized test scores, attendance, and sometimes discipline records. These are also the documents that are usually sent when a copy of a student's record is requested.

Special Education Records

Special education is "specially designed instruction, at no cost to the parents, to meet the unique needs of a child identified as having a disability and needing specially designed instruction to address the problems with learning that are a result of that disability" (IDEA, 1997). In addition to special education, a child may also be entitled to related services, which include "transportation, and such developmental, corrective, and other supportive services (including speech-language pathology and audiology services, interpreting services, psychological services, physical and occupational therapy, recreation, including therapeutic recreation, social work services, school nurse services designed to enable a child with a disability to receive a free appropriate public education as described in the individualized education program of the child, counseling services, including rehabilitation counseling, orientation and mobility services, and medical services, for diagnostic and evaluation purposes only), *as may be required to assist a child with a disability to benefit from special education,* and includes the early identification and assessment of disabling conditions in children" (IDEA, 1997).

Special education, like access to student records, is governed by federal law. The law, known as the Individuals with Disabilities Education Act ("IDEA"), 20 USC 1400, et seq mandates that public schools accepting federal funds provide a "free appropriate public education" to all disabled children living in the school district in the "least restrictive environment." Special education records include all documentation concerning a specific student that is related to identifying whether a child qualifies for special education and related services and the data concerning the development of the program of individualized instruction for the student, as well as the information concerning how the child is progressing in that program. A special education record includes (a) all psychological, psychiatric and physical and academic evaluations, assessments, and testing of a student; (b) documentation of the meetings to identify what evaluations, assessments and testing should be administered; (c) meetings to discuss the results of these evaluations, assessments and testing; and (d) documentation of meetings held to design or modify a program of instruction and related services and to discuss a student's progress within that specially designed program. However, certain special education records—usually psychological and psychiatric evaluations—are not always kept with the record's other parts. This occurs because some individuals believe that the psychological and psychiatric information is *more* confidential that the remainder of the student's record. *This is not true.* All information in a student's special education *and* regular education record is *equally* confidential, i.e. a student's attendance record is entitled the same level of confidentiality protection under the law as a student's psychological evaluation.

Depending on the age of the student and the level of services provided, a special education record can easily be several inches thick. Schools appreciate requests for information that are limited in scope to only that information that a counselor will use. However, do not hesitate to request the entire record if it is necessary to assure that a client receives appropriate treatment.

Child Welfare Records and Reporting

As previously stated, all records concerning child abuse investigations and treatment are subject to confidentiality. If a counselor has such records, regardless of how they are obtained, they remain subject to the state's statutes governing their release. It is also important to remember that information a counselor obtains during treatment concerning the abuse or neglect of a child *must be reported* to the appropriate authority (Confidentiality of Records, 42 U.S.C. §290dd-2(e)(2)).

Hospitals and Health Professionals Records

Hospitals and health care agencies can be sources of information needed by a counselor. Since the passage of HIPAA, the steps necessary to obtain information are fairly standard. While many agencies and hospitals prefer that a release of information that they have created be used, this is not required under the law. As long as the release of information contains the required notices, it complies with HIPAA. When information is required from a health care agency or a hospital, the release and a written request identifying the specific information needed should be sent to the record keeper of the agency or hospital. HIPPA release forms vary by state and examples for your situation are available readily on-line.

Legal Framework for the Counselor

Role of the Counselor in Legal Proceedings

When a counselor becomes involved in a legal proceeding as a witness, his/her role changes significantly. A counselor goes from having significant power and knowledge in the therapeutic relationship to having no power and very little knowledge about the legal process. Attorneys have one essential ethical responsibility in common with counselors: their sole duty is to advance the goal of their client. There are a few basic rules that a counselor should follow when required to testify in court while under oath. The counselor can be required to testify at a deposition, an administrative hearing, or a trial before a judge. A deposition is part of the information gathering that occurs after a lawsuit or criminal action is initiated but before the trial. Administrative hearings are similar to trials but are sometimes less formal and occur before hearing officers or administrative law judges. There are ten basic rules for witnesses when they testify, and all of them require practice.

1. *Always tell the truth.* The adjudicatory process relies upon the honesty of the individuals appearing before it. Additionally, this reliance is supported by stiff penalties for perjury.

2. *Take your time.* The witness must refrain from speaking until three events occur: (a) the attorney or judge completes their question and *stops speaking;* (b) you, as witness, have listened to everything that was said and (c) you think about whether you understand the question, whether you know the answer to the question, and what constitutes the briefest most complete answer. It is essential that the witness refrain from assuming facts necessary to answer the question asked if there are variables upon which the question relies. If you honestly do not understand the question, then you must say that to the attorney and, *if asked,* explain why.

3. *Remember that everything you say is being recorded.* This rule is important because *how* information is provided is as important as the information communicated. This is particularly true if the testimony either is before a jury or will be provided to a jury. If you tend to laugh or have another audible tic when nervous, practice controlling it. Speak slowly so that every word that you say can be recorded and understood by those in the courtroom.

4. *Always be polite.* Politeness is the hallmark of professionalism. Therefore, as a professional who has been called to testify, it is essential that you are polite to the judge, the jury (if there is one), *all* attorneys and all court personnel. Everyone who surrounds you as you testify has a particular and

essential role in the legal process. The counselor should project a calm and open demeanor, *never* speak unless asked a question, stop speaking as soon as the judge or attorney begins to speak and answer questions with complete sentences.

5. **Never guess or answer a question that you fail to understand.** It is the responsibility of the attorney asking the question of you to be clear. It is the counselor's responsibility to listen and ensure that he or she understands the question being asked of him/her. This means that while counselors listen to the question, they are ensuring that they understand the terms that the attorney uses; they understand all assumptions contained within the question and they are otherwise able to answer the question. It is also important to refrain from guessing. *If you do not know the answer, say so.*

6. **Admit it when you do not remember.** This is related to the preceding rule. Regardless of what an attorney may imply through either words or actions in response to a counselor's admitting that s/he does not remember a particular fact, it is essential that a counselor be honest. An event can be memorable to some and not others for a variety of reasons.

7. **Answer only the question.** It is essential that a counselor only provide a complete and concise response to a question posed by lawyers, judges or hearing officers. All answers must be verbal. Therefore, never nod or shake your head in response to a question. Counselors should not volunteer any information. When answering a question do so to avoid the use of technical terms and acronyms. For example, when explaining a diagnosis by axis, a counselor should include an explanation of what the axis means.

8. **Do not bring any documents with you that you cannot share unless required to because of a subpoena.** Attorneys can and will ask whether you have any documents with you when you appear to give testimony. Unless a subpoena has been issued for documents or unless you have an evaluation that was completed for purposes of the proceeding in which you are giving testimony, do not bring records with you. If you appear to rely upon records that are not available to the attorneys while you are testifying, those records could become part of the proceeding's record.

9. **Do not memorize your testimony.** Never memorize your testimony. Memorization should be avoided because you want your delivery to be natural and spontaneous. In addition, attorneys tend to change their questions and or the order of the questions continuously until the witness' testimony is delivered. Therefore, it is critical that the counselor listen to the question asked in order to assure that the counselor provides the answer to the question asked, rather than the question that s/he thinks was asked.

10. **Do not argue with the attorneys or the judge.** It is essential that a counselor remember that s/he is not in control of the situation when s/he testifies

under oath. Arguing only serves to undermine the counselor's credibility. If an attorney or the judge asks a question, including a question that purports to repeat what one just said, but is grossly inaccurate, the counselor should answer the question. If it is a question that requires a "yes" or "no" answer, that is all that should be given. Even if one's client is involved in the case, the only way that a counselor can help that client is by maintaining his/her credibility.

Final Comments on Ethical and Legal Issues for the Counseling Professionals

The issues regarding ethics and the law require careful consideration and constant vigilance for counselors and therapists. This chapter highlighted several components of the codes of ethics and laws for different mental health disciplines and the impact that these codes and federal and state laws have on the day-to-day operations within a counseling practice. It is the responsibility of the counselor or therapist to review and understand the code of ethics and laws that apply to their particular field of practice, and to remain vigilant for any changes made to these codes and laws.

While each profession has a separate code of ethics, every profession must be knowledgeable regarding the state and federal laws that protect the client's rights, such as the right to informed consent and confidentiality. The counselor also must understand all aspects of record keeping and access to records because the state and federal laws governing confidentiality affect this as well. Most importantly, however, is how state law requires the counselor to be a mandated reporter, an express exception to the laws concerning confidentiality. Mandated reporter laws create this exception when a helpless person, such as a child, elderly, physically or mentally disabled adult is possibly at risk of being harmed. These laws require that the counselor report their suspicions of abuse or neglect to law enforcement or the agencies charged with protecting these categories of individuals.

For a counselor, therapist or clinician, ethical dilemmas and legal questions arise frequently. Both require that the counselor understand the nature and breadth of the issue before taking any action. This chapter provides an overview of ethical decision-making models, a review of the literature concerning these models and a concise discussion of the law. The information presented is designed to assist the counselor in recognizing when an ethical or legal issue exists and to provide a framework for recognizing, evaluating, and resolving the issue. Ultimately, the counselor is responsible for the consequences of any course of action taken to resolve the situation.

References

Ahia, C. E. & Martin, D. (1993). *The danger-to-self-or-others confidentiality*. Alexandria, VA: American Counseling Association.

American Association for Marriage and Family Therapy (2001). *AAMFT code of ethics*. Washington, DC: Author.

American Counseling Association (2005). *ACA code of ethics*. Alexandria, VA: Author.

American Psychological Association (2002). Ethical principles of psychologists. Washington, DC: Author.

Bersoff, D. N. (1996). The virtue of principle ethics. In Eddington, N. & Shuman, R. (2005). *Law and ethics*. Retrieved November 27, 2007 from Continuing psychology education website: http://wwww.contpsyched@netzero.com.

Besharov, D. J. (1986) Child abuse and neglect: Liability for failure to report. In L. G. Schultz, Confidentiality, privilege, and child abuse reporting (1990). *IPT Journal*, 2. Retrieved November 23, 2007 from http://www.ipt-forensics.com/journal/volume2/j2_4_5.htm

Child Abuse Prevention and Treatment Act ("CAPTA") 42 U.S.C. §5106a (2006).

Corey, G., Corey, M. S., & Callahan, P. (2003). *Issues and ethics in the helping profession* (6ᵗʰ ed.). Pacific Grove, CA: Brooks/Cole.

Confidentiality of Records, 42 U.S.C. §290dd-2(e)(2)

Cottone, R. R., & Claus, R. E. (2000). Ethical decision-making models. A review of the literature. [Electronic version]. *Journal of Counseling and Development*, 78, 275-283.

Dansby-Giles, G., Giles, F. L, Frazier, W., Crockett, W. L., & Clark, J. (2006). Counselor ethics circles and sources of ethics information. [Electronic version]. *Vistas: Compelling perspectives on counseling*, 195-197. Alexandria, VA: American Counseling Association.

Eddington, N. & Shuman, R. (2005). *Law and ethics*. Retrieved November 27, 2007 from Continuing psychology education website: http://wwww.contpsyched@netzero.com.

Forester-Miller, H. F., & Davis, T. (1996). *A practionioner's guide to ethical decision making*. [Electronic version]. Alexandria, VA: American Counseling Association.

Frame, M. W., & Williams, C. B. (2005). A model of ethical decision making from a multicultural perspective. *Counseling and Values*, 49, 165-179.

Gladding, S. (2006). *Counseling: A comprehensive profession* (5ᵗʰ ed.). Upper Saddle River, NJ: Prentice Hall.

Green, S., Shilts, L., Bacigalupe, G. (2001). When approved is not enough: Development of a supervision consultation model. [Electronic version]. *Journal of Marital and Family Therapy*, 27(4), 515-525.

Herlihy, B. & Corey, G. (1996). *ACA Ethical standards casebook* (5th ed.). Alexandria, VA: American Counseling Association.

Hill, A. L. (2004). Ethical analysis in counseling: A case for narrative ethics, moral visions, and virtue ethics. *Counseling and Values, 48,* 131-148.

Individuals with Disabilities Act (IDEA) 20 USC §1401(29), (1997).

Kitchener, K. (1984). Intuition, critical evaluation and ethical principles: The foundation for ethical decision in counseling psychology. In H. F. Forester-Miller & T. Davis, *A practitioner's guide to ethical decision making* (1996). [Electronic version]. Alexandria, VA: American Counseling Association.

Family Education Rights Privacy Act ("FERPA")20 U.S.C. §1232g (1974).

Koocher, G. P. & Keith-Spiegel, P. (1998). *Ethics in psychology: Professional standards and cases* (2nd ed.). New York, NY: Oxford University Press.

Mappes, D. C., Robb, G. P., and Engles, D. W. (1985). Conflicts between ethics and law in counseling and psychotherapy. In Eddington, N. & Shuman, R. (2005). *Law and ethics.* Retrieved November 27, 2007 from Continuing psychology education website: http://wwww.contpsyched@netzero.com.*Journal of Counseling and Development,* 64(4), 246-252.

Mascari, J. B. & Webber, J. M. (2006). Salting the slippery slope: What licensing violations tell us about preventing dangerous ethical situations. In G. R. Waltz & R. K. Yep (eds.), *Vistas: Compelling perspectives on counseling 2006* (pp. 165-168). Alexandria, VA: American Counseling Association.

Miller, R. D., & Weinstock, R. (1987). Conflict of interest between therapist-patient confidentiality and the duty to report sexual abuse of children. In L. G. Schultz, Confidentiality, privilege, and child abuse reporting (1990). *IPT Journal,* 2. Retrieved November 23, 2007 from http://www.ipt-forensics.com/journal/volume2/j2_4_5.htm.

National Association of Social Worker. (1999). *Code of ethics.* Washington, CD: Author.

Remley, T. P., & Herlihy, B. (2005). *Ethical, legal, and professional issues in counseling* (2nd ed.). Upper Saddle River, NJ: Pearson Education, Inc.

Pope, K. S., & Bajt, T. R. (1988). When laws and values conflict: A dilemma for psychologists. In L. G. Schultz, Confidentiality, privilege, and child abuse reporting (1990). *IPT Journal,* 2. Retrieved November 23, 2007 from http://www.ipt-forensics.com/journal/volume2/j2_4_5.htm.

Schaffer, S. J. (1997). Don't be aloof about record- keeping, it may be your best liability coverage. In L. G. Schultz, Confidentiality, privilege, and child abuse reporting (1990). *IPT Journal,* 2. Retrieved November 23, 2007 from http://www.ipt-forensics.com/journal/volume2/j2_4_5.htm

Smith, D. & Fitzpatrick, M. (1995). Patient-therapist boundary issues: An integrative review of theory and research In L. G. Schultz, Confidentiality, privilege, and child abuse reporting (1990). *IPT Journal, 2.* Retrieved November 23, 2007 from http://www.ipt-forensics.com/journal/volume2/j2_4_5.htm

Social Security Act ("Title IV B") 20 U.S.C. §1232g (1974)

Southern, S., Smith, R. L., & Oliver, M. (2005). Marriage and family counseling: Ethics in context. [Electronic Version]. *Family Journal: Counseling and Therapy for Couples and Families, 13,* 459-466.

Somberg, D. R., Stone, G. L., & Claiborn, C. D. (1993). Informed consent: Therapists' belief and practices. In N. Eddington & R. Shuman, *Law and ethics* (2005). Retrieved November 27, 2007 from Continuing psychology education website: http://wwww.contpsyched@netzero.com.

Stadler, H. A. (1986). Making hard choices: Clarifying controversial ethical issues. In L. G. Schultz, Confidentiality, privilege, and child abuse reporting (1990). *IPT Journal, 2.* Retrieved November 23, 2007 from http://www.ipt-forensics.com/journal/volume2/j2_4_5.htm.

Stein, R. (1990). Ethical issues in counseling. In H. F. Forester-Miller & T. Davis, *A practitioner's guide to ethical decision making* (1996). [Electronic version]. Alexandria, VA: American Counseling Association.Buffalo, NY: Prometheus Books.

Tennyson, W., & Strom, S. (1986). Beyond professional standards: Developing responsibleness. *Journal of Counseling and Development, 14,* 298.

Weinstock, R., & Weinstock, D. (1988). Child abuse reporting trends: An unprecedented threat to confidentiality. In L. G. Schultz, Confidentiality, privilege, and child abuse reporting (1990). *IPT Journal, 2.* Retrieved November 23, 2007 from http://www.ipt-forensics.com/journal/volume2/j2_4_5.htm.

Zellman, G. L. (1990). Child abuse reporting and failure to report among mandated reporters: Prevalence, incidence, and reasons. In L. G. Schultz, Confidentiality, privilege, and child abuse reporting (1990). *IPT Journal, 2.* Retrieved November 23, 2007 from http://www.ipt-forensics.com/journal/volume2/j2_4_5.htm.

Section Three:

Counseling Strategies and Techniques

Group Counseling: An Effective Treatment Modality for Recovering Alcoholics
By: John L. "Jay" Allen Jr., Psy.D.

The structure of society, following both natural and social laws, is that people have a tendency to form groups (Coleman, 1990). From the earliest humans through today, individuals have discovered they can support each other, develop skills, and share problems better when they are in a group situation. Groups can help individuals to change self-defeating behaviors, such as alcoholism, and nowhere is it more evident than in group therapy, where members begin to understand and help themselves (McClure, 1990).

Perhaps one of the first group counseling sessions for alcoholics occurred when a few hearty individuals sat around a fire in front of a thatched hut and discussed problems caused by too much mead-quaffing among members of the group. Of course, it would be a few millenniums before it would be called group counseling; that term did not come into our language until 1905 when J.H. Pratt counseled discharged tuberculosis patients. Pratt, in his general-care instruction classes, soon realized that not only was he teaching hygiene, but patients were responding favorably to being counseled in a group setting (Columbia Encyclopedia, 2001).

Group counseling has become far more sophisticated in the over-100 years since Pratt held his first sessions; today we use research and statistical methods, for example, which make it easier to assess group progress (Riva, 2004). Group leaders realize they must be sensitive to the stage of development (Gladding, 1994) and are expected to have an understanding of group purpose, methods, and skills (Association for Specialists in Group Work, 2007).

Group therapy in general is too vast a topic to cover in one chapter; therefore, this chapter will focus on group therapy for recovering alcoholics. The historical context will be touched upon, as well as various theories, but primarily as they pertain to alcoholics. The somewhat-new online group counseling and its use with alcoholics will be mentioned. Also covered are ethical and legal issues—important in any counseling session, but even more so in a group that includes substance abusers, many of whom are there by court order. Free source material is mentioned, including ordering or downloading information.

Historical Context

Scientific Group Therapy

Pratt, mentioned above, is generally accepted as the first person to provide scientific group therapy. "His original intention was to boost (patients') morale through more effective cleanliness; soon, however, it became evident that his patients were deriving more benefit from being in a supportive group than from the actual lectures" (Berg, Landreth, & Fall, 1990, pp. 20-21).

About 20 years later Trigant Burrow—with Clarence Shields—opened up a form of therapy which Burrow first called mutual analysis, and then group analysis. Their joint efforts had a new approach, which required "the interpretation on the basis of a societal concept of consciousness, through the analysis of the social unconscious in its individual and social disguises" (Burrow, 1927, p. xvii). Burrow and Shields invited a group to join their "mutual analysis" experiment (Burrow, 1928) and the group stayed together for more than 30 years (Galt, 1973). The group called themselves The Lifwynn Foundation, breaking into smaller groups, with Burrow declaring that the optimal number in each group should be about 10 as "the object of group analysis is to give the individual the opportunity to express himself in a social setting without the inhibitions of customary social images" (Burrow, 1928, p. 199). (That number has remained rather constant; it is generally accepted today that six to 12 people is an optimal number. When there are more than 12, it becomes hard to include everyone at every session.)

First Documented Use of Group Therapy for Alcoholics

The first documented use of group therapy for alcoholics came about early in the now-famous Lifwynn years. Writing of the "pseudoalleviation provided by alcoholism and the euphoria of the drug addict," Burrow referred to "the call of the nest" (Burrow, 1926, p. 348) and how positively drug addicts and alcoholics respond to group analysis. The reasons are unclear, but Burrow was banned from publishing in most psychoanalytic journals; therefore, the work he did with alcoholics did not get its deserved attention. He did publish in other scientific reviews, though, and he exchanged opinions with eminent contemporary scholars in (among other disciplines) psychology, so his work was certainly not unnoticed (Gatti Pertegato, 1994).

First Use of Psychodrama in Group Therapy

Jacob Moreno worked with both children and prostitutes when he was a medical student in Vienna, finding that both groups responded well to storytelling and group work. In fact, Moreno organized the first self-help group for these disadvantaged prostitutes (Blatner, 1988). By 1921, when he had begun practicing psychotherapy and was treating patients in groups, he began experimenting with theatrical methods. However, it was not until he came to the United States in 1925, and began working with groups of prisoners at Sing Sing, that he first used the term *group psychotherapy* (Moreno, 1943). By 1934 he had introduced psychodrama to St. Elizabeth's in Washington, a hospital, which still exists as an innovative psychiatric facility. By the end of the decade, he had begun publishing *Sociometry: A Journal of Inter-Personal Relations*, which served as an outlet for professionals who were interested in role theory and group behavior (Narrative Psychology, 2007).

The 1920s, '30s, and '40s

At the end of World War I, Edward Lazell, a staff psychiatrist, began lectures at St. Elizabeth's Hospital for war veterans. Many of these men (and a few women) were suffering from the horrors of war; quite a few had turned to drugs and alcohol. Lazell reported many advantages of group counseling, which included socialization and reduction of fear of the analyst (Lazell, 1921). In the early '30s, L. Cody Marsh, impressed with Lazell's work, began similar sessions at Worcester State Hospital in Massachusetts (Marsh, 1931). Early on, Marsh used a public address system, which had certain advantages, but later he realized that having groups of 20 or less worked best in promoting rehabilitation (Marsh, 1935). Both Lazell and Marsh reported encouraging results with alcoholics; whether it was finding that others shared their problem, or even admitting there was a problem, the patients seemed to respond well when in a group setting (Marsh, 1935).

Many consider Alfred Adler and his co-workers to be the first to conduct group psychotherapy. While he never acknowledged being a group therapist, Adler's theories contributed to group therapy's initial conceptualizations. Adler saw people as being goal-directed (Fuhriman & Burlingame, 1994) and creative beings whose beliefs have purpose (Ansbacher & Ansbacher, 1956). Quite clearly the 12 steps of Alcoholics Anonymous, which would come along a few years later, are very compatible with Adlerian psychotherapy.

The Menninger Clinic made what was probably the first attempt to formally manipulate the patient's interpersonal and social environment (Menninger, 1936). In other words, the social milieu of the group itself could help with treatment (Kibel, 1992). At the same time, Florence Powdermaker and Jerome Frank, working with the Veterans Administration patients in Maryland, reaffirmed the importance of group cohesiveness. They believed group settings offered support, and that interactions among patients helped each individual develop a more accurate picture of himself or herself (Powdermaker & Frank, 1953).

During World War II, group therapy was being widely used in military and veterans hospitals. The first professional association for group therapists was formed—the American Society for Group Psychotherapy and Psychodrama (ASGPP). Counselors today who are interested in joining this group, or obtaining more information, may contact them at 609-452-1339 or at 301 N. Harrison St., #508, Princeton, NJ 08540. The ASGPP also publishes *The Journal of Groups in Addiction & Recovery*, which presents clinical, research, and training articles and which offers counselors an opportunity to keep up with the latest developments.

After World War II, many soldiers returned from the war with a propensity toward alcohol abuse. Group therapy, wherein the soldiers could discuss their wartime experiences among peers, was found to work well with these unfortunate men and women (Ruzek, 2003). A major step occurred in 1946, when A. Snedeker, then the Surgeon-General of the United States, instituted a policy to make group psychotherapy available in all Veterans Administration hospitals (Blatner, 2007).

The 1950s and Beyond

Excellent results were being reported concerning group psychotherapy as a form of psychiatric treatment for returning veterans, and this was a major reason increasing attention was being directed toward group therapy in mental hospitals (Mann & Semrad, 1948; Standish & Semrad, 1951). However, neuroleptic medication and biological treatments were now also becoming more viable and as a result a so-called "medical model" emerged, causing a de-emphasis on group therapy (Oldham & Russakoff, 1987). Also, there was a general feeling among some psychologists that patients might "already have too much insight" and that "focusing on feelings...often increases anxiety to a degree which impeded therapy" (Frank, 1963, p. 457). Consequently, there was an even further decreased emphasis on group psychotherapy. Some of these new medications, sadly, had disastrous consequences. One terrible example is the use of lysergic acid diethylamide (LSD) which was hailed in the 1950s as being an important breakthrough in the treatment of alcoholism. (Some reports claimed a 94 percent improvement rate.) Not until the 1960s did the real dangers emerge, and finally, in 1970, it was declared that no more trials of LSD for alcoholism would be held (Ludwig, Levine, & Stark, 1970).

Group psychotherapy then went into its period of innovation, with new therapies being tried (Gendlin, 1975). It was the time, for example, of Eric Berne's Transactional Analysis, or TA as it was generally called. TA proved to be yet another set-back for the treatment of alcoholism, as Berne and his followers believed that alcoholism is not a disease, and that it can be cured (Berne, 1964). About the same time—the mid-1960s—Gestalt therapy was the talk of New York, then became even more well-known after Fritz Perls moved to the Esalen Institute in California. Marathon group therapy also became popular, a 24-hour encounter group meeting where nonverbal methods were practiced (Gendzel, 1970). Hindu gurus, swamis, and Eastern spiritual teachers were fashionable, as was Arthur Janov's primal therapy, and Charles Diedrich's contribution to drug abuse, Synanon. This consisted of so-called games, which were near-violent (Blatner, 2007).

Some—such as yoga and meditation—are not unlike psychological working through, and Imagery therapy had Jungian origins (Sax & Hollander, 1972). Most, though, went the way of bell bottom pants and love beads. However, the period did bring a new awareness of groups—encounter groups, sensitivity groups, or whatever—which made people begin, once again, to see the advantages of group therapy. It was also a time of expansion for Alcoholics Anonymous (Wilcox, 1998). So despite some of the skepticism toward traditional group therapy that existed during this period, many clinicians were incorporating this modality as an accepted treatment. One study, for example, found that alcoholics appeared to have strong social fears, and while there might be resistance during the start of group therapy, there is improved adjustment in all aspects of the alcoholic's life. "Group therapy strengthens the ego by giving the alcoholic the opportunity to identify with other alcoholics...as well as aiding him to face the reality that he cannot drink," wrote therapist Charlotte Feibel (1960, p. 41).

The 1970s Through Today

In a review of 384 alcoholism treatment studies, Emerick (1974) found that peer-oriented care was highly successful, and further, the longer treatment is provided, the more likely the positive treatment effect (Backeland, Lundwall, & Kissin, 1975). Thus, it became clear that group counseling, especially when used with a 12-step program such as AA, offered an effective treatment modality.

As early as 1953, group psychotherapy was being hailed as a viable treatment in conjunction with AA (Thompson & Kolb, 1953). Time and studies have shown the combination to be successful. It must be pointed out, though, that group therapy is a complement to and not a substitute for AA. In AA, the idea is to help individuals attain sobriety; in group, clients work through conflicts that produce the alcoholic compulsion. The task is "to understand and alter their self-defeating styles of self-presentation" and help members overcome feelings of disengagement (Yalom, 1998, p. 118).

Freimuth (2000) indicates that group therapists can expect to treat an increasing number of recovering alcoholics who are already active in a 12-step program; he says that 12-step work appears to support the abstinence necessary for the focus on emotional growth (p. 299). Group therapy appears effective in increasing abstinence; Monras (2004) noted that its effect appeared from the 3rd month and increased from the 6th to 12th month. Monras also found that clients with medium education levels tend to abandon group therapy at a higher incidence than those of high or low education levels (p. 301).

More studies on that mid-range educational level should be done; the fact that they are the ones who drop out of group more often is intriguing. Counselors who are beginning their careers should take notice—this and other subjects need to be studied and reported. In fact, William Miller (Weiss, et al. 2004) suggested a need for group therapy studies in general, and outlined six types that are especially pressing: (1) group therapy versus no group therapy; (2) group therapy versus individual therapy; (3) group therapy plus individual therapy versus individual therapy alone; (4) group therapy plus individual therapy versus group therapy alone; (5) group therapy versus group therapy, examining theoretical orientation or content; and (6) more group therapy versus less group therapy. He felt variables such as type of group, education, treatment matching, and so on, should be studied and reported.

Long-term Effects of Group Counseling

Reviews in the 1970s and into the 1980s show group therapy to be effective (Bednar & Lawlis, 1971; Luborsky, et al. 1975). Among them are Malan, et al. (1976) who interviewed 42 patients from two to 14 years after termination of group therapy; results showed a very strong positive effect on all patients. Kaul and Bednar (1986) reviewed studies in over 900 journals and 1,500 books and monographs, concluding that group therapy results in client improvement. (Some but not all of the studies concerned alcoholics in group treatment.)

Small wonder, then, that group therapy is now the most common treatment modality for substance use disorders. It has been tried and proven effective for over 100 years (Price, et al. 1991). Group counseling provides individuals with the chance to see that their peers also have problems; it helps them learn new ways to solve problems. Individuals discover they are capable of understanding, accepting, and helping their peers (Berg, Landreth, & Fall, 1998, p. 41).

Various Theories of Group Counseling

Corsini (1957) indicates there are 25 distinct methods of providing therapy through the group process. Of course, any group leader must be aware of needs and limitations of his/her group, and be innovative in addressing the problems. Also, the group leader's own personality must be considered. Basically, though, Reality, Client-Centered, and Rational-Emotive counseling theories are three, which work extremely well in group therapy for alcoholics.

Reality therapy was developed by William Glasser and is based on a control theory, which focuses on problem-solving in the here-and-now. It seeks to help the client create a better future, instead of dwelling on the past. This makes it a very good therapy for the recovering alcoholic, because its cognitive-behavioral approach focuses on helping the client become aware of changes that are necessary in his/her life. It is a therapy of hope (Glasser, 1972).

Client-Centered counseling views the client as his/her own best authority and recognizes that individuals may lose touch with what their own experiences mean. Their identity may be undermined, due to pressure from others—something often found in the alcoholic population. Therefore, this is an especially good theory for group counseling; the alcoholic is usually quite receptive to a theory that offers unconditional positive regard along with empathic understanding. Carl Rogers, who published his conceptualization of Client-Centered Therapy in 1959, wrote that the counselor "must be non-judgmental, respond with understanding, set limits on behavior, and withhold from placing blame on the client" (Barrett-Lennard, 1998, p. 66). The client must feel free to explore his/her feelings without danger of the counselor (or others in the group) rejecting him/her (Barrett-Lennard, 1962).

Rational-Emotive Behavioral Theory (REBT) is Albert Ellis's contribution to counseling and is an excellent modality for treating alcoholics. REBT helps a client who verbalizes or exhibits irrational thinking, which is common among alcoholics. Ellis points out that the alcoholic may want to drink but does not want the undesirable consequences that come from such behavior. REBT is especially useful in this regard, because the counselor can help the group by creating realistic goals, establishing a relationship, and identifying key problems. Further, REBT teaches that clients can help each other model new beliefs (Ellis, 1982). Because its fundamental principles focus on beliefs and belief change, this is an especially good choice for individuals who are very religious (Nielsen, Johnson, & Ellis, 2001).

Of course, the process of conducting groups is dynamic. New ideas must be explored, old theories should be evaluated. The counselor must never remain static. As Mary Follett so famously wrote, "Never settle down within the theory you have chosen, the course you have embraced; know that another theory, another course exists and seek that" (Follett, 1934, p. 54).

Internet Group Counseling

Using Technology in Group Counseling

Follett's words are as true today as when she wrote them in 1934; the good counselor should never stop learning. The innovative counselor will look for ways to try new things. For example, it is essential that counselors learn how technology can enhance group counseling. The Internet has changed how people meet health needs, including mental health; many have turned to the Internet for online group counseling (Spaniol, Gagne, & Koehler, 1999).

Online counseling appears to help people with addiction problems, especially if it is used as an adjunct plan. For those in traditional treatment programs, many find that online counseling can add to their treatment. For example, they can go online at any hour of the day or night and "talk" with someone who shares their feelings of confusion, hurt, anger, or whatever. There is easy accessibility and the ability to re-read and edit communication (Cook & Doyle, 2001; Lange, van de Ven,

Schrieken, & Emmelkamp, 2001). There is a chance to access information in many databases and engage in moderated e-mail discussions (Ancis, 2998; Bitter, 1995). The Internet is especially useful for individuals with disabilities (Kenny & Murray, 1993). Geographically remote, underserved individuals may find it especially appealing (Mermelstein & Holland, 1991).

Internet Counseling: Not for Everyone

Addictions counselors should be especially aware that clients who are depressed and thinking of harming themselves or others should not go online for advice, but should seek immediate and appropriate help (Williams, 2007). Internet counseling is certainly contraindicated for those who suffer from disordered thought processes, such as paranoia and psychosis (Rochlen, et al. 2004). Homicidal patients and those who are under criminal investigation are also not suited for Internet counseling (APA, 2007).

The Internet is isolating; recovering alcoholics, for example, often need the camaraderie (now missing from their bar scene) which can be found in group therapy (Flores & Mahon, 1993). This is not to say that Internet counseling is contraindicated; however, the client should certainly be in a group that meets regularly, such as AA.

Additionally, confidentiality can be breached; viruses, hackers, and other threats are continually evolving. On the other hand, security measures are getting better; the key here is to stay up-to-date.

Remember, too, that the absence of nonverbal information can interfere in establishing therapeutic alliances (Cook & Doyle, 2002). However, Rochlen, Zack, and Speyer's (2004) review of online therapy found that clients did report strong alliances, and also reported disinhibition effects.

Counseling Ethics

The 2002 APA Ethics Code reflects the changes brought about by Internet counseling. For elements specifically relevant to Internet practice, go to Standards 9.03, Informed Consent in Assessments, and 10.01, Informed Consent to Therapy, both of which can be downloaded from the APA site: www.apa.org/ethics.

Since 1999, the members of the American Counseling Association have adhered to standards created to guide counselors who provide Internet counseling. Information may be obtained by contacting the ACA at 5999 Stevenson Avenue, Alexandria, Virginia 22304, or online: http://www.counseling.org.

Another valuable source of information is available from the International Society for Mental Health Online, which has published guidelines to assist counselors: http://www.ismho.org.

Overview of Ethical and Legal Considerations in Group Counseling

Confidentiality

Protecting patient confidentiality goes as far back as the Hippocratic Oath (Lasky & Riva, 2006). All these centuries later, it is still considered of utmost importance; the need to maintain confidentiality is "the essential groundwork of trust in treatment" (Hough, 1992, p. 106). Group counseling presents its own set of problems. For example, the counselor can assure the client that everything said in private is privileged, but when that same patient is in group, he/she might find that someone has talked or (in extreme cases) actually sold a story to the media. It becomes complicated, especially when we consider that self-disclosure is the very core of group therapy (Lasky & Riva, 2006).

The National Board of Certified Counselors (NBCC) provides guidance which helps clarify the problem: In Section B.16, the Code states:

> In group counseling, counselors clearly define confidentiality and the parameters for the specific group being entered, explain the importance of confidentiality, and discuss the difficulties related to confidentiality involved in group work. The fact that confidentiality cannot be guaranteed is clearly communicated to group members. However, counselors should give assurance about their professional responsibility to keep all group communications confidential (NBCC, 1998).

Trauma Suffered Within Group Counseling

Unfortunately, trauma can and often does occur within group counseling. NBCC addresses that problem in Section B.1 of the Code: "In a group setting, the counselor is responsible for taking reasonable precautions to protect individuals from physical and/or psychological trauma resulting from interaction within the group" (NBCC, 1998). Further, in Section B.16, the Code states that counselors should define confidentiality and the parameters "for the specific group being entered, explain the importance of confidentiality, and discuss the difficulties related to confidentiality involved in group work." Detailed guidance is provided; for example, the Code states that counselors must screen prospective group counseling participants to ensure compatibility with group objectives. Additionally, it is stated that counselors must be aware of the welfare of all participants, throughout the entire group process (NBCC, 1988).

Informed Consent

Since there is no binding assurance of confidentiality among group members, some counselors require consent forms, which waive liability against the counselor in the event that any group member violates confidentiality. Sample informed consent forms from the APA Insurance Trust may be downloaded at: http://www.

apait.org/apait/download.aspx.

The Association for Specialists in Group Work is another good source. They are a division of the American Counseling Association (ACA) and can be of special value to the counselor who is beginning his/her career: http://www.asgw.org. Because the substance abuser is often suspicious, the counselor should be especially aware that the client knows he/she is signing a standard treatment consent form. Also remind the client that he/she can refuse treatment (Walker, Logan, Clark, & Leukefeld, 2005). Safeguards must be maintained to keep client information confidential; the information should be retained on a safeguarded CD for a year after the counseling relationship has ended (Williams, 2007).

Group Therapy for Alcoholics

Leader's Language Expertise

Language must be employed properly. Figures of speech, for example, might easily be misunderstood; so can slang and verbal irony. The therapist should meet with the client before the first session and in plain, simple language prepare him/her for what lies ahead. Pregroup orientation can lead to much better outcomes (Yalom, Houts, Newell, & Rand, 1967). Explain to the client the importance of focusing on the here-and-now. Assure the client that confidentiality is expected, that all meetings must be attended, and that promptness is important. Ask about goals, and what the client would like to see changed in his/her life. Remember that the client is probably anxious about beginning group therapy, especially if he/she has never attended group. Details may be forgotten; therefore, the counselor might suggest to the client that he/she write the time, date, and place of the group sessions, and keep this information readily available. Yalom (1974) suggests urging clients to attend at least a dozen sessions before attempting to judge whether or not group is useful. Of course, many alcoholics are attending by court order, in which case the client should be reminded that attendance is imperative.

Structuring

Structure helps both counselors and clients work together effectively. Berg and Landreth (1990) suggest several points, the most obvious (and often most overlooked) being patience. The counselor should wait for responses, and be patient when members need time to think. Group members must show respect to each other. The counselor should recognize that he/she is not the authority with "correct" answers; instead, the counselor should help members respond to each other. When pressed for an opinion, the question should be referred to the whole group by saying, "What do the rest of you think?" The counselor must determine the central theme of the discussion; things can be pulled together by linking what one member says with what another has said, if it is related. If members appear confused, ask another member to summarize what he/she thinks the speaker has been saying. Listen to the tone behind the words, and not just to the words themselves (Berg & Landreth, 1990).

Structuring the Initial Session

Alcoholics present unique problems; therefore, structuring the initial session becomes very important. Yalom suggests going around the room and having each member discuss personal goals, guiding members so they interact with other members. For example, Yalom says you might try saying something like this: "Dave, I notice you are speaking to Ken but looking at me. Please look directly at the person you are talking to" (Yalom, 1974, p. 89). In other words, guide members so they interact directly with other members.

Structuring Continuing Sessions

Keep sessions in the here-and-now with discussions of what is happening in each member's life. Yalom reminds us that this focus consists of two tiers. In the first tier, there is experiencing, where members develop feelings toward other group members and the therapist, with immediate events taking precedence over events in the past. This focus facilitates "feedback, catharsis, meaningful self-disclosure, and acquisition of socializing techniques" (Yalom, 1995, p. 129). The second tier is the illumination process, where interpersonal learning is set in motion. The group begins to "examine itself and study its own transactions; it must transcend pure experience and apply itself to the integration of that experience" (p. 130).

Yalom (1995) suggests videotaping sessions. When these sessions are played back (usually at the next meeting) ask the group to identify which parts seem most important and which parts seem less important. By watching themselves, clients tend to be more self-observant and objective than when actually involved in the group interaction. Incidentally, clients often respond differently to the first playback session than to later sessions. Yalom relates, "In the first playback, patients attend primarily to their own image and are relatively less involved with the process of the group" (p. 427). For that reason, it is better to select certain segments rather than viewing an entire session indiscriminately. Also, some members resent time taken away from live group meetings. If they are too vocal about that, viewing time could be arranged outside the regular group meeting. Yalom notes that if a member has been drinking, videotape might show how he/she presents himself to others, and would also serve as notice that the individual has broken a cardinal rule by drinking.

Disruptive Clients

Alcoholics can be disruptive; working with this population is not easy. They exhibit numerous defense mechanisms such as "denial, deception, secrecy, minimization, intellectualization, displacement, and rationalization" (Miller & Glover-Graf, 2006, p. 166). Sometimes they become very angry; often, this anger is a way to divert attention from themselves (Saxon, Saxon, & Spitznagel, 1998). However, as van der Kolk noted (1989), a client who is angry might well be healthier than the client who idealizes the therapist. The therapist "must be able to 'take' such anger, as long as the anger never involves physical violence, and its basis is discussed openly in the concurrent or later session" (p. 390). The group setting is where clients can realize they may be allowed to express anger. George and Dustin (1988) recommend that emphasis should be placed on providing structures in the group. In this way, clients know they are safe to say what they wish. Remember, though, that such intensity often arouses anxiety; the leader must be careful that the clients do not respond by wanting to drink alcohol.

The counselor should be aware of any subgroups that are forming, as they can often provoke anxiety within the group. If a subgroup becomes disruptive, the counselor might do something as simple as change the seating arrangement. Of course, subgroups can also have a positive effect. Some clients—especially those who are marginally connected—may feel more comfortable with the help of a subgroup. It is up to the counselor to keep things positive.

Scapegoating (persecution, bullying) and leader roles often take place in group therapy (Horwitz, 1983), arising from the needs and personalities of the individuals (Gibbard, Hartman, & Mann, 1974). Again, these roles are not always bad, as they may serve functions for the entire group, including revitalization (Shields, 2000). Of course, scapegoating and damaging confrontation must be addressed, with the counselor making sure that things being said do not become hostile. The one being scapegoated should be allowed to present his/her opinions (Corey & Corey, 1997).

Clients who isolate themselves can become a frustration to others. Berg and Landreth (1990) report that avoidance behaviors range from absence to more active avoidances, such as the "Pollyanna" (unrealistically cheerful) or naive role. The Pollyanna is convinced that the world is "Disneyland, with a perpetual silver lining" (p. 180) and this group member will deny anything that is unpleasant. This is especially annoying when the individual glosses over and denies the pain of others. The counselor must, in that case, instruct the Pollyanna that out of pain we begin to understand ourselves. The naive member is similar, and needs to work on problem-solving skills. The entire group can help the naive member by sharing experiences and ideas.

The negative member who finds fault with everyone is actually quite easy to deal with. The anger is often linked to previous experiences, and this can be turned into a way of helping the individual open up and share with the group. The harmonizer is also disruptive: He/she avoids confrontation, but must come to realize that everyone is there to grow, which means that sessions (by necessity) must often be difficult (Berg & Landreth, 1990).

Alcoholics have a tendency to talk too much, which can be annoying and coun-ter-productive; however, this trait is usually easy to overcome. The client is often relieved when his/her talking is stopped; chances are, he/she simply does not know what to do or say. The counselor can simply say something like, "Lewis, some of us are having trouble following your train of thought. Maybe you could itemize, or put your thoughts into fewer words?" (Vannicelli, 1992). If this does not help, the group leader might go to the chalkboard and say something like, "I'll help you. Let's see, your first point is this" and so on until the points are made. In other words, the group leader gets all the thoughts down in black and white, without taking up too much time.

The alcoholic who talks too little can also become a problem; the fact that he/she will not share, though, may provide a clue to the client's problems. This can become a point of discussion, both privately and within the group. If the client is afraid of crying in front of others, the counselor should assure him/her that every-one there understands and nobody will laugh (Vanicelli, 1992).

Special consideration should be paid to clients who speak English as a second language; there might be a delay in their mental translation, or they might find it difficult to find the right words to express certain feelings. They often find it hard to pick up on subtle nuances of speech.

Sometimes a client, for no apparent reason, suddenly leaves a session, and this is especially true in the alcoholic population. The counselor might go after him/her and talk privately for a few minutes about the problem. Possibly the client wants reassurance and will readily return. If he/she does not return, the counselor should explain to the group that therapy requires members to remain in the session and that leaving a group session is rude and nonproductive (Vannicelli, 1992). Likewise, remind the group that if a person is constantly late or absent, this behavior is rude to other members and will not be tolerated (Corey & Corey, 1987).

When a client simply becomes too disruptive to keep in the group, he/she must be removed. This is not a subject for group discussion; the counselor must step up and take responsibility. Later the counselor should explain why the action was taken, and let members work through their responses (Center for Substance Abuse Treatment, 2005).

If a client is anxious after self-disclosure, he/she should be reassured by saying something such as, "Perhaps the fact that you have opened up…suggests that you are not feeling it is important to hide (your secret) any more" (Vannicelli, 1992, p. 161).

Because of the inherent problems with an alcoholic population, a highly spe-cialized approach must be taken when leading group therapy. The counselor should structure the group, see that productive work is maintained, and encourage group interaction. Members must never forget to focus on the here-and-now, which is important in any group session, but critical in one that is made up of alcoholics (Yalom, 1985).

A new Treatment Improvement Protocol (TIP) from the Center for Substance Abuse Treatment of the Substance Abuse and Mental Health Services Administration not only defines effective group therapy, but is especially helpful for improving skills of group leaders who work with an alcoholic population. The document, designated *"TIP 41, Substance Abuse Treatment: Group Therapy,"* is posted online at www.ncbi.nlm.nih.gov/books and is a free download. A free hard copy, designated as DHHS Publication No. (SMA) 05-3991, may be ordered by calling (800) 729-6686.

Group Therapy Sessions

Two Actual Sessions

The following are examples of actual group therapy sessions for recovering alcoholics, which took place at Welcome Home in Southern Maryland. (The name, location, and all identifying characteristics of people mentioned are changed to prevent recognition.) Welcome Home is a state-sponsored continuing-care facility, all male clients, with primary focus on alcohol and other substance abuse treatment services. Self payment is accepted; however, most of the men need payment assistance, which is available. The State purchased four large row houses on two adjoining blocks, and the main house has offices for the staff. It is also in that house, "The Main," as it is called, that all private and group counseling sessions are held. As full disclosure, this writer should mention that he did his Internship at Welcome Home, and that he is the group leader mentioned in the following sessions.

The locale is Welcome Home's main house, in a large room that is furnished with comfortable chairs, a couch, and several small tables. There is a sideboard that has a large coffee pot, hot water, tea bags, cups, cheese, and crackers. The lighting could be better: They use fluorescent fixtures, which seem to slightly agitate some of the men. The seating arrangement is semi-circular, with the group leader at the top of the open part. Every man can see everyone there, and the chairs are arranged so everyone is easily heard. Even though the first session began during daylight hours, the curtains were drawn; the house is located directly on a busy street, and this prevents distractions from whatever might be happening just outside the building. There is a clock on the wall, and a large chalkboard. A poster of the AA "Twelve Steps" is hung prominently.

The "Five-Minute" Session

The first session presented here was highly unusual: The men had become rather lackadaisical, perhaps from the lingering summer heat, or maybe because many had wanted summer vacations but weren't allowed to leave. Several had begun coming to group sessions late, offering feeble excuses. One man seemed on the verge of quitting and often stared out the window, then when the sessions were over he would bolt for the door. Whatever the reasons, it was felt that something drastic was needed in order to energize the group. Also, three members had shown anger and rising tensions; because of this, the group leader looked for a different way to moderate the anxiety. Thus, the idea for the "five-minute session" came into being. The group meetings after this session returned to the usual format; however, by then the men showed more interest and enthusiasm. Three of the men, since this session, have requested that the "five-minute game" (as they prefer to call it) be experienced again, perhaps on a monthly basis. (Two of the men were the ones mentioned above as being angry; the other was a lethargic man who hardly ever spoke.) All the men appeared to enjoy the spontaneity and fun of the experiment and since then the group has had much more productive meetings.

Eleven men were at this abbreviated session, which is one more than I consider optimal; however, even though the session lasted only five minutes, every man was addressed personally by name. Four men lingered afterwards to speak with me privately.

Transcript of Session

Group Leader: Hello, guys.

Commentary: We keep things very casual and friendly at Welcome Home, thus the formal greeting would be unnecessary. I refer to the group as "guys" and they call me "Jay." Also, the Executive Director said he finds it helps the men communicate better when they use given names.

Group as a whole: Hello, everyone. (Or words to that effect.)

GL: Is there anyone new to the group tonight? (The response indicated that no one was new.) Good, because we want to try something new tonight. How often do our sessions usually last?

Fred: Usually about a half-hour.

George: That's not so! They last a couple of hours.

Willie: Come on, man, they last anywhere from 30 minutes to an hour and a half, whatever Jay wants it to. He tells us when we're through.

GL: Willie is right. We are usually here from 30 minutes to an hour and a half, and sometimes even two hours, but tonight we're going to finish in five minutes!

Group: (Laughter)

Commentary: I did not explain my rationale to the men. The reason for the so-called "five minute session" was to create a trance through speed, and to make the men laugh, which I thought would elevate their mood. By moving quickly, the risk of responding to extraneous detail would be limited. This speed-session would also put the men in a time-bind and force them to say what was most important to them.

Bob: Man, that's a great idea. How come we never did this before? We have to go to AA at 6:30, and this gives us time to go get pizza between sessions.

Commentary: This was already encouraging. Bob is a contrarian; usually he manages to disagree with someone on even a minute point. I could already see that the five-minute session was unifying the men.

GL: Does anyone have anything pressing that they really want to talk about? We don't want anyone to leave here wishing he could have said something, but was rushed.

Ivan: I have something I need to get off my chest. I have to go home for the weekend, downtown Baltimore, and I don't have to tell you about my neighborhood. Anybody who has been listening to the last six or eight sessions can tell you that's what got me started down this path in the first place. I was a drunk by the time I was 16. You all know that. And the neighborhood is nothing but a (expletive) drug market. So what am I gonna do about it, guys? I don't want to face all that temptation. I don't feel I'm ready.

GL: What bothers you most? What do you feel is the worst trigger?

Ivan: I know it sounds stupid, but just thinking about the way the place looks. Looking at those buildings. It all brings it back, too many memories. Too much, man.

GL: Okay, who can help out here? Anybody else ever have this problem?

Clark: I think I know what he means. I had a bit of that the first time I went home from here. I got off the bus and walked home, 20 blocks, and every place I saw reminded me of something that I don't want to be reminded of. Where my aunt lived, where my old girlfriend still lives, all that (expletive).

GL: So do you think you could offer any advice to Ivan? You seem to share some of the same problems.

Commentary: It is Ivan's responses that interest me more than what Clark is saying. I do pay close attention, though, that Clark isn't saying something that could cause a relapse. I also want to be sure he is taking Ivan's problem seriously.

Clark: Sure. First off, I'd tell him this—don't walk 20 blocks. It's as easy as that. Just get in a cab and get yourself dropped off right at the door. And don't say you can't afford it, because I know you make good tips at that cafe where you work.

Commentary: All the men who live at Welcome Home are expected to hold at least part-time jobs. It provides structure in their lives, just as we attempt to provide structure in group sessions. The night sessions are primarily for the men who work during the day. Most of the men work at nights at hotels and fast-food restaurants, so we tend to have more daytime meetings. Incidentally, Ivan works at an upscale restaurant, which has caused jealousy among the men, as they feel his job is superior to theirs.

Ivan: You know, it's so stupid of me, but I never even thought about that. It would keep me from actually seeing all the old places, wouldn't it?

Clark: And the next morning, when you get up, don't go to the corner to see

142

your old friends. Don't have coffee with 'em. Don't mess around with 'em, man, that's all it takes. You going to see your mama? Well then, see your mama. Help her with stuff around the house. Maybe phone your grandma and see if she'll come over and see you instead of you going over there to see her. And if you need me—if you feel like you're gonna relapse—call me. I'll give you my cell number.

Commentary: Ivan has talked of his home life in many sessions. It is only natural that Clark feels like he knows the situation—Ivan has referred many times to his grandparents, who live a few blocks away from his mother. Also, I'd like to point out that Clark's advice—while basically sound—wasn't what interested me so much. What I was really interested in was how Ivan was responding to Clark. The two men had been somewhat unfriendly to each other in the past; this showed that a shared problem could be cohesive. They were helping each other, rather than coming to me for help—it is always a bit of a problem seeing to it that clients don't become dependent upon the counselor.

GL: I think there are some good things going on here. Why don't you two talk further after group? You're slowing the session—now let's look at the clock and see how many minutes we have left in this five-minute session!

Commentary: This amused the men. I was surprised that two or three men actually shouted out the number of minutes left—three!

GL: (continuing around the room) James, how are you doing?

James: Fine, Jay.

Commentary: James concerns me because I fear he is a splitting borderline, and have talked with the Welcome Home doctor about this. James often shows hostility, and his emotions can appear very labile—he switches up and down, very rapidly, day to day. In this particular session, though, James appeared to get into the session immediately, and seemed excited about trying something new. This pleased me.

GL: Anything you want to say?

James: No problems today, man.

GL: Are you sure? Sometimes your mood can get very down. By the way, Jim, that's a great shirt, very retro.

James: Hey, this is an original. It cost twenty dollars. It ain't from no thrift store. It's an original, and I got a piece of paper that says so.

Commentary: James thinks he has a problem, and he does, of saying exactly what is on his mind. He can appear very rude, and he knows this and has worked on it. Notice that I called him "Jim" instead of "James." He visibly perked up on that—he is almost childlike in his need to be liked. He has told us in group that he can say things that put people off, and he wants to work on this problem. I made a mental note to call him "Jim" from time to time.

Walter: Man, so your shirt is an original. Original what? Original shirt? That doesn't make any sense. Ask me what my problem is and let's get on with this Race the Clock game and stop talking about shirts.

GL: Okay, Walter, what is your problem today?

Walter: Nothing.

Group: (Much laughter.)

Commentary: Walter is a crowd favorite; he can usually make the men calm down when there is a problem. He can be quite funny, and seems to add joy to a lot of the meetings.

GL: Fine, Walter, now let's go to Paul. How are you today, Paul?

Paul: Uhhh, I dunno.

GL: Well thank you for sharing that with us, Paul! (The group laughed.)

Commentary: I could get away with dismissing Paul as I did because I know how well he's doing. He's close to the staff, and in the future will probably be employed at Coming Home.

GL: Who else has something they want to say? Nothing too depressing though—that's such a drag, man.

Commentary: The dated slang was done on purpose. The group had teased me once when I didn't understand one of their slang terms, so to "get in the game" I played along and would occasionally say something such as "solid" or "neat," which seemed to amuse them. Ordinarily, though, I wouldn't use slang with a client.

GL: Mike, how are you?

Mike: Okay today, who knows about tomorrow?

Commentary: I don't really trust Mike and fear he may be a psychopath. I have spoken to the Welcome Home doctor about this, and he says he'll keep an eye on things. The doctor did refer to Mike's anger as "prison behavior." Mike, I feel, is playing a game with us; he comes from the prison system, and thinks that by coming here he'll get his sentence reduced. On the positive side: Mike has an amazing ability to make newcomers feel at ease.

GL: Hey, by the way, Mike—thanks for making our newcomer, Pete, feel so good in the last session. I mean that. (Pause.) I really mean that. (Pete was not in this session; he is shifting to the night sessions.)

Commentary: As I talked to Mike, I slowed down and focused right on him. I allowed the mood in the room to settle, and become completely quiet—just for a moment—before I said "really." One advantage in working so quickly is that contrast can be created through sudden changes in tone, pace, or volume. It would be very hard to do this otherwise. This is what Milton Erickson called fractionation.

GL: Who has more to say? James?

James: No. No.

GL: Fine, I won't push it.

Commentary: Sometimes silence speaks louder than words. I made a mental note to pursue this with James at the next group session.

GL: William, please tell us how you feel today, and I hope you feel fine. (Emphasis was strong on "fine.")

Commentary: William has a terrible speech impediment, because of his teeth. He's nearly impossible to hear in group. This has been discussed with the doctor, who is trying to arrange free or low-cost dental care for William. As an aside, I should mention that William told me in a private session that the reason he got on drugs was because it was the only way he could bear to look at himself in the mirror. He said his family and everyone at school had imitated his speech. William never laughs or smiles, for a very obvious reason.

William: (loudly) I'm fine, Jay! (The entire group cheered.)

GL: Great. Now, don't say more, we're running out of time. Let's stop!

Commentary: Although the session was officially over, one of the things I like about this approach is its lingering effect. For example, James, who is one of the most difficult people in the group, came to me afterward and apologized for something he'd said two weeks earlier. Walter took me aside and described thoughts he'd been having that seemed to be obsessive. I'll discuss this with the doctor; it is possible that Walter has OCD, which might help explain why he became an alcoholic. We might be on the verge of a breakthrough with Walter. Finally, just as I was leaving the room, two other men, both of whom had rejected private counseling sessions, came to me and asked if they could make appointments. I left Welcome Home, feeling a great deal had been accomplished.

A Two-Hour Session

I entered Welcome Home and put a big bottle of hand sanitizer on the table, in clear view of all who entered the room. I smiled to myself when I thought about Pratt, and how group therapy actually began when he taught basic hygiene to groups of discharged tubercular patients. Here we are, over a hundred years later, and basic hygiene is still a problem: During the past month, colds have spread from person to person, with alarming regularity. Alcoholics can be terribly lackadaisical about personal hygiene; it occurred to me that a bottle of hand sanitizer—plus a sentence or two about avoiding germs—just might turn things around.

As always, before every session, I went over my notes from the previous session. Then I arranged the table, so light snacks and coffee would be readily available. The lights were adjusted.

It is now December and holiday lights are up all over town; our street is especially festive, so instead of pulling the blinds as I usually do (to prevent distractions) I decided to leave them open. The holiday lights, I felt, would offer a bit of needed cheer during this cold and rainy evening. Instead of the light classical music, which I usually play quietly during group therapy, I decided on Leontovych's upbeat "Carol of the Bells." The stage was set, and I felt optimistic, even though I realized that the holidays often cause people to return to drinking. I was determined that everything possible to help the men through this season would be offered. The group of 13 men arrived, greetings were said, and we began.

Group Leader: Does anyone have a pressing problem which we should address first?

Aaron: Yeah, as you know, I've been allowed to go home for Christmas. And I don't want to. My mother has stayed close to my wife, and not so much so to me, and I know she'll be there. Inez. She'll be there with the kids. Things are really rocky with me and Inez. She has told me when I get home we have to make big changes and I'm afraid that means she wants a divorce.

GL: Are they your kids, Aaron?

Aaron: First one probably is, second one probably isn't.

GL: Have you ever thought of getting a DNA test?

Aaron: Don't want to. Don't want to find out. I love the second one, that baby girl, just as much as I love Dustin. If Anna isn't mine, I don't want to know.

GL: Is there any real reason you feel Anna might not be yours?

Aaron: Yeah. Her and me—the wife—we didn't really get together much before she got pregnant with Anna. And she kept getting rides home from work, same guy, he came in once and I saw him. Didn't like him.

GL: Were you drinking at the time?

Aaron: Hell, yes! It was about that time that I got stopped for drunk driving. Had Dustin in the car with me. They threatened to take him away, and then I was given the chance to come here. A "last chance" they called it.

GL: How old is Anna?

Aaron: She's not quite a year old. And I know what you're thinking, that I couldn't really love a little baby that hasn't even learned to talk yet.

GL: I wasn't thinking that at all. Quite the opposite—I have no children, but I have friends who tell me that the minute the baby is born, it's yours and you love it.

Aaron: But what if she isn't mine?

GL: But chances are, she is. Look, you weren't thinking right when all that was going on. Go back in time a bit. Try to remember how you felt when your wife was driven home by somebody from her job.

Aaron: Well, first of all, I felt guilty. She was working, and I wasn't. And I should have been the one to take care of her, pick her up, stuff like that. But I was drunk a lot. Oh hell, let's be honest, I was drunk most of the time.

GL: Did it ever occur to you how hard your wife worked to support the family? And you say your mother has stayed close to her. Stop and think why. Maybe she knows that Inez needs family around her—your family. Instead of concentrating on the negative, why not look to the positive? Anna is yours; your wife is concerned about your marriage, but hasn't seen a lawyer yet. And she gets along with your mother—just think how many wives don't get along with in-laws!

Aaron: You make it sound so simple. But I see where you're going.

Commentary: It may have sounded simple, but of course it wasn't. Actually, Aaron might be in a crisis situation. Before he left, I arranged for him to get individual therapy before he went home for Christmas.

GL: What about it, group? Anyone want to share with Aaron on this?

William: Man, I just think you are so lucky to have a wife and children, and a mama and a house to go to at Christmas. Why can't you just stop and appreciate all that a little bit before you go off thinking she done played around on you. Where'd she work, some greasy spoon?

Aaron: Yeah. Place called "Sip and Chew."

William: Oh come on man! "Sip and Chew?" You gotta be kidding. Hey if she worked at some ol' "Sip and Chew" kind of place, I bet she didn't have time to do no running around on you. You oughta be glad somebody drove her home at night. You oughta been doing it.

Commentary: This is a very cohesive group, and while this may have sounded divisive, it wasn't. William spoke in good humor, smiling a lot. Aaron took it as it was meant—as positive criticism. A word about William: He is the person from the "Five-Minute Session" who had such bad teeth that he could barely be understood. Since that session, Welcome Home's doctor has arranged for him to get whole-mouth caps at a greatly reduced fee, and he has five years to pay the dental debt. It has made a world of difference in William. He smiles constantly, and speaks up in meetings. He is literally like a new man, and since getting his dental work, William has begun working in the kitchen at the best hotel in town. I have high hopes for William.

GL: David, let's hear from you. I know you celebrate Hanukkah. Do you think you'll have any problems over the holidays?

Commentary: David is the only Jewish member of our group, and was here when I was doing my Internship. He "graduated" and was doing fine, until he went to a rock concert one night and fell in with a group of so-called friends who were doing cocaine. He is one of the few men here who came on his own, and paid the entire fee. (Most are here by court-order, and few pay their own expenses.) When he woke up the next morning after the concert and realized he'd been doing lines of cocaine, he immediately called Welcome Home and asked to be placed in the program again. That certainly speaks well of him and everyone on the staff thinks he'll stay clean this time.

David: I can't deny that it will be a problem. I live in a very social neighborhood, and while there isn't much drinking, there is always wine.

GL: Interesting that you used the word deny.

David: Yes! I think I know what you're referring to. Last summer I told you that substance abuse is not high among Jews, but denial certainly is.

GL: That's right—you mentioned that many Jewish alcoholics do not get into treatment at all, or certainly not as early as they should. So you should be very proud of yourself: You sought treatment not once but twice. You came to us of your own accord. So we know you are really trying. Anybody want to say something to David about his?

Jeffrey: I just want to say that I think it's great that he came back here on his own, and that I just know he's going to do fine when he leaves here this time. Just stay out of those rock concerts!

David: Thanks. And you're right—I'll listen to CDs, but no more live concerts! No use asking for trouble.

GL: You've really hit on something there. And it's something I want all of you to remember over the holidays. You know, AA has a relapse tool that they call HALT. It's to remind you not to get too Hungry, Angry, Lonely, or Tired. H-A-L-T, see. It really helps, especially during the holidays. And I'd like to add to that: Know what your triggers are. David admits that rock concerts are his trigger. He gets in with the wrong crowd and does stuff he doesn't want to do.

Commentary: I walked to the chalkboard and wrote, in big, bold letters, "HALT." Then I wrote out what it stood for. I was pleased to see several of the men take out notepads and copy it down. I added, and underlined, **know what your triggers are.**

Darryl: I'd like to add something to that. I know what one of my triggers is, but there's nothing I can do about it. I simply can't talk.

Mac: What do you mean, you can't talk! That doesn't make any sense.

Darryl: You know what I mean. I can't have real conversations. Don't know how. Back when I drank, that was one of my triggers. I'd be with people and they were talking and I couldn't add anything, so I'd just wander off and get a drink. It made me feel better, and I guess I thought I was talking then, but I wasn't really.

GL: You mean real conversation, don't you, Darryl?

Darryl: Yes, a real conversation. The kind where I say something that makes sense and people want to talk to me. And over the holidays I'm going to be around a lot of people talking and I really just don't know how.

GL: Well, I can't say that we can make you a good conversationalist in the next few minutes, Darryl—but I do think we can give you enough skills that you can get through the holidays, and then you can start building on that. Help me out, guys. What do you want to say to Darryl about this?

Richard: I had an English teacher once who told me that the best way to talk was to listen.

GL: Good advice! Darryl—everyone—that is so true. To be a good conversationalist, you must really listen. Then you can take your cue from what was just said. Darryl, if somebody says to you, "I have an appointment tomorrow, which I think might lead to a job interview," what would you say?

Darryl: I guess I'd tell 'em "good luck."

GL: Okay, that's fine. But let's take it further. Maybe you could ask a question—I've found that an emotionally loaded question gets the best response. You might say, "I know you're looking for a job as a chef. What is it that inspires you about cooking?" When the person answers, it gives you yet another chance to continue the conversation. Before you know it, you won't be thinking of "what to ask" but rather, what the other person is saying. So we're back to the beginning: You must be a good listener.

I'd also keep in mind that very often in casual conversation, when people ask a question, it's not for the purpose of getting your answer, but in giving their own an-swer back. You can take advantage of that by saying something as simple as, "What do you think?" or "Please tell me more about that."

Commentary: This continued for several minutes. Then I suggested that he and I role-play. It rather surprised me, but Darryl got right into it, and actually came up with a conversational gambit: He asked if I'd been one of the volunteers who had decorated the street with Christmas flowers. I think he'll do fine over the holidays. I did suggest that he read the daily paper and have current information which he could discuss; I also reminded him that friends and relatives want to be asked about their own families, jobs, and so on.

Linc: You know, it's funny. Darryl has trouble talking—but people tell me to shut up! They say I talk too much.

GL: Well, Linc, as you know—talking too much can be as big a problem as talking too little. Maybe you could slow down a bit and wait for the other person to answer. Then pick up on subtle cues. For example, the person might want to change the subject. And try to talk less about yourself and more about the other person. Or simply describe something you saw.

Sydney: I saw something the other day that is good for an hour of conversation!

GL: What was it, Syd?

Sydney: It was this terrible show called "Celebrity Rehab" or something like that. All about these so-called famous people, like that guy who used to be in "Taxi." It showed him arriving at a clinic clutching a bottle of champagne and saying that he was loaded, as if we couldn't see that. Just a bad show! Oh—that girl who used to be married to Sly Stallone, she was in it. What do you think of that?

GL: I don't know guys—what do you think?

Drew: I think it makes fun of a situation that is very serious.

GL: I agree with you, Drew. It trivializes a serious illness.

Drew: I think a lot of people are making careers out of getting high. Look at all those young girls out there in Hollywood.

GL: Do you think any of them could serve as an example?

Raymond: I do. I think Amy Winehouse is an example of wasted talent. She has the greatest voice, man. And that song, "Rehab." Wow, wrong message, though—"no, no, no, I won't go."

Commentary: The conversation really got going at this point, and the men seemed to be enjoying it. Finally I stepped in and asked if anyone had anything else they'd like to say.

Eli: Yeah, I do. You know, some of you guys are going home for Christmas, but I'm not. I don't think it's fair.

GL: Well, Eli, you know that you've just begun your stay here at Welcome Home. The rule is you can't get leave until you've been here awhile. And you did break a rule last week—you missed Wednesday night group therapy, and that's the most important thing you do here.

Eli: Couldn't I make it up after Christmas?

GL: No, sorry. If it were just up to me, I might let you do it—but it isn't up to me. The Director specifically said that you must stay here. But remember, we'll have a special Christmas dinner here at the house, and if you want to join the other guys later, there will be caroling. Keep your nose clean and you'll go home for Easter, okay?

Commentary: The staff at Welcome Home is acutely aware of the high-risk situations facing alcoholics. They do everything they can to prevent relapse; for example, whenever there is a holiday, they arrange a schedule of pleasant activities.

John: Well, okay, I've waited to say my piece because it sounds plain silly.

GL: Nothing anyone says here is ever considered "silly," John. What is it?

John: Okay, here's the deal. I'm one of the ones going home for Christmas. But I'm scared for a reason I'll bet nobody has thought of. You see, my wife and I always go to a neighborhood community hall during the holidays, where they have this little four-piece band. Been doing it forever. Well, she likes to dance, and I can't dance a step. So then she dances with other guys, and I get jealous. In the past, I'd end up at the punch bowl, and you know where that got me. Anyway, I'm clean and sober now and intend to stay that way. And please don't tell me to stay away from the dance—it's the social event of the year for our neighborhood. Everyone is there from little kids to grandmas. About that punch bowl—I've got to admit I always added the booze myself, to my own drink that is. The punch is non-alcoholic.

GL: I'm glad you added that last part, John, because I definitely was going to suggest that you avoid the situation. But I see that it's a social event that everyone looks forward to. So I've got an idea. John, you may not believe this, but I helped pay for my first year of college by teaching ballroom dance. I was dating a young lady at the time who taught there, and she convinced me that with a few lessons I could also teach. Well, the girlfriend is long-gone, but the lessons have stayed with me. And here's a little secret they don't tell you: Anyone can be taught a basic dance step in a few minutes. So get up, and let's get started!

How about it, guys? Who else here knows how to do the fox trot? (Six men jumped up immediately.) Okay, so that means the rest of you don't know how to dance, right? Well, by the time you leave here tonight every one of you will be able to dance!

Commentary: This may seem like an unorthodox way to end a session, but it turned out to be one of the most productive we've ever had. Within an hour, John was dancing well enough to hold his own at any event. Dancing, after all, is one of the many coping skills that help us in our lives. Welcome Home's director heard about it the next day, and said that we were going to add several things to our schedule during 2010, beginning with weekly dance lessons. (He intends, among other things, to also have transcendental meditation classes, a baking course, conversational skills, and a computer workshop.)

The shining moment for me—and the sort of thing that makes counselors realize they've chosen the right profession—came when John called me on Christmas day and thanked me. He said his wife was thrilled that he'd learned to dance, and it was the best Christmas they'd had in years.

Summary

A single chapter cannot begin to cover the complexities of alcohol addiction and the therapies best suited for its treatment. Group therapy is the most popular treatment modality for recovering alcoholics, and for good reason. It helps normalize their lives, it gives them a chance to share and connect in a therapeutic environment. The aim of this writer was to simply present an overview of the subject, and even that is hard to do in a small amount of space. A look at the historical context shows us how far we have come; a look at today's problems shows us that we still have a long way to go.

Every counselor has his/her favorite reference books. However, this writer would like to list two of his favorites concerning group therapy; if the reader does not have them, they are worth checking out:

Corey, M.S., & Corey, G. (1992). *Groups: Process and Practice* (4th ed). Pacific Grove, CA: Brooks/Cole.

Gladding, S.T. (1994). *Effective Group Counseling*. Greensboro, NC: ERIC/CASS.

Practice Guidelines for Group Psychotherapy is a particularly good publication, and can be ordered free from American Group Psychotherapy Association, Inc., 25 East 21st Street, 6th Floor, New York, NY 10010 or phone them toll-free at (877) 668-2472. The publication can be downloaded through their Website: www.agpa.org.

References

Alcoholics Anonymous Services, Inc. (1991). *Twelve steps and twelve traditions,* (45th ed.). New York: Alcoholics Anonymous Publishing.

American Association for Marriage and Family Therapists (2001). *AAMFT code of ethics.* Washington, DC: AAMFT.

American Psychological Association (2002). *Ethical principles of psychologists and code of conduct.* Washington, DC: APA.

American Psychological Association (2007). Frequently asked questions about e-therapy. Retrieved November 2, 2007, from *www.psych.org/internet+counseling*

Ancis, J.R. (1998). Cultural competency training at a distance: Challenges and strategies. *Journal of Counseling and Development, 76,* 134-142.

Ansbacher, H.L., & Ansbacher, R.R. (Eds.). (1956). *The individual psychology of Alfred Adler.* New York: Basic Books.

Association for Specialists in Group Work. (2000). Professional standards for the training of group workers. Retrieved November 1, 2007, from *http://www. asgw.org/training-standards.html*

Baekeland, F., Lundwall, L., & Kissen, B. (1975). Methods for the treatment of chronic alcoholism: A critical appraisal. In Y. Israel, & J. Wiley (Eds.), *Research advances in alcohol and drug problems.* New York: John Wiley & Sons.

Barrett-Lennard, G.T. (1962). Dimensions of therapist response as causal factors in therapeutic change. *Psychological Monographs, 76*(43), 562.

Barrett-Lennard, G.T. (1998). *Carl Rogers' helping system: Journey and substance.* London, UK: Sage.

Berg, R.C., Landreth, G.L., and Fall, K.A. (1998). *Group counseling: Concepts and procedures.* London, UK: Taylor & Francis.

Berne, E. (1964). *Games people play.* New York: Grove Press.

Bittner, J.A. (1995). Technological resources for rehabilitation distance learning. *Journal of Rehabilitation Administration, 19,* 279-285.

Blatner, A. (1988). Spontaneity. In *Foundations of Psychodrama: History, Theory & Practice.* New York: Springer.

Blatner, A. (2007). A historical chronology of group psychotherapy and psychodrama. Retrieved November 2, 2007, from *http://www.blatner.com*

Buchbinder, J. (1986). Gestalt therapy and its application to alcoholism treatment. *Alcoholism Treatment Quarterly,* (3)3, 49-67.

Burrow, T. (1926). The laboratory method in psychoanalysis. *The American Journal of Psychiatry, 5,* 348.

Burrow, T. (1927). *The social basis of consciousness.* New York: Harcourt, Brace and Co.

Burrow, T. (1928). The basis of group analysis or the analysis of the reactions of normal and neurotic individuals. *British Journal of Medical Psychology,* 8:198-206.

Center for Substance Abuse Treatment (2005). *Substance abuse treatment:*

Group therapy, TIP Series 41, DHHS Publication (SMA) 05-3991. Rockville, MD: Substance Abuse and Mental Health Services Administration.

Coleman, J. (1990). *Foundations of social theory.* Boston: Harvard Press.

Columbia Encyclopedia (6th ed.). (2001). New York: Columbia University Press. Retrieved November 4, 2007, from *http://www.bartleby.com*

Cook, J.E., & Doyle, C. (2002). Working alliance in online therapy as compared to face-to-face therapy. *CyberPsychology & Behavior, 5*, 950-955.

Corey, M.S., & Corey, G. (1997). *Groups: Process and practice* (5th ed.). Pacific Grove, CA: Brooks/Cole.

Corsini, R.J. (1957). *Methods of group psychotherapy.* New York: McGraw-Hill.

Council for Accreditation of Counseling and Related Educational Programs (CACREP) (2001). *CACREP accreditation standards and procedures manual.* Alexandria, VA: Author.

Ellis, A. (1982). The treatment of alcohol and drug abuse: A rational-emotive approach. *Rational Living, 17*(2), 15-24.

Emerick, R. (1990). Self-help groups for former patients. *Hospital and Community Psychiatry, 41*(4), 401-407.

Feibel, C. (1960). The archaic personality structure of alcoholics and its implications for group therapy. *The Psychoanalytic Quarterly,* 30:604, 39-45.

Fisher, C.B. (2003). *Decoding the ethics code: A practical guide for psychologists.* Thousand Oaks, CA: Sage.

Fisher, C.B., & Fried, A.L. (Spring-Summer 2003). Internet-mediated psychological services and the American Psychological Association Ethics Code. *Psychotherapy: Theory, Research, Practice, Training, 40*(1-2), 103-111.

Flores, P.J., & Mahon, L. (1992). The treatment of addiction in group psychotherapy. *International Journal of Group Psychotherapy, 43*(3), 143-156.

Follett, M. (1934). *The new state, group organization and the solution of popular government.* New York: Longmans, Green.

Frank, J.D. (1963). Group therapy in the mental hospital. In M. Rosenbaum, and M. Berger (Eds.), *Group psychotherapy and group function.* New York: Basic Books.

Freimuth, M. (2000). Integrating group psychotherapy and 12-step work. *International Journal of Group Psychotherapy, 50*(3): 297-314.

Fuhriman, A., & Burlingame, G.M. (Eds.) (1994). *Handbook of group psychotherapy: An empirical and clinical synthesis.* New York: John Wiley and Sons.

Galt, A. (1973). Therapy in the context of Trigant Burrow's group analysis. *Group Process, 5*: 115-128.

Gatti Pertegato, E. (1994). *Behind the mask: On formation of true and false self.* (4th ed.) Milan, Italy: F. Angeli.

Gendlin, E.T. (1975). The newer therapies. In S. Arieti, D.X. Freedman, & J.E. Dyrud (Eds.), *Treatment.* New York: Basic Books.

Gendzel, I.B. (1970). Marathon group therapy and nonverbal methods. *American Journal of Psychiatry*, 127: 286-290.

George, R.L., & Dustin, D. (1988). *Group counseling: Theory & practice*. Paramus, NJ: Prentice-Hall.

Gibbard, G.S., Hartman, J., & Mann, R.D. (1974). The individual and the group. In G.S. Gibbard, J. Hartman, & R.D. Mann (Eds.), *Analysis of groups*. San Francisco: Jossey-Bass.

Gil, E. (1988). *Treatment of adult survivors of childhood abuse*. Walnut Creek, CA: Launch Press.

Gladding, S.T. (1994). *Effective group counseling*. Greensboro, NC: ERIC/CASS.

Glasser, W. (1972). *The identity society*. New York: Harper & Row.

Greenberg, I.A. (1974). Moreno: Psychodrama and the group process. In I.A. Greenberg (Ed.), *Psychodrama: Theory and therapy*. New York: Behavioral Publications.

Heinlen, K.T., Reynolds-Welfel, E., Richmond, E.N., & Rak, C.F. (2003). The scope of webcounseling: A survey of services and compliance with NBCC standards for the ethical practice of webcounseling. *Journal of Counseling and Development*, 81, 61-69.

Horwitz, L. (1983). Projective identification in dyads and groups. *International Journal of Group Psychotherapy*, 33, 259-279.

Hough, G. (1992). When confidentiality mandates a secret be kept: A case report. *International Journal of Group Psychotherapy*, 42, 105-115.

Kaul, T.J., & Bednar, R.L. (1986). Experiential group research: Results, questions and suggestions. In S.L. Garfield, & A.E. Bergin (Eds.), *Handbook of psychotherapy and behavior change: An empirical analysis*, 3rd ed. New York: John Wiley & Sons.

Kenny, S., & Murray, B. (1993). New home-delivered training prospects for people with disabilities. *International Journal of Rehabilitation Research*, 16, 195-208.

Kibel, H.D. (1992). Diversity in the practice of inpatient group psychotherapy in North America. *Group Analysis*, 25: 225-239.

Lange, A., van de Ven, J.P., Schrieken, B., & Emmelkamp, P.M.G. (2001). Treatment of posttraumatic stress through the Internet: A controlled trial. *Journal of Behavior Therapy and Experimental Psychiatry*, 32, 73-90.

Laskey, G.B., & Riva, M.T. (2006). Confidentiality and privileged communication in group psychotherapy. *International Journal of Group Psychotherapy*, 56(4), 455-476.

Lazel, E.W. (1921). The group treatment of dementia praecox. *Psychoanalytic Review*, 8: 168-179.

Leibert, T., Archer, J., Munson, J., & York, G. (2006). An exploratory study of client perceptions of Internet counseling and the therapeutic alliance. *Journal of*

Mental Health Counseling, 28(1), 69-71.

Luborsky, L., Singer, B., & Luborsky, L. (1975). Comparative studies of psychotherapies: Is it true that "Everybody has won and all must have prizes?" *Archives of General Psychiatry,* 32: 995-1000.

Ludwig, A.M., Levine, J., & Stark, L.H. (1970). *LSD and alcoholism: A clinical study of treatment efficacy.* Springfield, IL: Charles C. Thomas.

Mackewn, J. (1997). *Developing Gestalt counseling.* London, UK: Sage Publications.

Malan, D.H., Balfour, F.H., Hood, V.G,. and Shooter, A.M. (19076). Group psychotherapy: A long-term follow-up study. *Archives of General Psychiatry,* 33: 1303-1315.

Mann, J., & Semrad, E.V. (1948). The use of group therapy in psychoses. *Journal of Social Casework,* 29: 176-181.

Margolis, R.D., & Zweben, J.E. (1998). *Treating patients with alcohol and other drugproblems: An integrated approach.* Washington, DC: APA.

Marsh, L.C. (1931). Group treatment by the psychological equivalent of the revival. *Mental Hygiene,* 15: 328-349.

Menninger, W.C. (1936). Psychiatric hospital therapy designed to meet unconscious needs. *American Journal of Psychiatry,* 93: 347-360.

Mermelstein, H.T., & Holland, J.C. (1991). Psychotherapy by telephone a therapeutic tool for cancer patients. *Psychosomatics,* 32, 407-412.

McClure, B.A. (1990). The group mind: Generative and regressive groups. *Journal for Specialists in Group Work,* 15, 159-170.

Miller, E., & Glover-Graf, N.M. (2006). The use of phototherapy in group treatment for persons who are chemically dependent. *Rehabilitation Counseling Bulletin,* 49(3), 166-181.

Monras, M. (2003). Indications of group therapy for alcoholism treatment. *Actas Esp Psiquiatr,* 28(5): 298-303.

Moreno, J.L. (1943). Sociometry and the cultural order. *Sociometry,* 6(3), 299-344.

Moreno, Z.E. (1966). Evolution and dynamics of the group psychotherapy movements. In Moreno, J.L. (Ed.) *The international handbook of group psychotherapy.* New York: Philosophical Library.

Narrative Psychology. (2007). Theorists and key figures. Retrieved November 4, 2007, from *http://web.lemoyne.edu.html#moreno*

National Board for Certified Counselors. *NBCC code of ethics* (1998). Greensboro, NC: NBCC.

Nielsen, S.L., Johnson, W.B., & Ellis, A. (2001). *Counseling and psychotherapy with religious persons: A rational emotive behavior therapy approach.* Mahwah, NJ: Lawrence Erlbaum Associates.

Oldham, J.M., & Russakoff, L.M. (1987). *Dynamic therapy in brief hospitaliza-*

tion. Northvale, NJ: Jason Aronson.

Page, B.J. (2004). Online group counseling. In J. DeLucia-Waack, D.A. Gerrity, C.R. Kalodner, & M.T. Riva, *Handbook of group counseling and psychotherapy.* Thousand Oaks, London, & New Delhi: Sage Publications.

Powdermaker, F.B., and Frank, J.D. (1953). *Group psychotherapy: Studies in methodology of research and therapy.* Cambridge, MA: Harvard University Press.

Pope, K. (2007). Informed consent in psychotherapy & counseling: Forms, standards & guidelines. Retrieved October 29, 2007, from *http://www. consent+forms+counseling.com*

Price, R.H., Burke, A.C., D'Aunno, T.A., Klingel, D.M., McCaughrin, W.C., Rafferty, J.A., & Vaughn, T.W. (1991). Outpatient drug abuse treatment services, 1988: Results of a national survey. In R.W. Pickens, C.G. Leukefeld, & C.R. Schuster (Eds.), *Improving drug abuse treatment.* Rockville, MD: National Institute on Drug Abuse.

Rice, C.A., & Rutan, J.S. (1987). *Inpatient group psychotherapy: A psychodynamic perspective.* New York: Macmillan.

Riva, M.T. (2004). Current and historical perspectives on the field of group counseling and psychotherapy. In J.L. DeLucia-Waack, D.A. Gerrity, C.R. Kalodner, & M.T. Riva, *Handbook of group counseling and psychotherapy.* Thousand Oaks, CA: Sage Publications, Inc.

Rochlen, A.B., Zack, J.S., & Speyer, C. (2004). Online therapy: Review of relevant definitions, debates, and current empirical support. *Journal of Clinical Psychology, 60,* 269-283.

Ruzek, J.I. (2003). Concurrent posttraumatic distress disorder and substance use disorder among veterans: Evidence and treatment issues. In P. Ouimette & P.J. Brown (Eds.), *Trauma and substance abuse: Causes, consequences, and treatment of comorbid disorders.* Washington, DC: American Psychological Association.

Sax, S., & Hollander, S. (1972). *Reality games.* New York: Popular Library.

Saxon, M.S., Saxon, J.P., & Spitznagel, R.J. (1998). Identification of potential substance abuse behaviors in the rehabilitation client population. *Vocational Evaluation and Work Adjustment Journal, 31*(2), 36-41.

Shields, W. (2000). Hope and the inclination to be troublesome: Winnicott and the treatment of character disorder in group therapy. *International Journal of Group Psychotherapy, 50,* 87-103.

Spaniol, L., Gagne, C., & Koehler, M. (1999). Recovery from serious mental illness: What is it and how to support people in their recovery. In R.P. Marinelli, & A.E. Dell Orto (Eds.), *The psychological and social impact of disability,* 4th ed. New York: Springer.

Standish, C.T., & Semrad, E.V. (1951). Group psychotherapy with psychotics. *Journal of Psychiatric Social Work, 20:* 143-150.

Thompson, C.E., & Kolb, W.P. (1953). Group psychotherapy in association with Alcoholics Anonymous. *American Journal of Psychiatry*, 110: 29-33.

Understanding Gestalt (author), (January 2007). Retrieved November 27, 2007 from *http://www.addictionsearch.com*

van der Kolk, B.A. (1989). The compulsion to repeat trauma. *Psychiatric Clinics of North America*, 12, 389-411.

Vannicelli, M. (1992). *Removing the roadblocks: Group psychotherapy with substance abusers and family members.* New York: Guilford Press.

Walker, R., Logan, T.K., Clark, J., & Leukefeld, C. (2005). Informed consent to undergo treatment for substance abuse: A recommended approach. *Journal of Substance Abuse Treatment*, 29(4), 241-251.

Weiss, R.D., Jaffee, W.B., deMenil, V.P., & Cogley, C.B. (2004). *Group therapy for* substance use disorders: What do we know? Harvard Review of *Psychiatry*, 12(6), 339-350.

Wilcox, D.M. (1998). *Alcoholic thinking: Language, culture, and belief in Alcoholics Anonymous.* Westport, CT: Praeger Publishers.

Williams, J.E. (2007). Addiction and recovery: Can online counseling for drug and alcohol addiction problems be effective? Retrieved November 8, 2007, from *http://www.SelfGrowth.com*

Williams, M.B. (1994). In Sommer, J.F. (Ed.), *Handbook of post-traumatic therapy.* Westport, CT: Greenwood Press.

Yalom, I.D. (1974). Group therapy and alcoholism. *Annals of the New York Academy of Sciences*, 233(1), 85-103.

Yalom, I.D. (1995). *The theory and practice of group psychotherapy.* New York: Basic Books.

Yalom, I.D. (1998). *The Yalom reader: Selections from the work of a master therapist and storyteller.* New York: Basic Books.

Yalom, I.D., Houts, P.S., Newell, G., & Rand, K.H. (1967). Preparation of patients for group therapy: A controlled study. *Archives of General Psychiatry*, 17: 416-427.

Effective Counseling Using Integrative Psychotherapy

By: Robert F. Wubbenhorst, MA

Integrative psychotherapy is a widely utilized method of effectively inter-acting with clients. It is a counseling approach that goes beyond the use of single-theory techniques and allows the counselor to draw from many theories in order to find the right 'fit' for each individual client. This synthesis of various techniques offers several advantages for the client. According to Capuzzi and Gross (1995), ownership of an integrated theory is high as each counselor enhances their commitment to their approach while encouraging authenticity and congruence while being able to tailor their approach to best fit the client base that characterizes their practice.

History

The use of multiple disciplines in order to facilitate client change is not new. It can be argued that many theories are a combination of previous ones. According to Beutler and Clarkin (1990) "When a new theory is developed and compared with an old one, the comparison dims ones awareness of the fact that the new theory has incorporated some of the common knowledge to which the earlier theory contributed" (p.6).

As Stricker and Gold (1996) have noted, initial integration of concepts included conversion of Freud's theories into use by learning theorists in the 1930's. The breakout of psychotherapy integration didn't occur, however, until the late 1970's with Wachtel's (1977) *Psychoanalysis and Behavior Therapy*. This work is perhaps the most widely acknolwledged text relating theory and technique. Wachtel (1997) states:

> It is my general premise that psychodynamic and behavioral approaches to psychotherapy and the understanding of personality, are far more compat-

ible than is generally recognized and that an integration of the concepts and observations accumulated by these two approaches can greatly enrich our clinical work and our understanding of human behavior. (p.5)

It is not the psychotherapist's intention to piece together from various theories but to truly integrate other theories into a cohesive repetoire that benefits the client without strict adherence to each theory that underlies the process.

Theoretical Constructs

The basics of any successful therapeutic intervention lie in the rapport established with the client and the ability to maintain a therapeutic alliance. Also of high importance to the integrative psychotherapist is a knowledge of various theories of psychotherapy that they can build from in order to develop the most useful program for their client.

The three accepted integrative models of psychotherapy are the common factors approach, technical eclecticism, and theoretical integration. The common factors approach is essentially concerned with determining the factors that differing theories share. The ultimate goal is to create practical treatments based on shared aspects (Norcross & Newman, 1992).

Theoretical integration, according to Stricker and Gold (1996), "involves the synthesis of novel models of personality functioning, psychopathology, and psychological change out of concepts of two or more theoretical systems" (p. 51). Essentially a theoretical integtrationsist will combine many theories by blending the parts in order to create a new approach to practice.

Therapists who use a technically eclectic approach to integration are not concerned with the commonalities of theories, but rather with how particular aspects of those theories will best help the client alleviate their distress. Multimodal Therapy, developed by Arnold Lazarus is one such approach. According to Lazarus (1967):

Psychotherapists who function as eclectic theorists must inevitably embrace contradictory notions. To remain theoretically consistent does not require the rejection of promising techniques culled from other theoretical orientations. ...therapeutic competence depends upon an array of effective techniques rather than upon a mass of plausible theories. (p. 415)

Multimodal Therapy

According to Corey (2001a), "multimodal therapy is a broad-based, systematic, and comprehensive approach to behavior therapy that calls for technical eclecticism" (p. 161). Capuzzi and Gross (1995) state that, "the theory base is behaviorist, although a variety of interventions are applied to client treatment without regard for their theoretical origins" (p. 599). An important component, according to Corey (2001a) is that, "a genuine and empathic client/therapist relationship provides the soil that enables the techniques to take root" (p.161). Martin-Causey and Hinkle (1995) believe, "the multimodal approach assumes a systematic, holistic intervention with the intent being an implementation of long-term behavioral, cognitive, and emotional change" (p. 307).

Most of the therapeutic techniques used in multimodal psychotherapy are "drawn from the four major thrusts of the behavioral approach: classical, operant, social learning, and cognitive behavioral" (Corey, 2001b, p. 277).

The essential idea surrounding the multimodal approach is that human personality, or BASIC I.D., can be separated into seven functional areas: Behavior, Affect, Sensations, Images, Cognitions, Interpersonal relationships, and Drugs or biological functions (including exercise and nutrition). Therapy is comprehensive and brief in order to correct imbalances in a person's BASIC I.D (Lazarus, 1992). According to Corey (2001b), "irrational beliefs, deviant behaviors, unpleasant feelings, bothersome images, stressful relationships, negative sensations, and possible biological imbalances" (p. 278) can be corrected and the more a person learns, the likelihood of these problems reoccurring is diminished.

When a client chooses a multimodal therapist, the first step is a comprehensive assessment pertaining to his or her BASIC I.D. Corey (2001b) lists these as:

1. *Behavior.* This modality refers primarily to overt behaviors, including acts, habits, and reactions that are observable and measurable. Some questions asked are, "What would you like to change?" "How active are you?" "What would you like to start doing?" "What would you like to stop doing?" "What are some of your main strengths?" "What specific behaviors keep you from getting what you want?"

2. *Affect.* This modality refers to emotions, moods, and strong feelings. Questions sometimes asked include: "What emotions do you experience most often?" "What makes you laugh?" "What makes you cry?" "What makes you sad, mad, glad, scared?" "What emotions are problematic for you?"

3. *Sensation.* This modality refers to the five basic senses of touch, taste, smell, sight, and hearing. Examples of questions asked are: "Do you suffer from unpleasant sensations, such as pains, aches, dizziness, and so forth?" "What do you particularly like or dislike in the way of seeing, smelling, hearing, touching, and tasting?"

4. *Imagery.* This modality pertains to ways in which we picture ourselves, and it includes memories, dreams, and fantasies. Some questions asked are: "What are some bothersome recurring dreams and vivid memories?" "Do you have a vivid imagination?" "How do you view your body?" "How do you see yourself now?" "How would you like to be able to see yourself in the future?"

5. *Cognition.* This modality refers to insights, philosophies, ideas, opinions,

self-talk, and judgments that constitute one's fundamental values, attitudes and beliefs. Questions include: "What are some ways in which you meet your intellectual needs?" "How do your thoughts affect your emotions?" "What are the values and beliefs you most cherish?" "What are some negative things you say to yourself?" "What are some of your central faulty beliefs?" "What are the main 'shoulds,' 'oughts,' and 'musts' in your life? How do they get in the way of effective living?"

6. *Interpersonal relationships.* This modality refers to interactions with other people. Examples of questions include: "How much of a social being are you?" "To what degree do you desire intimacy with others?" "What do you expect from the significant people in your life?" "What do they expect from you?" "Are there any relationships with others that you would hope to change?" "If so, what kinds of changes do you want?"

7. *Drugs/biology.* This modality includes more than drugs, encompassing consideration of clients' nutritional habits and exercise patterns as well. Some questions asked are: "Are you healthy and health conscious?" "Do you take any prescribed drugs?" "What are your habits pertaining to diet, exercise, and physical fitness?" (pp. 278-279).

After the comprehensive assessment of the BASIC I.D. the therapist uses two procedures called *bridging* and *tracking* (Corsini & Wedding, 2000).

Bridging deals with a main tenet of multimodal therapy, which is "who or what is best for this individual" (Corsini & Wedding, 2000, p. 342)? In keeping with this belief, the therapist will begin by concentrating, at first, on what the client wishes to discuss and then bridging to more productive areas (Corsini & Wedding, 2000).

Tracking, according to Corsini and Wedding (2000), "refers to a careful examination of the 'firing order' of the different modalities (p. 343)." In other words, the order of importance, as ranked by the client, is very helpful in developing the appropriate treatment plan. Corsini and Wedding (2000) state, "our clinical observations suggest that when one selects techniques that follow the client's habitual sequence, the positive impact is greater than if one follows any other order" (p. 344).

When an individual, couple, or family enters into therapy with a multimodal therapist, the first step is to make certain that they are at ease. Corsini and Wedding (2000) suggest:

A therapist may begin the first session with small talk, noting formal details, such as name, address, phone numbers, marital status, and occupation. This gives the client the opportunity to adjust to the environment of the counseling room to experience a verbal interchange, and to be primed for the detailed inquiry that soon follows. After taking down formal details, the therapist may simply say 'so what seems to be troubling you?' (p. 355)

It is not uncommon for a therapist to suggest treatment options during the interview. It all depends upon what the client needs and if it is comfortable to do so. The following techniques may be used in Multimodal Therapy:

- *Anger-expression:* Many clients have difficulty in recognizing their anger; others are afraid of it. Once the anger is owned it can be eliminated through rational disputation, or channeled into appropriate assertive expression.

- *Anxiety-management training:* By using relaxation training, clients are encouraged to generate anxiety, producing negative imagery, etc. Immediately thereafter they are instructed to do the opposite: relax, dwell on calm sensations, serene images, etc. By learning to turn these feelings on and off, clients are apt to develop self-control and self-reliance.

- *Aversive imagery:* Technique of associating unpleasant thoughts and feelings with undesirable but self-rewarding behavior.

- *Bibliotherapy.*

- *Correcting misconceptions:* Clients are given facts to cope with the demands of daily living.

- *Contingency contracting:* The client agrees to increase, decrease or maintain a specific behavior, with the explicit understanding that rewards will ensue from fulfilling the terms of the contract, and negative consequences will be imposed for breaking them.

- *Feeling-identification:* Centered on exploring the client's affective domain in order to identify significant feelings that might be obscure or misdirected.

- *Focusing:* In a quiet, relaxed state, the client is encouraged to enter a contemplative mood and is gently coaxed into examining spontaneous thoughts and feelings until one particular feeling emerges as the focus of his or her full experiential awareness.

- *Goal-rehearsal or coping imagery:* A deliberate and thorough visualization of each step in a person's rehearsal of upcoming events. Deliberate picturing of oneself coping with situations will enhance transfer to the actual event.

- *Hypnosis.*

- *Modeling:* Learning by observation.

- *Paradoxical strategies:* Includes symptom prescription and forbidding a desired response.

- *Friendship training:* One identifies and discusses the prosocial interactions that constitute affectionate interactions, and the client is urged to put them into practice.

- *Meditation:* Helps to promote relaxation, lower blood pressure, and induces feelings of serenity and calmness.

- *Positive imagery:* Picturing a pleasant scene, real or imagined, past, present, or future in order to reduce tension and anxiety and enhance enjoyment.

- *Problem-solving:* Through modeling, coaching, and example the therapist enables his or her clients to apply scientific principles to the enterprise of problem resolution.
- *Positive reinforcement:* Praise, recognition, and encouragement will strengthen a given response.
- *Recording and self-monitoring:* Systematic recording, charting, and/or quantifying of target behaviors gives the client greater self-control in order to achieve the desired outcome.
- *Stimulus-control:* The presence of certain stimuli tends to increase the frequency of certain behaviors.
- *The empty chair:* The client faces an empty chair that he or she imagines is occupied by a significant other. The client commences by attacking, accusing, forgiving or requesting something of the 'other' person. The client then switches chairs and becomes the other person in response. This continues until some type of resolution is reached. It is especially useful in permitting clients to appreciate the other person's point of view.
- *Time projection:* Clients picture themselves going forward or backward in time and may experience relief after reworking and reliving past events.
- *Tracking:* Careful scrutinizing of the "firing order" of the different modalities. Clients are asked to take special note of the stimuli and events that precede and accompany any negative emotional reactions.
- *Relaxation training:* Several techniques are used to bring calmness to the client.
- *The step-up technique:* Picturing the worst thing that could happen in a stressful situation, then imagining oneself coping with it.
- *Thought Blocking:* Simple but effective way of combating some obsessive and intrusive thoughts by subvocally screaming 'STOP' over and over again (Lazarus 1989, p. 161).

Evaluation of treatment is a straightforward process. The profiles based on a client's BASIC I.D. are dynamic as therapy progresses, and evaluation is an important part of the client/therapist relationship. For example, a change in the Behavior aspect may include statements such as: 'client is less withdrawn or more assertive.' These changes may be noted at every therapy session or only on some occasions (Corsini & Wedding, 2000).

Treatment length in multimodal therapy varies according to the needs of the client. Brief therapy may be completed in ten or twelve sessions, while the average duration is approximately fifty. According to Corsini and Wedding (2000):

Regardless of the specific treatment format, multimodal therapy encompasses: (1) Specification of goals and problems, (2) Specification of treatment techniques to achieve these goals and remedy these problems, and

(3) Systematic measurement of the relative success of these techniques. In essence, this boils down to eliminating distressing and unwanted responses throughout the BASIC I.D. and also overcoming deficits that exist in any of these modalities (p. 363).

The multimodal approach to psychotherapy is a comprehensive, short-term approach that can efficiently change a client's outlook. It is a method that is very flexible and employs treatment options that fit each individual client. In multimodal therapy the client always comes first and the interaction between therapist and client is very important.

Possible Case Use:

As has been stated, Multimodal Therapy can be used with a wide variety of clients. It may be helpful for a beginning counselor to see how the initial interview might take shape.

BASIC ID Assessment:

In an example of a 13 year-old female referred for services due to depression and self-injurious behavior (SIB), establishing therapeutic rapport is essential to the progress of therapy. The client may be able to discuss some issues surrounding her feelings relating to the referral. She may note depression and SIB relating to her reactions to peer relationships. An example of questioning that may be used to facilitate this would be simply, "why do you think you are here to see me?" The client may acknowledge that she has experienced depressed mood, no interest or pleasure in activities, difficulty sleeping, loss of energy and feelings of worthlessness. Perhaps by her own account or through observations by parents and/or school staff you determine that these feelings are causing a significant impairment in her social and academic functioning. The next step would be the actual assessment of her BASIC ID, using a structured recording format. It may look something like this:

- **Behavior:** "When I become overwhelmed with the drama and stress of my friends I become depressed and cut myself in order to feel better."
- **Affect:** "I become overwhelmed with various emotions (sad, angry, scared) when I am involved with my friends' drama."
- **Sensation:** "I get headaches every day."
- **Imagery:** "I am overweight, ugly and wish I could change that."
- **Cognition:** "I am a caring person who must do everything for my friends."
- **Interpersonal relationships:** "I don't expect anything from my friends, but they expect a lot from me."
- **Drugs/Biology:** "I don't feel very healthy but I don't take any drugs."

Once the BASIC ID assessment has been completed, the counselor can ask the client what is the most important issue. This client may state that she is concerned with the SIB and would like to learn better ways to deal with her friends' drama and alleviate stress. Strategies to deal with this issue are various, but one may start with contingency contracting where the client agrees to reduce instances of SIB between sessions by practicing methods learned. Other approaches to follow with may be: Anxiety management, bibliotherapy, relaxation training and thought blocking.

This is only a basic introduction to the model. Where the therapist and client go from here is dependent upon their relationship and any influencing factors in the moment.

Conclusion

Multimodal Therapy works. It is very useful to therapists at any stage in their experience, but is especially useful for beginning counselors. With Multimodal Therapy a novice counselor has a structured framework available to begin their counseling sessions. Multimodal Therapy provides an organized way of getting an initial sense of a client's issues in a structured format. The BASIC ID format is an excellent way to begin a counseling relationship, by introducing a question and answer process that may be less intimidating to the client. Of course, to become proficient in this mode of therapy, a counselor needs to be thoroughly familiar with many theories of counseling. For a beginning therapist this may be a daunting task, however thorough knowledge of but a few theories is a great place to start.

References

Beutler, L. & Clarkin, J. (1990). *Systematic treatment selection: Toward targeted therapeutic interventions.* New York: Brunner/Mazel.

Capuzzi, D & Gross, D (1995). *Counseling & Psychotherapy: Theories and Interventions.* New Jersey: Prentice-Hall.

Corey, G (2001a). *Case approach to Counseling and Psychotherapy.* Belmont, CA: Wadsworth.

Corey, G (2001b). *Theory and Practice of Counseling and Psychotherapy.* Belmont, CA: Wadsworth.

Corsini, R & Wedding, D. (2000). *Current Psychotherapies.* Itasca, Illinois: Peacock Publishers, Inc.

Lazarus, A. (1989). *The Practice of Multimodal Therapy: Systematic, comprehensive, and effective psychotherapy.* Baltimore: Johns Hopkins University Press.

Lazarus, A (1992). The Multimodal Approach to the Treatment of Minor Depression. *American Journal of Psychotherapy Vol XLVI,* 50-57.

Martin-Causey, T. & Hinkle, J. (1995). Multimodal Therapy with an Aggressive Preadolescent: A Demonstration of Effectiveness and Accountability. *Journal of Counseling & Development, Vol 73, No. 3,* 305-310.

Norcross, J. & Goldfried, M. (Eds.), (1992). *Handbook of psychotherapy integration.* New York: Basic.

Norcross, J. & Newman, C. (1992). *Psychotherapy integration: Setting the context.* In J. Norcross & M. Goldfried (Eds.), *Handbook of psychotherapy integration* (p. 3-46). New York: Basic.

Stricker, G. & Gold, J. (1996). Psychotherapy Integration: An assimilative, psychodynamic approach. *Clinical Psychology: Science and Practice,* (3) 47-58.

Wachtel, P. (1977). *Psychoanalysis and behavior therapy: Toward an integration.* New York: Basic.

Wachtel, P (1997). *Psychoanalysis, behavior therapy, and the relational world.* Washington, DC: American Psychological Association.

A Matter of Timing: Guidelines for Utilizing Action-Oriented and Experiential Treatment Strategies
By: Elizabeth Strazar, MA., LPC

"Observe due measure, for right timing is in all things the most important factor." ~ Hesiod

While considered distinct theoretical paradigms, action-oriented and experiential methods of counseling share significant characteristics. Both emphasize the following tenets in their therapeutic approach (Caldwell, 1997; Gendlin, 1996; Greenberg, Watson, & Lietaer, 1998; Kurtz, 1990; Mahrer, 2004; Malcholdi, 2005; Wiener, 1999):

1. Embrace a growth and self-actualization model over a disease model.
2. Promote client-responsibility and empowerment.
3. Foster client/therapist collaboration.
4. Assume that human beings are self-regulating, self-healing, complex systems that are in the process of on-going creative change and re-definition.
5. Respect and utilize the healing attributes of the therapeutic relationship as a vehicle for offering clients an experience of acceptance and genuine interpersonal connection. This, in turn, supports clients to acquire the same self-acceptance and capacity for healthy relationships.
6. Reference the body as a source of information regarding a client's core beliefs, perceptions, attitudes, habits, and self-schemes.
7. Focus on present-tense experience as a means of clients' gaining a deeper awareness and understanding of valuable inner subjective body/mind information.
8. Utilize in-session experiments and exercises to increase clients' insights about feelings, thoughts, sensations, memories, images, and personal meaning.

169

Action-oriented and experiential strategies, although neither considered mainstream clinical approaches nor empirically supported, are gaining increased interest due to studies in the field of neuroscience, implicating the role of the emotional brain and non-verbal processes in experiences of trauma, depression, and anxiety (Cozolino, 2002; Ledoux, 1996). A correlation between these findings and the strength of action-methods can be seen in their use of the body and creative self-expression as a means of accessing non-verbal, emotion-based narratives, core beliefs, and habitual behaviors (Carey, 2006, Hudgins; 2002). Additionally, the proven effectiveness of using mindfulness in addressing the symptoms of affective disorders and borderline personality disorder has contributed to the efficacy of employing an experiential approach (Hayes, Follette, & Linehan, 2004).

Action Methods

Action-methods of counseling involve therapeutic interventions that utilize the use of the body in purposeful and expressive action within the therapy session (Wiener, 1999). Both verbal and non-verbal forms of expression and exploration are employed. The assumption of this method is that the body, in both expressive and creative action, retrieves kinesthetic and visual information that is not as readily accessed linguistically (Landy, 2008).

The category of action methods includes, but is not limited to, the following modalities: dramatic enactment (role-playing, behavioral simulations, psychodrama, drama therapy), dance/movement therapy, gestalt therapy, somatic therapies (body as metaphor/personal narrative), poetry therapy, play therapy, and art therapy. Through the use of these techniques, clients are supported to engage in creative, playful, and experiential exploration aimed at reconciling inner conflicts, thereby bringing about insight, resolution, and integration (Leveton, 2001). The integrated use of expressive modes is often utilized in action methods. This intermodal approach involves shifting from one expressive/action mode to another within a session. This framework allows clients to readily engage the creative/experiential modality that best aligns with their personality structure, the particular issue being addressed, and their innate style of self-expression (Knill, Barba & Fuchs, 2004).

The internal process of the client becomes an outer enactment and can be worked with in much the same way life is experienced—in action, reaction, and interaction—but with the added elements of therapist support, profound presence in the moment, and freedom of expression not usually available in the critical moments of daily life (Karp, Holmes, & Tauvon, 1998). Action methods both concretize and bring into the lived moment habitual patterns of behavior, difficult emotions, chronic conflicts, and key psychodynamic themes (Dayton, 1994).

Experiential Methods

Experientially oriented approaches have their roots in humanistic schools of psychology (gestalt, client-centered, existential, phenomenological). The basic strategy of this method is to gently guide clients toward an inner focused awareness of their present-tense experience (Greenberg, Watson, & Lietaer, 1998). This strategy entails coaching clients in the practice of mindfulness, thereby, giving them the valuable tool of inner attunement. Mindfulness is an observant state of awareness that allows clients to simply notice, without analysis or judgment, what they are experiencing in the present moment (Kabat-Zinn, 2005). Promoting emotional intelligence is key to this method.

The experiential process includes various techniques for evoking, deepening, and maintaining a client's contact with the flow of inner experience (Mahrer, 2004). The goal of this intervention is to enable clients to courageously and sensitively access information that is below consciousness. The assumption is that as clients become facile at mindfully following and understanding the fluctuation of their thoughts, feelings, images, memories, and sensations, they gain the ability to tolerate, express, study, and revise emotions and thoughts (Elliott, Watson, Goldman, & Greenberg, 2003).

Self-awareness leads to self-confidence and the capacity to creatively explore alternate cognitive, emotional, and behavioral options. The long-term goal of this experiential process is to provide clients with the tools of self-attunement, compassionate self-exploration, and authentic self-expression in addressing the moment-by-moment contingencies of their inner and outer lives.

The Art and Science of Counseling

To better understand why timing is such an important factor when utilizing action-oriented, experiential techniques in a counseling session, we must first look at the art and science of counseling itself. There is widespread consensus in the counseling field that there are two interdependent components that contribute to effective counseling: *specific* and *nonspecific* clinical factors (Goldfried & Davila, 2005). *Specific* treatment factors are grounded in standardized principles, theories, methods, and techniques. These factors are considered the toolbox of the therapist and often include empirically supported treatment strategies. Procedures, skills, and areas of study that fall into this category are easily transferable to both teaching and supervision and comprise the core training of all mental health counselors. These elements involve the objective, technical, scientific aspect of the counseling field (Hofmann & Weinberger, 2006).

Nonspecific treatment factors incorporate any counseling element involving both the working alliance between client and counselor and the stylistic expression of the counselor (Castonguay, Sonstantino & Holtforth, 2006). These factors represent the art of the therapy process. Art is defined in this context as the subjective, creative, innovative, and improvisational application of theoretical approaches and strategies (Hofmann & Weinberger, 2006). Due to its interpersonal focus, the art

171

of counseling necessitates a keen understanding of the value and mechanisms of the therapeutic relationship as a change agent. The sensitive use of the interpersonal dynamic between client and therapist is at the heart of non-specific treatment factors (Goldfried & Davila, 2005). Therefore, the art of counseling draws more heavily upon the domains of social and emotional intelligence (Goleman, 1995, 2006). Understandably, these constructs are less open to codification and instruction. Qualities that have been shown to enhance the therapeutic alliance (empathy, attunement, positive regard, and authentic presence/congruence) vary in both degree and style of expression from counselor to counselor (Cozolino, 2002). This poses a creative challenge when attempting to translate nonspecific treatment factors into a user-friendly, skills-training format for new counselors.

The way through this challenge is in acknowledging the vital interplay between the art and science of counseling. By understanding and utilizing the synergy between context (art/relationship) and content (science/technique), a counselor can hone an integrative and clinically sound practice. Decades of research indicate the positive correlation between therapeutic change and a counseling style that rigorously integrates theory/technique with alliance/relationship (Goldfried & Davila, 2005). Technical expertise, combined with a keen awareness of the therapeutic properties of the client/therapist relationship, is the current gold standard with practitioners from varying theoretical approaches (Castonguay & Beutler, 2005).

Timing and Attunement

Therapeutic timing is a key element to resolving the dialectical tension between the art and science of counseling. The elegance of timing is the integration of theory/technique with presence/relationship.

From a client-centered, experiential perspective, the notion of a well-timed therapeutic intervention hinges on the counselor's capacity for attunement (Bugental, 1999). Attunement, within this framework, is defined as the process of attending empathically to the internal process of the client (Siegel, 2007). Attunement requires mindfully listening to the narratives of clients and synchronizing with their natural pace and rhythm as they process external stimuli, access internal responses, and attempt to create order and meaning (Erskine, 1998). When a therapist models a high degree of attunement, clients learn how to attune to their own inner rhythms. The result is a greater capacity for empathy and understanding toward oneself and others (Kohut, 1984).

Conversely, the theory-driven choice of an intervention that is best suited for each client at every stage of the counseling process represents the technical aspect of the timing equation. Factors informing a therapist's clinical choices must include knowledge concerning the phases of therapy (exploration, insight, action), an awareness of a client's ego-strength and character structure, and an understanding of a client's degree of engagement in the change process (precontemplation,

contemplation, preparation, action, maintenance, termination) (Egan, 2001; Hill, 2004; Prochaska, Norcross, & DiClemente, 2002).

Considering these interacting factors, therapeutic timing can be defined as the synthesis of attunement with theoretical acumen. This integration results in the artful and intelligent use of timing in a therapy session. The art of timing supports clients' safety and engagement. The science of timing ensures that the chosen intervention has the desired result of creating maximum insight and change.

An essential goal for any counselor is developing a sense of what to say and do (science) and the best moment for both (art). As a skill, timing can also be described as the ability to sensitively track and decode a client's verbal and non-verbal cues (Kurtz, 1990). The information that is gathered through this tracking process helps the therapist to determine the client's core issues and evaluate a client's readiness to explore a specific topic or engage in a particular intervention. A focus on timing consists of leading and following, listening and responding, supporting and challenging. This improvisational process sets the stage for client/therapist collaboration and the development of a respectful and trusting therapeutic alliance (Siegel, 2007).

Once again, the synthesis of theory and relationship is critical to the topic of timing. Empathic attunement combined with sound clinical choices conveys to clients that they are understood and respected. This combination also provides an environment of acceptance and trust, promotes risk-taking, and enhances client confidence in the therapist's clinical judgment (Greenberg, Watson, & Lietaer, 1998). Within this environment, self-disclosure, openness to suggested exercises and experiments, and the accomplishment of therapeutic goals are enhanced. In summary, therapeutic change can be amplified through applying the technique of empathic and theory-driven timing.

In relation to action-oriented, experiential forms of counseling, timing poses a particular challenge for new therapists who might find it awkward to move from *talking about* to a *focus on* present-tense experience, in-session experiments, and the use of the body as a vehicle for creative self-expression and meaning-making. Gaining comfort with more action-oriented, present-focused methods is a gradual process of trial and error. Small blunders in timing are part of the territory of honing the craft of counseling. Yet there are preliminary guidelines that can support the comfort level of counselors interested in utilizing experiential, action-oriented interventions.

Guidelines and Case Example

In the presentation of these guidelines, emphasis will be placed upon the therapeutic element of timing as the guiding principle, the interplay of therapist techniques, and the therapeutic relationship. As previously stated, these elements are inextricably intertwined and need to be considered holistically in any discussion of the therapy process. A running narrative of a case example of an integrated experiential/action-oriented therapy session will be embedded in the presented guidelines. This is a simulated example that reproduces a realistic representation of a session. The purpose of this transcript is to illustrate the practical application of the proposed guidelines.

Education and Collaboration

Taking the time to educate clients about the basic tenets and interventions of experiential/action-modes is indispensable. It is advised to take the time to instruct and coach clients on the mechanisms of mindfulness (Germer, Siegel, & Fulton, 2003). Inward focused awareness is a core part of this counseling process. The more comfortable clients are with engaging inner reflection, the easier it will be for them to move in and out of inner study and outer action and dialogue (Leijssen, 1998).

While the initial sessions are the time to focus on an educational piece, ongoing instruction is part of this modality. The educational process naturally includes a component of collaboration. Engaging a client in the procedures of a counseling system allows them to be on-board with the theoretical aspects of the work. This takes the focus off of the therapist as an authority figure and sets up a dynamic of partnership and creative brainstorming during sessions. It also serves to empower clients and reinforce their strengths and inner resources (Rogers, 1993).

Case Narrative: Illustrating Education and Collaboration

John is a 32-year old white male. He has been coming to the counseling agency for one year when he opted to join a newly forming experiential/action-oriented group for a series of 10 sessions. His work in therapy had centered on his issues with low self-esteem, difficulty with intimacy, and general feelings of guilt around his lack of career accomplishments. During the course of his individual therapy, John had been able to amend negative belief patterns and make positive changes in his life. Due to his growing ego strength he felt ready to risk group work.

Linda meets with John for a preliminary session to determine if he will join the group. John's responsibility in the therapy process is immediately established as Linda explains that they will collaboratively decide if this modality is a good fit for him. Linda asks John if it is okay to explore in their session some of the techniques and tools that the group will be utilizing. The therapist empowers John by asking for his consent to experiment together.

Linda explains to John that action-oriented/experiential forms of counseling explore issues and concerns from a creative, expressive, and mindfulness-based approach. Linda's initial contact with John focuses on the educational process and enrolling him in collaboration. She doesn't introduce too much theory, but also wants to make sure he has a simple reference point for the process and is comfortable with the format. She makes sure to allow time for questions and concerns about the therapeutic approach.

Establishing Safety

Creating an environment of safety is the first task in any counseling format. There is a special finesse to facilitating curiosity, ease, and openness with clients who are unfamiliar with, or wary of, experiential or expressive modes. A client's skepticism or self-consciousness in relation to creative self-expression as a therapeutic tool is the first barrier the therapist must address. Therefore, a counselor's own comfort level with creative self-expression and mindfulness-based processes paves the way for the client to feel more at ease. A playful, experimental approach on the part of the therapist is a powerful tool for reducing a client's reluctance. It also stimulates the client's creativity and curiosity (Knill, Levine, & Levine, 2005).

Empathic timing is a key element in creating safety. The therapist's ability to attune to a client's readiness to engage is paramount. Similarly, opening to the immediacy of one's internal process requires the ability to be vulnerable and courageously attend to the flow of spontaneous experience. Engagement in deep inward focus is made possible by a therapist who moves slowly, with awareness and respect for the client's tempo and pace. This necessitates continual and close monitoring of a client's level of safety by the therapist (Mahrer, 2004). Offering a contact statement is a powerful way to track for safety, connect with the client's inner experience, and convey empathy (Kurtz, 1990). Contact statements are short reflective phrases illustrating support and understanding (Johanson & Kurtz, 1991). This intervention helps clients relax and stay with their process.

Choice of Intervention and Diving In

The most obvious method of choosing an exercise is to follow the client's lead. Emphasis is placed on trusting the client's intuitive choices. The role of the therapist is one of respectful companion, ever alert to subtle cues from clients as to which exercise or experiment will deepen their connection to their inner experience and support authentic self-expression. Supporting self-trust, self-exploration, and risk-taking is essential. This kind of collaboration will result in well-chosen interventions. Once again, if counselors are working with the principle of empathic attunement, they will be able to read a client's verbal and nonverbal signals as to which modality they are comfortable utilizing (Rogers, 1993).

Additionally, it is important to choose experiments and exercises as they relate to particular psychological issues, a client's ego-strength, and the stages of therapy. The topic of psychological issues and ego strength is complex and requires an in-depth case history and assessment process. Clients who have experienced early childhood trauma will need to be monitored more closely to prevent emotional flooding. Starting out slowly and tracking for signs of strong emotional states is recommended with clients who present a more fragile ego-structure (Hudgins; 2002,

Carey, 2006).

When attunement and timing are in place, there is less danger that the therapist will miss markers indicating extreme discomfort or fear on the part of the client. Similarly, the beginning stages of therapy will require the therapist to move with agility by balancing action, inner reflection, and conversation while a client's capacity for inner exploration and expressive action is gauged. As the therapy progresses, clients will be able to take more risks and broaden their repertoire of exercises and experiments.

After choosing an intervention, diving in simply requires returning to the guiding principle of empathic and intelligent timing. The therapist's own comfort level with the intervention will enable a relaxed entrance into the exercise/experiment. Diving in also entails stopping or shifting gears if the intervention falls flat or becomes too emotionally activating for the client (Kurtz & Minton, 1997).

Case Narrative: Illustrating Establishing Safety & Choice of Intervention and Diving In

The meeting between Linda and John takes place in the group room. An array of art supplies, musical instruments, and drama props are in plain view and readily available. The office environment is itself an invitation into the creative, playful zone and gives John permission to engage his imagination. When the time is right, John will be the one that makes the choice of which medium to use. Linda will not ask John to engage in expressive action until safety has been established. She will track changes in his breathing and bodily posture as indicators that he is feeling safe and ready to dive into expressive action. She is ever mindful to his tempo and rhythm. Linda's first task with John is to establish safety by offering herself as a non-judgmental witness. She models a relaxed and curious approach to their interaction.

LINDA: (*noticing John looking cautiously around the room*) So, what's going on for you as you look around the room?

JOHN: All this artsy stuff is making me nervous. I'm not an artist.

LINDA: That's fine. Lots of people feel that way. This kind of creative expression isn't about being an artist...it's about expressing your thoughts and feelings in another way other than talking. As I shared with you, the experiential/action-mode is flexible. You don't have to do anything you don't want to do.

This is another opportunity for Linda to broaden the educational component to the session. She is also gently moving through John's hesitation and skepticism by not enforcing any activity or asking him to focus on his nervousness. She is giving John the clear message that she hears his reluctance and, in this, is attending to timing and empathic attunement.

In the next passage, Linda utilizes the opportunity to determine which creative modality fits John's natural expressive tendencies.

LINDA: So, when you were a kid, what kinds of play did you enjoy?

JOHN: I loved fantasy play and pretending I was a superhero. I would spend hours alone just imagining scenes. But…I was also very physical…kind of hyper… liked to move a lot.

LINDA: Okay, so maybe some role-playing might be a better fit for you.

JOHN: Maybe.

LINDA: Well, we will not move into anything until you are ready. How about if we talk a bit about your thoughts and feelings about the group?

Again, Linda is applying empathic and intelligent timing, listening for cues, aligning with John's tempo. His reluctance is still strong and so she goes for more safety while also attempting to access his core thoughts and feelings.

JOHN: Right…well, I guess my main concern is that this whole thing is so new to me…the action, creative, mindfulness stuff…and I might not be as good as the other members at it…not good enough.

LINDA: I hear that…not good enough. It is a whole new thing for you. Apprehension is normal.

Linda is going for safety by utilizing empathic reflection and neutralizing John's hesitation. She then moves on a hunch (gained through John's body language and tone of voice) that fear might be surfacing for John. She offers John a contact statement to check out if she is on the right track.

LINDA: Is that a kind of scary feeling?

JOHN: Yeah, I'm definitely afraid to do this group thing.

Her hunch confirmed, Linda now moves toward helping John deepen the awareness of his experience. Notice Linda's use of language in referring to John's fear as 'the fear' instead of 'your fear'. This encourages John to have a witnessing stance instead of being over-identified with his experience. This little bit of distance from the fear wards off emotional flooding.

LINDA: Makes sense. Would you be willing to explore the fear a bit more through a mindfulness exercise?

Linda starts with a mindfulness experiment because of his reference to fantasy play when he was a child. This indicates that he has some comfort level with visual imagery and inner reflection.

JOHN: Yeah, I guess.

Linda attempts to move John into a more embodied connection to his fear of judgment by asking him to close his eyes and mindfully attune to his physical sensations. Linda coaches John through this process by deepening his connection to the immediacy of his experience.

She does this by asking him questions about the color, texture, movement, form, temperature, imagery, and feeling-tone of his fear. As he does this Linda continues to track for signals (breath, facial expressions, gestures, and posture) that his emotions are not flooding.

LINDA: Where do you feel the fear in your body?

JOHN: My stomach.

LINDA: Does it have a temperature or color?

JOHN: Hot and red.

LINDA: Is it moving or static?

JOHN: Moving…swirling…hyper…feels like I did when I was a kid…couldn't sit still sometimes. I had lots of strong emotions…too emotional.

As John reports his experience, his voice is timid and childlike. Linda is continually tracking for clues about John's inner state. She notices that John's body is contracted and his breath is shallow. Linda suspects that sadness is now emerging for John. Again, she offers him a contact statement to see if her attunement is correct.

LINDA: Some sadness there?

JOHN: Yeah, kind of sad *(pause, deep breath)*…actually, it's kind of intense, uncomfortable.

Linda then offers a reflective question to determine if John has reached a stopping point or is able to move on and go deeper. This is a crucial point where she must stay alert to balancing safety with diving in.

LINDA: Too uncomfortable?

JOHN: No. Just strong and familiar.

LINDA: Okay. Can we keep going with this?

JOHN: Yeah.

LINDA: Can you see an image of yourself as that boy?

JOHN: Yeah.

LINDA: How old are you?

JOHN: I don't know…maybe about seven.

Linda then offers a probe to evoke and gather more information about John's core beliefs about sadness.

LINDA: I'm going to say something to that boy…you just notice what happens when you hear me say: *It's okay to be sad.*

JOHN: *(very quiet)*. No, it's not okay. Not safe.

It is at this point that John spontaneously opens his eyes. Linda takes this as a cue that he needs to change modalities and wants to connect with her and determine if it is safe to proceed. John is in deep emotional waters quickly. This is common with experiential modes.

Clients will often come out of an inner focused state in order to anchor themselves in the interpersonal connection with the therapist. Linda attends to timing, safety, and the therapeutic alliance.

LINDA: Feelings got a little too strong?

JOHN: Yeah.

LINDA: It's great that you opened your eyes…taking care of yourself when the feelings got too strong.

JOHN: Yeah…feels like I'm taking care of that kid. Strange. Guess he needs that…needs attention.

Tracking and The Intermodal Process

Understanding how to shift from one expressive or experiential mode to another is a key factor in utilizing an intermodal approach. Empowering the client to choose modalities and a willingness to follow the lead of the client are essential tools. Tracking the client's process entails acknowledging what is there, deepening the experience, and offering possibilities for expanding inner awareness and authentic self-expression. By moving from one modality to another, the counselor/client dyad collaboratively accesses the client's inner resources and discovers new possibilities.

Additionally, it is recommended that counselors hone their capacity to improvise and shift gears when a client's inhibitions and/or fears are activated. Moving in and out of action, inner attunement, and authentic client/therapist interaction allows the process to stay grounded in present-centered experience while respecting the client's zone of safety (Knill, Barba & Fuchs, 2003).

Case Narrative: Illustrating Tracking and The Intermodal Process

Having been assured that John is able to continue studying the flow of his experience, she uses John's remark about the child needing contact and attention as a point of entry. Her goal is to engage the intermodal process and shift from inward focus to expressive action.

LINDA: Well, lets see if we can give that kid some attention. I have an idea… would you be willing to have a conversation with that seven-year old about how he feels about joining the group?

JOHN: I guess. Kind of like pretending…super hero stuff.

LINDA: Yes, exactly. We can set up two chairs and you can pretend you are the boy and then switch places and be yourself now…just see what happens. Sound okay?

JOHN: Yeah…that feels okay.

Again, Linda has chosen role-playing due to John's previous remark that this might be a more comfortable option. With this intervention, Linda is also integrating John's historical issues with his future fears while maintaining focus on present experience and action.

JOHN (*as seven-year old*) I don't want to go anywhere where I would be told I'm not good enough…made fun of…I can't do all that art stuff…and I might cry or get sad…scared.

LINDA: Okay, John, switch chairs and respond to him from your adult self.

JOHN: (*as adult John*) Don't be such a baby.

John turns to Linda. He is startled and taken off guard by his response to the boy.

JOHN: Wow, I would never say that to a seven-year old kid.

LINDA: Did someone say that to you when you were a kid?

John's breathing gets shallow. His body contracts and he gets very quiet. Linda offers empathic attunement.

LINDA: Sadness coming up again?

JOHN: Yeah, and some anger too. My mom said that. She was always pushing me to be more social...not shy away from people...but I felt like she didn't get how insecure I was. I needed more time...go at my own pace.

LINDA: This seems important...this feeling pushed and judged.

JOHN: Yeah. (*John becomes quiet again*)

Linda offers another probe to help John take in safety. She is also offering John a new option: experience his feelings with more compassion and understanding.

LINDA: It's okay to just let yourself feel the sadness and anger. We can go slowly, take your time.

JOHN: Yeah...that's good. (*John looks down but relaxes and opens up his breathing*)

With the emergence of this core issue, the therapeutic alliance is beginning to form and John is slowly allowing authentic self-expression. Client and therapist are seamlessly moving into an intermodal process due to Linda's ease at shifting gears, attending to timing, offering empathic contact statements, and integrating John's inward attunement with expressive action.

Support and Challenge

An experiential/action-oriented therapist does not consider a client resistant as much as in a protective process or hitting a barrier due to limiting core beliefs. The approach is informed by a humanistic philosophy and has respect for the function and purpose of the defensive posture. The key is to learn how to play with the defenses—and go in under the radar with probes (evoking experience), contact statements (a direct statement about a client's process—no interpretation), empathic attunement, reflective questions, and gentle support (challenge) to move into difficult emotions or experiences (Kurtz, 1990). Going in under the radar entails attending to safety, not pushing against the defenses, and aligning with a client's natural inclination toward insight and healing.

The deepest work can happen when a client is reaching an impasse. This is where the core issues reside (Mahrer, 2004). Working at the barrier (defensive posture) involves balancing safety and risk-taking. As clients give way to spontaneous expression it can be threatening and unfamiliar. To move through the impasse, the therapist can continue, or take over, the client's movement, words, enactment, or drawing as a way of keeping the process moving toward deeper awareness and insight. This also allows clients to see/hear their deepest feelings expressed from a safe distance, thus allowing further exploration in a container of safety (Levine & Levine, 1999).

Case Narrative: Illustrating Support and Challenge

JOHN: *(after a few moments of silence, John looks up at Linda)* But I do want to know what this sadness and anger is all about. It seems important.

John illustrates that he feels some degree of safety and support by making eye contact with Linda. His curiosity about his process is engaged and balancing his fear of encountering difficult feelings. John is giving Linda a clear verbal signal that it is okay to proceed. Linda stays with deepening the process.

LINDA: Yes, I agree…how about if we return to the inward focused place. Get some more information about what's going on.

JOHN: Okay.

LINDA: Can you close your eyes and allow your breathing to open up a bit? Just take your time and see where the feelings are in your body right now.

JOHN: My throat.

LINDA: Are there words that want to be spoken?

JOHN: No words. Just this tightness. Not sure. Strong feelings.

John is coming up against the boundaries of his comfort zone as therapist and client are entering deeper into his core material and working at the barrier. Linda is careful not to push him to do too much—respecting his defenses. Again, the delicate interplay between support and challenge—risk and safety is essential. Therapeutic timing leads the way. Linda gently challenges John to stay with the process by shifting gears and continuing the exploration by utilizing a doubling technique from psychodrama. Doubling involves the therapist giving voice to what the client cannot say or is unaware of feeling. This intervention has a dual effect of giving clients a sense of being seen and heard while also deepening their level of emotional truth and engagement (Dayton, 1994).

LINDA: Yeah, these are old feelings. Strong feelings. Would it be okay if I expressed the feelings you might be having? You can just listen and see if they fit. Does that sound okay?

Asking for permission to embody and take over John's inner experience empowers him to be instrumental in guiding the process of the session and tapping into his strengths during a time of vulnerability.

JOHN: Yeah.

In the next intervention, Linda is working with the information that John gave her about his mother. Her working theory is that he has internalized a negative self-view from his early experiences with a critical parent. She is mindful that he may be hesitant to enter into a realm where his earlier feelings of powerlessness, hurt, and anger might emerge. This theory-driven hunch informs the timing of Linda's intervention. She keeps the process in motion by entering the frightening place for him. She takes over the role of the seven-year old.

LINDA: I'm confused…feel sad…feel angry…and afraid to tell you what I'm feeling…you might yell at me…or tell me I'm a baby.

JOHN: (*John's face softens as he holds back tears*) That's it. Yeah, that's it. I have to hide what I'm feeling…not safe. Boys aren't supposed to be so sensitive…so emotional.

LINDA: Yeah, like right now…hard to let the tears happen?

JOHN: Oh yeah, not gonna let that happen.

John opens his eyes and takes a drink of water.

JOHN: (*looking at Linda*) That was weird.

He is organizing himself again around his old dynamic. He is judging and hiding the depth of his emotions—yet feeling the support of the therapeutic alliance enough to make contact with Linda again.

LINDA: Yes, it must feel weird to let yourself experience emotions that boys are not supposed to have.

JOHN: Ah, yeah!

LINDA: You did a great job. You let yourself try out something new and got in touch with some deep feelings. Very brave stuff.

JOHN: Yeah, definitely weird…but interesting.

LINDA: Okay, does this seem like a good place to stop?

JOHN: (*John laughs*) For sure.

Phases of a Session and Continuity

There are as many ways of defining the phases of a therapy session as there are styles or schools of counseling. Whichever framework a counselor adopts, it is important to track the arc of the middle, beginning, and end of a session in order to create a sense of continuity and safety. Several versions that are helpful for experiential/action-oriented sessions include the following frameworks:

1. Halprin (2003) defines a five-part process (identification, confrontation, release, change, and growth) and three levels of awareness that the therapist tracks (physical, emotional, and mental).
2. Rogers' (1993) phases include centering, sharing, engagement, and grounding.
3. Kurtz's (1990) model involves accessing, deepening, and processing.

It is important to note that the deep emotional experience and/or catharsis that often occur within an experiential/action-oriented mode must be followed with an identification of the themes revealed. Creating a bridge between a client's kinesthetic and linguistic processes supports order and meaning. Therefore, the grounding, integration, or summary phase of the session is of vital importance with this method. This stage of the session also serves to link the work of the session with a client's current life issues and goals (Gendlin, 1996).

Case Narrative: Illustrating Phases of a Session and Continuity

As mentioned, an essential stage of the experiential/action-oriented mode includes a time to ground and integrate the less verbal insights gained during the earlier phases of the session. The final exchange between Linda and John illustrates that less is often more when wrapping up a session.

LINDA: So, you got in touch with lots of feelings rather quickly.

JOHN: Yeah, that usually doesn't happen.

LINDA: This way of working can be quite powerful.

JOHN: I get it.

LINDA: Does it make sense that this old dynamic with your mom would make you want to shut down and protect yourself?

JOHN: Yeah, totally…it stops me from taking risks, being myself…and feeling close to people. Woman people. (*John laughs*)

LINDA: Great insight. And joining a group would certainly bring up some of these old feelings.

JOHN: Yeah. I know this issue…but am feeling it now in a way that makes more sense. I guess being in the group might help to finally work this one out.

LINDA: I think the format would work great for you. Do you want to give it a try?

JOHN: Why not…I already know the ropes…just don't make me draw anything. (*John smiles*).

LINDA: Absolutely not. And who knows…that seven-year old part of you might surprise you and want to pull out the crayons.

John once again expresses his fears, but this time with less self-judgment. He is playful and Linda responds in kind. She both assures him that she respects his boundaries and supports and empowers his ability to take risks.

In the following exchange, Linda brings closure to the session by empowering John to identify the key learning from the session. Supporting John to clarify his insights helps him move toward behavioral change. It also helps John anchor his newly acquired inner resources and define how he can use them in a future challenging situation (entering the group).

LINDA: So, what did you learn today that could help you be in the group with more ease?

JOHN: That's clear…go at my own pace. Not do anything that doesn't feel right for me. That might make it less anxious.

LINDA: Fantastic. I'll remind you if you forget.

JOHN: (*laughs*) I'm sure I will.

Humor is a sign of comfort and safety and signals that the session was moving in the right direction. John was able to gain an embodied sense of his issues and identify future goals and objectives. He also gained a valuable tool for monitoring his safety levels and supporting more authentic presence and self-expression.

Throughout the course of this session the therapist was mindful of the stages of the process. She made sure the flow of the session allowed for safety, contact, exploration, and integration. She knew when to deepen the client's emerging core material (physical, emotional, and cognitive) and when to pause and allow the client to manage and organize new information. The session goal of determining if the client would join the group was never lost during the deeper emotional work.

In addition, the therapist kept her focus on the crucial element of timing in moving from one action/experiential modality to another. She offered probes, reflective questions, empathic attunement, supportive acknowledgements, contact statements, collaborative suggestions, and nonjudgmental coaching to navigate through the client's barriers. It is through an integration of these elements that an action/experiential process sensitively unfolds.

Conclusion

The synthesis of attunement with sound clinical judgment results in the skill of therapeutic timing. The centrality of timing in the counseling process is offered as a fundamental guiding principle for new counselors as they hone their unique style of integrating the art and science of counseling. As noted, timing is especially important when utilizing action-methods and experiential approaches. Therefore, it is of vital importance that novice counselors attune to their own natural rhythm and tempo, be patient, and lead with a spirit of creative, mindful exploration. The presented guidelines and case narrative are meant to serve as a springboard. It is hoped that this brief introduction to this dynamic modality will engender further study and professional training by interested counselors.

References

Bugental, J. F. T. (1999). *Psychotherapy isn't what you think: Bringing the psycho-therapeutic engagement into the living moment.* Phoenix, Arizona: Zeig, Tucker & Co., Inc.

Caldwell, C. (1997). *Getting in touch: The guide to new body-centered therapies.* Wheaton, Illinois: Quest Books

Carey, L. (Ed.) (2006). *Expressive and creative arts methods for trauma survivors.* London: Jessica Kingsley Publishers.

Castonguay, L. G., & Beutler, L. E. (2005). *Principles of therapeutic change that work.* NY: Oxford University Press.

Castonguay, L. G., Sonstantino, M. J., & Holtforth, M. G. (2006). The working alliance: Where are we and where should we go? *Psychotherapy: Theory, Research, Practice, Training, 43 (3), 271-279.*

Cozolino, L. (2002). *The neuroscience of psychotherapy: Building and rebuilding the human brain.* New York, NY: W. W. Norton & Company.

Dayton, T. (1994). *The drama within: Psychodrama and experiential therapy.* Deerfield Beech, FL: Health Communications.

Egan, G. (2001). *The skilled helper: A problem-management and opportunity-development approach for helping* (7th ed.). Belmont, CA: Wadsworth Hill, Publishing.

Elliott, R., Watson, J. C., Goldman, R. N., & Greenberg, L. S. (2003). *Learning emotion-focused therapy: The process-experiential approach to change.* Washington, DC: American Psychological Association.

Erskine, R. G. (1998). Psychotherapy in the USA: A manual of standardized techniques or a therapeutic relationship? *International Journal of Psychotherapy, 3,* 231-234.

Gendlin, E.T. (1996). *Focusing oriented psychotherapy: A manual of the experiential method.* NY: Guilford Press.

Germer, C. K., Siegel, R. D., & Fulton, P. R. (2005). *Mindfulness and psychotherapy.* NY: The Guilford Press.

Goldfried, M. R., & Davila, J. (2005). The role of relationship and technique in therapeutic change. *Psychotherapy: Theory, Research, Practice, Training, 42 (4),* 421-430.

Goleman, D. (1995) *Emotional intelligence.* NY: Bantam Books.

Goleman, D. (2006). *Social intelligence.* NY: Bantam Books.

Greenberg, L. S., Watson, J. C., & Lietaer, G. (Eds.). (1998). *Handbook of experiential psychotherapy.* New York: Guilford Press.

Halprin, D. (2003). *The expressive body in life, art and therapy: Working with movement, metaphor and meaning.* London: Jessica Kingsley.

Hayes, S. C., Follette, V. M., & Linehan, M. M. (Eds.). (2004). *Mindfulness and acceptance: Expanding the cognitive-behavioral tradition.* NY: Guilford Press.

Hesiod. (1999). *Theogony, works and days.* M. L. West (Trans.). USA: Oxford

University Press.

Hill, C.F., (2004). *Helping skills: Facilitating exploration, insight, and action.* Washington, D.C.: American Psychological Association.

Hofmann, S. G., & Weinberger, J. (Eds.). (2006). *The art and science of psychotherapy.* NY: Routledge.

Hudgins, M. K. (2002). *Experiential treatment for ptsd: The therapeutic spiral model.* NY: Springer Publishing Co.

Johanson, G., & Kurtz, R. (1991). *Psychotherapy in the spirit of the tao-te ching.* NY: Bell Tower

Kabat-Zinn, J. (2005). *Coming to our senses: Healing ourselves and the world through mindfulness.* NY: Hyperion.

Karp, M., Holmes, P., & Tauvon, K.B. (Eds.) (1998). *The handbook of psychodrama.* London: Brunner-Routledge.

Knill, P. J., Barba, H. N., & Fuchs, M. N. (2003). *Minstrels of the soul: Intermodal expressive therapy* (2nd ed.). Toronto: E.G.S. Press.

Knill, P. J., Levine, E. G., & Levine, S. K. (2005). *Principles and practice of expressive arts therapy.* London: Jessica Kingsley.

Kohut, H. (1984). *How does analysis cure?* Chicago: University of Chicago Press.

Kurtz, R. (1990). *Body-centered psychotherapy: The hakomi method.* Mendocino, CA: LifeRhythm.

Kurtz, R. & Minton, A. (1997). Essentials of hakomi body-centered psychotherapy. In C. Caldwell (Ed.). *Getting in touch: The guide to new body-centered therapies* (pp. 45-60). Wheaton, Illinois: Quest Books.

Landy, R. J. (2008). *The couch and the stage: Integrating words and action in psychotherapy.* New York: Jason Aronson.

LeDoux, J. (1996). *The emotional brain: The mysterious underpinnings of emotional life.* NY: Simon & Schuster Inc.

Leijssen, M. (1998). Focusing microprocesses. In L. S. Greenberg, J. C. Watson, & G. Lietaer (Eds.). *Handbook of experiential psychotherapy* (pp. 155-177). NY: The Guilford Press.

Leveton, E. (2001). *A clinician's guide to psychodrama, 3rd edition.* NY: Springer Publishing Company.

Levine, S. K., & Levine, E. G. (Eds.) (1999). *Foundations of expressive arts therapy: Theoretical and clinical perspectives.* NY: Jessica Kingsley Publishers.

Mahrer, A. R. (2004). *The complete guide to experiential psychotherapy.* Boulder, Colorado: Bull Publishing Company.

Malchiodi, C. A. (Ed.). (2005). *Expressive therapies.* NY: Guilford Press.

Prochaska, J. O., Norcross, J. C., & DiClemente, C. C. (2002). *Changing for good.* NY: Quill.

Rogers, N. (1993). *The creative connection: Expressive arts as healing.* Palo Alto,

CA: Science & Behavior Books.

Siegel, D. J. (2007). *The mindful brain: Reflection and attunement in the cultivation of well-being.* NY: W. W. Norton & Company.

Silverstone, L. (1997). *Art therapy: The person-centered way* (2nd ed.). London: Jessica Kingsley.

Wiener, D. J. (1999). *Beyond talk therapy: Using movement and expressive techniques in clinical practice.* Washington, DC: American Psychological Association.

An Overview of Counseling Theories and Interventions
Psychoanalytic, Humanistic, and Cognitive-Behavioral Perspectives
By: *Frank E. Vargo, Ed.D.*

*L*inda is a 46 year-old woman who has recently been undergoing a range of emotional and related physical difficulties, in conjunction with very significant personal events and changes in her life. A recent divorce, professional disappointments and job adjustments, a current diagnosis of cancer that is being successfully treated, grown children and subsequent family system changes, and issues and responsibilities related to aging parents have all cumulatively and progressively impacted Linda's emotional, social, and vocational functioning. Linda's recent emotional and physical symptomologies have included strong elements of depression and anxiety. Her decline in general emotional and physical well being have prompted Linda to seek professional help with a counselor to better enable her to understand and resolve her current life issues and emotional difficulties.

A Wide Range of Counseling Models and Options
As Linda pursues her goal to proactively utilize counseling/therapy to address her current life issues and difficulties, she will likely find herself initially bewildered and even possibly confused at the options and many styles of counseling interventions and therapists that are available to her. With even a minimal amount of personal investigation and research, Linda will come to realize that there are numerous theories and models of counseling and therapy, based on the foundations of various theories of personality that have developed and evolved over the many past decades (Corey, 2005; Capuzzi & Gross, 2007; Corsini & Wedding, 2007; Burger, 2004; Seligman, 2006; Sharf, 2003; Fadiman & Frager, 2002).

This chapter will provide a brief overview of the counseling theories and models, and related theories of personality development that are generally accepted in the "mainstream" of the modern counseling professions and governing professional organizations. The article is intended to be used by beginning graduate students in clinical mental health counseling, counseling psychology, and related professional fields. A succinct overview of accepted counseling models can be utilized as a starting point for more extensive and thorough studies and research in counseling theories and practice, in the context of formal graduate studies and training. The counseling theories that will be overviewed will include psychoanalytic therapies, existential therapies, person centered/humanistic therapies, behavioral therapies, and cognitive-behavioral therapies.

The Value of Understanding Multiple Models of Counseling and Personality

As counselors initially train and then develop and evolve as professional mental health providers, it is common for each professional to accept and assimilate one or several counseling models and related personality theories as a primary foundation for the basis of practice and intervention. It is also very common, and quite appropriate, for professional counselors to utilize an *eclectic approach* to therapy: That is, an integration and utilization of numerous counseling models and strategies which are appropriate to a particular client and therapeutic situation (Capuzzi & Gross, 2007; Corey, 2005; Seligman, 2006). For instance, a therapist using a more eclectic and *theory integrated* model of counseling while working with "Linda" may initially frame an understanding of emotional difficulties from a *psychoanalytic* perspective, while concurrently utilizing a *behavioral/classical conditioning* model to counter condition acquired phobic and related anxiety responses, and finally then develop and employ specific *cognitive behavioral* strategies to address established dysfunctional patterns of thinking and reasoning that are contributing to patterns of depressive feelings and thought.

To better facilitate the understanding of numerous and diverse professionally established counseling and personality models for graduate level study, this chapter will focus on each selected model of counseling theory with a specific focus on *each individual theory by itself*, one at a time. Each counseling theory section will also reference the hypothetical case study of "Linda", to provide further understanding and clarification of concepts and principles.

Psychoanalytic Theory and Therapy

When the term "psychology" is considered today, a majority of individuals in Western society may concurrently refer to the theories of *Sigmund Freud* and his model of therapy known as *psychoanalysis*. Freud's writings and related clinical work, developed and implemented approximately one hundred years ago, laid a solid foundation for the entire related fields of psychotherapy and counseling. Freud's expansive body of work and his pivotal theories strongly impact, to varying degrees, virtually all areas of modern clinical theories and interventions (Corsini &

Wedding, 2007; Seligman, 2006; Corey, 2005).

Freud developed what is widely considered to be the first comprehensive theory of personality. Although some of his concepts and ideas predated his own specific ideas, Freud has been noted to be the first person in relatively modern times to integrate, organize, and codify some previous rather loosely related ideas of others into a cohesive and unique comprehensive theory of human behavior (Burger, 2004).

Sigmund Freud's theories and insights regarding the nature of human behavior and personality were revolutionary and brilliant for his time. His understanding and importance of the *unconscious mind* regarding most aspects of human psychological functioning were pivotal positions in his theories on mind and human behavior, which continue to reverberate in many counseling and therapy theoretical frameworks to this day (Capuzzi & Gross, 2007; McWilliams; 1994; Greenberg & Mitchell, 1983; Bernstein & Warner, 1981). Some of the primary principles of Freudian psychoanalysis, which permeate even modern clinical thinking, include the concepts of ego-defense mechanisms, emotional developmental stages, transference and countertransference phenomenon, the impact of unconscious mental processes on behavior, and the importance of early life experiences and development (Corey, 2005; Capuzzi & Gross, 2007; Corsini & Wedding, 2007; Burger, 2004; Seligman, 2006; Sharf, 2003; Fadiman & Frager, 2002; Bernstein & Warner, 1981).

Psychoanalysis can be understood within the framework of a psychology of *conflict,* with the mind (and human psyche) constantly struggling with conflicting inner emotional conflicting forces (Corsini & Wedding, 2007; Greenberg & Mitchell, 1983; Bernstein & Warner, 1981). Burger (2004) outlined a brief narrative outline of major psychoanalytic principles developed by Sigmund Freud. A synopsis of that summarization is as follows:

+ According to Freudian psychoanalytic theory, human personality can be divided into *conscious, preconcious,* and *unconscious* components. The human psyche can also be understood within the related frameworks of the *id, ego,* and *superego*. Psychological activity is then manifested by a psychic energy within the form of *libido.* Psychoanalytic theory further posits that intrapsychic tension between the elements of human personality creates psychological tension and subsequent psychopathology. The ultimate and ongoing goal of all human behavior (and psychoanalytic psychotherapy) is a return to a tensionless state.

+ Freud concluded and believed that a healthy personality involves the primary capacity to utilize the ego to mediate and successfully control id impulses and superego demands. To accomplish those functions, the ego commonly will utilize a range of psychological *defense mechanisms,* such as *repression, denial, sublimation, displacement, reaction formation, projection,* and *intellectualization.*

+ The therapeutic goal of psychoanalytic psychotherapy, then, is to bring *unconscious sources and components of a client's problems into conscious awareness*. Typical strategies to accomplish those goals include a long term "talk therapy" utilizing *free association techniques, analysis of dreams* (which Freud felt were directly related to the unconscious mind), *various projective tests*, and even *hypnosis*.

Freudian psychoanalysis laid the foundation for concurrently developed alternate psychoanalytically related models of personality, as well as for more current neo-Freudian models of psychoanalytic theories and psychotherapies (Corey, 2005; Corsini & Wedding, 2007; Burger, 2004; Greenberg & Mitchell, 1983; McWilliams; 1994; Bernstein & Warner, 1981). Two of Freud's early students and colleagues, Alfred Adler and Carl Jung, digressed from some of Freud's initial theories, and eventually developed their own psychoanalytically oriented models of personality and therapy (Fadiman & Frager, 2002; Burger, 2004; Corey, 2005; Capuzzi & Gross, 2007; Corsini & Wedding, 2007; Seligman, 2006; Sharf, 2003).

Later developed models of personality and subsequent models of psychotherapy included the developmental psychology theories of Erik Erikson (Burger, 2004; Fadiman & Frager, 2002; Guntrip, 1973), and the various models of more contemporary *Ego Psychology* and *Object-Relations Theory* (Bernstein & Warner, 1981; Greenberg & Mitchell, 1983; McWilliams; 1994; Fadiman & Frager, 2002; Burger, 2004; Corey, 2005; St. Clair, 2000). Contemporary models of Ego Psychology posit a stronger focus on emphasizing the *striving of the ego for mastery and competence throughout the human life span*. Object-Relations theories work within a primary framework that involves *intrapsychically represented interpersonal and early life relationships*.

Linda and Psychoanalysis

If Linda chooses to address her difficulties by utilizing a range of psychoanalytically oriented models of counseling, she will typically undergo variations of insight oriented therapy interventions, with a focus on developing an increased awareness of unconscious processes, and subsequent psychological mechanisms, that are *underlying and driving her feelings and behaviors*.

Existential Psychotherapies

While the various psychoanalytic approaches to therapy can be framed within the context of common theoretical core concepts, the same is not as true for the understanding of the various psychotherapies grouped under the collective model of *existential therapies*. It is more appropriate to understand the existential therapies within the framework of a *philosophical approach* to therapy, which then strongly influences an individual counselor's therapeutic practice (Corey, 2005; Capuzzi & Gross, 2003). Existential psychotherapy, as such, does not have a unified collective approach regarding specific techniques and interventions, and is in fact not even considered an independent school of therapy. Techniques and interventions from other therapeutic models, integrated within an existentialistic framework, are quite acceptable and commonly utilized (Corey, 2005).

What then, are some of the similarities consistent with various counseling models that are associated with existential philosophies? The following are some of those commonalties, outlined by Corey (2005):

- Existential therapists, in general, *do recognize* and acknowledge many of the foundational tenets of other theories of personality, such as in the psychoanalytic and behavioral orientations. However, existential philosophies and therapies in general do not agree with the strong *deterministic* views of human nature that are framed by psychoanalytic and behavioral traditions.

- A basic premise of virtually all existentialistic models of counseling is that as individuals, *we are free and therefore responsible for our choices and actions.* We are, quite literally, the authors of our lives, and our choices determine who and what we ultimately choose to be. As such, a primary focus of most existential therapies is to explore with clients and then encourage them to recognize that they can *consciously and purposefully shape their lives*, and to concurrently explore and choose options in their lives.

Yalom (1980, 2003) emphasizes that the first step in the therapeutic journey is for an individual to *accept responsibility for his or her life* and previous (and future) life choices. Existentially oriented therapy, then, can also be understood as a process of *searching for value and meaning in life* (Sharp & Bugental, 2001; Frankl, 1963; Yalom, 1980; May, 1961). Another therapeutic goal, therefore, in an existentialist counseling framework is to encourage a client to explore options and choices for better creating an individualistic meaningful existence.

In existentially oriented models of therapy, the direct relationship between the counselor and the client is paramount to the success of the therapy. The therapeutic relation itself is intrinsically important to the counseling process to facilitate positive change in a client (Capuzzi & Gross, 2007; Corey, 2005).

While there are many prominent psychotherapists and clinical scholars who could be considered to have strong or at least partial existential leanings to their individual counseling models, four individuals have clearly embodied and promoted existentialistic views of therapy. They are *Viktor Frankl, Rollo May, James Bugental,* and *Irvin Yalom*. Counselors who aspire to include existential views and philosophies into their own therapy models would do well to read and study from those four individuals, who each developed their own therapeutic models from various existential philosophies and philosophers, as well as from drawing on models of humanistic psychology (Corey, 2005).

Linda and Existentialistic Psychotherapy

If Linda chooses to address her difficulties by utilizing a range of Existentialistic oriented models of counseling, she will typically undergo variations of insight oriented therapy interventions, with a focus on developing an increased awareness that she can consciously and purposefully direct and shape her life journey, help her to take more direct responsibility for her life to make more effective and positive choices, and to assist her in exploring and choosing life options to enable her to better create subjectively enhanced meaning, value, and purpose to her existence.

Person Centered Therapy

Compared to the wide range of *current* models of personality and therapies, the options of established therapies in the first half of the twentieth century may today seem quite limited, with a then primary focus on highly structured and deterministic psychoanalytic or behavioral philosophies and applied therapeutic models (Capuzzi & Gross, 2007). In direct reaction to the established therapy models that were seen by some as too directive, impersonal, and deterministic in nature, alternate theories and models of counseling began to develop, that integrated a more *humanistic* and existential approach to the understanding of human nature, and subsequent applied models of psychotherapy. One such model, pioneered initially in the 1940's by *Carl Rogers*, was *Client Centered Therapy*, later to be more widely known as *Person Centered Therapy* (Capuzzi & Gross, 2007; Corsini & Wedding, 2007; Corey, 2005; Rogers, 1951, 1942).

The *Person Centered* approach to therapy, which is also referred to as *Rogerian Therapy* (reflecting the primary influence of Carl Rogers) emphasizes the power of an individual to affect change in his or her life, and the importance of the attitude and personal characteristics of the therapist in the therapeutic relationship (Rogers, 1951, 1942). Rogers believed, and as such framed his therapeutic model, that people have a great potential to understand themselves to solve their individual problems and life challenges. As such, most individuals are very capable of *self-directed growth*, with a limited amount of (high directive) intervention from the therapist, *if the therapeutic relationship provides a certain type of client-therapist relationship* (Rogers, 1951, 1942; Corsini & Wedding, 2007; Corey, 2005). From the very beginning of his work and the early development of Client/Person Centered Therapy, Rogers posited that the attitudes of the therapist in the therapeutic framework, and the client's perceived personal characteristics of the therapist (e.g., empathetic, caring, genuine, etc.) *were critical* components to a positive outcome in the counseling/therapy process (Corsini & Wedding, 2007; Capuzzi & Gross, 2007; Corey, 2005; Rogers, 1951). Other concepts central to Person Centered Therapy models (Rogers, 1961, 1980; Corsini & Wedding, 2007) include the understanding that each individual perceives the world and life from a unique perspective that the therapist must try to understand (a *phenomenological* view of reality), and that individuals commonly want to obtain the maximum amount for themselves in all areas of their lives (a ongoing process of *self-actualization*).

In summary, the following are the major conditions that Carl Rogers (and virtually all Person Centered therapies) posited that are necessary for successful change to occur in the therapy process (Corsini & Wedding, 2007; Capuzzi & Gross, 2007; Corey, 2005; Rogers 1951,1961,1980):

- The Therapist-Client Relationship: A positive relationship between the client and the therapist, which facilitates two people in a genuine and meaningful psychological contact.

- Client Incongruence: When there is a discrepancy between an individual's perceptions of his/her world (one's *phenomenological* view) and one's true positive nature and/or actual world reality, a state of *incongruence* may result, and diminished psychological, emotional, and social functioning may result. Such a state of emotional/psychological disequilibrium often precedes the search for change through the processes of therapy and counseling.

- Therapist Congruence: The therapist is *congruent* in the therapeutic relationship, as he/she continuously strives to understand the client's unique phenomenological worldview.

- Therapist Unconditional Positive Regard (UPR): The therapist genuinely accepts the client unconditionally, without any degree of judgment, disapproval, or even approval.

- Therapist Empathetic Understanding: The therapist continuously strives to experience an understanding of the client's unique perceptions of his/her world based on a specific internal frame of reference, *and* the therapist consistently communicates that understanding back to the client.

- Client Perception: The client must perceive, at least to some degree, that the therapist does indeed have a notable degree of empathy for him/her, and that a condition of unconditional positive regard (UPR) does exist with the therapist within the context of the therapeutic relationship.

It has been understandably stated by many that Carl Rogers and his humanistic psychology movement revolutionized the profession of psychotherapy, by developing and promoting the concepts and related applied clinical theories that involved the *client* being the most important agent for self-change and personal growth in one's life (Bozarth, Zimring, & Tausch, 2002; Corsini & Wedding, 2007; Corey, 2005).

Linda and Person Centered Psychotherapy

If Linda chooses to address her difficulties by utilizing a range of Person Centered oriented models of counseling, she will typically undergo variations of insight oriented therapy interventions, with a focus on developing her own personal capacity to affect change in her life and enable self-directed growth, within the context of a trusting, empathetic, non-judgmental, and limited therapist directed model of counseling.

Behavior Therapy

While psychotherapy in the early part of the twentieth century was dominated by psychoanalytic theories of personality, the dominant paradigm from approximately the 1950's to the late 1960's was *behavioral psychology* (Olson & Hergenhahn, 2008; Hergenhahn & Sordi, 2004; Hergenhahn & Olson, 2006; Corey, 2005; Fadiman & Frager, 2002; Burger, 2004; Gardner, 1987). While behavioral psychology had its precursors and related theorists earlier in the twentieth century, such as John B. Watson and Ivan Pavlov, the most prominent theorist in behavioral psychology was B.F. Skinner (Olson & Hergenhahn, 2008; Burger, 2004; Hergenhahn & Sordi, 2004).

A broad comparison of behavioral psychology and humanistic/person centered models of therapy may lead many to the conclusion that both theoretical philosophies and models were polar opposites of each other. The following fundamental theories and premises of behavioral psychology and related behavioral therapy, as reflected by numerous writers and Skinner himself (Olson & Hergenhahn, 2008; Corsini & Wedding, 2007; Miltenberger, 2005; Spiegler and Guevremont, 2003; Kazdin, 2001; Corey, 2005; Mazur, 2005; Sprinthall et.al., 1997; Masters et.al., 1987; Skinner, 1953, 1971, 1974), are as follows:

- Behavioral psychology and therapy posits that individuals become "what they are" through complex and cumulative processes of *learning*, that occurs through environmental interactions. Innate genetic factors in individuals are acknowledged in behavioral psychology/therapy, but are not emphasized as primary factors in psychological and personality development. Behaviorism, in philosophy and practice, defines an individual's "personality" as the end result of that person's individual and cumulative history of conditioning.
- Behaviorism, in its most traditional form, identifies two basic types of conditioning that facilitate learning: *classical conditioning* and *operant conditioning*. Classical conditioning, based on the early work of Ivan Pavlov, is defined as the process of pairing a new stimulus with an existing stimulus-response bond. Operant conditioning, by definition, results when a behavior is followed by either reinforcement or punishment. While the basic definitions of both classical conditioning and operant conditioning may

initially appear rather fundamental and simple, the actual process and applications of those behavioral principles in reality can be complex. For example, "reinforcements" in an operant conditioning model may encompass diverse and complicated variations of reinforcement schedules, patterns, and options.

Behavior therapy is based on the principles and procedures of the scientific method of study and research. As such, *empirical data* is the focus and hallmark of behavioral psychological and all behavior therapy practice. In fact, behaviorism only recognizes *observable and measurable* data. Consistent with that notion is the behavioral premise that "internal cognitive processes" (e.g., information processing "between" stimulus-response connections) are not only irrelevant, but for all intents and purposes do not even exist. While the most radical behavioral philosophies may be arguably constrictive in regard to the actual complexity of human behaviors and personality functions, the focus on empirical data in behaviorism over decades has resulted in an enormous corpus of solid validating research.

In contrast to other more insight oriented psychotherapies (especially psychoanalytically oriented therapy models), behavior therapy *primarily deals with changing behaviors in the present.* While understanding how past behaviors and learning have been acquired, such an understanding and analysis is not really important to facilitate new learning and subsequent behavior change. The focus of therapy is on current environmental and subsequent learning factors that maintain problem behaviors, and the introduction of new learning procedures to affect behavioral change.

While behaviorism may be construed as a highly deterministic theory of personality, and behaviorally oriented therapies have by nature a high degree of therapist direction and control, *behavioral therapy **clients** are expected to assume an active role in the therapeutic process,* within the context of a strong "partnership" between therapist and client. As such, behavioral therapy is considered to be highly action-oriented. That is, the client does not just "talk of and about their problems", but is expected to participate in and follow through with procedures (in and out of the actual therapy time) to affect behavioral change. Consistent with core behavioral principles, *learning* (e.g., new learning, re-learning, etc.) is the very foundation of behavioral therapy processes. Learning results from the collaborative development of individualized goal directed behavioral programming that involves ongoing client participation, monitoring, evaluation, adjustment, and ongoing self-management.

Based on decades of extensive clinical research and sound empirical evidence, behaviorally oriented therapies have demonstrably been proven as very effective interventions for a diverse range of psychological, psychiatric, behavioral, and medical populations, and in many types of clinical and educational settings (Olson & Hergenhahn, 2008; Corsini & Wedding, 2007; Miltenberger, 2005, 2004; Spiegler and Guevremont, 2003; Kazdin, 2001; Corey, 2005; Mazur, 2005; Sprinthall et al., 1997; Masters et.al., 1987). Some of the more common behavioral procedures utilized in behavioral therapy, as well as in more eclectic therapies that utilize behavioral principles when warranted, include counterconditioning procedures to address phobic responses, systematic desensitization exercises to counter anxiety, and various progressive relaxation techniques (Mazur, 2005; Sprinthall et.al., 1997; Masters et al., 1987; Wolpe, 1990).

Linda and Behavioral Therapy

If Linda chooses to address her difficulties by utilizing a range of behaviorally oriented models of therapy, she will typically participate in systematic therapy sessions that will enable her to develop appropriate individualized behavioral programs to diminish identified problematic emotional responses and behavioral patterns, and to establish new and more positive behaviors and emotional states.

Cognitive-Behavioral Therapy

The role of behaviorism as the dominant psychological and therapeutic paradigm in the middle of the twentieth century laid the foundation of the newer and most recent paradigm of psychological theory and related applied psychotherapy, *Cognitive-Behavioral Therapy*, also known by the abbreviated term of *CBT* (Capuzzi & Gross, 2007; Corey, 2005; Sprinthall et.al., 1997; Gardner, 1987). Cognitive-behavioral therapy can be understood as a general category of theories and related clinical theories and models that involve *both* behavioral psychology and cognitive psychology. The combination of the two clinical models and subsequent intervention strategies results in a combination of behaviorally based strategies and cognitive interventions. The primary goal of cognitive-behavioral therapy, then, is the achievement of both *behavior* and *cognitive* change (Dobson, 2001; Capuzzi & Gross, 2007). CBT interventions are directive, well structured, goal directed, and time limited.

A central tenant to all cognitive-behavioral therapies is the relationship between cognitions (thoughts, beliefs, etc.), and emotions and emotional states (Capuzzi & Gross, 2007; Corey, 2005; Sprinthall et.al., 1997). Irrational thoughts (conscious, unconscious, or automatic) can elicit specific negative emotional responses. For example, a thought such as "I am never successful at anything" may have a direct emotional response and experience that is subjectively depressive in nature. If an individual continues to consciously or unconsciously "repeat" that thought, *even if it is for the most part inaccurate*, a repeated negative emotional experience will continue and can perpetuate.

Cognitions (thought, beliefs, etc.), then, can be (according to CBT proponents) *direct mediators of emotional and behavioral change* (Dobson & Dozois, 2001;

Craighead et al., 1995). As such, virtually all CBT interventions involve the goal of behavioral and emotional change *by influencing thinking*, and related cognitive structures such as self-perpetuating irrational beliefs, attitudes, and conclusions (Dobson & Dozois, 2001).

To date, there have been more than twenty different therapies that have been recognized under the headings of "cognitive therapy" or "cognitive-behavioral therapy" (Corey, 2005; Dattilio & Freeman, 1992; Dattilio & Padesky, 1990; Mahoney & Lyddon, 1988). To provide concrete examples, this section will present an overview of several of the most prominent proponents and theorists of cognitive-behavioral therapies, specifically involving the CBT models of *Albert Ellis* and *Aaron T. Beck*.

Various CBT models approach changes in cognition/thinking in different ways. In Albert Ellis' *Rational Emotive Behavior Therapy* (REBT), a technique identified as the "ABC's of Irrational Beliefs" is utilized to help enable an individual to (A) identify a situation that could elicit a high emotional response and possible negative thinking, (B) identify and record subsequent negative and/or negatively irrational thoughts, and (C) identify the connections between the identified negative thoughts and dysphoric emotional states. A subsequent therapeutic process of cognitive *reframing* would then be utilized to facilitate more positive cognitive restructurings (Corsini & Wedding, 2004; Ellis, 2001).

Aaron Beck's model of cognitive therapy posits a number of actually categorized types of illogical thinking examples, or *cognitive distortions* (Beck, 1963, 1976, 1987, Corey, 2005;) that are commonly encountered in the process of CBT. They are as follows:

+ Arbitrary inferences: making conclusions without supporting and relevant evidence.
+ Selective abstraction: forming conclusions based on one or several isolated details of an event.
+ Overgeneralization: holding extreme beliefs on only the basis of a single incident or personal experience, and then inappropriately generalizing those conclusions.
+ Magnification and minimization: perceiving a situation in a greater or lesser context of understanding than is actually appropriate.
+ Personalization: when an individual relates external events to himself/herself, when there is no actual basis for making such a connection.
+ Labeling and mislabeling: inappropriately and inaccurately defining oneself or another based on past mistakes or imperfections that may not apply in the present.
+ Polarized thinking: a tendency to understand and/or interpret events, people, etc. in a very extreme, "all or nothing" manner.

Linda and Cognitive-Behavioral Therapy

If Linda chooses to address her difficulties by utilizing a range of cognitive-behavioral oriented models of therapy, she will typically participate in systematic therapy sessions that will enable her to identify patterns of negative thinking, help her to understand the relationships between irrational thought patterns and dysphoric emotions and emotional states, and enable her to restructure negative cognitive patterns and beliefs into more positive and reality based accurate thought and perceptions.

Summary

Linda will ultimately achieve success regarding her therapeutic goals. Like many individuals in her situation, she will participate in a counseling process with a therapist who integrates a range of clinical philosophies and multi-faceted therapeutic interventions. That *eclectic* approach to therapy over time afforded Linda the opportunity to utilize insight oriented therapy to understand early life influences and related unconscious processes that unconsciously motivated her behaviors, as well as helped her to understand and change acquired patterns of inaccurate, dysfunctional thinking patterns that affected her emotionally. Linda learned to accept more responsibility for her own life, and over time she developed an awareness of a deeper meaning to her life and life experiences. She was able to achieve those goals in a therapeutic relationship that was genuine, caring, empathetic, and non-judgmental.

References

Beck, A.T. (1963). Thinking and Depression: Idiosyncratic content and cognitive distortions. *Archives of general psychiatry*, 9, (324-333).

Beck, A.T. (1976). *Cognitive therapy and emotional disorders.* New York: Universities International Press.

Beck, A.T. (1987). Cognitive Therapy. In J.K Zeig (Ed.), *The evolution of psychotherapy*(pp.149-178). New York: Brunner/Mazel.

Bernstein, A., & Warner, G. (1981). *An introduction to contemporary psychoanalysis.* New York: Jason Aranson

Bozarth, J.D., Zimring, F.M., & Tausch, R. (2002). Client-centered therapy: The evolution of a revolution. In D.J. Cain & J. Seeman, (Eds.), *Humanistic Psychotherapies: Handbook of research and practice* (pp. 147-188). Washington, DC: American Psychological Association.

Burger, J. M. (2004). *Personality* (6th ed.). Belmont, CA: Wadsworth.

Capuzzi, D., & Gross, D. (Eds.). (2007). *Counseling and psychotherapy: Theories and interventions* (4th ed.). Upper Saddle River, NJ: Prentice Hall.

Corey, G. (2005). *Theory and practice of counseling and psychotherapy* (7th ed.). Belmont, CA: Wadsworth.

Corsini, R. J., & Wedding, D. (2004). *Current psychotherapies* (7th ed.). Belmont, CA: Wadsworth.

Craighead, W.E., Craighead, L.W., & Ilardi, S.S. (1995). Behavior therapies in historical perspective. In B. Bongar & L.E. Beutler (Eds.), *Comprehensive textbook of psychotherapy: Theory and Practice* pp. 64-83). New York: Oxford University Press.

Dattilio, F.M., & Freeman, A. (1992). Introduction to cognitive therapy. In A. Freeman & E.M. Dattilio (Eds.), *Comprehensive casebook of cognitive therapy* (pp.3-11). New York: Plenum.

Dattilio, F.M., & Padesky, C.A. (1990). *Cognitive therapy with couples.* Sarasota, FL: Professional Resources Exchange.

Dobson, K.S. (2001). *Handbook of cognitive-behavioral therapies* (2nd ed.). New York: Guilford Press.

Dobson, K.S, & Duzois, D.J.A. (2001). Historical and philosophical bases of the cognitive-behavioral therapies. In K.S. Dobson (Ed.), *Handbook of cognitive-behavioral therapies* (2nd ed., pp.3-39). New York: Guilford Press.

Ellis, A.E. (2001). *Overcoming destructive beliefs, feelings, and behaviors.* Amherst, New York: Prometheus Books.

Fadiman, J., & Frager, R. (2002). *Personality and personal growth* (5th ed.). Upper Saddle River, NJ: Prentice Hall.

Frankl, V. (1963). *Man's Search for Meaning.* Boston: Beacon.

Gardner, H. (1987). *The Mind's New Science: A history of the cognitive revolution.* New York: Basic Books.

Greenberg, J., & Mitchell, S. (1983). *Object Relations in Psychoanalytic Theory.*

Cambridge, MA: Harvard University Press.

Guntrip, H. (1973). *Psychoanalytic Theory, Therapy, and the Self.* New York: Basic Books, Inc.

Herhenhahn, B.R., & Olson, M. (2006). *An introduction to theories of personality.* New Jersey: Prentice Hall.

Herhenhahn, B.R., & Sordi, M. (2004). *An introduction to the history of psychology.* New York: Wadsworth.

Kazdin, A.E. (2001). *Behavior modification in applied settings (6ᵗʰ ed.).* Pacific Grove, CA: Brooks/Cole.

Mahoney, M.J., & Lyddon, W. (1988). Recent development in cognitive approaches to counseling and psychotherapy. *Counseling Psychology.* 16, 190-234.

Masters, J., Burish, T., Hollon, S., & Rimm, D. (1987). *Behavior Therapy.* San Diego: Harcourt Brace Jovanovich.

May, R. (Ed.). (1961). *Existential psychology.* New York: Random House.

Mazur, J. (2005). *Learning and behavior (6ᵗʰ ed.). New Jersey: Prentice Hall.*

McWilliams, N. (1994). *Psychoanalytic Diagnosis.* New York: Guilford Press.

Miltenberger, R.G. (2004). *Behavior modification: Principles and procedures (3ʳᵈ ed.).*Pacific Grove, CA: Brooks/Cole.

Olson, M. & Hergenhahn, B.R. (2008). *Introduction to the theories of learning.* New Jersey: Prentice Hall.

Rogers, C. (1942). *Counseling and psychotherapy.* Boston: Houghton Mifflin.

Rogers, C. (1951). *Client-centered therapy.* Boston: Houghton Mifflin

Sharf, R. S. (2003). *Theories of psychotherapy and counseling: Concepts and cases* (3ʳᵈ ed.). Belmont, CA: Wadsworth.

Sharp, J. G., & Bugental, J.F.T. (2001). Existential-humanistic psychotherapy. In R.J. Corsini (Ed.). *Handbook of innovative therapies* (2ⁿᵈ ed., pp. 206-217). New York: Wiley.

Skinner, B.F. (1953). *Science and human behavior.* New York: Macmillan.

Skinner, B.F. (1971). *Beyond freedom and dignity.* New York: Knopf.

Skinner, B.F. (1974). *About behaviorism.* New York: Knopf.

Spiegler, M.D., & Guevremont, D.C. (2003). *Contemporary behavior therapy(4ᵗʰ ed.).* Pacific Grove, CA: Brooks/Cole.

Sprinthall, R., Sprinthall, N., & Oja, S. (1997). *Educational psychology: A developmental approach (7ᵗʰ ed.).* New York: Mc Graw-Hill.

St. Clair, M. (2000). *Object Relations and Self Psychology: An introduction* (3ʳᵈ ed.). United States: Brooks/Cole.

Walsh, R.A., & McElwain, B. (2002). Existential Psychotherapies. In D.J. Cain & J. Seeman (Eds.) *Humanistic psychotherapies: Handbook of research and practice* (pp. 253-278). Washington, DC: American Psychological Association.

Wolpe, J. (1990). *The practice of behavior therapy (4ᵗʰ ed.).* Elmsford, NY: Pergamon Press.

Yalom, I.D. (1980). *Existential psychotherapy.* New York: Basic Books.

Yalom, I.D. (2003). *The Gift of therapy: An open letter to a new generation of therapists and their patients.* New York: Harper Collins.

Section Four:

Developmental Issues in Counseling

When the Child Is the Client

By: Sharon Hoferer, MA

Working with children in psychotherapy can hold unique challenges. While the child is the client and must be the primary focus in therapy, the family and extended community are integral components in understanding the child's situation and problems. It behooves the beginning therapist to understand the role of the family and community in the child's life and to make them allies in the treatment process. Additionally, because children each have different developmental levels, therapy cannot be a one-size-fits-all treatment. This chapter looks at some of the challenges therapists may face when working with children and provides suggestions on how to achieve a successful outcome in the therapy process.

Conducting an Initial Intake Interview

Since children rarely are voluntary clients, they seldom have a sense of what therapy is about or even that they need therapy. Usually, an adult sees that a problem exists and recommends treatment. Sometimes a parent or guardian is having trouble with the child and decides to seek help. When conducting a first interview, knowing who the referring source is will be an important first step in understanding what the problem may be. It is also equally important to find the answer to the question "Why now?" What has been happening recently in the child's life that is causing concern?

Before beginning an initial intake interview, be sure the room is arranged appropriately. Try to make the space as quiet and as free of distractions as possible. There should be enough chairs available for the child and all the members of the family. Because children have not yet developed sufficient capacity for describing their lives through their words, they need an alternate outlet for expression of feelings and thoughts. Play is the language that children most often use to communicate. Although it is not essential, you may find it helpful to have a few toys available as well as crayons or markers and some paper.

While it is important to meet with the child's caregivers and get background information on the situation that brings them to therapy, you will also get useful information from your observation and interaction with the child. Remember that your relationship with the child and family begins the moment you start to interact with them and this often occurs in the waiting room.

Observe as much as possible how the child behaves when you walk out to greet the family. Where is the child sitting? Are the parents interacting with their child or is the child alone in a separate corner of the room? Is the child sitting in a chair or are books and magazines being tossed about in the waiting room?

How do the parents and child respond to the invitation to come with you? You also need to decide if you will meet with the child or the parents first, or if you want the entire family to come in together. If you ask the child to meet with you prior to the parents, how does the child respond? Does he separate easily from his parents? Observe how the child moves as you walk to your office. How is she dressed? Is her attire appropriate for the weather? Is she well groomed or are her clothes soiled? How do her communication skills seem? Observe if the child speaks and acts appropriately for his age.

When doing an initial assessment with a child it is important to get an in-depth developmental history that should include information about the mother's pregnancy, the child's birth, the developmental milestones in the child's life and a sense of the temperament of the child as an infant.

Next, you should enquire about the child's educational history. Does the child have an IEP (individualized education plan) or learning disability? Has the child ever repeated a grade? Does the child have any behavioral problems in school? What type of classroom is he in?

It is important to get a comprehensive family history that should include information about any psychiatric illness or treatment, medical illness, and substance abuse problems for the parents and siblings. It is also important to get a comprehensive health assessment of the child to determine if any of the current problems may have a biological basis to them.

Find out with whom the child lives. Has anyone in the family experienced a problem with physical or sexual abuse? Have there been any recent deaths, incarcerations, or CPS (Child Protective Services) involvement? Find out if the family is experiencing any particular stresses such as unemployment, homelessness, a recent divorce, or separation. What is the relationship like between the child and parents or other caretakers? What is the relationship like between the siblings?

Another important aspect of the intake process is reviewing the child's social history. How does the child get along with peers? Do the parents approve of the child's friends? Does the child have any friends? Does the child see them outside of school? What activities is the child involved in? How does the parent discipline the child? What are the child's eating and sleeping habits?

Besides getting the background history on the child and family, find out from both the child and the family members what they see as being the presenting problem. That is, what is bringing this family into treatment at this time in the child's life? The amount of information needed during an initial interview can seem overwhelming to both the family as well as the therapist. Allow for sufficient time to go over information on confidentiality and informed consent as well as for questions and concerns that the child and family might have.

Finally, before the end of the session, determine the frequency and timing of future sessions, explaining the importance of consistency in keeping appointments (along with your policy for missed and late sessions) and set an appointment for a follow-up session. Leave yourself time to make notes of your observations following the initial interview and fill out any necessary paperwork as soon as possible after the session, while the information is still fresh in your mind.

Informed Consent

The relationship between client and therapist is a professional one, whereby the therapist agrees to provide a service (therapy) in exchange for a fee. Therefore, it is important for both parties to understand the nature and extent of this relationship. Part of the therapist's job is to explain the therapeutic process and relationship during the initial interview. It is important that the child and the family understand their rights and responsibilities as these apply to the child's therapy.

The parents or legal guardians normally make the decision of consenting for treatment of younger children. Informed consent is a right of the client and family of a child or adolescent. Discussing rights and responsibilities in the therapeutic setting provides an opportunity for building trust in the practitioners and helping create a therapeutic alliance (Gustafson, McNamara, & Jensen, 1994).

The question arises when working with children and adolescents as to how competent a minor individual is in giving consent to treatment. Most legal guidelines are based on children's developmental needs and rights and apply the best-interest-of-the-child standard in cases of competing rights between parents and children (Halasz, 1997). There is no magic age when a person is either able to give consent or is incompetent to consent to treatment. In fact, giving consent is not an all-or-nothing ability. Even very young children can agree to some portion of the work with a therapist if the therapist explains the situation properly to them.

Some therapists like to send forms out following a telephone inquiry with a request for the client and family to bring them to the initial interview. Other practitioners prefer to have the client and/or family fill out the forms together with the therapist present. Either way, it is helpful to have the entire family present as you explain the issues of confidentiality and informed consent.

Your explanation of the client's rights and responsibilities should include an explanation of the type of psychological services you are able and willing to offer the family. Do you primarily work with the child or do you also offer services to the parents and family? Is group therapy available to the child? A parent support group? You should give a brief explanation of the type of therapy you plan to offer the family. Do you use play therapy with younger children? Is your focus cognitive behavioral? If a court system is involved with the family, be sure to help the parents understand what you are willing to offer them. Will you prepare an evaluation for the court? Will you attend court proceedings? Are they looking for an expert witness? Do you qualify for that?

You will want to discuss the frequency and length of sessions with the family along with deciding on the fees. Explain your policy regarding phone conversations and emergency contact. Will you charge for phone sessions? If the family expects you to prepare documents for court or attorneys, what are your fees? If you consult with other professionals such as law guardians, CPS workers, school officials, or teachers, what is your fee for such services? Will you bill for your services or do you expect payment at the time of the session? How will you handle late or non-payment for services rendered? What happens if a client needs to miss a session? How much advance notice do you require? Will you still charge for the session that the client misses?

Do you accept insurance? Which ones? If you do accept insurance, let the family know that insurance does not normally cover missed appointments and that the family will be responsible for those charges if that is your policy. Encourage the family to explore what the insurance company will cover regarding therapy and for how many sessions they will pay. Depending upon the number of sessions, you may want to discuss what the family's options are if insurance coverage is limited.

What hours are you available for phone contact? What should the family do if they are experiencing a psychological emergency with their child? If you need to contact them, what number should you use? Do they want you to leave a message on an answering machine if you cannot reach them directly?

What type of records do you keep? Who has access to them? What rights does the family have regarding access to the records? In the case of a minor child, it is important to review with the parents the information about their child's treatment that they have access to and what information is not available to them. For example, while you may give them an overview of what goals you are working on with the child, you will not normally share specifics of your discussions with their child, unless requested to by the child. Let the child know that when you do speak with the parents, you will mention this beforehand, and that you will share with the child what you intend to discuss with the parents.

Finally, it is important to discuss with the parents the risks of therapy, such as the limits of confidentiality (which will be discussed more fully in the next section), the fact that therapy may not work and that the problem may get worse. It is equally important to share the benefits as well, such as the possibility that the parent-child relationship may improve, that parenting skills may improve, and that therapy may indeed help with some of the problems the family is experiencing.

Just as it is important for the parents to understand their rights and responsibilities as well as how therapy will work for their child, it is equally important that the child understand, as much as possible, how the process works. It is helpful to start by asking if he knows why his parents have brought him to your office. It is important for you to understand what the child is thinking about why he is there. Next, ask the child how *he* feels about being there. He has probably heard his parents speaking about why they feel he must be there, but what are *his* feelings about starting therapy? When you greet the family in the waiting room, remember to address the child as well and introduce yourself to her. This lets her know that you recognize her as a person in her own right—not just as a child of her parents. If the child has never seen a therapist before, you may want to explain a little bit about how you do your work with children. Speak to the child in age-appropriate language, but do not speak down to her. Children are very attuned to how adults interact with them. Be respectful of the child during the interview process and be aware of how the parents speak of the child in your presence. While you want to maintain a therapeutic relationship with the parents, the child is your client and your primary relationship is with her.

A sample psychotherapist-patient contract that can be adapted for your practice or agency is available at http://www.apait.org/apait/applications/INF.doc.pdf.

Limits of Confidentiality

One of the reasons that a therapeutic relationship works is because the information that individuals share during the therapy session is private. Confidentiality by the therapist is required. It is both an ethical as well as a legal violation when you share privileged information without permission. However, there are certain instances when therapists not only are allowed to breach confidentiality, but are required by law to do so.

It is important to explain to both the child and the family the extent—and limits—of confidentiality. It is equally important to inquire whether the child understands what you are telling him.

Explain that under normal circumstances, what the child tells you during therapy is confidential, that is private. You, as the therapist, will not share details about what the child tells you with anyone else, not even the parents, without the child's permission. However, in most cases, there are some exceptions to that rule. Explain to the child (and to the parents) that if you believe the child is threatening serious harm to another person, or is acting in a way that is likely to harm the child that you must let the parents and sometimes other people know about the situation. If there is an emergency where the child's life or health is in danger, you may give another professional the necessary information to protect the child's life. If you believe or suspect that someone is abusing the child, or the child is hurting an elderly, or disabled person you are required to file a report with a protective agency.

When working with children, the limits of confidentiality may vary from state to state. Morris (1993, p. 11) suggests seeking local answers to the following questions:

1. Is a child in psychotherapy accorded legally-protected privileged communication in your state?
2. If yes, what are the exceptions to privileged communications for a child in your state?
3. Is there a common usage lower age limit for children legally granting them privileged communication?
4. Is there legal precedent in your state that has tested the constitutionality of the privileged communication granted to children and adolescents?

The answers to these questions should guide you in your policy regarding confidentiality with the children in your practice.

Another instance where the rules of confidentiality may not hold is if a judge or court requires you to testify when a child custody or adoption proceeding is involved. You, as the therapist, may be called upon to render your opinion as to the fitness of a parent.

If the family has been required to enter therapy as a condition for the return of a child because of child protective services (CPS) removing the child from the home, you will be asked by CPS to file a report from time to time. You will be asked to comment on how the therapy is progressing and if the parents are in compliance with the mandate. This will also be the case if a child is in therapy due to a criminal act and is involved in probation. The court system will want to know how the child is doing in treatment. Explain these exceptions to the client and family if it applies to them. If you are working with a foster child, help the foster parents understand that social services can request information from you regarding the child's therapy. Be aware that, in most instances, the social worker assigned to the case, and not the foster parent, must sign any required signatures such as for release of information or consent to treat.

Another exception to confidentiality comes into play when a family uses either a health insurance company or Medicaid to pay for therapy. Insurance companies have a right to access certain information about the client and the therapy. Go over the HIPAA (Health Insurance Portability & Accountability) form if you are insurance reimbursable and help the parents understand what information will be available to their insurance company.

If you work in an agency or are still under supervision, let the family and child know that you will be discussing certain aspects of the therapy with your supervisor and colleagues in order to provide the family with the best service available to them.

Ordinarily, clients must give written consent before a third party can receive psychotherapy notes (Reamer, 2005). Review with the parents during the first few sessions, what information might be necessary to get and/or receive from other providers to the child. These can include, but are not limited to, teachers, guidance counselors, childcare providers, medical doctors, probation officers, CPS workers, psychiatrists, social workers, lawyers, court appointed advocates and other family members. Get signed releases for any agency or person with whom the parent wishes you to converse before you share any information about your client.

A new concern regarding confidentiality that has come to the foreground in recent years is the issue of e-mail. It is possible for other than the intended party to read information that you share via the Internet. Additionally, any e-mail you receive from a client becomes part of the client's record and is open to scrutiny should the client's records be subpoenaed. If you choose to share an e-mail address with your client, it is important that s/he understand the limits of confidentiality regarding his or her e-mails.

Networking

The idea of collaborating with a child's extended community is based on a systems theory of therapy (Salmon & Faris, 2006). Systems theory is an awareness that the client functions in a larger community that has its own set of social networks and professional systems. This is particularly true for children who are dependent on the systems of which they are a part. Most children who enter the mental health network arrive there because they are not functioning well in a number of settings. Generally, several adults have expressed concern due to either behavioral or emotional expressions of distress by the child.

The child may be experiencing difficulties in school, home, day-care, or after-school activities. A coach, scout leader, or spiritual leader may have raised concerns about the child. The family may be involved in a custody dispute, or may simply be a split family with several stepparents involved. All of these people will have their own relationship with the child and will be able to bring a different perspective of their experience of the situation.

During the initial interview, discuss with the parents what people in the child's life spend time with him and with whom the parents may wish you to speak. If the child is having difficulty in school, you may want to network with the teacher, principal, or guidance counselor to explore their concerns regarding the child. If the child has had any medical problems you may want to request a report from the medical doctor. Additionally, if a doctor has not seen the child for a physical within the last year, suggest to the parents that they schedule an appointment to rule out a biological basis to whatever is going on with the child.

If the child has been having difficulties with siblings, you may want to consider having some sessions of family therapy that involve the entire family. Ask the parents who the primary caretaker for the child is. If both parents are working, a grandparent or other relative may spend the most time with the client. The information they have to share may provide important insights into the family dynamics and about what has brought the child into therapy at this time.

Some parents may not be very comfortable with the idea that you want to discuss their child with people outside of the family system. It is important that you be understanding of their concern while at the same time, explaining that you would encourage them to consider your request as it would be beneficial to their child and help the therapy move forward. If you propose that your goal is to have all the professionals sharing a common purpose (Briggs, 1999), that of helping the family help the child to achieve a successful therapeutic intervention, the majority of the parents will be supportive of your request for information.

As stated previously, it is important to get signed releases from the parent or legal guardian for each person or agency from whom you wish to request or release information. The parents have a right to know what information you will be sharing and what information some agencies may request of you, particularly when a court or social service provider has mandated therapy.

In sharing information with other providers, continue to be mindful of the issues of confidentiality and only share the information that will be helpful to your client. It is important that you share with your client, dependent on his or her developmental stage, the information that you are giving to others. Doing so helps maintain a sense of trust between you and the client. It is also helpful to remember that in all exchanges, you are advocating for your client and his best interest.

Some agencies have coordinated service providers on site who manage the exchange of information between professionals. This allows for ease of services, prevents duplication of services, and offers an opportunity for the family and service providers to come together to discuss what services are available to the family. If your agency does not provide this service, or if you are in private practice, you may want to consider investigating what services are available in your community so when the need arises, you can make the proper referral. Helping the family reach out to other service providers in the area will give them additional support as they work with you to help their child.

The Therapist's Position of Power

By its very nature, the role of therapist contains a position of power. Our ethical guidelines tell us that we must never exploit our clients; they are vulnerable and it is part of our job to protect them (Zur, 2008). We have the power in controlling the time, the frequency, the place, the length of the session and the cost. We establish the pace of the therapy and the type of therapy that we offer the client. We structure the sessions. We ask the client very personal questions at times, while never sharing intimate details about ourselves. Simply put, one person is in charge, the other is not (Rose, n.d.).

Frequently, therapists are seen as experts, and in some ways, there is truth to that belief. Because of our training, we have become experts in the techniques of helping people to engage with themselves, disclose themselves, and change themselves (Rose, n.d.). We use our power best when we work with people to enact their freedom and therapists have the ability to do just that.

Because families frequently seek therapy at a time when they are in crisis and vulnerable, we need to be especially mindful of our position of power when working with children. Myriad adults tell children daily what to do, where to go, and how to behave. In our relationship with the child, it is important to empower the child with the ability to be the instrument of change. We can do this by asking permission before we share information with the parents. We do this when we tell children that they have a right not to answer a question if they do not want to. When we help them talk about all of their feelings without judging them, we are acknowledging their right to feel. They learn that they can be angry, be hurt and that they can let another person know what is inside of them. Our therapy room may be the only place where it is safe to do this.

When parents bring their child to therapy, they frequently feel "at the end of their rope." Most parents try to cope with whatever situation is happening for as long as they can. Therefore, when they appear in your office, they are looking for someone to tell them how to help their child. It is important to remind the parents that you are there to help them in their relationship with their child, but that *they* are the expert of their child. They know their child better than you do. Most parents who bring their child to therapy, care about their child. They simply may not know how to help him. It is important to work with the parents and engage them in the process of their child's therapy. This may include parent education and family sessions. Sometimes it is helpful for you, as therapist, to model the way to interact with the child so the parents can learn better skills.

It is equally important not to take sides during a therapy session between a parent and the child. If you take sides either through your thoughts, words or actions, you may make one family member calmer, but you are also likely to make the other family member more upset. If you can remain objective and listen and be understanding, you can help each member of the family hear the other. Doing so will allow the family members to resolve their own problems with you supporting them in the process.

By educating our clients and families, listening carefully to them and understanding their needs and concerns, and by following a collaborative style of decision making, we can equalize the power in psychotherapy.

Understanding Culturally Different Families
Different cultures have different expectations of the roles of children.

Understanding some of these nuances are helpful when working with families whose culture differs from the therapist. Because demographics in the United States are changing rapidly, there is an increased number of children from culturally different backgrounds who are coming into the mental health system (Harry, n.d.). Many of these families have beliefs and practices that differ from those of mainstream American families. Unless the therapist has at least a basic understanding of some of these differences, the clinician may experience difficulties in working with these families.

The view of the professional as "expert" is common among many Hispanic, Southeast Asian, and Native American groups, as well as most low income American groups of any cultural background (Harry, n.d.). Parents who come from societies that have rigid hierarchical structures tend to show deference to experts in any field. Many of these families expect their children to do the same.

While traditional modern American families may struggle with the concept of a psychiatric disability, traditional beliefs among some cultural groups regarding this issue can become a source of disagreement between the families and the professional. Helping educate the family on the ability to treat their child can enable them to accept the services that are needed.

Therapists need to recognize that there are different concepts of family structure that exist within the various cultures as well as the families' understanding of the line of responsibility. Are you dealing with a culture that follows a patrilineal or matrilineal line? Is this a family where the elders are to be respected or are children given free reign of expression? When we use the word "family" we may assume this to mean biological family, but in some working class cultures for example the word "family" includes godparents, extended family, and even friends. In Native American families, the family frequently extends to tribal members as well as namesakes. These variations in family systems can influence the understanding of the meaning of the individual. Indeed, some cultures place more value on the rights of the group than on the rights of the individual.

Parenting styles vary among the different cultures as well, and therapists need to be informed as to the traditions of the cultures that they serve. Judgments they make and suggestions that they give will be more readily accepted if they are grounded in the acceptable practices of the group with whom they are working.

One way to acknowledge these cultural differences is to discuss them directly. If you are working with a child and family who are culturally different from you, you may want to let them know it may be hard for you to know what their life is like since you come from a different background than they do. Another way to be culturally aware is to have materials in your office that reflect the various cultures with whom you work. Dolls, books, and sandtray items should not reflect only families of European descent.

Be mindful that some clients come from a background of oppressive relationships that can affect the ability to establish trusting relationships with the therapist (Brown, 1997). Cultural values can also affect the importance that parents place on problems. Knowing that Asian American and Native American families are very concerned when their children break from tradition, that Japanese families prefer interventions that allow for more familial harmony, and that British families look favorably on treatment that focuses the child on autonomy and the establishment of clear personal boundaries will enable the therapist to create treatment plans that will work. Be aware of those cultures that emphasize self-control as consultation strategies that require high levels of self-disclosure will feel too threatening to those parents.

When working with families of different cultures, miscommunication and misunderstanding can be a barrier to effective treatment of the children. Therapists who are aware of these differences and are willing to work with the families and make necessary modifications in their treatment strategies to accommodate the differences will be able to achieve a more successful outcome in the therapy.

For those therapists who are interested in reading a more in-depth discussion of the differences in cultures and the effects that those differences can have on the therapy, the book *Ethnicity and Family Therapy* by McGoldrick, Giordano, and Garcia-Preto (2005) is highly recommended.

Child Abuse, Neglect and Trauma

When working with children, it is important to be aware of the possibility of child abuse and/or neglect. The therapist needs to know the law regarding the reporting of such incidents as well as being able to recognize the signs and symptoms of abuse. One aspect of this issue is that as a therapist, in most instances, you are a mandated reporter, meaning the law requires you to report any suspicion of abuse or neglect. It is important that you realize you are not required to prove the existence of the abuse. Simply being concerned that it may exist is cause for a report to the appropriate authority. If you are in doubt if there is something you need to report, it is helpful to discuss your concern with either your supervisor or another colleague.

Each state has its own laws defining abuse and neglect, as well as its own designation for reporting it. As a therapist, you are responsible for knowing and following the law of your state. Know the phone number of the contact person you would call in order to make a report. If you work within an agency, be familiar with the protocol and chain of command for making such a report.

Since several diagnoses common to children have a trauma history at their basis, it is important to do a trauma and abuse assessment with the child as part of your screening process. An excellent version of such a tool is the UCLA PTSD Index for DSM IV. Copies of this tool are available at the International Society for Traumatic Stress Studies (ISTSS) at http://www.istss.org/resources/UCLA.cfm.

217

There are versions available for children and adolescents, as well as one that parents of younger children can take for the child. Additional resources and assessment tools are available at http://www.istss.org/resources/browse.cfm under "Resources for Clinicians." A trauma and abuse assessment will help you determine if trauma or abuse has occurred and, if it has, the specific affects it has had on the child's ability to function and develop. Once you are able to get this information, you will be able to make recommendations for treatment that meets the needs of the child and family.

It is important not to overwhelm the child by requesting too much information at once. Before beginning this task, give the child some tools to help stay grounded. Letting the child know that he can say he does not want to answer a question will give him a sense of control of the situation. You can also remind him that he can ask you to stop at any time. Be sure to do so if he asks.

Some symptoms of trauma in younger children that may not be recognized include confusion, bullying, acting out in class, hyperactivity, loss of acquired skills, regression, somatic symptoms such as stomach aches or headaches, repetitious play, a preoccupation with danger, aggressive behavior, angry outbursts, school avoidance, inability to concentrate, and lower performance at school. In adolescents, symptoms such as rebellion at home, depression, social withdrawal, sexual acting out, risk-taking behavior, accident proneness, withdrawal, and a change in relationship with friends can be symptomatic of an experience of trauma.

Researchers of evidence-based practices have determined that trauma-focused cognitive behavioral therapy works best for children who have experienced abuse or trauma. If you are unfamiliar with this form of therapy, there is a free on-line course you can access at http://tfcbt.musc.edu/ to learn how to use this technique in your practice.

Assessing for Suicidality/Self-harm in Children

Because children do not have a clear understanding of the finality of death, the necessity of correctly assessing for suicidality and self-harm is of primary importance. Suicide among children has become much more common than it used to be. Intentional suicides have occurred in children as young as four years old (Lukas, 1993), however it is more common for individuals over the age of 12 to actually commit suicide. About 1-2 out of every 100,000 children in the United States under the age of 15 will commit suicide. The rate goes up to 11 out of 100,000 for those who are 15-19 years of age. Among children ages 10-14, suicide is the fourth leading cause of death and the third leading cause of death for teenagers between the ages of 15-19.

The rate of suicide attempts is even higher. In any given year, 2-6% of children will attempt suicide and 1% will be successful on their first try. Children with a history of a major depressive disorder, mood disorder, anxiety disorder or substance abuse problem have a higher than average rate of suicide attempts. Children who have a family history of suicidal behavior and guns have an increased risk for suicide themselves. 90% of children and adolescents who attempt suicide have a history of psychiatric disorders, so suicide risk needs to be carefully assessed on a regular basis.

There are two myths about suicide of which clinicians should be aware. The first is that a person who is thinking about killing herself will never tell anyone. Most people do give some indication, either verbally or behaviorally, that they are thinking of taking their own life. This may be in the form of an off-handed remark, such as "I wonder what it would be like to be dead" or by a comment such as "What difference does it make that I didn't get on the team?" Adolescents may make reference to their thoughts of suicide in school assignments, particularly creative writing or artwork. A young child may start to have a serious interest in what heaven might be like, where there was no previous interest in the topic. There are also non-verbal ways that an individual may indicate a loss of interest in staying alive. If a teenager stops eating, or starts to give away cherished possessions, or stops participating in activities, or starts having frequent accidents and injuries, this may mean that the teen is thinking of suicide. Additionally, younger children may provide indirect clues in the form of acting-out or violent behavior, often accompanied by suicidal threats.

If children are continuously thinking about death and believe that being dead would be nice, they are more at risk of making a serious suicide attempt. Be particularly concerned if there has been a recent suicide within the child's school or circle of friends. There sometimes exists the possibility of a suicide pact among children that you will want to explore. Self-injurious behaviors can occur in children as young as elementary school-age with common behaviors including running into traffic, jumping from heights, and cutting, scratching or marking one's body. These actions are a cry for help that a therapist needs to listen to.

The second myth that some therapists believe is that talking about suicide will put the idea into someone's head and actually cause a person to commit suicide. This is not the case. Most people who are considering suicide are actually relieved to find someone they can talk to about it.

Before the situation actually occurs, know what procedures exist for managing potentially suicidal clients. With whom will you speak? What telephone numbers do you need to have available? How will you deal with the client if you are waiting for the police or ambulance to arrive? Be aware of your legal obligations in such a situation. Know what the limits of confidentiality are regarding a suicide threat. Is there anyone you need to notify? One important aspect as a clinician is to take careful and thorough notes when you suspect a client is seriously considering suicide.

Take all talk of self-injury and suicide seriously. It is important here, to trust your instinct. If you are concerned about a child, follow up on your concerns, as the consequences for not doing so could be disastrous. Be aware that there are several levels of suicidal risk. The first is suicidal thinking or ideation. This is where someone states that she has been thinking of hurting herself. Therefore, you need to begin to ask some questions to determine how serious the risk may be.

You will first want to determine if s/he has a plan. How does he imagine he will hurt himself? Find out how frequently the client thinks about the plan. When was the last time he considered it? Has she ever attempted suicide in the past? How comforting is the thought of suicide? Does she currently have a plan? How lethal is the method he has planned? Does she have the means to accomplish her goal?

Depending on the answer to each of the above questions, determine your own plan of action. If a child responds that he wishes he were dead, but has not decided how he plans to do it, there is less of an imminent threat than if he says he plans on using the gun that is in his parent's closet. Remember, the greater the planning, the greater the potential. Additionally, if the child is currently on anti-depressants for a mood disorder, be aware that the risk of suicide increases during the first few weeks of medication management and there is a higher potential that the child will follow through on the threat.

At this point, if you have determined that there is a serious risk of harm to the child you will want to involve the parents or caregivers in the process. First, explain to the child that because you are concerned about the information she has told you, you are going to share your concern with her parents. Let her know that you are glad she has shared the information and that together you will all decide the best way to keep her safe. Be prepared that the parents or caregivers will be upset when they hear that the child is thinking of suicide. Acknowledge that while this is a scary situation for all of them, there are ways to help the child be safe. If you have determined that the threat is serious, ask the parents if they feel they can transport their child to the emergency room to be seen by a physician. If you or the parents feel that transportation in the family car is not safe or possible, arrange for emergency transportation to the hospital. If you can determine that the situation does not warrant immediate hospitalization, you can then proceed to put an emergency plan in place with the parents.

First, access whether you believe the parents can adequately respond to the situation. If the family is already in crisis or there is a history of parental drug or alcohol abuse, you may want to send the child to the hospital to be assessed by a psychiatrist, rather than allow her to return to her home. If you feel that the parents are capable of supervising the child, decide together what steps to take to provide a safe enough environment for their child. If the child has indicated that there are lethal methods available to her, such as drugs, alcohol, knives and/or guns, ask the parents if they can remove them from the house or lock them up where the child cannot have access to them. Arrange for the child always to have someone with her until she can return for a follow-up visit with you. Check that the parents have phone numbers available for emergency transportation, the hospital emergency room as well as either your emergency number or a crisis number for times when you may not be available for consultation.

Before the family leaves your office, determine that the parents are comfortable assuming care for their child, that they understand the seriousness of the threat, and that they know the steps to take if their concern level rises. You should have a plan set in place for the child to be assessed by a physician along with a scheduled appointment with you for a follow-up visit.

The National Hopeline Network at 1-800-SUICIDE provides access to trained telephone counselors, 24 hours a day, 7 days a week. This can be a helpful resource to families and children during times of crisis. If you wish to offer a family the resource of a crisis center in your area, you can find which ones are available at www.hopeline.com/ries.asp.

Conclusion

Working with children and their families does offer some unique challenges but it also offers many rewards to those therapists who choose to work in this field. Being aware of the challenges and having the resources and support you need will make your job easier. The following suggested resources and forms are only some of the aids that are available. It is helpful to find a professional listserv, as well as a supervisory group where you can share your concerns about your clients and gain additional knowledge about the techniques that will best serve your clients.

Further support can come from joining the professional association for which you qualify as a member. Continued education in the form of workshops and conferences will help you network with other professional members in your line of work as well as give you the benefit of staying abreast of the knowledge in your field. Using all of these resources as you need them will allow you to continue to enjoy your work and be an effective source of help to your young clients.

Resources for Therapists

Recommended Books to use with children:

- Bang, M. (n.d.). *When Sophie gets angry-really, really angry... .* New York: Scholastic.(Ages 3-7: Storybook)
- Bisignano, J. (1991). *Living with death: Journal activities for personal growth.* IL: Good Apple. (Grades 5-9+: Workbook)
- Davis, D. (1984) *Something is wrong in my house.* Seattle, WA: Parenting Press. (Ages 8-12: Storybook)
- Girand, L.W. (1984). *My body is private.* IL: Albert Whitman & Co. (Ages 5-10: Storybook)
- Heegaard, M. (1991). *When something terrible happens: Children can learn*

to cope with grief. MN: Woodland Press. (Ages 6-teen: Workbook)
+ Holmes, M.M. (2000). *A terrible thing happened*. Washington, DC: Imagination Press. (Ages 5-10: Storybook)
+ Lovell, C.M. (1999). *The star: A story to help young children understand foster care*. Published by author. (Ages 4-7: Storybook)
+ Malecka, J. & Bunnell, S. (1997). *Making the most of me*. Michigan: Instructional Fair. (Grades 5-8: Workbook)
+ Nemiroff, M.A., & Annunziata, J. (1990) *A child's first book about play therapy*. Washington, DC: American Psychological Association(Ages 4-9: Storybook)
+ Pincus, D. (1990). *Feeling good about yourself: Strategies to guide young people toward more positive, personal feelings*. CA: Good Apple, Inc.(Grades 3-8: Workbook)

Recommended Reading/Resources for Therapists

+ American Psychological Association. (2007) *Record keeping guidelines* Available at http://www.apa.org/practice/recordkeeping.pdf
+ American Psychological Association. (1993). Guidelines for providers of psychological services to ethnic, linguistic, and culturally diverse populations. *American Psychologist, 48,* 45-48. Available at http://www.apa.org/pi/oema/guide.html.
+ Harris, E. & Bennett, B.E. (n.d.) *Information about the sample psychotherapist-patient contract*. Available at http://www.apait.org/apait/applications/INF.doc.pdf
+ Malloy, J., Malloy, M., & Taub, J. (2007). *Children's mental health in New Hampshire:Evidenced based practice*. Copies are available at no charge on the Center's web site: www.nhpolicy.org
+ Reznick, C. (2007).*The healing power of children's imagination for medical procedures: Help for pain, anxiety, and fear*. Available at http://www.imageryforkids.com/art_healingpower.html
+ Zuckerman, E.L. (2003) The Paper Office. New York: Guilford Press.
+ Zur, O. & Nordmarken, N. (2008). *To touch or not to touch: Exploring the myth of prohibition on touch in psychotherapy and counseling*. Available at http://www.zurinstitute.com/touchintherapy.html

Websites with Resources for Therapists Working with Children

+ http://www.selfhelpwarehouse.com/: Carries a variety of self help and educational tools.
+ http://www.childtherapytoys.com/store/index.html: Toys to use with children in therapy
+ http://www.annastoydepot.com/: Source for sandtray items and therapy

toys
- http://www.ncpamd.com/books.htm: Books that deal with children's mental health issues
- http://www.maginationpress.com/bbytopic.html: Books for children in therapy
- http://www.childswork.com/: Books, games, and supplies for therapy sessions
- http://www.ssww.com/artsandcraftsupplies/: Art and craft supplies
- http://www.compassionbooks.com/store/: Books on grief

Web sites with Links to Articles for Therapists
- http://www.empty-memories.nl/www_1.html: Related to psychological trauma, dissociative disorders and the mind
- http://www.traumacentral.net/: Links on trauma, resources for professionals and the public
- http://psychclassics.yorku.ca/topic.htm: Classics in the history of psychology
- http://www.trauma-pages.com/resources.php: Trauma resources
- http://scholar.google.com/: search engine for scholarly articles and websites
- http://www.clinicalsocialwork.com/articles.html: articles on various professional topics
- http://www.psybc.com/library-categories.php: on-line continuing education courses
- http://www2.library.ucla.edu/search/765.cfm?su=69: links to databases related to psychology

References

Briggs, M. H. (1999) Systems for collaboration: integrating multiple perspectives. *Child and adolescent psychiatric clinics of North America, 8,* 365–377.

Brown, D. (1997). Implications of cultural values for cross-cultural consultation with families. *Journal of counseling & development, 76,* 29-35.

Greenwald, R. (2005). Child trauma handbook: A guide for helping trauma-exposed children and adolescents. New York: Haworth Press.

Gustafson, K. E., McNamara, J. R. & Jensen, J. A. (1994). Parents' informed consent decisions regarding psychotherapy for their children: Consideration of therapeutic risks and benefits. *Professional Psychology: Research and Practice, 25(1),* 16-22

Halasz, G. (1997). The rights of the child in psychotherapy. *American Journal of Psychotherapy,50 (3),* 285-297.

Harry, B. (n.d.)Developing cultural self-awareness. Retrieved from internet on January 11, 2008 from http://www.casanet.org/library/culture/culture-aware.htm

House, A.E. (2002). *The first session with children and adolescents: Conducting a comprehensive mental health evaluation.* New York: Guilford Press.

Jones, A. M. (2002). An account of play therapy with an abused child from a different ethnic background to the therapist. *Children & Society, 16,* 195-205.

Lukas, S. (1993). *Where to start and what to ask: An assessment handbook.* New York: Norton & Co.

McGoldrick, M., Giordano, J., & Garcia-Preto, N. (Eds.). 2005. Ethnicity and family therapy, (3rd Ed.). New York, NY: Guilford Press.

McNeil-Haber, F. M. (2004). Ethical considerations in the use of nonerotic touch in psychotherapy with children. *Ethics & Behavior, 14(2),* 123–140.

Morris, R.J. (1993). Ethical issues in the assessment and treatment of children and adolescents. *Register Report, 19(1),* 4-12.

Reamer, F. G. (2005). Update on confidentiality issues in practice with children: Ethics risk management. *Children & Schools, 27(2),* 117-120.

Rose, N. (n.d.). Power in therapy: Techne and ethos. Academy for the Study of the Psychoanalytic Arts. Available at http://www.academyanalyticarts.org/rose2.htm

Salmon, G. & Faris, J. (2006). Multi-agency collaboration, multiple levels of meaning: Social constructionism and the CMM model as tools to further our understanding. *Journal of Family Therapy, 28,* 272–292.

Zuckerman, E.L. (2003) The paper office. New York: Guilford Press.

Zur, O. (2005). Ethical and legal aspects of touch in psychotherapy. Available at http://www.drzur.com/ethicsoftouch.html

Zur, O. (2008). Zur Institute: Innovative resources and continuing education. Retrieved from the internet on January 1, 2008 at http://www.zurinstitute.com/

clinicalupdates.html

Zur, O. and Nordmarken, N. (2008). *To touch or not to touch: Exploring the myth of prohibition on touch in psychotherapy and counseling.* Retrieved January 5, 2008 from http://www.zurinstitute.com/touchintherapy.html

When to Let 'Em See You Sweat: Therapist Self-Disclosure with Adolescent Clients
By: Jennifer A. Smith, MA, Clinical Mental Health Counseling

Helping professionals who work with adolescents, particularly the innumerable young people who have been labeled 'at-risk' by their parents and schools, are familiar with the awkward rites of passage one must survive before gaining entry into the adolescent world. To glimpse beyond the walls, you must master a complex form of power-dancing where the steps change for every partner, the tempo varies continuously, and instruction is given in a foreign language—and is rarely offered in the halls of graduate schools. Add to that the adolescent partner's tendency to smash your toes and dismiss you mid-song, and you begin to imagine the bewilderment often felt by novice practitioners seeking to enter the field of adolescent treatment. Luckily, like the Zen of Adolescent Therapy, the secret lies within you.

It is a widely-held belief that adolescents are challenging to work with; however, given the high rates of mental health problems experienced by this population, and evidence suggesting that untreated issues may worsen in adulthood, it is critical we as professionals learn to engage with adolescents successfully (Baruch, 2001; Malekoff, 2004; Meeks & Bernet, 2001; Oetzel & Scherer, 2003; Richardson, 2001; Rubenstein, 1996). Many effective techniques used with children or adults don't work with adolescents, and worse yet, can create unintended wedges between therapist and client (Baruch, 2001; Edgette, 1999; Malekoff, 2004; Meeks & Bernet, 2001; Richardson, 2001). Challenging us to prove ourselves immediately, adolescents demand to know who we really are. They size us up with the keenest sense for whether we can be trusted based on our clothes, our gait and stance, and the somehow telltale look in our eyes (Edgette, 1999; Oetzel & Scherer, 2003; Rubenstein, 1996). They require that we be authentic, or as it's more likely to be put, that we 'get real' (Edgette, 1999; Malekoff, 2004; Richardson, 2001; Rubenstein, 1996).

Communicating authenticity to clients can be achieved through the use of therapist self-disclosure (TSD). TSD, broadly defined as any personal information shared by a therapist with a client, includes not only verbal statements about one's life, thoughts or feelings, but also those subtler messages revealed through nonverbal communication, and things like how our offices are decorated and what traditions we observe (Burkard, Knox, Groen, Perez & Hess, 2006; Curtis, Field, Knaan-Kostman & Mannix, 2004; Davis, 2002; Edgette, 1999; Kim et al., 2003; Klein, Kolden, Michels & Chisholm-Stockard, 2001; Myers & Hayes, 2006; Peterson, 2002; Richardson, 2001; Rubenstein, 1996). Some disclosures are inadvertent and perhaps unavoidable, but direct responses to client queries are particularly challenging for new practitioners to formulate, given the traditional caveat in training programs to avoid unduly influencing the therapeutic process (Davis, 2002; Peterson, 2002). Fear of making an inappropriate disclosure coupled with our need to appear as if we know the 'right' thing to say, sometimes leads helping professionals to re-enact a scene out of a parent's worst nightmare, stammering, "And how would you feel about it if I *did* smoke pot when I was your age?"

Since few programs offer training in TSD, many beginning clinicians feel unsure of how to respond to the first impressions flaying they're subjected to during initial contact with adolescent clients (Burkard et al., 2006; Davis, 2002). This peeling open of who we are begins with sharp observation and may proceed quickly to direct questioning by adolescent clients, demanding we justify ourselves convincingly before making another move (Baruch, 2001; Edgette, 1999; Oetzel & Scherer, 2003; Richardson, 2001; Rubenstein, 1996). And with the instincts of a natural predator, they strike with amazing accuracy. Writes Edgette (1999), "When he would catch me hesitating, discombobulated and searching desperately for the 'right' response, he would smile coldly and move further in. 'You don't have a *clue*, do you?'" (p. 38). As with any dance, faltering and uncertainty about where to step not only confuses our partner but may leave us standing alone on the dance floor.

Although the use of TSD is becoming more accepted as a potential intervention, therapists are often unsure how to use it, when and with whom (Curtis et al., 2004; Davis, 2002; Klein et al., 2001; Myers & Hayes, 2006; Peterson, 2002). This chapter begins by discussing significant developmental factors affecting adolescents, and how to meaningfully engage them in therapy, knowledge that serves as the basis for implementing TSD with adolescent clients. The author then explores research on TSD, the ethics around its use, and how to decide when TSD may have beneficial effects. By offering practical suggestions regarding what to say, and perhaps more importantly what *not* to say, the author provides a guide for how to effectively use TSD to demonstrate genuineness and authenticity as a means for building therapeutic alliances with adolescents—even if it means that sometimes they'll see you sweat.

Adolescent Clients

Challenges of Working with Adolescents

Compared to adult and child populations, relatively little empirical research has been conducted regarding effective therapy practice with adolescents (Baruch, 2001; Malekoff, 2004; Meeks & Bernet, 2001; Oetzel & Scherer, 2003; Richardson, 2001; Rubenstein, 1996). According to Oetzel and Scherer (2003) however, "the prevalence and impact of mental health issues among adolescents are astonishing" (p. 215). Reports that 10-20% of adolescents experience significant mental health problems are concerning when coupled with the fact that "fewer than one in five youths in need of mental health services receive the needed treatment (National Institute of Mental Health [NIMH], 1999)" (Oetzel & Scherer, 2003, p. 215; Rubenstein, 1996). This combination of sparse research and low rates of engagement among adolescent clients have led in part to adolescent therapy's reputation as being 'challenging,' a euphemism for what others might refer to as a maddening, white-knuckle roller coaster ride (Baruch, 2001; Edgette, 1999; Malekoff, 2004; Richardson, 2001; Rubenstein, 1996). However, for those willing to experience the rush, engaging in work with adolescents offers an opportunity to explore the potential for success via alternative approaches. Writes Malekoff (2004), "My experience advises me…[that] work with adolescents is not for the faint-hearted, but rather for the young at heart" (p. xi).

Without an established empirical base, adolescent development research, studies of general therapeutic factors, and accounts from practitioners in the field may serve as the best available guide for proceeding in our work with adolescent clients (Baruch, 2001; Oetzel & Scherer, 2003; Richardson, 2001; Rubenstein, 1996). It is important to note that as with any population, adolescents present with a broad range of characteristics and abilities, and not all of them are beyond the reach of traditional therapies (Baruch, 2001; Edgette, 1999; Malekoff, 2004; Meeks & Bernet, 2001; Richardson, 2001; Rubenstein, 1996). Writes Edgette (1999), "Some adolescents are a genuine pleasure to work with, comfortably accepting the therapy setting and our offers of help" (p. 38). This is not to suggest, however, that young people who reject traditional approaches are unpleasant or categorically resistant to treatment. In explaining why he avoids such terms as 'at-risk,' 'behaviorally disordered,' and 'oppositional defiant' to describe adolescent clients, Richardson (2001) writes, "The term challenging puts the impetus on the relationship between helping professionals and the youth and challenges us adults to adjust our style to meet the needs of the youth" (p. 4). One such necessary adjustment is the need to view adolescent behaviors in therapy within the context of their larger experiences with adults, as well as through the lens of developmental striving.

According to Rubenstein (1996), "Adolescents are beyond the play room and most do not have much patience of the traditional 'talk therapies'" (p. 355). Other practitioners (Baruch, 2001; Edgette, 1999; Malekoff, 2004; Richardson, 2001) echo this statement, and share accounts of adolescent clients who respond to talk therapy only with sighs and grunts, by rambling incessantly about seemingly mundane topics, or by firing questions and provocative statements boldly back at therapists without so much as blinking—and then storming out of the office to have a cigarette. Given our society's paradigm for the difficult teenager, "it is easy to chalk up the challenge of working with adolescents to their time-honored 'authority issues'" (Edgette, 1999, p. 38). However, as Edgette (1999) goes on to say, "there is a far more critical difference between working with adults and working with teens that we rarely come to grips with: few teenagers come willingly to therapy in the first place" (p. 38). Given the involuntary nature of most adolescent referrals, it is therefore imperative that engagement and therapeutic alliance building be our primary goals (Baruch, 2001; Edgette, 1999; Meeks & Bernet, 2001; Oetzel & Scherer, 2003).

Adolescents as 'Culturally Different' from Adults

As adolescents straddle the worlds of childhood and adulthood, eager to reject early dependencies but not quite having mastered adult responsibilities, they also face "...rapid and pervasive developmental changes involving physiological, cognitive, emotional, and social transformations (Holmbeck & Updegrove, 1995; Weisz & Hawley, 2002)" (Oetzel & Scherer, 2003, p. 218). Indeed, this active period of adolescent development involves some massive tasks, including: a search for one's identity; striving for autonomy from parents; and developing a sense of belonging (Baruch, 2001; Edgette, 1999; Malekoff, 2004; Meeks & Bernet, 2001; Oetzel & Scherer, 2003; Richardson, 2001; Rubenstein, 1996). While adolescents are faced with figuring out who they are and how they fit into the world around them, hormonal and neurological changes simultaneously ensure they're beset with intensified emotional experiences and unstable abilities to self-regulate or use advanced reasoning (Malekoff, 2004; Meeks & Bernet, 2001; Oetzel & Scherer, 2003; Richardson, 2001). Add to this a societal context in the United States where families and communities are increasingly disconnected (Baruch, 2001; Malekoff, 2004; Rubenstein, 1996), and it is easy to imagine that adolescents, caught between worlds, must rely on a strong peer culture to survive.

According to Meeks and Bernet (2001), "the adolescent's view of adult, organized society contains inherent elements of ambivalence" (p. 17). The developmental tasks of separating from parents and forming a unique identity lead adolescents naturally toward rejecting their parents and other authority figures while at the same time longing for the autonomy and power associated with the adult world (Baruch, 2001; Edgette, 1999; Oetzel & Scherer, 2003; Richardson, 2001). In addition, adolescents' tendency to scrutinize themselves and assume that others cast a similarly glaring spotlight on their every move, increases the likelihood of feeling isolated and defensive when experiencing problems. For this reason, group work with adolescents can be a powerful intervention, one that allows adolescents to see they are not alone, and that "others express similar concerns, fears, and life experiences" (Richardson, 2001, p. 164). This sense of universality has been identified by inpatient adolescents as a valuable therapeutic factor (Richardson, 2001), and suggests that many adolescent clients consider themselves misunderstood outsiders. Furthermore, this sense is not mere paranoia as indeed many adults have difficulty accepting the different styles of dress, language, and expression with which adolescents experiment. Write Meeks and Bernet (2001), "Adults may view adolescents as a minority group and respond to them, as a group, with stereotyped attitudes and expectations that could only be described as prejudicial" (p. 18).

Research exploring cross-cultural counseling yields interesting similarities in client reports of mistrust and ambivalence when engaging in therapy with dominant-culture therapists (Burkard et al., 2006; Kim et al., 2003). Although admittedly the experiences of culturally different clients are distinct from the trials suffered by the adolescent population, there may be useful parallels to be made between the use of TSD with each group. Write Burkard et al. (2006), "Many people of color have experienced prejudice and discrimination in their contact with European Americans at individual, cultural, and institutional levels and consequently may be distrustful of future contacts (Terrell & Terrell, 1984)" (p. 16). Position this statement next to Edgette's (1999) assertion that "adolescents have lost faith in the power of words to help them deal with their misery. They have already 'talked' with parents, teachers and police, and have been met with lectures, punishment, accusations of lying or all of the above" (p. 38), and it seems plausible to suggest that cross-cultural counseling research might have something to offer regarding work with adolescents.

Issues of Power

All human beings have basic needs, including a need for power and a sense of competence (Baruch, 2001; Edgette, 1999; Malekoff, 2004; Oetzel & Scherer, 2003; Richardson, 2001; Rosenberg, 2003; Rubenstein, 1996). During the transition from childhood to adulthood, adolescents are keenly attuned to issues of power, and gain heightened awareness of the ways in which adults exert control in home, school and professional settings (Baruch, 2001; Oetzel & Scherer, 2003; Richardson, 2001). For youth who have suffered abuses of power by the trusted adults in their lives or who lack an experience of themselves as competent (i.e., 'challenging youth'), Richardson (2001) asserts, "the need for love and belonging and the need for power and achievement [are] particularly crucial...[and] it is rare to find a challenging youth who does not struggle on a daily basis to responsibly meet these two needs" (p. 39). Since traditional therapy settings require skills and behaviors that most adolescents have not yet mastered, and since parents or courts often 'force' them to attend sessions in the first place, it is understandable that many adolescent clients enter our offices as if entering a boxing ring; they are like defensive bragga-docios, determined to hold their own and exert whatever power they can (Baruch, 2001; Edgette, 1999; Oetzel & Scherer, 2003).

Those adolescents who come in swinging, however, are usually my favorites. Their willingness to engage in battle is at least a willingness to engage, and they are demonstrating a strength of spirit that's necessary for later therapeutic gains. Although it's the most obvious manifestation, however, this type of head-on con-frontation is not the only way power issues play out with adolescents in therapy. Writes Baruch (2001):

> For the young person entering therapy, especially when it is for the first time, the ranking difference can exacerbate those factors that make ther-apy and the therapist seem threatening. This in turn can evoke the more primitive responses to a sense of being under threat: namely to fight back, behave submissively or flee. Whilst fighting back or being submissive can be worked with, the latter option leaves the therapist with an empty chair. (p. 18)

What is important to note here is that adolescent clients' expressions of power are both normal and developmentally-driven. We must acknowledge that a need for control over our own lives is human nature, and that upon perceiving threats to our personal liberty, adults, too, are likely to assert themselves in defense (Baruch, 2001; Edgette, 1999; Richardson, 2001).

In addition to understanding that adolescents are "developmentally hard-wired for independence, for hyperbole, for cloistering among their own kind and defin-ing themselves through opposition..." (Edgette, 1999, p. 38), as practitioners we must also be aware that the same set of behaviors might be attempts by clients to escape emotional pain (Baruch, 2001; Edgette, 1999; Richardson, 2001). Writes Edgette (1999), "many of these kids have abandoned words, choosing instead to act out their pain by running away, cutting themselves, fighting, failing in school, drinking and taking drugs" (p. 38). Whether engaging in risky behaviors to dis-tract themselves from personal concerns or 'sabotaging' sessions to avoid having to talk about the issues, provocative behavior by adolescents might also be as much about the adults around them as it is about client problems. Writes Baruch (2001), "[adolescent aggression] may also reflect a maladaptive struggle to achieve a sense of safety by rendering the adult ineffective and powerless" (p. 118). The ability to frame both verbal jabs and self-destructive behavior in adolescent clients as imper-fect attempts to claim power and cope with problems assists us in preserving our own power, hopefully from a centered stance where the focus remains on control-ling ourselves versus further triggering our clients (Baruch, 2001; Edgette, 1999; Oetzel & Scherer, 2003; Richardson, 2001; Rubenstein, 1996).

A note is in order, at this point, regarding how we define power. Given that adolescents' shocking or unsavory behavior in our offices might be designed specifically to knock us off our feet, how are we to respond from a place of power that doesn't further threaten the adolescent clients' stand? Richardson (2001) reminds us that "aggressive behavior from youth often elicits hostile and counterproductive behavior from adults, and hyperactive behavior often yields impulsive, irrational adult responses (Long, 1991)" (p. 101). Despite our occasional illusions of grandeur, the fact remains that we are all human, and unless therapists practice responding consciously, our own instincts to protect ourselves may play out just as adolescent clients fear and expect they will—with a failure to connect and further proof that we can't do anything right (Baruch, 2001; Edgette, 1999; Oetzel & Scherer, 2003; Richardson, 2001; Rosenberg, 2003; Rubenstein, 1996).

The type of power I'm encouraging you to foster has been described by Rosenberg (2003) as 'power with' as opposed to 'power over.' It is similar to the power emanated by an advanced student of the martial arts, characterized by attunement to the other, confidence in one's ability to respond reflexively, and a lack of compulsion to use undue force. Writes Rosenberg (2003), "It's a power based on mutual trust and respect, which makes people open to hearing each other and learning from each other, and to giving to one another willingly out of a desire to contribute to the other's well-being..." (p. 7). Although the establishment of trust takes time, it is possible to demonstrate mutual respect and qualities of trustworthiness from the beginning of our interactions with adolescent clients. Edgette (1999) describes the moment when she first realized her power with an adolescent client, and writes:

> When I finally spoke the truth of our awkward, awful situation—a truth both of us were experiencing but that neither of us, until then, had spoken out loud—I gave Carl a reason to respect me. As a person worthy of respect, I could then begin to matter to him. And once *I* mattered, what I said to him could matter. (p. 40)

Practitioners who are skilled in engaging adolescent clients do not exert or take power; they *give rise to it* by demonstrating a genuine desire to connect with clients, and a willingness to participate in the dance authentically (Edgette, 1999; Malekoff, 2004; Richardson, 2001; Rosenberg, 2003; Rubenstein, 1996).

Importance of Genuineness

Research literature and practitioner accounts indicate that adolescents place a high value on the quality of genuineness in helping professionals (Edgette, 1999; Malekoff, 2004; Meeks & Bernet, 2001; Oetzel & Scherer, 2003; Richardson, 2001; Rubenstein, 1996). Writes Edgette (1999), "...most of them [adolescents] haven't yet adopted the adult custom of measuring their words and choosing politeness over genuineness. As such, these kids are far more sensitive than adults to any form of disingenuousness" (p. 39). During the developmental stage of adolescence, young people are learning to form more intimate bonds and, as such, are often preoccupied with the minute details of social cues and figuring out their meaning (Meeks & Bernet, 2001; Richardson, 2001). Although their ability to interpret other people's behavior is not perfected, adolescents nonetheless tend to have strong feelings about whether or not someone is friend or foe. Quips Richardson (2001), "Kids who have been exposed to a lot of B.S. inevitably develop their own sophisticated B.S. detectors. These devices look like a tiny freckle, are barely visible to the human eye, and are located just behind the ear" (p. 19). I can personally attest to the presence of these refined receivers because, like many others, I have heard their sirens wail when on distracted occasions I said the 'right' thing to a youth without feeling the truth of it in my heart.

All the same, a commitment to genuineness is not just the result of a youthful perspective. The ability to sense whether adults are sincere in their efforts to help is an important survival skill for adolescents who have suffered abuse, perhaps repeatedly, by adults in their lives in whom they had innocently placed their trust (Edgette, 1999; Malekoff, 2004; Richardson, 2001). For this very reason, the adolescent clients with the highest needs are often the toughest to engage; lacking the real power to protect themselves in the adult world, young people hone their abilities to avoid future attack through a judicious use of trust (Baruch, 2001). Richardson (2001) illustrates this point with an account from one young woman who says:

> You know, I've been in seven different foster homes so I've seen lots of shrinks and social workers. Some of them were pretty cool, but most of 'em, you could tell, they were just punching the clock. I don't blame them; if I was them I would probably do the same thing, but Lisa's different. When I tell her something, she's really listening. But what I like best is she ain't bogus. She's real. I know she's going to shoot straight with me. I don't know how I do it, but I can usually tell right away if they're real or not.—Keisha, age 13 (p. 20)

The difficulty lies in the fact that with many adolescent clients, their 'bullshit detector' relies on a hair trigger, one that is far too sensitive to be accurate all the time. In other words, some well-meaning practitioners trip the alarm by accident, cutting off a relationship that may have been of benefit to the adolescent client if given the chance to develop.

Practitioner awareness of the adolescent's need for genuineness is critical to the therapeutic process, as is an understanding of what 'trips the trigger' or is perceived by clients as a sign of being 'fake' (Edgette, 1999; Meeks & Bernet, 2001; Oetzel & Scherer, 2003; Richardson, 2001; Rubenstein, 1996). Genuineness or authenticity may be described as congruence between what we say or do and what we really think, communicated to adolescent clients through honest disclosure and a straightforward bearing (Baruch, 2001; Edgette, 1999; Malekoff, 2004; Oetzel & Scherer, 2003; Richardson, 2001; Rubenstein, 1996). Writes Edgette (1999),

> Nothing in our therapy training prepares us to work with clients like these—ones who have zero interest in sitting across from us, want no part of 'mutual goal setting,' find our warmth claustrophobic, our empathy suspect and our favored interventions a manipulative joke. So what's left? What's left, I have discovered, is an enormously underutilized resource in working with adolescents—candor. (p. 39)

According to Oetzel and Scherer (2003), "Therapist candor is intriguing to adolescents because of the personal and nondefensive stance assumed by the therapist" (p. 217). Furthermore, it is clear that adolescents have little patience for artificial attempts to connect by feigning interest or pretending to be a part of their world (Edgette, 1999; Meeks & Bernet, 2001; Oetzel & Scherer, 2003; Richardson, 2001; Rubenstein, 1996). Writes Edgette (1999), "Teenagers instinctively dislike the therapist who tries too hard, who solicits approval, who minces words or who harbors grand designs for their 'recovery' other than to be as useful as possible, as defined by the teen him- or herself" (p. 39).

Literature discusses the value placed on therapist authenticity in humanistic orientations, including that practiced by Carl Rogers, who stressed the importance of genuineness and a positive regard for clients (Burkard et al., 2006; Klein et al., 2001; Myers & Hayes, 2006; Peterson, 2002). Having positive regard for, or liking, our clients has been shown to be an important factor both in developing a therapeutic alliance as well as promoting beneficial outcomes for clients across populations (Burkard et al., 2006; Edgette, 1999; Klein et al., 2001; Myers & Hayes, 2006; Richardson, 2001). The ability to sincerely like our adolescent clients, then, appears to be a key factor in whether they perceive us as genuine, and has been cited as "'the single most central matter at the core of helping'" (Morse, 1996; as cited in Richardson, 2001, p. 19). However, given challenging adolescents' propensity for mistrusting adults, feelings of positive regard for clients alone may not be sufficient to forge a bond—*what is crucial is our ability to communicate this caring effectively.* Writes Richardson (2001), "...while most professionals do care, obstacles such as struggling for control and focusing on symptom behaviors sometimes make communicating this caring quite difficult" (p. 19). Genuine positive regard helps protect against knee-jerk reactions to judge or criticize clients, and makes it easier for therapists to express empathy for client struggles (Edgette, 1999; Klein et al., 2001; Richardson, 2001). Writes Edgette (1999), "...You can't exercise benevolent candor unless you genuinely like the kid you're sitting across from. The saving paradox is that authenticity helps to clear a space for genuine affection and caring to grow" (p. 40).

Therapist Self-Disclosure (TSD)

TSD Defined

Although research studies sometimes limit the definition of TSD to "'therapist statements that reveal something personal about therapists (Hill & Knox, 2002, p. 256)'" (Burkard et al., 2006, p. 15), literature exploring TSD also commonly includes nonverbal elements such as how offices are decorated, how therapists dress, and what holidays are observed (Burkard et al., 2006; Curtis et al., 2004; Davis, 2002; Kim et al., 2003; Klein et al., 2001; Myers & Hayes, 2006; Peterson, 2002). Taking an even broader view of TSD are those who argue that age, gender, level of education, and in-session behavior also constitute disclosures, albeit unavoidably (Davis, 2002). Writes Davis (2002), "According to Singer (1977), even interpretations, the epitome of psychoanalytic interventions, 'are neither exclusively nor even primarily comments about...clients' deeper motivations but first and foremost [are] self revealing remarks' (p. 183)" (p. 438). In other words, taken to an extreme, TSD might be said to apply to every aspect of therapy, given that each practitioner draws attention to or involuntarily responds to different aspects of the client's presentation (Davis, 2002). Furthermore, Davis (2002) suggests that even moments when therapists choose to withhold a response are occasions of active intervention, writing, "In not answering a patient's question, or in remaining silent, a therapist is very much doing something (Lipton, 1977). The patient, in turn, responds to the analyst's silence by giving his or her own meaning to it" (p. 439).

Ongoing debate about whether the therapist can provide an anonymous 'mirror' to clients, removing his or her own reflection from the pool, has been happening for at least one hundred years, dating back to Freud's theorizing about the role of the analyst and effects of countertransference (Davis, 2002; Myers & Hayes, 2006; Peterson, 2002). Current literature indicates that the use of TSD is becoming more acceptable as a valid therapeutic technique, yet research suggests only 1-13% of therapist interventions constitute overt TSD (Burkard et al., 2006; Davis, 2002; Myers & Hayes, 2006; Peterson, 2002). However, while therapists may not be using TSD multiple times within sessions, research by Simi and Mahalik (1997; as cited in Peterson, 2002) suggests that 60% of clients report that therapists self-disclosed personal information at some point during therapy. Rates of TSD use also vary depending on therapists' theoretical orientations (with more frequent use occurring in humanistic or feminist therapy, for example), as well as with different client populations (Burkard et al., 2006; Davis, 2002; Kim et al., 2003; Klein et al., 2001; Myers & Hayes, 2006; Peterson, 2002). Writes Davis (2002), "Renik (1995) suggests that even those psychoanalysts who still consider a stance of anonymity to represent superior analytic technique would nevertheless acknowledge that self-disclosure is unavoidable with certain types of patients (e.g. *adolescents...* [italics added])" (p. 438).

While this author agrees that even small details serve to communicate who we are to clients, in order to practically analyze when and how to use TSD appropriately TSD's can be further broken down into categories based on content, level of intimacy, or therapist intentions (Davis, 2002; Kim et al., 2003; Myers & Hayes, 2006; Peterson, 2002). Four categories developed by Wells (1994; as cited in Peterson, 2002) that are based on TSD content include: information related to therapist training and theoretical orientation; insights regarding personal struggles the therapist overcame; admission of therapist feelings towards client behavior or the client as a person; and acknowledgment of errors the therapist made in session that may have impacted the client negatively. Writes Peterson (2002), "One distinction that authors often make, consistent with Wells' (1994) categories, is between disclosures of within-session reactions and disclosures about other personal experiences of the therapist" (p. 23). For example, there is a distinct difference between a therapist's commenting, "I'm sensing that maybe what I just said was off the mark for you," versus sharing, "I struggled with Bulimia when I was in my 20's and found support groups very helpful." Davis (2002) points out that even within in-session and personal remarks there can be differences in the intensity of TSD's, writing, "the deliberate disclosure of countertransference feelings or personal facts can have very ordinary content (e.g. 'I'm feeling confused' or 'I'm originally from the Midwest') or extraordinary content (e.g. 'I am sexually attracted to you' or 'I have cancer')" (p. 439, footnote).

Dangers of Using TSD

Two commonly cited dangers of using TSD are interference with a client's freedom of association, and potential boundary violations (Davis, 2002; Kim et al., 2003; Klein et al., 2001; Myers & Hayes, 2006; Peterson, 2002). Because psychoanalytic traditions place emphasis on uncovering hidden conflicts through a process of free association, critics contend that TSD may unduly change the direction of a client's train of thought, and/or might cause the client to be fearful that if certain information is shared during therapy it will result in the therapist's judgment or rejection (Davis, 2002; Peterson, 2002). In addition, since psychoanalysis relies on the therapist's ability to use transference issues as a way of increasing client insight into intrapsychic conflicts, the more clients are personally responsible for the direction of therapy content, the more likely they are to accept suggestions that what has been discussed reveals something about themselves (Davis, 2002). For example, if a therapist were to self-disclose that her own dreams about the sea represent a desire to wash away the guilt she feels about her mother, a client might either adopt this interpretation for him or herself too readily, or in contrast, refuse to believe the therapist's suggestion that client dreams indicate a similar conflict. When engaging in therapy with adolescents, the danger of a client's withholding information out of fear of therapist judgment may have merit (Baruch, 2001; Edgette, 1999;

Richardson, 2001). TSD's that reveal a therapist's disapproval or moral stance on behaviors in which the adolescent client may engage (e.g. sexual intercourse or substance use) may prevent the formation of a trusting relationship, as well as the client's likelihood of addressing such issues in therapy (Baruch, 2001; Edgette, 1999; Richardson, 2001).

The danger of violating professional boundaries with clients through TSD is another important consideration. Not only would this type of breach represent unethical practice, but it may also result in failure to create a therapeutic alliance as well as possibly causing psychological harm to clients (Kim et al., 2003; Myers & Hayes, 2006; Peterson, 2002). Boundary violations through the use of TSD may include sharing details that are more intimate than the client is comfortable with, or sharing personal information so liberally that the focus of therapy shifts away from the client (Myers & Hayes, 2006; Peterson, 2002). For example, a therapist might inappropriately share, "my partner and I have sex several times a week" with a client experiencing shame related to past sexual abuse, or the therapist might spend half a session recounting a personal story that relates to the client's presenting issue but is also an unresolved conflict for the therapist. According to Myers and Hayes (2006), "Self-disclosure may be considered akin to the use of touch in therapy: A double-edged sword that can be either of great benefit or damage depending on its use" (p. 175).

Some possible effects of boundary violations include: generating negative emotions in clients; critically reducing a client's faith in therapist competence; interfering with a client's autonomy; or inviting an inappropriate relationship between therapist and client (Curtis et al., 2004; Kim et al., 2003; Klein et al., 2001; Myers & Hayes, 2006; Peterson, 2002). While at minimum, improper TSD may cause client reactions of fear or disgust, gross violations can lead to suicidal behavior linked to feeling exploited by the therapist (Myers & Hayes, 2006; Peterson, 2002). In addition, Peterson (2002) cites research by both Epstein (1994) and Brodsky (1989) that warns against personal self-disclosures based on indications that sexual involvement with clients (a serious ethical breach) is often preceded by boundary violations through TSD. Rather than suggesting that TSD directly causes therapists to become sexually involved with clients, Epstein (1994; as cited in Peterson, 2002) writes, "'Extensive personal disclosure may be a sign of a severe impairment in the therapist's ability to understand and maintain the professional role' (p. 201)" (p. 24). Other indications that TSD might be dangerous include lack of a strong alliance between client and therapist, and client characteristics such as weak boundaries, poor reality testing, inability to regulate emotions, fear of intimacy, and presenting issues that are 'characterological' in nature (Myers & Hayes, 2006; Peterson, 2002).

Benefits of Using TSD

Despite the potential dangers of TSD, its use in therapy is becoming more accepted as a valid intervention, and studies show positive effects on the therapeutic alliance when self-disclosure is used appropriately (Burkard et al., 2006; Curtis et al., 2004; Davis, 2002; Kim et al., 2003; Klein et al., 2001; Myers & Hayes, 2006; Peterson, 2002). In addition, as Davis (2002) points out, certain client populations actively seek TSD from practitioners, making it nearly impossible to avoid with adolescents and clients who exhibit paranoid or narcissistic tendencies. Interestingly, while the primary impetus for using TSD must always be potential benefits for clients, Klein et al. (2001) also offer brief discussion regarding positive effects of TSD on therapists when used to promote congruence. Klein et al. (2001) write, "Rogers (1967) spoke of feeling 'twisted...perhaps I am responding socially, smiling, while actually I know we are avoiding something' (p. 396) and then used the twisted feeling as a cue for the need for self-examination and a return to a more genuine and direct way of relating" (p. 399). This statement by Rogers suggests that a possible secondary benefit might also be TSD's ability to maximize practitioner effectiveness by reducing the distraction and distress caused by a therapist's suppression of difficult feelings in-session.

Many potential benefits of TSD have been identified for clients, including: strengthening the therapeutic alliance; modeling disclosure for clients; gaining new insights; and providing practical advice or solutions to problems (Burkard et al., 2006; Curtis et al., 2004; Davis, 2002; Kim et al., 2003; Klein et al., 2001; Myers & Hayes, 2006; Peterson, 2002). A review of the literature by Myers and Hayes (2006) indicates that, "on the whole...research suggests that therapist disclosure tends to have favorable effects" (p. 175). Client reports commonly indicate that TSD improved the therapeutic relationship by increasing feelings of trust, providing validation, and communicating an empathic connection with practitioners (Burkard et al., 2006; Davis, 2002; Kim et al., 2003; Klein et al., 2001; Myers & Hayes, 2006; Peterson, 2002). In addition, research suggests that appropriate use of TSD may relax clients, make therapists seem more attractive, human and genuine, and serve to equalize power within the relationship (Curtis et al., 2004; Kim et al., 2003; Myers & Hayes, 2006; Peterson, 2002). Writes Davis (2002), "this is inevitably true, in Singer's view, because 'the basic precondition for empathic communication is...personal knowledge of the experience under scrutiny—or as common language has it, 'it takes one to know one'" (pp. 182-183)" (p. 438). Although findings vary regarding whether in-session versus personal TSD's are more likely to improve the therapeutic alliance, it appears that what is most important is a match between particular client needs and the type of TSD employed (Burkard et al., 2006; Curtis et al., 2004; Kim et al., 2003; Myers & Hayes, 2006). One potential limitation of the research that has been identified is the difficulty determining whether TSD directly affects the therapeutic alliance or whether it merely serves as a vehicle for previously identified factors such as congruence, positive regard, and a belief in therapist competence (Burkard et al., 2006; Curtis et al., 2004).

In addition to positive effects on the therapeutic alliance (which inevitably improves the chance of future therapeutic gains), TSD has been found to serve as a way of modeling self-disclosure both within and outside therapy settings (Burkard et al., 2006; Kim et al., 2003; Myers & Hayes, 2006; Peterson, 2002). In other words, appropriate use of TSD demonstrates to clients how they might express their own feelings later in therapy as well as in their own lives. Peterson (2002) cites research by Knox et al. (1997) indicating, "Disclosures helped normalize the clients' problems, and...the therapists' disclosures facilitated the clients' own open expressions" (p. 24). Research regarding cross-cultural use of TSD further supports this finding, suggesting that therapists' ability to communicate understanding of cultural issues promoted trust leading to increased client disclosures (Burkard et al., 2006; Kim et al., 2003; Peterson, 2002). Furthermore, Burkard et al. (2006) point out, "some clients may come from cultural backgrounds that leave them unfamiliar with psychotherapeutic processes, such as client self-disclosure, or may hold cultural values that stigmatize help-seeking behavior for psychological difficulties" (p. 16). Again, whether TSD's take the form of explaining the therapy process through informed consent or contain more personal disclosures regarding the therapist's immediate experience in-session, resulting levels of trust or social learning seem to lead to increased client disclosure. However, cross-cultural counseling may heighten the need for awareness regarding an appropriate fit between TSD and client expectations, as is illustrated by research indicating that Mexicans viewed counselors as more expert and trustworthy when they did *not* self-disclose (Burkard et al., 2006).

Another benefit of TSD explored by cross-cultural researchers is the transmission of practical advice or solutions to problems (Burkard et al., 2006; Kim et al., 2003). Write Kim et al. (2003), "Asian American clients tend to view professional counselors as authority figures and may expect counselors to share about their life experiences and the lessons learned from these experiences" (p. 325). Being able to cite past success in overcoming obstacles can increase clients' sense of hope, as well as indicate concrete, practical steps toward reducing their own problems. Rubenstein (1996) identifies the benefit of offering practical, quick solutions when working with adolescents as well. Writes Rubenstein (1996), "We need to model, facilitate, and teach them appropriate ways of getting the attention of those who appear to have turned a deaf ear" (p. 358). Additionally, when therapists are able to self-disclose countertransference issues or personal experiences with past problems, clients sometimes benefit by gaining insight into their own difficulties (Curtis et al., 2004; Kim et al., 2003; Klein et al., 2001; Peterson, 2002). A study of 600 analysts who engaged in therapy themselves identified "'helped provide me with new meanings of my experiences'" as one of the top ten most helpful counselor behaviors (Curtis et al., 2004, p. 187). New insight may also be related to the candor appreciated by adolescent clients, or the willingness of therapists to 'call a spade a spade' (Edgette, 1999; Meeks & Bernet, 2001; Richardson, 2001). Writes Peterson

(2002), "Matthews (1988) reported that therapists practiced disclosure...to help clients recognize boundaries between what they think and feel and what others think and feel" (p. 26). This type of reality testing through TSD can assist clients in gaining insight into ways that distorted thinking contributes to their difficulties (Peterson, 2002).

Ethical Decision-Making and TSD

When faced with the question of whether or not to self-disclose to clients, practitioners typically consider the potential dangers or benefits to clients themselves, and may also reflect on established ethical guidelines (Davis, 2002; Myers & Hayes, 2006; Peterson, 2002). Peterson (2002) asserts that guidelines set forth by the American Psychological Association (APA) related to client exploitation, autonomy, and value conflicts may be particularly salient, and suggests that practitioners considering TSD adhere to the ethical principals of Beneficence, Nonmaleficence, and Justice. According to these principles, therapists are expected to pursue the goal of helping clients, refrain from causing harm to clients, and act in a fair and ethical manner with all clients in similar situations (Davis, 2002; Myers & Hayes, 2006; Peterson, 2002). Despite the APA's attempts to provide clarity regarding ethical mandates, however, therapists' theoretical orientations lend a certain subjectivity to how they view their actions with regard to TSD (Davis, 2002; Kim et al., 2003; Klein et al., 2001; Myers & Hayes, 2006; Peterson, 2002). For example, Peterson (2002) writes, "humanistic therapists see self-disclosure as an ethical necessity because it promotes not only the principal of beneficence but also the principal of fidelity" (p. 23). In a similar vein, practitioners influenced by feminist theory consider TSD essential to the process of informed consent, as well as the need to minimize power differentials with clients (Myers & Hayes, 2006; Peterson, 2002). Traditional psychoanalysts, in contrast, strive to maintain anonymity and free association with a client, as discussed earlier, which contraindicates the use of TSD (Davis, 2002; Myers & Hayes, 2006; Peterson, 2002).

Given APA guidelines against the exploitation of clients, some practitioners focus primarily on the distinction between in-session versus more personal content revealed through TSD (Peterson, 2002). According to Peterson (2002), "Wachtel said that a therapist's disclosures about his or her life outside of therapy introduce material that is a distraction from the client's experience, which is the only issue of importance in therapy" (pp. 23-24). TSD about in-session experiences, on the other hand, may be more acceptable to therapists across orientations because the focus remains on client issues and the immediate therapeutic process. However, as Myers and Hayes (2006) point out, "nevertheless worth considering before disclosing are hosts [of] other contextual factors, including but not limited to client diagnosis, presenting concerns, phase of therapy, skill level of the therapist, and others" (p. 182). Considering the complexity of factors affecting the use of TSD, and Davis' (2002) assertion that "the ultimate impact on the therapeutic process of this decision often only can be evaluated and understood well after the fact," leaves practitioners with several questions. How are therapists to prepare for ethical decision making around TSD? And what might be useful to therapists in the moment when TSD is elicited by clients themselves, and they are compelled to make quick decisions?

Besides recommendations to familiarize oneself with established ethical guidelines, and to raise self-awareness regarding how TSD fits into one's theoretical and personal value systems (*before* facing a decision in-session), Peterson (2002) suggests asking the following questions before making personal disclosures:

(a) Is this information necessary to protect the client's informed consent? (b) Is my purpose in disclosing this information to benefit the client or to benefit myself? (c) Will this particular client use this information in a way that is helpful? [and] (d) Will disclosing this information interfere with our therapeutic progress…? (p. 30)

In addition, therapists are encouraged to consider what their intentions are for using TSD, and how comfortable they are with disclosing the information (Davis, 2002; Myers & Hayes, 2006; Peterson, 2002). For example, in presenting two cases from his earliest days of practice, Davis (2002) describes how TSD can be used to regulate the distance between therapists and clients, and how later reflection revealed that he was trying to avoid strong countertransference feelings by disclosing and non-disclosing in various situations. Fear that clients are relying heavily on us and we may not be skilled enough to protect them could result in our pulling back unwittingly through refusal to disclose (and/or through choosing to disclose, depending on the context).

Attempts at self-protection might also apply in situations when TSD content is emotionally charged for therapists, as is the case when therapists are grieving or have been diagnosed with a serious illness. Peterson (2002) writes, "Vamos said, 'At the simplest level, it was some time before I felt in control of my emotional responses when talking of my husband's death, and I would have felt uncomfortable weeping openly in front of my patients' (p. 304)" (p. 29). Although acknowledging that the therapist's ability to discuss difficult personal experiences might provide benefit to clients, Peterson (2002) contends, "regardless of whether the therapist chooses to disclose or withhold information, he or she should work to minimize any potential harm to clients" (p. 29). In this manner, a therapist who is grieving might seek support with another professional or outside support network, and a practitioner experiencing illness could arrange for a colleague to provide back-up during absences. In addition, Peterson (2002) raises the question of whether therapists are indeed obligated to disclose personal information of a private nature, and writes, "the therapist must be comfortable and secure enough to acknowledge his or her need for privacy in a non-defensive manner and to help clients understand that decision" (p. 29). In all cases, the therapist's ability for self-reflection and clinical consideration regarding client welfare is the key to an ethical approach to TSD decision-making.

Using TSD with Adolescent Clients

What to Say

How therapy works. While informed consent procedures are important with every client population, explaining what to expect and how therapy works is particularly crucial with adolescents (Malekoff, 2004; Meeks & Bernet, 2001; Oetzel & Scherer, 2003; Richardson, 2001). Write Oetzel and Scherer (2003), "Adolescents, and sometimes their families, often have inaccurate impressions of psychotherapy and the therapy process, which are generally made by media and stereotype" (p. 222). Offering information to adolescent clients, such as, "Our sessions will last for about an hour each week, and mostly we'll talk about how things are going for you and what you'd like to see change," can reduce anxiety by letting adolescents know what to expect. Sharing other specifics, like telling adolescent clients that they can choose where (or whether) to sit in your office, or that it's okay to take a break if they need to use the restroom, further defines the 'rules' of the therapy process. Also, according to Oetzel and Scherer (2003), "Directly addressing the stigma associated with psychotherapy early in treatment is often necessary to engage adolescents" (p. 222). Communicating to clients that some symptoms and behaviors they worry about are within the normal range of experience, or that other adolescents struggle with similar problems, may decrease feelings of shame or embarrassment associated with participating in therapy (Oetzel & Scherer, 2003; Richardson, 2001). Casual interjections of, "'That sounds familiar,'" "'Welcome to the club,'" or "'So, what else is new?'" may be enough to normalize experiences for some adolescents (Richardson, 2001, p. 108). In order to understand what type of disclosures would be helpful to clients, therapists may sometimes need to pose questions. For instance, Baruch (2001) suggests asking adolescents to imagine what the future relationship between client and therapist might be like (i.e. how much will the client like or dislike the therapist, or what kinds of conversations will they have?), as a way of revealing fears or misconceptions.

Since young people are generally referred to therapy by their parents, schools or state agencies, another area of critical concern for adolescent clients is confidentiality (Baruch, 2001; Malekoff, 2004; Meeks & Bernet, 2001; Oetzel & Scherer, 2003; Richardson, 2001). For example, practitioners might state to adolescents: "Most people are curious whether I'll keep what we talk about private, that is, just between the two of us, or whether I'd tell their parents what we talk about. If you know ahead of time what I'd have to share with someone else then you won't feel like I've broken our confidence, and you can decide if there are things you're not ready to talk about."

Discussing confidentiality in clear and concrete terms not only informs adolescents that there are limits to privacy but also that they have a choice about what to share. Meeks and Bernet (2001) suggest asking adolescents, "'Of all the things we have talked about [today], what is okay to discuss with your parents and what things do you not want them to know about?'" (p. 53). While it's important to be open about parents' rights to know (in general) what problems are being addressed in therapy, what might help improve the situation and how serious it is, entering into dialogue with adolescent clients about specific therapy content increases the likelihood of informed consent with regard to confidentiality. In addition, therapists may reassure adolescent clients that nothing will be shared without their knowledge, and that if something must be reported, the therapist will focus on the facts rather than revealing a client's private feelings or statements (Baruch, 2001; Malekoff, 2004; Meeks & Bernet, 2001).

How you work. In addition to disclosing general information about the therapy process, practitioners working with adolescents may describe their own working style and how they view the therapist's role (Oetzel & Scherer, 2003; Richardson, 2001; Rubenstein, 1996). Writes Rubenstein, "I work for them and with them. They are the captain and I am the first mate" (p. 356). Using metaphors is an effective way of communicating role expectations to adolescent clients that avoids lengthy discourse that could be viewed as lecturing (Meeks & Bernet, 2001; Rubenstein, 1996). To show that he is open to TSD, Richardson (2001) suggests asking adolescents early in the session, "'Do you have any questions for me? [No?] Okay, let me know if you think of anything'" (p. 121). This not only demonstrates the therapist's willingness to self-disclose, but it also implies the client can assist in directing the flow of sessions. Another common type of TSD that is important with adolescent clients is the therapist's ability to admit mistakes (Malekoff, 2004; Richardson, 2001). Writes Malekoff (2004), "I confessed: 'I'm not sure I handled things right. I've been wondering what you thought about it'" (p. 332). A simple confession of this nature reveals many things to an adolescent client, including that the therapist: is human, doesn't always need to be right, reflects on what happens in sessions, and values the client's ideas.

Rubenstein (1996) recommends TSD's that communicate the client's freedom of choice. Writes Rubenstein (1996), "I usually begin by telling them about my three strikes and I'm out rule. In translation, it means that if, after three meetings, they do not see any point in coming, for whatever reason, I will support them" (p. 356). Other practitioners (Baruch, 2001; Meeks & Bernet, 2001; Oetzel & Scherer, 2003; Richardson, 2001) echo the importance of disclosing that the therapist will offer choices to adolescent clients. Baruch (2001) reports asking clients to commit to only six initial sessions, framing therapy as an experiment that is time-limited. Write Oetzel and Scherer (2003), "Allowing adolescents to choose their therapist, or giving them treatment options from which to choose, or offering them the choice of what to discuss in therapy may enhance the relevance of and motivation for psychotherapy... (Church, 1994; Hanna & Hunt, 1999; Liddle, 1995; Loar, 2001; Rubenstein, 1996)" (p. 222). Writes Baruch (2001), "I...posed it as a question 'how should we decide what to focus on?'" (p. 19). Although based on a broad definition of TSD, it is nonetheless clear that proposing options to adolescent clients can communicate how the therapist's personal style affects the therapy process.

Therapy-process related TSD may also include sharing assessment information or recommendations for additional services (Edgette, 1999; Meeks & Bernet, 2001; Richardson, 2001; Rubenstein, 1996). Writes Rubenstein (1996). "... I share with them [adolescent clients] everything I have been told about them; from parents, teachers, courts or whomever. I want them to know what I know. They have entered an uneven playing field. I want to level it..." (p. 356). Careful that this not backfire and be viewed as the therapist's pre-judging the adolescent, Richardson (2001) suggests saying, "'To be honest, I've only had time to glance at what was sent. And besides, I would rather hear your story'" (p. 121). Reviewing results from assessment tools, looking at school records, and being open about the referral source's concerns are also forms of TSD that effectively empower adolescent clients. In addition, providing referrals for other services may give practitioners an opportunity for TSD. Writes Rubenstein (1996), "Few adolescents are comfortable calling a place. Many more are willing to call a person, particularly if we can tell them something about who they are calling" (p. 359). Saying things like, "Oh yeah, Jeff is a good guy and he's really easy to talk to. Most of the young people I send to Jeff tell me he's really funny," reduces the adolescent client's anxiety about meeting a new person. Therapists must remember, however, not to paint a too-rosy picture of the colleague, as this could reduce the adolescent client's ability to trust disclosures in the future (Edgette, 1999).

Truth and values disclosure. Meeks and Bernet (2001) assert that a therapist has a "responsibility as an adult to offer his ethical conclusions [to adolescent clients]..." (p. 159). Richardson (2001) echoes this sentiment, writing, "We are not helping anyone if we deny the reality of living in a world with problems, consequences, and limitations" (p. 77). Truth and values-related TSD's with adolescent clients may include content about 'how the world works,' or may offer information regarding therapist values and/or boundaries (Edgette, 1999; Malekoff, 2004; Meeks & Bernet, 2001; Richardson, 2001). Rubenstein (1996) describes sharing knowledge about societal rules, writing, "I will tell them how I use my 'dress up' clothes to help insure my access to respect, attention and, when I need it, power. I want them to know how the adult world works" (p. 356). Not all TSD's about the world are as neutral, however. Write Meeks and Bernet (2001), "Adolescent patients frequently test the therapist's willingness to call a spade a spade. The adolescent who is engaging in behavior that is either extremely antisocial or very bizarre may ask the therapist's opinion about the seriousness of the problem" (p. 51). Indeed, 'acting out' is one of many ways that adolescent clients invite TSD, and may be, as Peterson (2002) points out, "aimed at identifying their place in the world" (p. 27). Writes Richardson (2001), "We need to find ways to reaffirm the youth's worthiness and also clearly communicate our expectations" (p. 77).

One example can be found in Edgette's (1999) description of working with an adolescent who was insistent her parents move back to their old neighborhood since the recent move had significantly upset her social life. Although careful to offer genuine empathy toward the adolescent, Edgette (1999) recounts eventually 'calling the client out,' by saying:

> "I can't imagine that anyone has a problem with Jenna being unhappy about the move," I told them at a family session. "What amazes me though, is Jenna's belief that you, her parents, would take her demand that you move back so seriously!" Jenna looked at me sharply... Seems no one had ever told Jenna that she can sometimes push the envelope too far and lose ground. (p. 41)

Luckily, the existence of a strong therapeutic alliance prevented this candid challenge from damaging the relationship, and Edgette (1999) describes how the adolescent was then able to move on to productive problem solving with parents around adjusting to the move. Take note, however, that the therapist merely expressed her sense that the client's stance was out of line with 'how the world works' —had the therapist literally said, 'You sometimes push the envelope too far,' it may have been counterproductive. Writes Edgette (1999), "I've found candor to do a better job of pressing. Same message, but you don't lose the kid" (p. 40).

In addition to providing TSD's about societal mores, practitioners who work with adolescents often find themselves faced with having to assert their own personal values or maintain appropriate boundaries. With regard to adolescent threats to break therapist, home or institutional rules, Richardson (2001) suggests ways of maintaining client choice while simultaneously disclosing limits—for example, by saying, "'If you do choose to run away, I will have to call the police'" or, "'That chair you are sitting on cost $75 and will need to be replaced if it is broken'" (Richardson, 2001, p. 78). At the same time, Richardson (2001) contrasts these positive responses with less effective ones, like "'I forbid you to leave this house'" and "'This is my office. You break that chair and you pay for it!'" (p. 78). The preferred statements are direct and non-coercive. As Edgette (1999) describes it, "The therapist sitting across the room isn't telling him what to do; she's just telling him what she thinks. And she's not even trying to make him agree" (p. 39). In validating adolescent choices, therapists must be careful not to tacitly condone antisocial or risky behavior (Edgette,

1999; Meeks & Bernet, 2001; Oetzel & Scherer, 2003; Richardson, 2001).

Sometimes challenges to therapist values are more direct and involve client attempts to enlist the therapist in dishonest or unethical activities (Meeks & Bernet, 2001; Oetzel & Scherer, 2003; Rubenstein, 1996). Meeks and Bernet (2001) present a case when an adolescent client told his mother the therapist recommended buying a 'flashy car' to enhance her son's self-esteem; based on this account, the mother gave her son a large sum of money. When the client asserted this was no big deal, the therapist replied, "'It isn't okay with me. I don't want to be part of your con game. Besides, you are throwing away your chances in therapy for a bunch of chrome and steel. I can't go along with that'" (p. 157). Rather than triggering adolescent authority issues, this type of frank, nonjudgmental disclosure of the therapist's values tends to intrigue adolescent clients, and invite more dialogue (Edgette, 1999; Meeks & Bernet, 2001). In the above case, the therapist was given the opportunity to say, "'Do you have any idea of how much that lousy car is really costing you? If you want to live the life of a con artist, that's your business, but let's at least be honest about what you're doing when you come here [to therapy]'" (p. 157).

Personal disclosures. Although there is wide-spread agreement that certain types of personal disclosures are inappropriate with adolescent clients (e.g. explicit sexual material, accounts of drug use that might be construed as glorification), some personal information may be shared with therapeutic results (Edgette, 1999; Meeks & Bernet, 2001; Oetzel & Scherer, 2003; Peterson, 2002; Richardson, 2001; Rosenberg, 2003). Furthermore, failing to answer questions posed by adolescent clients can be viewed as evidence that therapists are phony and can't be trusted (Edgette, 1999; Oetzel & Scherer, 2003; Peterson, 2002; Rubenstein, 1996). Modeling one's ability to trust someone with personal information can also communicate to adolescent clients that the therapist respects them, resulting in a stronger therapeutic alliance (Oetzel & Scherer, 2003; Peterson, 2002). Richardson describes using TSD to validate an adolescent's need for privacy and to build trust early in the relationship by saying, "'Sounds like you have to get to know someone before you tell them your business. Is that true? [Youth answers, 'Yeah'] I don't blame you. I'm that way too'" (p. 120). TSD's might also serve to inform adolescent clients about the therapist's temperament, valuable information for the client who has experienced explosive adult reactions or weak boundaries in the past. Meeks and Bernet (2001) describe a scenario with a client who attempts to intimidate the therapist, saying, "'What would you do if I came over there and knocked the shit out of you?'" (p. 322). Rather than be tricked into ending the session or making a power play, the therapist replies honestly that, "' I'd holler for all the help I could get. I don't see that hitting me would help you. I'd try to get enough people here to keep you from hurting me or getting hurt yourself'" (p. 322). This personal disclosure seems genuine in that the therapist admits he would need help defending himself, and that his concern would remain on keeping the client safe. TSD's recounting how the therapist overcame obstacles in the past may have beneficial effects with adolescent clients (Baruch, 2001; Malekoff, 2004; Meeks & Bernet, 2001; Peterson, 2002; Richardson, 2001). In addition to potentially normalizing client experiences, adolescents who identify with the therapist strongly enough may be induced to adopt new strategies in addressing similar problems. Malekoff (2004) writes, "I became acutely aware that my own experience was lurking in the back of my mind the whole time…The question of self-disclosure is always tricky" (p. 244). When attempting to convince an adolescent client that he should seek emergency medical treatment after a fight, Malekoff (2004) successfully used TSD to convey the potential seriousness of the client's injuries as well as to free the adolescent from having to admit weakness in seeking help. The model provided by the therapist gave the adolescent permission to make a different choice without risking his autonomy (Baruch, 2001; Malekoff, 2004; Meeks & Bernet, 2001).

In-session disclosures. In-session disclosures include content related to the practitioner's immediate experience of what is happening during therapy, and are generally considered to be less risky than personal disclosures, since they reinforce a focus on the client and/or the therapeutic relationship (Oetzel & Scherer, 2003; Peterson, 2002). Therapists may comment directly about something the adolescent client shares, might express how they are feeling toward the client, or may be an attempt to offer an alternative view of the adolescent's problem (Edgette, 1999; Meeks & Bernet, 2001; Oetzel & Scherer, 2003; Peterson, 2002; Richardson, 2001). Writes Edgette (1999), "We'd talk about whatever was happening in the moment: the fact that we had nothing to talk about; his belief that he didn't have any problems to talk about; the problems he thought *other* kids talked about in session" (p. 40). Although as Malekoff (2004) points out, people sometimes view this type of work with adolescents and wonder, 'where is the therapy in that?' being with clients 'where they are' in the moment lays a foundation for the rare and life-changing times when adolescents will actively seek support for more serious problems. It's unlikely an adolescent client will ever enter your office and say, 'I've really been looking forward to our session today because I've got a problem I need your help on.' What is more often the case is that after forty minutes of fits and starts, and listening to a story about what happened in the cafeteria that day, your client will casually say something like, 'Well, my mom kicked me out last Saturday and I've been sleeping on the couch at Jack's house. I had to wear these jeans three days in a row, but it's cool.' The point is, despite the practitioner's laudable drive to maximize each therapy hour and accomplish measurable progress toward treatment goals, with adolescent clients, sometimes taking the long way around is the best route to where you want to go; if the only way you can get them to stay with you is to talk about the birds that are dancing outside your window, so be it (Edgette, 1999; Malekoff, 2004; Meeks & Bernet, 2001; Richardson, 2001). In the absence of meaningful discourse, talking about anything teaches adolescents they are capable of connecting

248

and that you're there with them (Edgette, 1999).

Perhaps the most important role TSD can play for adolescents in therapy is to counterbalance their view of the world with alternative perspectives (Baruch, 2001; Edgette, 1999; Meeks & Bernet, 2001). Although this might be done with truth- and values-disclosures (discussed previously), other times the therapist may choose to reflect on an in-session reaction, saying something like, "I'm confused. You're talking about this fight like it's no big deal but you once told me that Tammy's your best friend, the only one you can talk to. Can you help me 'get' this?" Meeks and Bernet (2001) suggest observing that the client is describing a difficult scene "as though he were recounting a story about a friend" and then wondering aloud "why [he] is so disinterested in [his] own welfare" (p. 51). Disclosing genuine curiosity when a client's story has contrasting elements suggests to adolescents that a more favorable perspective could apply to the situation, and may give them permission to admit stronger feelings that the client feared were unacceptable (Baruch, 2001; Edgette, 1999; Meeks & Bernet, 2001).

Challenging client perspectives might also occur through more direct TSD's when the therapist offers personal interpretation of a client's situation. Telling adolescents what you think is 'really going on' is most effective when a positive therapeutic relationship has already been established, and you are able to candidly state an opinion without triggering client shame or defensiveness (Baruch, 2001; Edgette, 1999; Malekoff, 2004; Meeks & Bernet, 2001; Richardson, 2001). Writes Edgette (1999), "'Tell her that you think she's gotten herself painted deep in a corner—that perhaps she actually wouldn't mind going back to school, if she could find a way to make it *her* choice'" (p. 41). The skillful therapist chooses words carefully, offering a tentative explanation that leaves room for the possibility of future solutions. Saying something like, "Wow, that's such a dilemma, because on the one hand if you do what your mom wants it's like admitting that she's right, but I also see you're not psyched about being around Mark and Sean when they're drunk," indicates an ability to see the adolescent's perspective while still acknowledging the client's right to choose how to respond. The next logical question is, "What do you think you'll do about it?" TSD's that accurately reflect to clients what you know about them as a person may help to reinforce positive aspects of their identity (Meeks & Bernet, 2001; Oetzel & Scherer, 2003; Richardson, 2001).

Another type of in-session TSD that includes nonjudgmental observation relates to the interpersonal dynamics occurring between client and therapist (Edgette, 1999; Meeks & Bernet, 2001; Richardson, 2001). When utterly stumped about how to proceed, Edgette (1999) reports plainly saying, "'What a crazy situation we've gotten ourselves into. After weeks of meeting, we still don't know how to have a simple conversation with each other. Don't you think that's crazy?'" (pp. 39-40). This frank acknowledgement that they were both struggling exposed the 'elephant in the room' and freed them to relax with each other (Edgette, 1999). In addition, practitioners may use TSD to express caring for adolescent clients as well as un-easiness with risky behaviors. Writes Richardson (2001), "it is often a good starting point to offer a personal statement of concern—but only if we mean it. Don't forget, kids know" (p. 76). Saying something like, "I really care about you and right now I'm feeling concerned," communicates positive regard to clients while at the same time suggesting the therapist would like to see things change (Meeks & Bernet, 2001; Richardson, 2001). Since adolescents often feel misunderstood and defensive about their problems, clients may have difficulty accepting therapist support; however, Richardson (2001) writes, "If we offer a genuine statement of concern, it will often be appreciated and remembered even when their initial reaction suggests otherwise (p. 76).

How to Say it

Share power. As Edgette (1999) points out, "the art of authenticity with kids looks easy enough to master: you track your experience of the session and of your client, and you selectively share it" (p. 41). However, given the importance of autonomy for adolescents, accurately assessing a client's level of development is the key to choosing appropriate TSD's (Edgette, 1999; Oetzel & Scherer, 2003; Peterson, 2002). Writes Edgette (1999), "...it [therapy] needs to respect their na-tures—proud, sensitive to criticism, wanting contact and care as long as it isn't too obvious—at the same time that it commands respect in return for being an honest and purposeful process" (p. 56). Healthy adolescent development encompasses a broad range of abilities and does not always proceed in a straightforward manner (Baruch, 2001; Malekoff, 2004; Meeks & Bernet, 2001; Oetzel & Scherer, 2003; Richardson, 2001). For example, some adolescents may demonstrate advanced rea-soning skills while social abilities are slow to develop, or may be able to apply skills in some settings but not others, acting one way at home but differently at school or in therapy (Oetzel & Scherer, 2003). Therefore, what pushes one adolescent's 'autonomy button' may have a very different effect on another client of the same age. Write Oetzel and Scherer (2003), "cognitively immature adolescents require...con-crete examples, and guidance in how to establish therapeutic rapport. On the other hand, talking too concretely to an adolescent who prefers higher order reasoning may result in the adolescent's feeling infantilized" (p. 220). In addition, therapists may want to consider an adolescent's attachment style when trying to engage clients in therapy (Baruch, 2001; Oetzel & Scherer, 2003). Understanding how an ado-lescent client might perceive the therapist's attempts at alliance building, as well as how the adolescent responds to being in a heightened emotional state, can provide helpful cues regarding whether TSD will have a positive effect on clients (Baruch, 2001; Davis, 2002; Oetzel & Scherer, 2003; Peterson, 2002; Richardson, 2001).

Despite the fact that adolescents are still mastering the ability for advanced reasoning, most adolescent clients appreciate the opportunity to explore their ideas and debate value systems through open dialogue (Malekoff, 2004; Meeks & Bernet, 2001; Oetzel & Scherer, 2003; Richardson, 2001). Writes Richardson (2001), "Youth want counselors who are honest and genuine; however, they do not want someone who believes they have all the answers. Any conversation that resembles a lecture will often be tuned out" (p. 33). Edgette (1999) warns against "rolling out the latest treatment technique for xyz disorder—a disorder that a teenager may not even believe he or she has, much less think is even marginally relevant" (p. 38). Although adolescents' dangerous behaviors trigger fearful, and sometimes overbearing, adult responses, fostering adolescents' ability to weigh the options themselves ultimately increases their safety more than lecturing or coercive tactics (Edgette, 1999; Malekoff, 2004; Richardson, 2001). Writes Edgette (1999):

> We do best when we invite youngsters, through our candor, to take a different look at themselves with no obligation. They learn that temporarily suspending their world view doesn't mean they're giving up or giving in. No one is going to pounce on their attempts to explore and then hold them to that path. They can go back. They're not stuck *even if they were to agree that another way could be a better way.* (p. 56)

TSD's that originate from an objective stance and encourage flexible thinking represent developmentally appropriate interventions with adolescent clients.

Maintaining a neutral stance, though, not only promotes better decision making in adolescent clients, it also allows the therapist to access 'power with' a client (Baruch, 2001; Edgette, 1999; Meeks & Bernet, 2001; Richardson, 2001; Rosenberg, 2003). Edgette (1999) describes how working with adolescents sometimes resembles riding horses, writing, "Both processes involve influencing without frank displays of power, yet come quickly and horribly undone by tentativeness" (p. 39). Here is where beginning therapists are most at risk, as a lack of confidence in professional abilities may be subtly conveyed to clients through a self-conscious bearing. The ability to cultivate inner assurance—the Zen of Adolescent Therapy —if expressed through genuine use of TSD, can be a practitioner's saving grace. Therapists who are relaxed enough to laugh at themselves, and centered enough to step blithely around adolescent traps, demonstrate both confidence and trustworthiness. Write Meeks and Bernet (2001), "Adolescents…are very critical of adults who are too stiff and self-important" (p. 50). Richardson (2001) describes a scene when an adolescent client in therapy group "opened his hand, revealed a hundred little pieces of paper, which used to be his [behavior] card, sprinkled the pieces on my head and said, 'Here, Brent, sign this!'" (p. 27). Rather than take the bait, Richardson wisely started laughing and congratulated the adolescent on 'a good one.' Writes Richardson (2001), "In this line of work, there's too much big stuff to sweat the small stuff. Laugh at yourself. Laugh at funny situations. Laugh with… adolescents, not *at* them" (p. 50). The ability to choose a response that honors the playful nature of adolescents discloses to the client a willingness to follow their lead in the therapy dance (Meeks & Bernet, 2001; Richardson, 2001).

Show me. Finally, because challenging adolescents are pre-disposed to distrust what adults say, TSD's with adolescent clients must move beyond lip-service and transform into action in order to make a lasting impression (Edgette, 1999; Malekoff, 2004; Richardson, 2001; Rubenstein, 1996). Rubenstein (1996) offers several examples of how to demonstrate genuineness to clients through action, including: setting up a comfortable office with no desk to hide behind; meeting with clients at school or attending a court date for support; inviting a client's friend to join the session if it's relevant to exploring issues; and dressing comfortably, often in jeans or bright colors. Practitioners who are skilled at forming therapeutic alliances with adolescents act in ways that disclose their willingness to put the client's needs before their own, even when it contradicts the norms of adult culture (Edgette, 1999; Malekoff, 2004; Richardson, 2001; Rubenstein, 1996). Rubenstein (1996) describes what I consider to be a brilliant move, one that costs very little and yet accomplishes so much:

> I know of few adolescents who do not consider eating to be their first priority when they finally get out of school or get off from work. Therefore, my first therapeutic intervention is simply to feed them. With this in mind, I have stocked a small, closet-like room, which is separate from my office, with juice drinks, chips, pretzels, granola bars, and the like…It delivers a short but powerful message about the availability of nurturance. (p. 355)

In addition to demonstrating that the therapist cares about a client's needs (and tastes), a ritual of this kind starts the relationship off in more neutral territory, gives the adolescent a chance to casually observe the therapist, briefly delays the start of 'dreaded' therapy, and provides an outlet for nervous energy when at last entering the office (Rubenstein, 1996). Although most likely saying very little, the therapist instantly discloses that therapy might contain both interesting and valuable tidbits.

Conclusion

Adolescents are a challenging population to engage in treatment, and warrant continued attention in therapy process literature. Adolescent client needs for genuineness and authenticity dictate willingness on the part of practitioners to engage in TSD both early on and throughout therapy, as a way of engaging clients and forming therapeutic alliances. Consideration of developmental factors in adolescence is critical to the appropriate implementation of TSD with this population; however, therapists who focus on developing positive regard for clients and, what Edgette (1999) calls, 'benevolent candor' will quickly learn to master the steps required for entering the adolescent world. By carefully revealing oneself through the dynamics of TSD, practitioners may hope to model a healthy self-image, qualities of trustworthiness, and a path toward healing.

References

Baruch, G. (2001). *Community-based psychotherapy with young people: Evidence and innovation in practice*. Philadelphia, PA: Taylor & Francis, Inc..

Burkard, A. W., Knox, S., Groen, M., Perez, M., & Hess, S. A. (2006). European American therapist self-disclosure in cross-cultural counseling. *Journal of Counseling Psychology*, v53, n1, pp. 15-25. Retrieved September 8, 2007 from EBSCO Host database.

Curtis, R., Field, C., Knaan-Kostman, I., & Mannix, K. (2004). What 75 psychoanalysts found helpful and hurtful in their own analyses. *Psychoanalytic Psychology*, v21, n2, pp. 183-202. Retrieved September 8, 2007 from EBSCO Host database.

Davis, J. T. (2002). Countertransference temptation and the use of self-disclosure by psychotherapists in training. *Psychoanalytic Psychology*, v19, n3, pp. 435-454. Retrieved September 8, 2007 from EBSCO Host database.

Edgette, J. S. (1999). Getting real: Candor and connection with adolescents. *Family Therapy Networker*, v23, n5, p. 36. Retrieved September 8, 2007 from EBSCO Host database.

Kim, B. S., Hill, C. E., Gelso, C. J., Goates, M. K., Asay, P. A., & Harbin, J. M. (2003). Counselor self-disclosure, East Asian American client adherence to Asian cultural values, and counseling process. *Journal of Counseling Psychology*, v50, n3, pp. 324-332. Retrieved September 8, 2007 from EBSCO Host database.

Klein, M. H., Kolden, G. G., Michels, J. L., & Chisholm-Stockard, S. (2001). Congruence or genuineness. *Psychotherapy: Theory, Research, Practice, Training*, v38, n4, pp. 396-400. Retrieved September 8, 2007 from EBSCO Host database.

Malekoff, A. (2004). *Group work with adolescents: Principals and practice* (2nd ed.). New York: The Guilford Press.

Meeks, J. E., & Bernet, W. (2001). *The fragile alliance: An orientation to psychotherapy of the adolescent* (5th ed.). Malabar, FL: Krieger Publishing Company.

Myers, D., & Hayes, J. A. (2006). Effects of therapist general self-disclosure and countertransference disclosure on ratings of the therapist and session. *Psychotherapy:Theory, Research, Practice, Training*, v43, n2, pp. 173-185. Retrieved September 8, 2007 from EBSCO Host database.

Oetzel, K. B., & Scherer, D. G. (2003). Therapeutic engagement with adolescents in psychotherapy. *Psychotherapy: Theory, Research, Practice, Training*, v40, n3, pp. 215-225. Retrieved September 8, 2007 from EBSCO Host database.

Peterson, Z. D. (2002). More than a mirror: The ethics of therapist self-disclosure.

Psychotherapy: Theory, Research, Practice, Training, v39, n1, pp. 21-31. Retrieved September 8, 2007 from EBSCO Host database.

Richardson, B. (2001). *Working with challenging youth: Lessons learned along the way*. Philadelphia, PA: Brunner Routledge.

Rosenberg, M. B. (2003). *Raising children compassionately: Parenting the nonviolent communication way*. Encinitas, CA: Puddle Dancer Press.

Rubenstein, A. (1996). Interventions for a scattered generation: Treating adolescents in the nineties. *Psychotherapy: Theory, Research, Practice, Training, v33, n3*, pp. 353-360. Retrieved September 8, 2007 from EBSCO Host database.

Counseling the Geriatric Client
By: Terry Ruby, Ph.D.

"…Above all, now is the time to alleviate the suffering of older people with mental disorders and to prepare for the growing numbers of elders who may need mental health services" (**Administration on Aging, 2000**).

At what age does one classify a client as geriatric? Is 65-years old a magic entry into old age? Aging is a ubiquitous process; it is happening to everyone and continues to happen until death. How to grow old with grace and dignity? How to compress illness to the last days of life? How to insure the highest quality of life into old age? These universal questions have individual answers. The answers depend on a complex array of variables, some which can be controlled and some which control.

By virtue of statistics if you do not have an elder on your caseload at this time, the chances are in the next five years you will, unless you are exclusively a child practitioner. In any case you may have an elder in your life who you witnessed growing old or you may want to be proactive about your own aging. This chapter offers insights and quality of life measurements to guide the counselor working with the elder population. It also offers these same guidelines as personal awareness to your own aging process. Getting old is a good thing; getting sick is not.

The older population is on the threshold of a boom. According to the United States Bureau of Census projections, a substantial increase in the number of older people will occur during the 2010 to 2030 period, after the first baby boomers turn 65 in 2011 (He, Sengupta, Velkoff, & DeBarros, 2005). A well-functioning, healthy, active older citizen contributes a host of services to the community. This same person requires less in the way of economic and medical assistance. Behavioral and preventive medicine researchers have documented scientific evidence to justify telling patients their mental attitudes can affect their health (Kubzansky, Sparrow, Vokonas, & Kawachi, 2001).

There is a growing problem in the quality of life of the aging population of our nation. Currently, research about healthy aging is capturing news headlines and mass media (Cruikshank, 2003; Dannefer, 2000: Holstein & Gubrium; 2000: Katz, 2000). However, there persists an epidemic of obesity, heart disease, diabetes, and depression in this very population (Colcombe & Kramer, 2003). This gap between knowledge and application impacts both the current generation of elders and the upcoming baby boom generation, which will exponentially increase our senior population (Birren & Schaie, 2001). The impact of poor quality of life for elders encompasses individual suffering, medical demand, and economic burden (Strawbridge, Deleger, Roberts, & Kaplan, 2002). There are many factors contributing to this problem, among which are limited, practical knowledge about healthy aging, barriers to accessing comprehensive geriatric healthcare, apathy on the part of elders about the aging process, and cultural norms associated with aging (Friedan, 1993: Fry, 2001; Hay & LaBree, 2002).

Role of Health-Related Beliefs in Counseling Elders

Mental health counselors are trained to acknowledge the role culture plays in diagnosing and treating clients. Connecting health-related beliefs and culture to elders who experience depression, anxiety, pain, psychoses, and personality disorders are increasingly important components of effective counseling interventions. Often, elders are not aware that they have specific health-related beliefs that affect their choices related to health decisions. Four approaches to health-related beliefs are outlined below.

The Health-Belief Model

The health-belief model helps to explain the relationship between beliefs and attitudes about health behaviors, such as optimal adjustment to aging and quality of life. There are two dimensions to the health-belief model: the impetus to take a health action and the path of action. The impetus to take action is related to the client's beliefs about his/her susceptibility to chronic disease or age-related emotional adjustments. Educating clients about the risk factors associated with emotional conditions of aging can delay the onset and provide the stimulus to take a health action such as beginning a regular exercise program for physical and emotional well-being. Another action-oriented behavior centers on recognizing the differences among independence, dependence and interdependence especially as it relates to aging. The concept of interdependence helps elders reconcile the adjustment to inevitable life changes secondary to the aging process. Interdependence represents the dynamics of a healthy life style. For example, when an elder strives for independence he/she may appear rigid; a dependent elder may be considered malleable; an interdependent senior demonstrates flexibility. The rigid and malleable characteristics lead to feelings of isolation and apathy, which can be interpreted as failures. These failures in later life contribute to anxiety, loss of self-esteem, and depression.

The preferred path of action is related to the client's belief about the benefits and barriers to positive health changes. The client must believe the proposed program is worth participation and there are no barriers to participation. Does the client believe that talking about his/her feelings only makes them worse? Does the client consider mental health care only for those who are "really crazy?" If the client agrees to services, can s/he secure transportation to the counseling center? These questions affect an elder's decision to seek mental health care and alert the counselor to potential obstacles to effective care.

The Social Cognitive Model

Social cognitive or self-efficacy helps to explain another example of health-related behaviors. This model suggests that behavior is determined by expectancies about what happens next, expectancies about the outcome of a behavior, expectancies about one's own competence to perform a behavior, and incentives about the value of a particular outcome (Rosenstock, Strecher, & Becker 1988). Expectancies about what happens next are related to a client's perception of his or her susceptibility to age-related conditions such as depression and adjustments to physical and emotional losses. A client's expectancies about his or her ability to perform a behavior are referred to as self-efficacy.

Self-efficacy is one's belief that s/he is able to perform a specific behavior: in this case demonstrate a positive attitude about aging. Those with higher self-efficacy are more likely to manifest a positive adjustment to the aging process (Rowe & Kahn, 1998). Self-efficacy theory can facilitate a client's participation in counseling by questioning the client about past health behaviors and discussing the positive or negative outcomes associated with these behaviors. Defining the client's strengths by using past successes bolsters the energy necessary to take on present issues.

The Transtheorectical Model

A third model of health-related behaviors is the transtheoretical model, delineating stages of change that can be applied to aging gracefully. This model was developed by Prochaska to explain the stages individuals experience prior to making a health-behavior change (Prochaska & Velicer, 1997). This model outlines five stages in the process of changing behaviors: (a) precontemplation, (b) contemplation, (c) preparation, (d) action, and (e) maintenance. Accurate staging of the client will facilitate effective treatment planning. Smoking cessation programs often use this model. Does the elder have no intention of quitting (precontemplation) or has s/he thought about quitting but doesn't have a plan in place (contemplation)? Both of these stages are future oriented and become ideas to include in a treatment plan. However, does the client have nicotine patches and/or smoking cessation medication at home (preparation); did the client indicate a date on the calendar to mark the beginning of the cessation program (action)? The preparation and action stages of health-behavior changes allow interaction with the counselor to focus on goal setting, define social supports, and formulate contracts and commitments. The maintenance stage represents six months or more of a sustained behavior change. If achieved, this accomplishment can then be applied to another problematic behavior as a prototype for success.

Intrinsic and Extrinsic Factors Related to Health Behaviors

Intrinsic and extrinsic factors related to the client also affect health behaviors. Intrinsic factors might include biomedical characteristics, personality attributes, and psychological makeup. Biomedical factors such as comorbidity can lead to poor adherence (Boyette, Lloyd, Boyette, Watkins, Furbush, & Dunbar, 2002). Frequently missed appointment attributed to physical illnesses and multiple medical appointments occur often with the elderly population. Positive attitudes and outlook about one's ability to manage the changes of aging relate to better participation in the counseling process. However, negative personality attributes, whether life-long or of recent onset, help to define the work of counseling. Psychological factors such as high levels of depression, anxiety, and confusion present more of a challenge for the counselor. Every elder has encountered and managed some hardship in life. Using past experiences and recalling emotionally stronger times feed a sense of integrity. These attitudes and thought processes are necessary for successful aging.

Extrinsic or environmental characteristics include the level of motivational feedback in the counseling design. Studies have demonstrated how the use of motivational feedback by the program director, participants, or, in this case, the counselor significantly improved participation (Lazarus, 1966; Merrill, 1994). Extrinsic influences that are counselor based include confidence, enthusiasm, trustworthiness, warmth, genuineness, and empathy. Social support from family and/or friends is another important extrinsic consideration.

Quality of Life Measurements

In the interplay of elder mental health, social health, perceived health and self-esteem, anxiety, depression, the combination of depression and anxiety, pain, and disability combine to form many considerations of quality of life measures. Awareness of these diverse elements adds depth to the counseling process.

Mental Health

Mental health care for elders rarely becomes a priority unless a manifest mental illness is evident. Addressing mental health issues of aging when they first present saves health care dollars and improves the quality of life of the elder. A Harvard Medical School Division on Aging study tested the hypothesis that among community-dwelling older adults with relatively low and high socioeconomic status (SES), low SES is associated with both poor emotional well-being and physical function (Rios, Abdulah, Wei, & Hausdorff , 2001). The authors found that health status was not significantly different in the two groups. However, in contrast, participants with low SES tended to have an increased tendency towards depression. According to the authors, this effect may be due to different compensatory mechanisms. Compensatory mechanisms or defense mechanisms are any behavior pattern that protects the psyche from anxiety, shame, or guilt (Birren & Schaie, 2001). The implication is that the lower SES group had fewer compensatory mechanisms. These deficits can be positively affected with the counseling process.

Gradual memory decline is part of normal aging. Many elders believe falsely that they have poor memory or worry that they have dementia. Loss of memory is influenced by physical health, lifestyle habits, and education (Kawashima, 2005). Most older people are capable of maintaining an adequate memory by exercising their minds frequently and using appropriate memory skills. Mental health counselors can assist elders in distinguishing the difference between normal forgetting and dementia by completing the Mini Mental State Examination and using the age and educational norms to score the results. Also, discussing the difference between "where are the keys" as opposed to "what are the keys," assures elders who are not demented.

Social Health

Social health, according to some researchers, (Kawamoto, Doi, Yamada, Oguni, Okayama, & Tsuruoka 1999; Kennedy, 2000; Masuchi & Kishi, 2001) exemplifies the most essential ingredient in elder health. They refer to the need to reduce isolation and encourage social interaction. Consider what it takes to be social; one must have some functional memory, ability to communicate, and desire to stay connected to others. Elder housing complexes offer opportunities for independent living as well as built-in socialization.

Studies that focus on the social, economic, emotional, and spiritual contexts of aging call for policy changes that reflect the need for affordable and quality healthcare that includes all these aspects of aging (Nampudakam, 1999). The author recommends any policy for the aged should aim at addressing physical and social health problems from the beginning of the age continuum to enable people to grow old with minimal disability and chronic disease. The American Mental Health Counselor Association has an active legal advocacy network, which alerts members to pertinent legislation (www.amhc.org).

Perceived Health and Self-Esteem

Perceived health and self-esteem are considerations in the counseling process with all ages; however, with the elder client self-perception of aging influences pre-

259

ventive health behaviors (Levy & Myers, 2004). Self-esteem, expressed as a sense of self, impacts the aging process. Recognizing that healthy aging includes a variety of losses, perceived health and self-esteem are topics of importance when treating elders. Validating the losses may be the beginning of establishing the counseling relationship. Helping the client to move on to the task of living with his or her losses becomes the work of counseling.

A Spanish study (Azpiazu, Cruz, Villagrasa, Abanades, Garcia, & Valero de Bernabe, 2002) was designed to identify the main factors, which have an impact on the quality of life and the perceived health conditions of those over age 65. Main factors related to the perception of poor health condition and poor quality of life were anxiety disorders, depressive disorders, lack of exercise, and dependence for basic everyday living activities. The authors concluded that mental health functioning capacities are the factors that have the greatest bearing on the perception of health condition and quality of life of an individual over age 65. Why does one elder with multiple comorbidities see the possibilities when a similar elder sees the obstacles? The counseling process can facilitate an elder's focus on his or her remaining strengths and how those strengths can be nurtured to add quality of life to each day. A famous quote from Satchel Paige comes to mind, "How old would you be if you didn't know how old you were?"

Anxiety

Anxiety and depression are the most frequently diagnosed mental health illnesses among the elder population. Research on both the course and treatment of anxiety in older adults lags behind that of other mental health conditions such as depression and Alzheimer's disease. Until recently, anxiety disorders were believed to decline with age (Sampson, 2006). However, current research shows that aging and anxiety are not correlated. Anxiety is as common in the old as in the young, although how and when it appears is distinctly different in older adults (Sampson).

Older adults with an anxiety disorder had some level of anxiety when they were younger (Lang & Stein, 2001). According to the authors, elders managed their early-life anxiety by manipulating the environment, perhaps by avoiding situations or by having a spouse perform certain activities. Late-life stressors and vulnerabilities unique to the aging process, such as chronic physical problems, cognitive impairments, and significant emotional losses may manifest as late-life anxiety disorders. Older persons are less likely to report psychiatric symptoms and more likely to emphasize their physical complaints (Robichaud & Lamarre, 2002). Separating a medical condition from the physical symptoms of an anxiety disorder is more complicated in the older adult. Anxiety may manifest itself in cognitive symptoms (extreme frustration and fear of losing control), behavioral symptoms (restlessness and hyperkinesis), or physical symptoms (sweating and palpitations) (Lang & Stein, 2001). These same authors suggest that an anxiety disorder should be considered in any elder with depressive symptoms or with physical symptoms that are not explained by a physical problem. Counselors treating elders with anxiety disorders should address both physical and emotional symptoms, such as the ability to concentrate, comfort around others, sleep, fatigue, and nervousness.

Depression

Diagnosing and treating depression in elders has improved (Birren & Schaie, 2001; Crimmins, 2004). The challenge for elders and their healthcare providers focuses on discriminating among presented somatic physical symptoms, which may mask depression. From another perspective, some researchers have studied optimism as a means of protecting elders from depression. Dispositional optimism has been linked in previous studies to better health and outcomes (Achat, Kawachi, Spiro, DeMolles, & Sparrow, 2000). This Harvard School of Public Health study examined the independent association of dispositional optimism and depressive symptoms. The findings for optimism and depression were statistically significant, and optimism and depression were determined to be independent predictors of functional status among aging men (Achet et al., 2000). Addressing the role of optimism in healthy aging and setting treatment goals centered on optimism would be appropriate for most elders seeking mental health care.

Anxiety and Depression Combined

Oftentimes depression and anxiety manifest simultaneously, or one may lead to the other (Jeste, Alexopoulos, Bartels, Cummings, Gallo, & Gottlieb, 1999). The consequences of these disease processes negatively affect the elder as well as his/her friends, family, healthcare providers, and the healthcare system at large. A Japanese study (Kawamoto et al., 1999) suggested that improving certain background factors with health, medical, and welfare services will alone show an improvement in depressive and anxiety states of community-dwelling older persons. Without a personal connection or a more sustaining contribution to personal change, which a counselor can offer, these background factors may represent a symptom, not a cause of depression in the elderly.

Pain

Pain affects quality of life. Impaired life quality secondary to pain can lead to depression, anxiety, and increased suicide (Hunter, 2005). Effective treatment of pain in older people requires specialized knowledge and training in pain management. A number of factors make it potentially difficult to effectively treat pain in the elderly. Psychological factors, as well as drug interactions, are some considerations when reviewing current medications of an elder. The psychological aspects of pain management in the elderly should demand as much attention as the medical aspects of pain management (Hunter, 2005). Addiction to pain medications should always be a consideration and should not be ruled out because the client is older.

Disability

The picture of disability is changing. Disabled people of all ages join the mainstream in society and now have legal grounds to demand accessibility. Elders might find early or late onset disability physically and emotionally less challenging based on more acceptable and accessible environments. Living with a disability and emotional vitality are no longer mutually exclusive. The protective effect of emotional vitality on adverse health outcomes in disabled older women was studied at Wake Forest University School of Medicine, Winston-Salem, North Carolina (Phenninx, Guralnik, Bandeen-Roche, Kasper, Simonsick, & Ferrucci, 2000). The findings suggest positive emotions can protect older persons with manifest disabilities against adverse health outcomes. Acknowledging a late-life disability for some elders raises the risk of developing depression and anxiety disorders. Mental health counselors who establish a relationship with medical providers who treat elders can facilitate the potential for elder referrals. It is a well-studied phenomenon that most elders present to their medical providers with somatic symptoms regardless of the origin of the pain or complaint.

Clinical Considerations in Treating Elder Clients

The challenges to treating elders begin before they arrive for the initial intake. Accessibility to care might include stigma, transportation, denial of need, lack of information about available care, financial hardship, abusive living arrangement, and extreme frailty. Once an elder agrees to treatment what considerations should come to mind when engaging with elders in the counseling process? Transference and countertransference studies with elders and counselors raise the consciousness of expectations and the dynamics of the counseling relationship. Treatment plans for elders differ in some ways from those designed for a young or middle-aged adult. The life-review process and reminiscence assist elders in summarizing and presenting pertinent information that drives treatment goals. Coordinating care across the continuum of healthcare becomes essential with elders. Exploring Erikson's (1982) stage of late life adds depth to a counselor's geriatric knowledge. These subjects will be considered from a clinical perspective in this section.

Accessibility to Elder Mental Health Care

Before an elder arrives for counseling, or in the case of homecare, when the counselor arrives at the elder's home, much consideration or coordination of care from the medical, familial, and possibly social service agencies has already taken place. This can facilitate or sensitize the elder to the counseling process. Being aware of basic needs to participate in counseling becomes the initial focus; can the elder hear and see to his or her best potential? Can the elder understand and sign releases to communicate with all necessary parties? A minimal cognitive evaluation, such as the Mini Mental State Examination, should be routine in an elder evaluation. Information about recent medical interventions, a complete list of all prescribed and over-the-counter medications, including home remedies, should be noted.

Accessibility may center on transportation; many elders rely on family members who work during the day for rides to appointments. Home visits, local senior ride programs, or social service agencies that sponsor volunteer ride programs may help get the elder to the counseling center.

It is a well-documented phenomenon that elders usually present to the primary care provider with somatic complaints when the main issues are depression, anxiety, or both. Denial on the part of the elder, as well as lack of information about elder-focused mental health care, prevents elders from seeking, recognizing the need, and obtaining necessary services.

Another accessibility issue is financial; Medicare co-payments for mental health services are not at parity with medical co-payments. Elders must pay a 50% co-payment for outpatient mental health services; visits to other types of care require a 20% co-payment. The American Psychiatric Association and other mental health organizations regularly advocate in Congress to end Medicare's higher cost for mental health care (Daly, 2007).

Elder abuse and extreme frailty represent other areas of accessibility obstacles. Much work has been accomplished in the area of recognizing and reporting elder abuse, but abuse at all levels still exists. Mail delivery persons, neighbors, hairdressers, bank personal, and others can make anonymous reports to elder abuse hotlines. Timely responses are demanded by law and usually result with the elder being connected to a variety of services, including counseling.

Engaging in the Counseling Process

Reducing barriers to treatment begins with recognizing the stigma attached to mental health intervention. Most elders respond to a more conversational approach, to statements that imply adding quality to life, to facilitating communication among healthcare providers, and to securing community services if needed. Stigma is reduced further with a life review or reminisce method of treatment. Butler (1963) defined and described the life review process as "a naturally occurring, universal mental process" with certain characteristics that help recall past life events. For some individuals the life review is experienced only as brief insignificant thoughts. For others, the process may take the form of mild nostalgia or regret. Still for others, it can be experienced as anxiety, guilt, and/or depression. Contraindications to using the life review process, as identified by Butler (1963), are elders who look to the future and avoid the past and present, individuals who have severely and consciously injured others (guilt is real), and the narcissistic elders who interpret late life as an insurmountable threat.

Another strategy for engaging elders in treatment involves Erikson's theory that aging represents a stage of development. The later adulthood stage, as identified by Erikson (1982) is represented by the psychological crisis of integrity versus despair. This stage begins when the elder experiences a sense of mortality. This may be triggered by retirement, the death of a spouse or close friend, or may simply result from a changing social or familial role. Like the life review, the elder considers his/her life career to determine if it is was a success or a failure. According to Erikson (1982), this reminiscence or introspection is most productive when experienced with significant others. The mental health counselor may play the part of an objective significant other and one to whom the elder trusts information kept hidden from family and friends.

Ego integrity is the positive result leading to wisdom; wisdom as defined by Erikson (1982) is "informed and detached concern with life itself in the face of death itself" (p.61). Conversely, despair is the negative result leading to a fear of death, a sense that life is too short, and depression. This information helps the elder and the counselor plan treatment goals, search for strengths, and effectively target quality of life issues.

Aging is not a disease to be cured. Older adults live in various stages of health, happiness, and ability. They are more different from each other than are members of any other age group and deserve to be treated as individuals. Counselors who recognize the greater probability of loss (physical, cognitive, social, financial, personal, familial, and environmental) for this age group will be better positioned to recognize mental health risk factors, thereby facilitating engagement in the counseling process.

Transference and countertransference may be insidious for both the counselor and the elder client. Transference that is brought to the therapeutic relationship represents what is learned in the context of other relationships; it usually represents signs of unresolved difficulties concerning the earlier relationship (Knight, 2004). Especially for the older client, transference has its roots in the family-of-origin. The counselor is identified with an emotionally significant other, including family members and persons from the client's past. The counselor is more likely to be identified with a family member of similar age and sex. Gently probing the elder with questions such as "Who do I remind you of?" or "Have you felt this way about someone else?" helps the counselor and the client realize the dynamics that may affect outcomes.

Countertransference is the linkage between the counselor's personal feelings and his/her professional work (Genevay & Katz, 1990). "Overhelping" or "underhelping" elder clients represents the counselor's own denial and/or fear of growing old, being helpless, or dying, as well as his or her anger related to death and loss and the need for control. The counselor who works with elders will learn to confront and examine his/her own aging process; this may be the best gift an elder can offer to a young, middle-aged, or older clinician.

Suicide and the Elder Population

Approximately one of every five suicides in the United States is committed by a person over 65 (Smyer & Qualls, 1999). The history and statistics of suicide in the elderly usually points to a recognizable and probably treatable situation. Health care providers are in a prime position to help with prevention because 75% of older adults who commit suicide visited their medical provider within one month prior to the suicide (Smyer & Qualls, 1999). Applicable to the mental health counselor, the majority of older persons who commit or attempt suicide were experiencing their first episode of depression without significant complications, a condition that would be readily treatable. Counselors should always questions elders about suicide ideation and/or plans and behaviors that may indicate suicide. Is the elder giving away treasured items? Is the elder expressing worthlessness? Is this same person making statements that lead one to believe that the world and the elder's family would be better without him or her?

Other Mental Disorders in Late Life

Dementias

Dementias increase with age. Types of dementing illnesses to consider are dementia of the Alzheimer's type, vascular dementia, Lewy Body dementia, and mixed dementia. Usually, these clients come to the counseling process from outside sources looking for documentation and verification of capacity. Counselors can suggest environmental changes that address client's safety, as well as home based care. Also, pharmacological interventions such as antipsychotics, antidepressants, and cholinesterase inhibitors might add to the quality of life for the elder and all associated with the elder. The counselor may facilitate a medication referral if needed.

Substance Abuse

Types of substance abuse encountered with elders might include alcohol, recreational drugs, and prescription and over-the-counter medications. Counselors should always include a substance use and abuse screen with the intake visit. As with the adult population, elders might benefit from group therapies, individual counseling, and behavior modification centered on substance use and abuse. Diagnosis and treatment would be approached differently if the client has had a long history of substance abuse or began as an adjustment to a late-life change. This difference might dictate the type of non-pharmacological and pharmacological interventions suggested. An antidepressant may eliminate the need for substance abuse to treat an elder's depression. Also, pharmacological "debridement" of poly-pharmacy may be what is needed for many elders who are swallowing handfuls of prescribed pills each day.

According to a February 2008 research article published in The Journal of the American Geriatrics Society the authors report that almost one in ten elderly Medicare beneficiaries exceed recommended drinking limits (monthly use exceeding 30 drinks per typical month and "heavy episodic" drinking of four or more drinks in any single day during a typical month in the previous year) (Merrick, Horgan, Hodgkin, Garnick, Houghton, Panas, & Saitz, 2008). These results reflect a self-reported Medicare Current Beneficiary Survey of 12,413 elders. Unhealthy alcohol consumption is more common among older Americans than previously thought. The authors suggested screening for alcohol abuse to be especially important in the elder population, given a higher susceptibility to illness and interactions of alcohol with medications.

Psychoses

It was once thought that persons over 50 years could not develop schizophrenia. Today, schizophrenia is an equal opportunity diagnosis. Types of schizophrenia to consider with elders are early onset, late onset, and schizoaffective disorder. Other psychoses include mania and delusional disorders. Engaging in treatment might be the elder's first encounter with someone identifying a psychotic disorder. It is not usual for an elder to have increased paranoid tendencies; it becomes the work of the counselor to identify this paranoia as a real threat to autonomy or a possible psychosis.

Interventions to consider with elder psychoses involve cognitive behavioral therapy and social skills training, as well as engaging and educating the family about the disease process and setting loving limits. Pharmacological interventions are best managed by family member who can be depended on to administer antipsychotic, anticonvulsant, and mood stabilizing drugs as prescribed.

Summary

The geriatric population is growing exponentially; as an adult and a counselor thoughts and actions about how to age "gracefully" become important and essential. Taking mental and physical action now, recognizing these same needs in your clients, and considering health-related beliefs all affect current and future functioning. Anxiety, depression, and/or both combined are the most prevalent mental health diagnoses in elders; however, one must consider psychosis, substance abuse, and dementia. The suicide rate in the United States is highest in males over 65-years who had visited their primary care provider within one month prior to suicide. Elders tend to somatasize ill feelings; how to differentiate between a heart attack and a broken heart becomes the work of an alert health care provider.

Old age is not an illness looking to be cured and more drugs do not usually mean better care. Suffering is unnecessary at the end of life. Effective mental health care for elders includes assistance from others and community agencies, protecting our elders, and practicing evidence-based medicine. Depression is not inevitable but a treatable diagnosis regardless of age. Quality of life for elders, measured as physical and emotional well-being, are amenable to counseling interventions. Quantity of years lived is no longer the best measure of successful aging.

References

Achat, H., Kawachi, I., Spiro, A., III, DeMolles, D. A., & Sparrow, D. (2000). Optimism and depression as predictors of physical and mental health functioning: The normative aging study. *Annals of Behavior Medicine, 22*(2), 127–130.

Azpiazu, G. M., Cruz, J. A., Villagrasa, F. J. R., Abanades, H. J. C., Garcia, M. N., & Valero de Bernabe, F. A. (2002). Factors related to perceived poor health conditions or poor quality of life among those over 65 years of age. *Salud Publication, 76,* 683–699.

Birren, J. E., & Schaie, K. W. (Eds.). (2001).*Handbook of the psychology of aging.* New York: Academic Press.

Boyette, L. W., Lloyd, A., & Boyette, J. E., Watkins E., Furbush L., Dunbar S.B., et al. (2002). Personal characteristics that influence exercise behavior of older adults. *Journal of Rehabilitation, Restoration, and Development, 39,* 95–103.

Butler, R.N., (1963). The life review: An interpretation of reminiscence in the aged. *Psychiatry, 26,* 65-75.

Colcombe, S., & Kramer, A. (2003). Fitness effects on the cognitive function of older adults: A meta-analytic study. *Psychological Science, 14,* 125-130.

Crimmins, E. (2004). Trends in the health of the elderly. *Annual Review of Pubic Health, 25,* 79–98.

Cruikshank, M. (2003). *Learning to be old.* Lanham, MD: Rowman & Littlefield.

Dannefer, D. (2000). The regulation of the self in the postmodern state. In Schaie, K.W. & Hendricks, J. (Eds.), The evolution of the aging self: The societal impact of the aging process, 269-280. New York: culture, and subjective well-being: Emotional and cognitive evaluations of life. *Annual Review of Psychology, 54,* 403–425.

Daly, R. (2007). APA tells congress: End Medicare's higher copay for mental health treatment. *Psychiatric News,* 42,9,1.

Erikson, E. (1982). *The life cycle completed.* New York: W.W. Norton.

Friedan, B. (1993). *The fountain of age.* New York: Simon and Schuster.

Fry, P. S. (2001). Predictors of health-related quality of life perspectives, self-esteem, and life satisfactions of older adults following spousal loss: An 18 month follow-up of widows and widowers. *The Gerontologist, 41,* 787–799.

Genevay,B., & Katz,R.S.(1990).*Countertransference and older clients.* Thousand Oaks,CA: Sage Publications, Inc.

Hay, J., & LaBree, L. (2002). Cost-effectiveness of preventive occupational therapy for independent-living older adults. *Journal of the American Geriatric Society, 50,* 1381–1388.

He, W., Sengupta,M., Velkoff,V.A., & DeBarros, K.A., (2005). *United States Census Bureau, Current population reports,* United States Government Printing Office, Washington, D.C.

Hunter, N. (2005).*Pain in the elderly*. Retrieved January 9, 2006,from http://www.irishhealth.com/?level=48id=8397.

Jeste, D., Alexopoulos, G., Bartels, S., Cummings, J., Gallo, J., Gottlieb, G.,(1999). Consensus statement on the upcoming crisis in geriatric mental disorders research agenda for the next 2 decades. *Archives of General Psychiatry, 56,* 848–853.

Kawamoto, R., Doi, T., Yamada, A., Oguni, T., Okayama, M., Tsuruoka, K., et al. (1999). A study of depressive state and background factors in community-dwelling older persons. *Nippon Ronrn Igakkai Zasshi, 36*(10), 702–710.

Kawashima, R. (2005). *Train your brain: 60 days to a better brain.* Teaneck, NJ: Kumon.

Kennedy, G. J. (2000). Geriatric mental health care: A treatment guide for health professionals. New York: Guilford.

Knight, B., (2004). *Psychotherapy with older adults, 3rd Edition.* Thousand Oaks, CA: Sage Publications, Inc.

Kubzansky, L., Sparrow, D., Vokonas, P., & Kawachi, I. (2001). Is the glass half empty or half full? A prospective study of optimism and coronary heart disease in the normative aging study. *Psychosomatic Medicine, 63,* 910–916.

Lang, A.J., & Stein, M.B. (2001). Anxiety disorders: How to recognize and treat the medical symptoms of emotional illness. Geriatircs, 56,24-27.

Lazarus, R. (1966). *Psychological stress and the coping process.* New York: McGraw-Hill.

Levy, B., & Myers, L. (2004). Preventive health behaviors influenced by self-perceptions of aging. *Preventive Medicine, 39,* 625–629.

Masuchi, A., & Kishi, R. (2001). A review of epidemiological studies on the relationship of social networks and support to depressive symptoms in the elderly. *Japanese Journal of Public Health, 48*(6), 435–448.

Merrick,E.L., Horgan, C.M., Hodgkin, D., Garnick, D.W., Houghton, S.F., Panas, L., & Saitz, R.(2008). Unhealthy drinking patterns in older adults:Prevalence and associated characteristics. *Journal of the American Geriatric Society, 56*(2),214-223.

Merrill, B. A.(1994). A global look at compliance in health/safety and rehabilitation. *Journal of Orthopedic Sports Physical Therapy, 19*(5), 242–248.

Nampudakam, M. (1999). Greying blues. *Health Millions, 25*(5), 3–5.

Penninx, B. W., Guralnik, J. M., Bandeen-Roche, K., Kasper, J. D., Simonsick, E. M., Ferrucci, L., et al. (2000). The protective effect of emotional vitality on adverse health outcomes in disabled women. *Journal of the American Geriatric Society, 48,* 1359–1366.

Prochaska, J. O., & Velicer, W. F. (1997). The transtheoretical model of health behavior change. *American Journal Health Promotion, 12,* 38–48.

Rios, D. A., Abdulah, D. R., Wei, J. Y., & Hausdorff, J. M. (2001). Disparate effects of socioeconomic status on physical function and emotional well-being in older adults. *Aging, 13,* 30–37.

Robichaud, L., & Lamarre, C. (2002). Developing an instrument for identifying coping strategies used by the elderly to remain autonomous. *American Journal of Physical Medcine and Rehabilitation, 81,* 736–744.

Rosenstock, I. M., Strecher, V. J., & Becker, M. H. (1988). Social learning theory and the Health Belief Model. *Health Education Quarterly, 15,* 175–183.

Rowe, J. W., & Kahn, R. L. (1998). *Successful aging.* New York: Pantheon Books.

Sampson, S. (2006). New thinking on anxiety and aging: Anxiety disorders common in the elderly. Retrieved from the WWW on January 16, 2006. http://www.adaa.org/aboutADAA/newsletter/AnxietyandAging.htm

Smyer J. & Qualls S., (1999). *Aging and mental health.* Massachusetts: Blackwell.

Strawbridge, W. J., Deleger, S., & Roberts, R. E. (2002). Physical activity reduces the risk of subsequent depression for older adults. *American Journal of Epidemiology, 156,* 328–334.

Section Five:

Crisis and Self-Care

Developing a Professional Mindset: Individual and Organizational Crisis Intervention Strategies
By: Andy Vengrove, Ed.D. & Scott Rice, Ph.D.

Crisis counseling skills are a necessary part of a counselor's repertoire. The traumatic events that have occurred within our schools, places of employment, and society at-large have prompted many professionals in the field to focus on increasing crisis intervention skills within those in the helping profession. Counselor trainings have focused on crisis theory and specific models of intervention; topics have included multi-stepped models of crisis intervention, suicide assessments, grief work, and system-wide approaches to sudden death and catastrophic events. Specific counseling skills are taught that enable professionals to conduct risk assessments through face to face and telephone contact.

While these specific techniques and practices are extremely valuable and a vital part of the learning process, it appears that less emphasis is often given to an important part of the training process. More specifically, we contend that developing the proper mindset or mental preparedness for crisis counseling should be the first step in the learning process and that crisis intervention training should place more emphasis on helping counselors develop this awareness. The distinction between specific crisis skills, and an effective crisis intervention mindset, is a distinction of the "what" vs. the "how". In this conceptualization, our contribution to the crisis counseling literature will be to focus on those techniques, procedures, and mental preparations, which concern *the manner and mindset* by which a counselor engages in crisis intervention. For example, concerning the individual clinician, we will focus on how to avoid "catching the crisis", so that one can maintain a detached, objective, problem-solving stance both individually, and within a team or organization. We will also make a distinction between the typical mindset, style, and techniques utilized by counselors to help people, and the orientation that one must adopt in order to be effective in a crisis. Once the proper mindset is established, the counselor will be better prepared to employ the specific crisis intervention counseling skills needed to be effective during a variety of crisis situations. Further, we present important considerations for organizations seeking to prepare for crisis situations. Through implementation of a crisis team, we present one way that organizations can improve group functioning within a crisis. While an in-depth discussion of crisis theory and individual and organizational intervention strategies are beyond the scope of this chapter, it is important to begin by establishing a shared perspective of the term "crisis" and then move further into the manner and mindset by which counselors engage in crisis intervention.

Defining Crisis

Generally speaking, the term "crisis" has been defined in various ways, however many of the definitions tend to share similar qualities. For example, Caplan (1961), who is considered one of the pioneers in crisis intervention theory and intervention, presented the crisis event in its most simplistic form by stating, "...it is an upset in the steady state of the individual" (p. 18). Caplan expands upon this by stating that,

> People are in a state of crisis when they face an obstacle to life goals-an obstacle that is, for a time, insurmountable by the use of customary methods of problem solving. A period of disorganization ensues, a period of upset, during which many abortive attempts at solution are made. (p. 18)

Brammer (1985) presents crisis as a,

> ...state of disorganization in which people face frustration of important life goals or profound disruption of their lifecycles and methods of coping with stressors. The term crisis usually refers to a person's feelings of fear, shock, and distress about the disruption, not the disruption itself. (p. 94)

James (2008) presents a summary of several definitions and highlights the severe consequences that may ensue by stating that,

> Crisis is a perception or experiencing of an event or situation as intolerable difficulty that exceeds this person's current resources and coping mechanisms. Unless the person obtains relief, the crisis has the potential to cause severe affective, behavioral, and cognitive malfunctioning. (p. 3)

Lastly, Kanel (1999) keenly points out that crises share three major points that are all reflected in the preceding definitions; the precipitating event, the subjective distress caused by the perception of this event, and the failure to employ normal coping methods to alleviate the situation leading to lower psychological, emotional, and behavioral functioning. Kanel refers to this as the "trilogy definition" (p. 1).

With the onset of a crisis event, humans are hard-wired to experience an anxiety response, with hormonal releases that assist our brain and bodies with preparing for an active behavioral response. The capacity for immediate, emotionally driven action exists today because of its survival benefit. Natural selection working within our species has meant that those individuals not capable of mobilizing resources to answer the body's call to action in "fight or flight" scenarios perished during times of crisis. Those that were quick to successfully perform some survival-driven action, survived, and bred, passing on the capacity to act quickly when alarmed to their descendants. The result is a species in which individual members share a common biological response when encountering situations of severe and immediate danger. The behavioral response that results from the action of biological mechanisms will vary from individual to individual, as will the thoughts associated with the immediate alert to danger.

Basic Goals of Crisis Work

Unlike traditional psychotherapeutic approaches to counseling, crisis work/counseling is very focused and somewhat limited in its intent. The conceptual approach of restoring one's level of equilibrium to pre-crisis levels is one of the more basic principles of crisis intervention. The equilibrium approach is based on some of the early bereavement research by Lindemann (1944) who focused mainly on the grief responses after the loss of significant others and Caplan's (1964) expanded view of crisis states resulting from the blockage of life goals and the inability to overcome these obstacles through familiar means. James (2008) refers to this as the equilibrium/disequilibrium model and suggests that this is the, "...purest model of crisis intervention and is most likely to be used at the onset of the crisis" (p. 14). Keeping in mind Kanel's trilogy definition noted above, this model assumes that the individual in crisis has been in a sense, "shaken" from their normal psychological and emotional functioning and moved to an unfamiliar place where they perceive the situation (i.e. internal and external) to be insurmountable. This frame of mind leads to an increase of distress and a decrease of psychological functioning; hence a state of disequilibrium ensues (James, 2008; Kanel, 1999; Caplan, 1961). Therefore our initial focus as crisis workers is to help individuals regain a sense of pre-crisis equilibrium (i.e. to stabilize their psychological functioning).

The Proper Mindset to Avoid Catching the Crisis

It is during this initial phase of crisis work that our clients tend to feel that they or the situation at-hand is "out of control" or out of "their" control. From our experience working with people and with larger systems in crisis, creating a structure around the perceived or real internal and/or external "chaos" is one of the keys to success in crisis work. In order to be an effective crisis worker, we contend that the crisis worker must maintain their own equilibrium in that they must enter the crisis situation with the proper mindset. We must be able to maintain our professional stance while also being able to enter into chaotic, emotionally charged, and potentially dangerous situations. For example, crisis situations may include emotionally charged issues including but not limited to rape, suicide, death, murder, sexual and physical abuse. These issues tend to evoke strong feelings within ourselves and we must maintain our professional objectivity, poise, and framework in order to be effective counselors (James, 2008; Halpern & Tramontin, 2007; Corey, 2005). Simply stated, the first "rule" of crisis intervention is to not "catch the crisis."

One of the authors recalls a powerful example of a counseling supervisor remaining calm and effective during a crisis situation. Note the words that describe the overt behaviors of the supervisor, and the effect these behaviors had on the supervisees. The following vignette illustrates this point; the intended results of establishing the proper mindset for crisis counseling will follow.

In the early 1980's the author interned in a college counseling center located within the Health Services Department on campus. While in weekly supervision with two other interns, the supervisor answered his phone, listened attentively to the caller and calmly (i.e. low tone of voice, no overt change in his outward appearance) acknowledged that he understood the information that was being communicated. The supervisor calmly hung-up the phone and turned slowly to the group of interns and provided us with the following information: It was reported that a shooting just occurred in the cafeteria and that there may be a fatality; campus security will call back momentarily. The supervisor suggested that we continue with our supervision. As young undergraduate interns, we all noticed a dramatic rise in our anxiety levels, as in most crisis situations, we were unprepared for the news and unsure of ourselves; we looked at each other and we did not know quite what to do or say (i.e. we were experiencing our own sense of disequilibrium). We focused on our supervisor who was waiting for us to continue, urging us to talk about what we were currently experiencing in the immediate moment. It was at that point that we also noticed that our supervisor was calm and attentive to our needs; he appeared to be using the potential crisis situation itself to model the proper mindset needed for crisis counseling. The phone rang again and our supervisor responded with the same calm, reassuring affect that he previously demonstrated during the initial call. As the call ended, he once again turned slowly and calmly towards us and provided us with the following information in a serious tone, using language that was clear and uncomplicated: There was a confirmed shooting in the cafeteria. An ex-boyfriend entered the cafeteria, approached a table full of students where his ex-girlfriend was eating her breakfast and shot her at point blank range. The shooter walked out of the cafeteria and waited to be arrested by the police. He then stated that the students who were sitting at the table and witnessed the shooting were being brought to the health and counseling center where we were presently located. As young interns, our anxiety levels increased dramatically, and we were all filled with self-doubt as we felt the situation was beyond our capabilities. Our natural instinct was that we should do something, yet we were unsure of just what to do and how to do it. In a very succinct and calm manner, our supervisor prepared us to just "be" with the witnesses and "listen and attend." He assured us that we were certainly capable of this. It was the modeling of our supervisor, and the reassurance he provided, that kept us from "catching the crisis". This instilled us with confidence and helped us to regain a sense of equilibrium. More specifically, our supervisor modeled the following behaviors: He maintained his composure upon hearing the news; he appeared calm, kept a low voice tone and his physical movements were deliberate. He appeared in control and confident. He appeared to have the proper "mindset" established before entering into this situation. He addressed our anxieties and relayed his confidence in us to proceed effectively. He provided a structure by giving us brief but clear instructions on how to proceed.

Discussion

These actions taken by the supervisor mirror those that characterize effective therapy, despite the immediacy and sense of urgency brought by the crisis situation. What may be difficult for therapists in general, and beginning therapists in particular, is the ability to make sound judgments within such a constricted timeframe. When not involved in crisis situations, reflection and planning are a necessary and essential part of effective intervention with clients. In fact, the type of thinking utilized by therapists requires a set of bi-level processing skills that are highly specialized. This processing, on one level, involves being "present" with a client, utilizing verbal and nonverbal communication skills that convey warmth, openness, and positive regard. This first level also includes the manifest content of the verbal dialog.

The second level of processing is characterized by the reflection, analysis, and interpretation of the flow of verbal and nonverbal information coming from the client, and the effect of therapist words or actions on the client. The result of this analysis and interpretation is the formulation of a question, comment, or gesture (or a decision to withhold an overt action or statement), which will convey meaning to the client. These actions are the "tools" by which the therapist can, over time, empower change in the client. In utilizing the second level of processing, a therapist must always weigh the impact of any given action on a client, and determine if it will enhance or interfere with a desired therapeutic outcome. These metacognitive processes are essential to good therapy, and although difficult to measure, are most likely characteristic of the most effective therapists. For such helping professionals caught in a crisis, the ability to engage in thoughtful planning in a controlled way is suspended. For helping professionals involved with a crisis, the urge to act, and to act immediately, is compelling.

Like all humans in crisis situations, predictable thoughts accompany a hormonal release. As these thoughts are "attached" or associated with the emotional impulses, they represent "automatic thoughts" (Beck, 1976). These are emotionally based cognitions, which give immediate meaning to the feeling, a cognitive judgment that can lead to action. In crisis situations, these automatic thoughts can lead an individual toward action aimed at surviving, and helping others to survive, an emergency. These automatic thoughts involve neural pathways that may be different from those typically involved with decision-making processes associated with the frontal lobes. Due to the hormonal involvement and time urgency, such processing is being overridden by survival mechanisms.

Informational processing which involves the frontal lobe includes activities such as: reflection on the problem, consideration of available options for solving the problem, evaluating the quality of the options for action, selecting a course of action, and finally, acting. These cognitive activities are usually not possible, or are condensed into a very brief time span. This time pressure can drastically reduce the use of logical thinking, as the full range of available options does not get considered, when "tunnel vision" takes over.

For therapists and others in the helping profession, being effective in a crisis involves being aware of typical automatic thoughts in advance of the crisis. Careful planning and preparation ahead of a crisis will allow procedures and pre-planned behaviors to override the impulsive and often ineffective actions associated with urgent automatic thoughts. For the counselor or helping professional within a crisis, the automatic thoughts may typically come in the form of "I should be..." followed by some type of action impulse. Immediate thoughts will involve assessment of risk of immediate danger to self and others. These thoughts can range from any immediate need to protect oneself, to immediate needs of loved ones (family responsibilities), needs to function properly as a clinician (professional responsibilities), and depending on the nature of the crisis, specific actions involving safety to self or others. Perhaps the most compelling urge to some type of action results from automatic thoughts regarding real or imagined consequences of inaction. These thoughts take the form of an "if...then" contingency, e.g. "If I don't (take some type of immediate action), then...(some type of unwanted consequence will occur). These automatic thoughts for the beginning counselor may also reflect concerns with professional competence, "I'm supposed to know what to do now."

In crisis situations, often the initial, prevailing cognitive urge is to know more. An initial piece of information will be obtained, and this information is often incomplete, and likely to raise many further questions. The thought, "I should know more", is often accompanied by an action urge, "I must do something to know more". This can result in hasty actions: physically leaving to go to a place where more information may be obtained; making telephone inquiries; urgently questioning others for what they know, etc...All actions within a crisis have implications. Each individual involved in a crisis will have their own set of independent "automatic thoughts" and resulting action urges. The result is often hasty and uncoordinated independent actions by many individuals. At a minimum, these scattered actions can result in inefficiency, and a failure to solve the crisis. In some situations, such actions can actually worsen the crisis. At times when communication with others *before* acting is most essential, communication often receives the lowest priority.

To counter some of the more impulsive and scattered actions that can typify individual humans functioning within a crisis, it is necessary to address both individual and group functioning within a crisis. This can be accomplished through a dually focused intervention plan: one focus being the mindset of the individual counselor or crisis worker within the crisis, and the other to pre-establish organizational structures and procedures which can enhance the performance of individuals and the group, during a crisis event.

Preparation for the individual counselor or crisis worker involves training that helps clinicians to draw upon knowledge and expertise in a clear and logical manner, allowing them to maintain their equilibrium. This also involves an increased level of self-awareness, as clinicians need to know how to monitor their level of effectiveness in crisis situations. The creation of structure around a perceived chaotic situation communicates to clients and fellow counselors or crisis workers, both verbally and nonverbally, that we have the confidence to effectively help them with the crisis at hand.

Organizational Interventions

Training in crisis work will foster the development of a professional crisis mindset in counselors and crisis workers. In addition to this type of preparation, there are group and organizational interventions which, when implemented, can greatly benefit individual and group functioning within a crisis. Pauchant and Mitroff (1992) described the differences between "crisis prone" and "crisis prepared" organizations, making comparisons with functional and dysfunctional families. Part of an individual's ability to avoid "catching the crisis", and function well within a crisis, is related to the degree of preparedness for crisis made by their organization. An example of such an intervention is the development of integrated and coordinated plans established between organizations and public safety institutions (police, fire, hospital, disaster relief agencies).

In addition to planning between organizations, developing crisis plans within organizations is a critical component to assure more efficient crisis functioning of individual professionals within the organization. One such intervention utilized within an organization is the crisis team. Crisis teams, effectively designed and organized, address each of the four goals addressed toward individual counselor functioning listed above. In addition, they provide a communication and planning structure that allows an organization to utilize its strength and provide effective intervention.

A crisis team is a defined group within an organization, whose members come together before, during, and after a crisis, for the purpose of planning interventions, following up on their effectiveness, and revising initial crisis plans. The crisis team may include members from outside the organization as well, in order to maximize effectiveness. Characteristics of crisis teams include: interdisciplinary or diverse roles among team members, shared communication and initial planning, ongoing assessment which allows for coordinated amendments to plan, post-crisis follow-up intervention, post-crisis debriefing and performance evaluation. Crisis team composition, functions and procedures vary by organization type.

Essential procedures for crisis teams include a mechanism for immediate notification of members, with a time to meet for an initial consultation. In most crises, this initial consultation will happen with immediacy. The initial contact should originate from a pre-designated person, with clearly assigned back-up personnel specified with pre-established and ideally rehearsed communication plans. The beginning counselor should become acquainted with these plans within the organization in the event that his or her client, or an unforeseen community disaster might require the efficient communication between organization members.

After the decision to call together crisis team members has been made, and the crisis team meets to share information and develop an initial action plan, counselors and team members within the crisis team experience the potential for impaired communication, due to the various emotional states of individual team members.

Perl (2008) wrote about the "people" elements of crisis management, stating, "Be aware that in a crisis, your crisis team's core personality traits will be accentuated. I have seen internal politics, competitiveness, jealousy, insecurities, and a whole host of other issues all bubble to the surface within crisis management teams" (p. 1). As discussed earlier, the hormonal triggers within individuals create emotional and cognitive changes that, in the group setting, are multiplied and are cumulative. Perl (2008) advocates for strong leadership during a crisis; a workable plan, clearly defined organizational expectations; education for the crisis team regarding how individuals react during a crisis; training for the crisis team on specific crisis procedures to be followed; and the development of relationships with personnel outside the organization who will function alongside the crisis team in a crisis. Athey and Moody-Williams (2003) stress the importance of cultural competence for effective crisis teamwork.

Team members in general, and the team leader specifically, must make preparations, and take action, which helps the team to communicate. One person should speak at a time. The speaker should be heard by other group members, and asked clarifying questions before the next idea is presented. The leader must insure that accurate initial information has been gathered, or identify the gathering of specific further information as part of the initial action plan. The leader must also insure that communication is clear and direct, and that the team present information that is only relevant to the accurate understanding of the situation, or helps to develop the plan. Ideally, there is a balance within the team between strong leadership, and participation by all team members. Schonfeld and Newgass (2007) wrote of crisis teams in schools.

> Team members realize that group process allows for deliberation from multiple vantage points and permits compromise that respects potentially competing priorities, such as ensuring order and security, providing the school community with accurate information, and promoting emotional recovery and optimal coping. (p. 1)

The structural procedures in crisis teams, like the particular constituent members, will vary between organizations. But two tenets essential to improving the functioning of individual team members are:

1. Clear assignment of tasks or responsibilities to specific, named group members.
2. A plan for when and where to reassemble the team after the execution of the initial action plan.

Generally, a team member is pre-appointed to document the facts of the crisis, and any subsequent action plans developed. Dates and times are recorded, and key interventions spelled out in specific, but simple terms, and include the name of the team member assigned to each task. Pre-established forms assist with the comprehensiveness of the action plan. Perl (2008) writes of the use of checklists to assist crisis team function. Each team member can ask any essential clarifying questions regarding the demands of their responsibility. Because of the pressing demands of the crisis, team members may need to be dispatched prior to the end of the meeting, but efforts to have all members together for the essential details of plan development can pay dividends later regarding more coordinated and effective plan execution. The team does not adjourn until all members are clear as to their responsibilities, and a follow-up meeting time and place is arranged.

The follow-up meeting involves the reconvening of the team to report back on the outcomes of the individual components of the action plan executed by each team member. The format of each follow-up crisis meeting is the same—to review the status of the interventions implemented from the previous crisis meeting, and any new needs that must be added to the follow-up plan. An advantage of such a model, characterized by brief initial crisis team meetings and brief follow-up meetings is the wider net of possible needs and interventions that get considered by the team, based on their experiences in carrying out initial crisis responsibilities. New needs, and sometimes new resources, are identified in the time that elapses between meeting and follow-up meeting. Crises which are ongoing, and which require a sustained and evolving intervention by counselors and crisis team members, may involve multiple follow-up meetings, possibly over multiple days. For crises that are not multi-faceted, and are of short duration, the follow-up crisis team meeting can serve as the post-crisis debriefing.

The importance of intervention with the crisis team following the crisis has been stressed by previous authors (Weinberg, 1989; Mitchell, 1987). The stress of a crisis creates thoughts and feelings that can be lasting, in the form of rumination and obsessive thoughts, judgment (and misjudgment) of performance of self and others in the crisis, and lasting emotional reactions stemming from the crisis. McCann and Pearlman (1990) coined the term "vicarious trauma" to describe the trauma reactions found in counselors following their experiences with clients who recount traumatic events.

Mitchell (1987) referred to post-crisis debriefing sessions as "de-mobilization sessions". Everly and Mitchell (1999) included Critical Incident Stress DeBriefing (CISD) as a component of their overall crisis management plan model. In this model (CISM), CISD is to occur within the first twelve hours, post-crisis, and is a group intervention that targets symptom reduction, and is designed to help with psychological closure. Weinberg (1989) identified procedures common to post-crisis debriefing sessions. Writing from the standpoint of a consultant to an organization, he suggested that the consultant should first facilitate a discussion among team members in order to bring forth their thoughts and feelings stemming from the recently passed crisis. Secondly, he indicates the importance of the need to be attentive for, and help fellow crisis team members with their personal reactions to the crisis.

> Occasionally, team members disclosed what they believed to have been mistakes or regretful statements or actions. It is important for a counselor's long-term peace of mind to dispel these beliefs if the beliefs are irrational, or at least to frame them in such a way that they are easier to accept. (Weinberg, 1989, p. 307)

A final advantage of the post-crisis de-briefing is the ability for crisis team members to learn from the experience, and improve future crisis team functioning. Pagliocca, Nickerson and Williams (2002) advocate the development of an "evaluation mindset". As applied to crisis teams, team members seek to evaluate the various response components that occurred during and after the crisis, and whether or not these actions met the intended goals. Improvements in policies and procedures can then be made for the future.

In conclusion, both individual and organizational preparations are important to helping develop a proper and effective "mindset" for crisis counseling. These preparations are particularly important for beginning counselors, as automatic thoughts and their subsequent actions may affect their equilibrium and render them less effective in emotionally charged situations. Beginning and seasoned counselors alike benefit from being mentally prepared prior to engaging in crisis counseling. As illustrated in the presented vignette, establishing the proper mindset can be contagious. Our behaviors affect those around us, from other helping professionals to the clients that we serve. The crisis planning and structures we proactively create (e.g. crisis teams) to address crisis situations will relate directly to our ability to maintain professional demeanor and mindset within a crisis. When we avoid "catching the crisis", we engage in clear and logical thinking that will allow us to function effectively within the chaotic situation, while conveying a sense of calmness and confidence that suggests that we can work through the most difficult of circumstances.

References

Athey, J. & Moody-Williams, J. (2003). *Developing cultural competence in disaster mental health programs: Guiding principles and recommendations.* Washington, D.C.: U.S. Department of Health and Human Services.

Beck, A.T. (1976). *Cognitive Therapy and the Emotional Disorders.* New York: International Universities Press.

Brammer, L.M. (1985). *The helping relationship: Process and skills* (3rd ed.). Upper Saddle River, NJ: Prentice Hall.

Caplan, G. (1961). *An approach to community mental health.* New York: Grune & Stratton.

Caplan, G. (1964). *Principles of preventive psychology.* New York: Basic Books.

Corey, G. (2005). *Theory and practice of counseling and psychotherapy* (7th ed.). Belmont, CA: Thompson Brooks/Cole.

Everly, G.S. (2000). Crisis management briefings (CMB): Large group crisis intervention in response to terrorism, disasters, and violence. *International Journal of Emergency Mental Health, 2(1),* 53-57.

Everly, Jr.,G.S., & Mitchell, J.T. (1999). *Critical incident stress management (CISM): A new era and standard of care in crisis intervention (2nd Ed.).* Ellicott City, MD: Chevron.

Halpern, J., & Tramontin, M. (2007). *Disaster mental health: Theory and practice.* Belmont, CA: Thomson Brooks/Cole.

James, R.K. (2008). *Crisis intervention strategies* (6th ed.). Belmont, CA: Thompson Brooks/Cole.

Kanel, K. (2007) *A guide to crisis intervention* (3rd ed.). Belmont, CA: Thompson Brooks/Cole.

Lindemann, E. (1944). Symptomatology and management of acute grief. *American Journal of Psychiatry, 101,* 141-148.

McCann, I.L. & Pearlman, L.A. (1990). Vicarious traumatization: A framework for understanding the psychological effects of working with victims. *Journal of Traumatic Stress, 3,* 131-149.

Mitchell, J. T. (1987). Effective stress control at major incidents. *Maryland Fire and Rescue Bulletin, June,* p. 3-6.

Pagliocca, P. M., Nickerson, A. B., & Williams, S. (2002). Research and evaluation directions in crisis intervention. In S. E. Brock, P. J. Lazarus, & S. R. Jimerson (Eds.), *Best practices in school crisis prevention and intervention* (pp. 771–790). Bethesda, MD: National Association of School Psychologists.

Pauchant, T. C., & Mitroff, I. I. (1992). *Transforming the crisis prone organization.* SanFrancisco: Jossey-Bass.

Perl, D. (2008). *Crisis management: Don't forget the people!* Retrieved April 8, 2008 from http://www.continuitycentral.com

Trippany, R.L., White Kress, V.E., Wilcoxon, S.A. (2004). Preventing vicarious trauma: What counselors should know when working with trauma survivors. *Journal of Counseling and Development*, 82, p. 31-37.

Weinberg, R.B. (1989). Consultation and training with school-based crisis teams. *Professional Psychology: Research and Practice*, 20(5), 305-308.

Coping with the Intensity of Trauma Treatment: Managing Counselor Wellness
By: Raven Kim, RN, MA

Eager to make a difference in the field, individuals new to the therapeutic process may feel fueled by their passion for the work and a discussion on burnout and compassion fatigue can appear premature—more appropriate for the "seasoned clinician"—or, for a much later date. Susceptibility is often as simple as what brought us to this life's work and we owe it to ourselves and to our clients to remain vigilant. Work with trauma survivors can be motivated by a fascination with the neuropsychobiological mechanisms that shape us, or compassion born of personal experience. Whatever fuels the empathic process, the helper becomes immersed in a relationship examining the impact of trauma. As stories unfold, it is with awe that we witness inner resources emerging and the strengths of survivors. Somewhere in this state of amazement, and often, not far into a career, helpers begin to experience textbook symptoms that are easy to deny or attribute to various generic stressors. Excellent supervision can assist in working through the more profound responses, helping to enhance a practice, as well as the ability to be fully present for clients. It can also hone instincts and teach valuable life lessons, which prove necessary in maintaining personal wellness, but there is far more to understand.

The therapeutic relationship with trauma survivors can feel as if Pandora's Box has been opened, as various presentations and comorbid conditions surface during the treatment process. Disordered attachment among trauma survivors challenge the therapist's ability to maintain strong boundaries, as this may be the first trusting relationship the client has experienced. Borderline traits, developed in response to trauma, test the will of all involved in treatment and tap into the therapist's energy reserves. A common constellation of comorbid conditions may include, Depression, Anxiety, Anger, Aggression, Borderline Personality Traits, Substance Use Disorder, Eating Disorders, Cutting, Dissociation, Somatization, along with suicidal ideation and/or attempts. One client can feel like a full caseload as stabilization is embarked upon. The success of this phase will determine if the client can engage in the therapeutic process. Historically, therapist reactions to treating trauma survivors has often been categorized as contributing to burnout or looked at through the lens of countertransference (Figley, 1995). Over the last decade, the paradigm has shifted from exploring, naming, and defining the impact of treating trauma survivors on the therapist, toward preparing those in the helping professions to anticipate the personal impact inherent in this work. The absence of widespread trauma informed services inhibits the development of universal wellness programs for treatment providers. Secondary Trauma and Vicarious Traumatization are widely accepted terms linked with empirical evidence, which supports findings of neurobiological changes occurring in the helper. These changes mimic those of the trauma victim's and are elicited in response to direct exposure to the information presented by the therapist's clients.

Differentiating burnout and compassion fatigue from secondary and vicarious traumatization is essential in managing counselor wellness. Working with difficult clients can result in burnout in any career. Vicarious or Secondary Trauma present as more specific, in that the helper is impacted by direct exposure to trauma survivors and the details of what they process. The actual communication of traumatic events from the victim to the helper can quite suddenly produce symptoms. As the counselor witnesses the victim's descriptions, neurological and physiological responses are elicited. Events of simultaneous burnout are not unusual and the helper's own trauma history, if present, will create an atmosphere where the counselor is more susceptible. To this end, burnout and countertransference can create an environment where the helper is most vulnerable. Terminology in the field is often used interchangeably and as research progresses a more defined understanding evolves. The day-to-day exposure to a client's stories can often produce such a gradual layering of neurological changes that the impact may go unrecognized. Alterations in sleep, energy levels, or tolerance can change subtly, over time, and never be attributed to the impact of the therapeutic relationship. Shared feelings that occur in this relationship are labeled and interpreted differently in the context of different schools of thought and disciplines in the field. Countertransference, often used to explain changes in body states and emotional responses in the therapist, and the integration of projective identification, often claimed to be masterfully implemented by experienced psychoanalytically trained clinicians moving the client toward their goal, may each be blamed for changes in the clinician, easily missing the underlying impact of secondary trauma. There is the possibility here for the blame to be placed on the individuals we are meant to serve. Discovering ways in which empathy can empower the therapist is the challenge. Focus placed on cognitive, emotional and somatic empathy can establish a more effective therapeutic intervention.

A more inclusive view of countertransference in contemporary thought is offered by Johansen (1993), describing the impact of all the emotional reactions of the therapist toward the patient, regardless of the source. Life stressors experienced by the therapist, past or present, are included, in addition to what is absorbed by the therapist from the trauma processed by the client (Johansen, 1993, as cited in Stamm, 1999). Figley notes the contrasts to the more traditional view of counter-transference as being the therapist's conscious and unconscious responses to the transference of the client, often as it connected to the therapist's past experiences (Stamm, 1999). As countertransference remains an undesirable consequence of the therapeutic relationship that we strive to eliminate to avoid distortion on the part of the therapist, secondary traumatic stress is a natural consequence of this rela-tionship (Stamm, 1999) and necessitates effective management. An updated view of countertransference incorporates the difficulty of the individual client and the material they present with the impact of the therapist's past experiences and life stressors (Figley, 1995). A 1991 study evaluated therapist qualities that appear to help manage countertransference most effectively. The five predominant qualities identified were: having more insight into and explanations for their feelings; pos-sessing a greater capacity for empathy and understanding for his/her client's emo-tional experience; having a greater ability to differentiate between the needs of self and the needs of the client; being less anxious with clients; and having an ability to conceptualize client dynamics in the past, as well as the present. Therapists rated the most important qualities to be self-integration and self-insight (Figley, 1995, as cited in Stamm, 1999).

Although different sources over the last 15 years have categorized, assigned and used terms interchangeably, recent clarification linked to advances in research, has defined the impact of the therapeutic process on the helper more succinctly. Babette Rothschild (2006), in her book, *Help for the Helper: Self-care Strategies for Managing Burnout and Stress*, helps to clarify the cause and effect in each category. The term that has been in the public consciousness over the longest period of time appears to be burnout. From many perspectives, it holds a negative connotation with more than a hint of blame for the helper. The label is used to categorize an individual who often performs in a less than dedicated manner, an individual often fed up with his or her job and those that it serves. There is a negative undercurrent here, indicating that the helper should have prevented this state before it occurred. In the context of this chapter, burnout is an overall state of extremes that results from the impact and intensity of the work, resulting in compromised health and/ or a negative view of life (Rothschild, 2006). Research has indicated that burnout is responsible for a decrease in concern and esteem for clients, often resulting in a compromised quality of care (Raquepaw & Miller, 1989; as cited in Trippany, White Kress & Wilcoxon, 2004). In 1985, the term Vicarious Traumatization was introduced describing a vulnerability to trauma, perceived as if it had been per-sonally experienced. At the same time, Secondary Traumatization was described

(Rosenheck & Nathan, 1985, as cited in Rothschild, 2006) as a rather contagious set of symptoms that were experienced by family members of trauma survivors, as a result of the closeness of the relationship and how it has been impacted and altered as a result of trauma. An integrated definition that has evolved has added the therapist that is witnessing what the victim is experiencing and the stories that are told. The therapist becomes a secondary victim as the impact of witnessing overwhelming information and emotion is shared in the therapeutic process. Figley introduced the Term Compassion Fatigue (Figley 1995), which described the exhaustion that can be inherent in compassionate work. Rothschild (2006) further defines this as a description of the impact on an individual suffering as a result of serving in a helping capacity. Vicarious traumatization differs in that the therapist experiences the client's trauma in his or her own nervous system responses. This holds similarity to the feelings that may be evoked while watching a suspense or horror movie or engaging in a high risk sport. If the therapist has a personal history of trauma that is triggered during the therapeutic process, the historic trauma is primary and the traumatic stress experienced is vicarious (Rothschild, 2006).

Monitoring body states and implementing stress management tools requires a basic understanding of the stress response in the body. A more in depth understanding of neurobiological responses to trauma is integral in working with the impact of past trauma on clients, as well as how that trauma may be reactivated in every day situations and therapeutic interventions. *The Body Keeps the Score: Memory and the Evolving Psychobiology of Post-traumatic Stress* is a comprehensive and very readable article that can offer concise insight into the basics. (van der Kolk, B., Harvard Review of Psychiatry, 1994, 1(5), 253-265).

Empathy has become a topic of research allowing us to trace the imprint left as we vicariously feel what another is feeling. The obvious benefits span survival of, and bonding within, the species. The risks are magnified in the therapeutic relationship. We have become more aware of our unique susceptibility to the risks as a modern Western society, since the horror of 9/11. We suddenly had the desire to reach beyond our valued cocoon of independence and privacy to touch one another. We were driven toward a sense of safety through community, and traces of ritual and traditions born of tribal roots were resurfacing with renewed meaning. It was a glimpse of the power of the empathic process. For some, the impact triggered something from their personal past; for others the vicarious experience impacted the way they were wired. Perhaps the news media, with its repetitive tone of horrors, became unmanageable, or the response to other trauma was met with a diminished affect.

Mirroring is utilized to establish rapport and gain information within the therapeutic relationship. Mirror neurons, or brain cells that can mimic the activity of another's brain cells, are a topic of study that offer insight into the powerful responses of observing the experience of another and the identical neuron response to direct experience (Gallese, 1999, 2001, as cited in Rothschild, 2006). Postural echoing or emotional contagion (Morris, 1979 and Hatfield and colleagues, 1992, 1994, as cited in Rothschild 2006) have been systematically observed and described in studies on unconscious mirroring. This behavior activates the Autonomic Nervous System and explains the responses manifested in the clinician in response to traumatic processing. Because this occurs on an unconscious level, the impact is often not realized unless the clinician remains acutely aware of his or her own body states. Studies related to copying another's facial expression directly correlated to experiencing the associated feelings and emotions (Hess & Blairy, 2001 and Levenson & Ruef, 1997, as cited in Rothschild, 2006). The therapist mimics body posture, facial expression and muscle tension frequently during sessions involving intense emotion. Unintentional mimicry leaves the helper largely unaware of this response, as a chain reaction begins in the nervous system of the therapist.

Differences in individuals may make it easier to notice arousal or changes in clients for some, and for others, changes in self-states will be more readily noticed. Either way, a basic knowledge of arousal signs and symptoms will assist the clinician in monitoring his or her own state of wellness. A recent study indicates that therapists focusing on body awareness had lower incidences of vicarious traumatization (Forester 2001, as cited in Rothschild, 2006). A conscious effort to be aware of respirations, heart rate, and muscles tension will assist the helper in consciously making effort to change the effect of stress. "Unmirroring" or consciously changing position, breathe rate, or body posture can become a habit by taking a drink, changing position while seated, alternating muscle tensing and relaxation, and recording changes of expression in the client or self during the session.

Awareness can make all the difference in the therapist's ability to think clearly. Hyperarousal will impact this ability as the passing of information from the hippocampus to the prefrontal cortex is altered in response to stress. The vulnerability to the stress hormones, epinephrine and norepinephrine, suppresses hippocampal activity. Feeling spacey or fearful during sessions may indicate hyperarousal but individual assessment comes with emotional awareness. Neurological studies by Damasio (1994) indicate that emotions are necessary to make rational decisions, and feeling the consequences of the decisions in one's body is what informs our decisions (Rothschild, 2006). Somatic markers guide decisions and provide the basis for "gut feelings" that are consciously or unconsciously used in the decision making process.

Communication is yet another variable and communication styles that are compatible can provide support and validation, fostering mental health. Conflicting styles will contribute to the stressors and leave both the therapist and client frustrated and sorting through negative emotions. Harris and Linder outline core senses utilized under stress and how identifying them can facilitate effective communication (Stamm, 1999). A predilection for visual, auditory, or kinesthetic associations establishes the primary core senses used to gather information which are used most often for decision-making, motivation and abstract thinking. In traumatic stress, this sensory sorting style is most often utilized to the exclusion of all others. Verbs used can indicate core sense associations and 12 sorting styles are categorized, as outlined by Densky and Reese, (1989). The helper needs to be able to diffuse the barriers created by conflicting sorting styles with a sense of knowing and a tolerance for individual differences. It is an interesting exercise to establish a working knowledge of personal communication styles and those of individuals with whom one communicates regularly. Within the therapeutic process, conflicting styles can create further vulnerability to compassion fatigue and burnout. The importance of this awareness is in gaining control of how information presented is being processed.

Peer support and regular contact is essential in maintaining counselor wellness. Accessing objective viewpoints, professional supervision, and consultation assist the helper in maintaining objectivity and provide an arena where emotions can be shared that may be inappropriate elsewhere. A professional peer group can provide emotional support, information, social companionship, and instrumental support. These are the key elements identified by Flannery (1990) to be essential in a supportive system. If a helper is suffering from Secondary Traumatic Stress, it places both the helper and the client in jeopardy. Many specialists in the field of trauma maintain that practicing without a professional support system is unethical (Munroe, 1994, as cited in Stamm, 1999). Provisions of tangible supports, clarification of insights and validation of feelings, can assist the therapist with Secondary Traumatic Stress (STS). Clarification of responsibilities and insight into limitations are essential to ethical practice. Assisting the helper with the ability to reframe the trauma and providing an appropriate response to the emotional experience of the helper maintain a professional empathic link. Figley (1989) outlined components of a healing family environment and they hold true for the professional support environment, as well.

1. Stressors are accepted as real and legitimate.
2. The problem is viewed as a problem for the entire group and not as a problem that is limited to the individual.
3. The general approach to the problem is to seek solutions, not to assign blame.
4. There is a high level of tolerance for individual disturbance.
5. Support is expressed clearly, directly, and abundantly in the form of praise, commitment, and affection.
6. Communication is open and effective; there are few sanctions against what can be said. The quality of communication is good and messages are clear and direct.
7. There is a high degree of cohesion.
8. There is considerable flexibility of roles and individuals are not rigidly re-

stricted from assuming different roles.

9. Resources—material, social, and institutional—are utilized efficiently.
10. There is no subculture of violence (emotional outbursts are not a form of violence).
11. There is no substance abuse (Figley, 1989, as cited in Stamm, 1999, p 85).

Symptoms of Secondary Traumatic Stress, Vicarious Trauma, and Compassion fatigue mimic those of traumatic stress. They may include, but are not limited to, alteration in sleep patterns and insomnia, irritability, anxiety, emotional withdrawal, avoidance of certain tasks, isolation from coworkers, feelings of helplessness and inadequacy, and flashbacks. Left without intervention they may contribute to burnout. As mentioned earlier, helpers with a personal history of trauma are at increased risk for a high severity of symptoms. Job performance may suffer and substance abuse may be utilized as a coping mechanism. Symptoms of depression are not unusual. The personal impact of treating trauma can alter relationships and have sexual side effects. Intrusive thoughts and guilt often negatively impact intimacy (Trippany et al., 2004). Noting the changes and symptoms in colleagues opens an opportunity to normalize the experience as inherent in the work and offer professional support in the form of groups or informal conversation. Acknowledging the impact of the work from the outset establishes an atmosphere where individual creativity and inner resources can manifest to manage the effects of stress. Offering professional resources without marginalizing the individual is essential to providing a safe environment. What we have come to know about treating trauma in our clients needs to be extended to the helper affected by secondary traumatic stress, vicarious trauma, and compassion fatigue. Flexibility in symptom management techniques will support the individual in recovery. According to Williams (1994), ethical trauma work involves symptom management and in the formula for working with trauma clients, common practice utilizes the rule of thirds. One third of the time is devoted to present issues, one third is for memory/trauma work and one third is for processing (Williams, 1994, as cited in Stamm, 1999). Counselor wellness requires a foundation of similar balance and an examination of driving forces within the therapeutic relationship. The right combination of self-awareness, knowledge, intuition, and theory can provide a measure of ethical practice, according to Williams and Sommer (Stamm, 1999).

Issues of ethics are outlined prolifically in the field of psychology but there is a glaring absence regarding issues of self-care incorporated in ethical guidelines. Munroe speaks to issues associated with Secondary Trauma in therapists and notes that the focus on protecting the client has, until recently, excluded protection of the helper as in the best interest of the client. An observation presented by the author is imperative to consider. If the helper does not make self-care a priority, reinforcement of internalized negative belief systems among abuse survivors are inadvertently reinforced (Munroe, 1994, as cited in Stamm, 1999). We become part of the problem, not the solution.

Effective "empathy management" is at the core of maintaining counselor wellness. A vigilant synthesis of insight, self-awareness, relaxation techniques, intact support systems, and balance are essential components. Physical shifts can consciously maintain counselor choice, as the body-to-body resonance can be broken as needed. Shifting position or stepping back is immediate yet subtle. A simple change in furniture proximity can alter the dynamics of a session by offering the helper an enhanced sense of protection. A willingness to explore similarities and feelings evoked from personal experience can help maintain the insight needed to seek supervision and therapeutic intervention. Knowing your own baseline is the foundation. If that destabilizes, a state of imbalance prevails and a healthy therapeutic alliance becomes impossible.

Prevention methods for Vicarious Trauma (VT) range from limiting trauma clients per caseload to engaging in peer supervision groups. The socialization of these groups combined with the normalization of experiencing VT is reported to lessen the impact while helping to maintain objectivity (Catherall, 1995; as cited in Trippany et al., 2004). Agencies employing counselors providing services to clients with a trauma background have a responsibility to assist their clinicians in decreasing the impact or occurrence of VT (Pearlman & Saakvitne, 1995b; as cited in Trippany et al., 2004). Variables such as supervision, consultation, staffing and continuing education are reported to impact occurrence and outcome positively as they are provided. Benefits for employees providing insurance coverage for personal counseling, paid vacation, and limitations placed on the number of clients with a trauma background per caseload, were indicated as significant in prevention or minimizing symptom severity of VT. Several studies indicate that a counselor's sense of spirituality and meaning makes him or her less vulnerable to VT (Trippany et al., 2004).

There are guidelines available, tests and scales that can offer some assessment, but overall, you will provide the most accurate indicator by paying close attention to mind-body wellness. If you are suffering from your work, seeking help is your professional responsibility—to yourself and your clients.

The Professional Quality of life Scale: Compassion Satisfaction and Fatigue Subscales—Revision IV authored by B. Hudnall Stamm, may be freely copied, as long as the author is credited, no changes are made and it is not sold. ProQOL-R IV can be accessed at http://www.isu.edu/~bhstamm. This can be used as a self-test with self-scoring directions available. The PTSD Checklist Civilian Version (PCL) can be used to evaluate your level of vicarious trauma (F.W. Weathers, J.A. Huska, and T.M. Keane, 1991 for DSM-IV. Boston: National Center for PTSD, Behavioral Science Division). For further information the PILOTS database may be consulted http://www.ncptsd.org/PILOTS.html.

The Social Readjustment Rating Scale: Stressful Life Events evaluates general levels of life stressors (Holmes & Rahe, 1967; as cited in Rothschild, 2006). These and other scales are also available in the appendix of *Help for the Helper: Self-care Strategies for Managing Burnout and Stress.*

Resources are mounting as the impact of treating trauma is examined. Studies are validating experiences of clinicians whose lives have been altered by their empathic work and we are encouraged to reconnect with our inner selves, practicing mindfulness and common sense life rhythms that have become unnatural living in a fast paced society and immersed in empathic work. Providing an environment of mental health is what we have diligently prepared for but the focus must shift to the source—the self—as the place to begin.

References

Densky, A. B. & Reese, M. (1989). *Programmer's pocket summary*. Indian Rocks Beach, FL: Southern Institute Press.

Figley, C. R. (1995). *Compassion fatigue: coping with secondary traumatic stress disorder in those who treat the traumatized*. New York: Brunner/Mazel.

Rothschild, B., (2006). *Help for the helper: Self-care for managing burnout and stress*. New York; W.W. Norton & Co., Inc.

Stamm, B.H. (Ed.) (1999). *Secondary traumatic stress: Self-care for clinicians, researchers, & educators*. Baltimore, MD: Sidran Press.

Trippany, R. L., White Kress, V. E., & Wilcoxon, S. A. (2004). *Preventing vicarious trauma: What counselors should know when working with trauma survivors.* Journal of Counseling & Development Vol. 82, Winter 2004.

van der Kolk, B. (1994). *The body keeps the score: Memory and the evolving psychobiology of post-traumatic stress*. Boston: Harvard Review of Psychiatry 1 (5), 253-265.

"We are Human": Collective Advice on Personal Resiliency for New Helping Professionals

By: Christine Michael, Ph.D. & Nicholas Young, Ph.D., Ed.D.

Recently, seasoned helping professionals and graduate students pursuing advanced education and credentials graciously took time out of their busy personal and professional lives to offer advice to new and aspiring practitioners. More than seventy counselors at different stages of their careers took part in this formal qualitative research project, which was purposely designed to gather the "practitioner voice." The authors felt that practitioners themselves were in the best position to share their experiences and wisdom on how to successfully sustain oneself in the helping field over time. While there is no shortage of pundits who volunteer their perspectives, this research sought to consider how those in the field on a daily basis view a number of important issues. Asked in an open-ended survey to reflect upon aspects of professional stress and personal resiliency, respondents described the pressure points of practice and shared advice aimed at helping others gain health and well-being while engaged in demanding work with human beings in need. Their viewpoints were captured using grounded qualitative research methodology, which resulted in the formation of themes or "common views or advice" that would be most reflective of the perspectives of the co-researchers—the practitioners who were engaged in the research.

Compassion Fatigue and the Pillars of Resiliency

This topic has drawn attention in the scholarly literature in recent years, as what Figley (1995) described as "compassion fatigue" has become more prevalent. Increased client loads, paperwork, regulations, insurance company demands and requirements, and fiscal concerns tax practitioners more than ever. Professional isolation, the recognition of the staggering mental health needs of so many populations in our communities, and the struggle to keep too many personal and professional balls in the air at one time threaten to stress even the most skillful practitioners, especially as fiscal resources available to support therapeutic intervention continue to wane further and further.

The field of resiliency studies offers many glimpses into the factors that help individuals survive, and even thrive, in stressful situations that persist over time. Gordon and Wang's (1994)work with "the defiers of negative prediction" found that those who maintained optimal well-being and productivity under adverse conditions shared common outlooks and traits. They were self-directed, they possessed a "spirit life" or "religious ideal," and they viewed change as both possible and rewarding. Even in the face of obstacles and challenges, they maintained a "healthy anger," which motivated them to fight injustice without becoming depressed by it. Their progress in life was aided tremendously by the real-life presence of a mentor or guide.

Garmezy and Rutter (1983) describe the "competency indices" of resilient individuals in terms of six attributes. Such individuals are "effective in work, play, and love, " as well as having healthy expectations for themselves and maintaining a positive outlook on life, even when confronting challenges. They possess a sense of self-esteem and an internal locus of control. Additionally, they are self-disciplined. Powerful components of their competency include highly developed problem-solving and critical thinking skills. Finally, they are buoyed by a lively sense of humor.

Wolin and Wolin (1993) identified the "seven resiliencies" in their work. Among these were personal independence, initiative, and morality. When an individual could hold true to these three aspects of self, he or she increased personal resiliency in the face of adverse conditions. Further, resilient individuals brought to bear creativity, humor, and insight when faced with challenging problems. As with others' works, these authors found that positive relationships empowered resilient individuals and offered them support and guidance that were crucial to their development.

There is a substantive body of literature on the qualities of resilient individuals that reiterates many of the aforementioned factors (Werner & Smith, 1992; Werner, 1990; Rutter, 1979) Among common variables are: an active, evocative approach to problem solving; an optimistic view of the future, even amidst personal suffering; and the ability to attract others' positive attention, which led to mentoring and other valuable relationships. The researchers also found resilient individuals to be those who had a tendency to seek novel experiences—lifelong learners who were not afraid to challenge themselves to change. Such individuals also possessed a "proactive perspective" that allowed them to anticipate and plan for future events. They had a sense of their own identity and "roots" and were able to separate themselves from "unhealthy situations and persons."

From the classic literature on resiliency, other scholars and researchers have looked at applications of such work on the helping professions. Henderson and

Milstein (2002), who have examined resiliency in educational settings extensively, articulate the "personal characteristics of the resilient." While some of the traits such as an "easy temperament" may, in part, be biological in nature, others are skills and attitude-based. Highly developed communications and problem-solving skills are essential, as is the ability to know how to institute environmental conditions to promote resiliency. Resilient practitioners have high expectations for themselves and others, a sense of purpose for the future, and strong social skills that allow them to recruit other individuals to their causes. As well, they are highly attuned to others and able to empathize with them, while holding them to high standards.

Professional Stressors

Mullenback and Shovolt (2001) speak to a number of professional stressors that can tax the individual and lessen his/her work outcomes and personal satisfaction. The primary stressor is being challenged by issues and cases that require a degree of competence that the individual does not possess. This lack of competence affects not only the professional care that can be given, but also one's sense of esteem and worth. Practitioners also suffer in therapy processes that are "frozen." A survey of helping professionals conducted by the American Psychological Association in the late 90's concluded that one of the most stressful circumstances for a psychologist or counselor involves a situation where a client is not progressing adequately. Being professionally stuck is simply not an enviable situation and leads to emotional and, at times, physical discomfort associated with distress. "Breaches in peer relationships" also are highly stressful in the workplace, and intrapersonal crises, when they intrude upon the professional sphere, threaten professional roles, as well.

Promoting Personal Resiliency

Skovholt (2001), writing on the "resilient practitioner," identified "factors that sustain the professional self." One cluster of factors centered on meaningful participation in the lives of others, a feeling of success in being able to help them, and a reverential recognition of the "creativity, courage, ingenuity, tolerance of pain" that attends human life. Strong professional boundaries, good peer support, and supportive supervision and mentoring also were key factors. Maintaining humor and playfulness, curiosity, and the desire to continue learning and growing as a professional were also traits related to resiliency. Individuals who grew and thrived were astute in differentiating between "idealism" and "realism," and they also were able to tolerate professional ambiguity, loss, and "normative failure" in their work. Other, external, contributors to professional sustenance included adequate pay, benefits, and professional development opportunities and a work environment characterized by a "low level of organizational conflict."

Building resilience is the "primary prevention for career burnout," writes Simon (2009) in an article on the chiropractic profession. Arguing that professional resilience can be "built" over time, Simon highlights the consistent themes among the studies mentioned above: resilient individuals, he says, engage in caring relationships; hold high expectations for success; find positive meaning in their work; set clear boundaries; and have strongly developed business practices and life skills. Simon argues for greater emphasis on practicing self care, managing time effectively, working on developing strong Emotional Intelligence, balancing long-term goals with shorter ones, maintaining perspective, and being aware of how to manage one's own resistance to aspects of professional practice as the keys to developing and nurturing resilience.

Career Life Cycle

Another lens through which to view the promotion of professional well-being is that of the "career life cycle." Taking this approach, one casts a "career" as a series of developmental stages, in which there are specific tasks for the individual to resolve, and potential pitfalls if those tasks are not resolved successfully. When resolution is not successful, stress on the individual increases. Fessler and Christensen (1991) conducted early work with teaching professionals, finding eight stages of professional development: pre-service; induction; competency building; enthusiastic and growing; career frustration; career stability; career wind down; and career exit. At the competency building stage, for example, a practitioner enters the stage needing to build skills to be able to function professionally in a seamless manner. In the early part of the stage, s/he is merely acquiring those skills, feeling at times as though s/he is "treading water" professionally; a successful resolution of this stage sees the practitioner with a large "tool kit" and skills to function almost automatically, freeing more energy for creativity and building professional self esteem and confidence. This sets the stage for desiring greater roles beyond simple mastery. A practitioner who cannot become proficient in skills building and application easily could become frustrated, feeling low esteem and high potential for burnout.

Skovholt's (2001) stages of practitioner development are similar in nature, moving from imitation stage, through conditional autonomy, exploration, integration, individuation, and finally integrity. In the same vein as the schema mentioned above, his model poses a balance/risk dilemma at each stage. For example, a professional at the individuation stage is at risk for becoming stale or bored if s/he does not integrate new roles, such as mentoring younger practitioners or contributing to the dissemination of knowledge through teaching or writing, into his/her repertoire. Challenge and change are necessary components of developmental health.

The Practitioners' Perspective on Resiliency

To initiate this study, eighty-eight seasoned counselors and psychologists were surveyed and asked to complete a series of questions related to professional stressors and their advice on how to best cope with them. Seventy-four of those practitioners opted to participate in this study and thus had their viewpoints carefully considered. All information provided was narrative and analyzed using grounded qualitative research methodology espoused by Patton (2002), which resulted in the selection of the most prominent themes offered by the participants. The authors contend that those prominent themes can be viewed as the best advice from the field to current and aspiring practitioners alike on the topic of personal resiliency. Such themes or suggestions may be considered appropriate to emulate, depending upon one's personal circumstances.

What did our participants suggest were stressors and best practice coping strategies? Five "stressor" themes and six "self care" themes were identified. We took it as a positive sign that our subject sample placed greater emphasis in their responses on self-care after noting the "issues" and "obstacles" that cause them frustrations that lead to stress. As appropriate, verbatim quotes are offered as part of the explanation of select themes, as in those instances the direct quote was found to be indicative of the views of the majority of respondents.

Stressors that take a toll on personal health and well being: What the respondents said about professional practice

Regardless of the many satisfactions that survey respondents reported when working with their clients and social service agencies, there are myriad aspects of their job that have the potential to take a toll on their personal health and well being. These may include:

"The Juggling Act"

Not surprisingly, a frequently-reported stressor involves "juggling responsibilities of work, practicum, courses, children, home, marriage...There's no down time...I'm trying to find or make time for self care and not feel guilty about it." The Juggling Act also involves "the many different needs and requirements of different work situations." For women, in particular, the home/family/work dilemma results in a sinking sense that nothing is every done fully or as well as they would like.

"Drowning in a Sea of Emotions"

That which draws practitioners to work in the helping professions and provides them with their greatest job satisfaction is also experienced as that which threatens to overwhelm them. The sheer "stress of being caught up in clients' emotions" wears on one day after day. And the frustration of "the overwhelming numbers of painful situations which are often beyond my help" can diminish one's sense of efficacy, and joy in the work role. This can be experienced even within the office as "feeling helpless while listening to multiple problems in a session." Exacerbating these frustrations is the act of "seeing good people beaten down by a system that does not seem to favor those it's supposed to be helping."

"The Focus on Paper instead of the Client"

A common lament of contemporary practitioners is the inordinate amount of time devoted to paperwork, documentation, files, and payment protocol. Such tasks often obscure the real purpose of their profession, respondents say. "The background work—insurance, promotion, documentation, time management," one notes. "This foundational work is more difficult for me than the actual 'work' of teaching and seeing clients!" Being consumed with such mundane duties leads to a "decreased ability to be proactive and creative" in one's work.

"Unhealthy Aspects of the Health Professions"

Many helping professionals noted the unhealthy aspects of their work environment, even as they recognize that their role is to promote well-being in others. Too often, a workday is "totally sedentary," or one rushes from one professional commitment to another. There is little down time on the job and the ever-present "tendency to walk into others' problems and want to help." Social service agencies rarely have the luxury of on-site fitness centers or healthy cafeterias, so practitioners scramble to squeeze exercise regimens and nutritious meals into precious few free moments.

Fatigue in the Field

How do helping professionals experience the aforementioned threats to their health and well-being? Common responses to this question highlight the dangers of prolonged practice without attending to one's own needs. According to respondents, the following are typical reactions to the wear and tear experience on the job:

- "An overload and a difficulty allowing downtime for myself"
- "Feeling like I'm falling into the "martyr trap""
- "Irritability, problems with sleep"
- "Loss of a sense of humor"
- "Muscle tension in the neck, shoulders, back"
- "Emotional exhaustion and burnout"
- "Loss of time given to people in my life"

While humorous in its description, this final response sums up the multiple aspects of living that lead practitioners to become potential victims of professional exhaustion: "stress, overwhelm, depression, isolation, weight gain, very messy apartment, slightly grumpy husband."

Care for the Caregivers

When asked how to meet the demands of professional life, while keeping one's personal life balanced and healthy, those surveyed offered the following advice, clustered in themes that were common among the respondents' answers.

Pay attention to your physical, mental, and spiritual health needs

Every respondent mentioned some variation on the theme of carving out time for physical exercise and taking care to eat a nutritious diet. "An overweight and out of shape practitioner is a disaster waiting to happen," wrote one. "Just add stress and look out!" Veterans believed that learning stress management and stress reduction techniques was critical to high functioning and longevity on the job. As was frequently pointed out, there is no "time" to be "found" in a busy workday, so it is imperative to "find something that is relaxing to you and schedule that regularly." Maintaining a sense of humor also was linked to good health. Encouraged to "laugh everyday at something," new practitioners were warned: "if you do not have a good sense of humor, do not become a helping professional." Humor, respondents felt, was often the only way to deal with problems, diffuse tensions, and model perspective for yourself and those around you. It is additionally important to nurture a spiritual life—however that is defined and expressed—because "a solid spiritual foundation is crucial in providing help and support in a job that is often very lonely regardless of the number of people you work with." Survey participants also spoke of the value of meditation, self-reflection, and frequent life review. Even in the busiest schedules, others found time to volunteer, particularly in arenas unrelated to their daily practice.

Maintain connections to others

Personal connections, respondents believed, provide a social buffer against the stressors inherent in the job. First, practitioners should build support networks of individuals they can trust. As mentioned in the previous quote, serving as a helping professional is a lonely job. Being able to openly and honestly share ideas, explore dilemmas, and seek advice from colleagues are ways to inoculate against isolation. It is especially crucial to have sounding boards for examining the messy problems of Schon's "swampy lowland" where "messy, confusing problems defy technical solutions" (1987, p. 4). "Critical friends" groups or peer supervision may mitigate some of the uncertainty and anxiety involved in launching into practice. In addition to colleagues, former faculty members are important connections to cultivate. They are familiar with one's work and can help one to bridge the transition from novice to more experienced practitioner by continuing to "teach" in more informal ways. " Seek mentors and be a mentor yourself," respondents urge; mentors can be invaluable guides during the early years of work role acquisition and mastery. And when mastery has been achieved, there is great satisfaction in the generativity that accompanies mentoring someone else.

Strive for personal and professional growth.

While those in the helping professions are responsible for the growth of clients in their charge, they are equally responsible for nurturing and supporting their own growth. Setting annual personal and professional development goals along with dedicating time to intellectual renewal are mandatory if one is to avoid stagnation and burnout. Warns one leader, "if you are limiting your reading, you are in the wrong profession!" New practitioners are strongly urged to cultivate personal interests and hobbies outside of work and devote time to them on a regular basis. Although a foreign concept to some, veteran practitioners promote articulating annual professional goals that are personal, as well as professional. This is the key to sustaining a balanced life. As one notes: "As I set professional goals with my staff, I include specific goals related to family and personal time. As we review these monthly, it is a good reminder of balance." A part of remaining "enthusiastic and growing" is keeping the meaningful parts of previous jobs alive in one's present job. Many helping professions who currently are administrators were drawn from the ranks of counselors and therapists, so it makes sense to stay connected to client populations or causes that they cared about prior to moving into administrative ranks. Teaching, coaching, or supervising are other ways to "remind yourself of why you are in the profession."

Hold to your principles and values.

One's principles and values should be the guiding force in deciding what is worth standing up and fighting for, veterans say. Stay out of institutional politics as much as possible, and instead, "try to keep your eye on the big picture." Choosing political battles wisely will conserve energy for those issues that are at the heart of one's belief system. "A solid set of core values and a very well developed sense of character are essential," a seasoned leader writes. "You must know what you believe in, both your personal values and what you believe in professionally." This knowledge also assists one in evaluating whether or not the job has "goodness of fit" at critical developmental points in one's life. Compromising one's most deeply held values to hold on to a job may be a key factor in professional distress and disease.

Balance your personal and professional worlds.

Keeping both worlds in harmony demands certain skills. First among them is prioritizing, because too easily, a practitioner can be absorbed into the life worlds of his/her clients and their issues, or a helping professions administrator can "fall to the wants and demands of every group for professional time...it is essential to remember that one individual cannot do and be everything." One's personal and professional goals should be used as the litmus test for whether or not something is of high priority. Delegating also is a critical skill. Finding skilled people and trusting them to assume meaningful parts of the work role is difficult for those who confuse control with effectiveness, or who believe that they should handle all difficult tasks themselves. Rather than feeling guilty about not be able to do it all, savvy practitioners learn to see delegating as an opportunity to develop others' individual talents and leadership capacities. Healthy leaders also have perspective; they do not mistake their job for their life. Finding balance entails being "selfish" at times. Use extended vacation time and don't allow work to devour weekends or days off completely, veterans say. "Set aside a week end day that is just for you, every week if possible." Avoid the fallacy of believing that "working 20 hours extra per week will reduce the workload."

Before beginning any professional post, it is imperative to talk to significant others about the realities of the job. "Your spouse or significant other must be involved from the beginning when you first become interested. Agreements must be made relative to time and how it will be divided between work and home and family, and the demands must be discussed in great detail." Whenever possible, include family members in appropriate professional activities, and as one's own children go through school, always take time to attend their activities." Perhaps the most valuable piece of advice is to draw an impenetrable line between work and home life, taking care to be present to family when one is with them. "Turn off the job and its worries when not on the clock" and spend quality time with partners, children, and others. Maintain a "home is home, work is work" compartmentalized approach. Build in time and rituals that are "sacred," such as family mealtime, down time with your partner, a morning hike with your dog, or a monthly activity with friends. "Put your all into each as passionately as possible," a veteran leader pleads, "for you have only one soul to share."

Recognize that "we are human"

The temptation to expect more than is humanly possible of oneself seems to be part and parcel of entering the helping profession. Yet, one cannot connect with every client, steer all sessions towards finding solutions, assist each individual in attaining greater attunement, or diagnose each distress or disease accurately. As one individual wrote, a useful strategy for promoting greater health and well-being is "forgiving myself a little for not being 'perfect.'"

Prioritizing one's needs and responsibilities is another aspect of humanity. It can be as basic as "boundary setting and just saying no" and "values prioritization-both in work arenas and in the larger balance of life needs." This activity also can be expressed symbolically, such as "keeping a file of things I'd like to do in the future, but that I don't have time for right now."

A component of such prioritization involves recognizing the primacy of certain life cycle events and embracing them as fully as possible when they occur. While there may be other opportunities for advancing in one's profession or taking on a leadership position, the same cannot be said for being present during a partner's illness or parent's death, or celebrating in first achievements of a young child. Recognizing life's passages and "truly appreciating what is around us" are likely antidotes to the stresses of living life without mindfulness.

Conclusion

Seasoned practitioners believed that the topic of professional health and wellness was a critical one—one that too frequently is ignored. Their suggestions lead to possible recommendations that may mitigate the harsh effects of job demands on individual and family health and well-being. First, at the professional preparation stage, it seems imperative that schools that prepare helping professionals must adopt a more overt curriculum dealing with human development, health and well being. Requiring coursework that integrates research and techniques to deal with time management, stress reduction, physical health and spiritual renewal may be the first step in preparing more resilient practitioners. While there is no question that there is a certain amount of cognate knowledge and sets of practitioner skills that must be inculcated, ignoring the "human curriculum, from a practitioner standpoint, can result in grave consequences. Second, the curriculum also should include honest presentations on strategies for seeking a balanced life; the most obvious seminar leaders would be current helping professionals who have achieved such balance. Information about the importance of understanding the career life cycle and its attendant developmental tasks could assist professionals in better gauging their place in the cycle and the types of strengths and needs that reside in each stage. Such awareness also allows one to "normalize" developmental experiences, thus lessening the feeling that one is isolated and alone in undergoing these passages.

Mentors are identified as the key partners in developing human resiliency in every major study on that topic. Professional mentoring at all stages of the career cycle is critically important as a model for how one can go about constructing a meaningful professional path. At the later stages of the career cycle, mentoring also provides a vehicle for seasoned veterans to leave a legacy to the profession by shaping and nurturing those who will follow them. Engaging in mentoring may help veterans avoid stagnation, cynicism, and lack of purpose at the end of their career.

In addition to good mentoring, honest evaluation must occur throughout the stages of the career cycle. Beginning with appraisal at the pre-service stage, teachers, mentors, and internship supervisors must be willing to assess not only theoretical knowledge and diagnostic skills, but also the "soft" skills necessary for practice. While knowledge can be increased and skills developed and refined, such attributes as empathy, genuine regard for others, humor, compassion, the ability to communicate effectively, and the will to change oneself and inspire others may not be "teachable." Given that these also are related to resiliency, the absence of such qualities may be early indicators of a lack of fit between an individual student and his/her chosen field.

At the job search stage, prospective practitioners should be helped to take stock of their values and family life cycle needs and use these as guidelines in finding jobs that fit them well. In professional development networks, participants should spend as much time on discussion and reading involving the above topics as on the "usual fare." Strategies for addressing impending boredom, burnout, or fatigue must be shared. For example, Skovholt (2001) suggests four primary ways of creating more "novelty, challenge, and energy" professionally: changing one's work tasks; changing one's methods; changing one's population of practice; and changing one's time allocation to certain roles. In the long run, unhealthy practitioners are not assets to the helping profession. Finally, leaders in human services agencies, schools, and other mental health settings must be educated themselves to recognize their responsibility in creating healthy environments so that they can protect their own health and attract and retain high quality practitioners for their institutions. As one respondent notes, "We are human." Yet rarely are contemporary helping professionals encouraged to operate by the principles that are known to encourage optimal human development.

References

Anthony, E.J. & Cohler, B.J. (1987). *The invulnerable child.* New York: The Gilford Press.

Fessler, R. & Christensen, J.C. (1991). *The teacher career cycle: Understanding and guiding the professional development of teachers.* San Francisco, CA: Jossey-Bass.

Figley, C. (1995) (ed). *Compassion fatigue: Secondary traumatic stress disorder in those who treat the traumatized.* New York: Routledge

Garmezy, N. & Rutter, M. (1983). *Stress, coping and development in children.* New York: McGraw-Hill.

Henderson, N. & Milstein, M. (2002). *Resiliency in schools.* Thousand Oaks, CA: Corwin Press.

Mullenback, M. & Shovolt, T. (2001). Burnout prevention and self-care strategies of expert practitioners. In Shovolt, T. (2001). *The resilient practitioner: Burnout prevention and self-care strategies for counselors, therapists, teachers and health care providers.* Needham, Heights, MA: Allyn and Bacon.

Patton, M. (2002). *Handbook of qualitative research.* (3rd ed). Thousand Oaks, CA: Sage Publications, Inc.

Rutter, M. (1979). Protective factors in children as responses to stress and disadvantage. *Primary Prevention in Psychopathology, 3,* 49-74.

Schon, D. (1983). *The reflective practitioner: How professionals think in action.* USA: Basic Books, Inc.

Shovolt, T.M. (2001). *The resilient practitioner: Burnout prevention and self-care strategies for counselors, therapists, teachers and health professionals.* Needham Heights, MA: Allyn and Bacon.

Simon, S. (2008). Primary prevention for career burnout: Building resistance. *Dynamic Chiropractic, 26,* (3). 1-4.

Wang, M.C., & Gordon, E.W. (1994). *Educational resilience in inner-city America.* London, England: Routledge.

Werner, E.E. (1982). *Vulnerable but invincible: A longitudinal study of resilient children and youth.* New York, NY: Adams, Banniser & Cox.

Werner, E.E. (1990). *Protective factors and individual resiliency: Handbook of early childhood intervention.* Cambridge, MA: Harvard University Press.

Werner, E.E., & Smith, R.S. (1992). *Overcoming the odds: High-risk children from birth to adulthood.* Ithaca, NY: Cornell University Press.

Wolin, S.J. & Wolin, S. (1993). *The resilient self: How survivors of troubled families rise above diversity.* New York: Villard.

Biographies of Chapter Contributors

Biographies

Co-Editors/Contributors

Nicholas Young, Ph.D., Ed.D.

Dr. Young holds a B.S. from Austin Peay State University and an M.A. in Clinical Psychology, an M.A. in Human Resources with a focus in Industrial and Organizational psychology, a Masters of Public Administration, a CAGS in School Psychology, and a Doctor of Education in Educational Psychology from American International College. He finished a post-doctoral fellowship in clinical psychology and earned an M.Ed. in Educational Administration and an M.Ed. in Curriculum and Instruction at AIC. Dr. Young completed individualized graduate studies in school counseling as well as a CAGS in Educational Administration at Westfield State College before obtaining a MBA from Western New England College. Dr. Young also holds a Ph.D. from Union Institute & University with a specialization in educational administration. He also earned a Fellowship in Advanced Educational Leadership, a Senior Fellowship in Advanced Educational Leadership and an International Diplomate in Educational Leadership from American International College.

In the broad helping profession, Dr. Young has had significant experience working in school, clinical and education settings. He is a nationally certified counselor, a nationally certified school psychologist, a licensed educational psychologist, a board certified health services provider, and a licensed psychologist with clinical and educational specialties. Dr. Young is also an experienced educator and educational administrator, having served in building and district level school leadership positions. In the field of education, he holds certifications as a superintendent of schools, school principal, special education director, and pupil services administrator, special education teacher, guidance counselor and school psychologist. He participated in, and completed, the prestigious Japan Fulbright Program; and he was appointed as an Associate Editor to the journal "*Insights on Learning Disabilities:*

From Prevailing Theories to Validated Practices.

Dr. Young is a regular presenter at state and national conferences, and he has published in various practitioner journals and books. Prior to joining the graduate faculty at Norwich University in the early 90s, which later became Union Institute & University, he taught graduate level education, counseling and psychology courses at American International College. Dr. Young pioneered the Department of Graduate Psychology and Counseling and has been its Director since its inception in December 2001.

Christine Michael, Ph.D.

Dr. Michael holds an A.B. in British and American Literature from Brown University, an MAT from Brown in secondary English, a M.Ed. from Rhode Island College in developmental reading, and a Ph.D. from the University of Connecticut in education/human development and learning. She also completed post-doctoral studies in school administration and is licensed as a principal/superintendent. Prior to joining Vermont College on the faculties of the M.A. and CAGS Programs, she taught at Antioch/New England Graduate School, Castleton State College, Southern Vermont College, North Adams State College, and Rhode Island College.

Dr. Michael also served a seven-year stint as a higher education administrator, first as academic coordinator and then as the Academic Dean at Southern Vermont College. She has taught at the middle school and secondary levels, has been on the faculty and has supervised Upward Bound and transitional summer programs for minority students, and is an independent consultant to schools systems.

She also has been committed to family and early childhood literacy through projects for Head Start, the Center for the Book, and the Council on the Humanities. Currently, she is a National Program Director for the Foundation for Excellent Schools. Recent publications and national presentations have centered on such topics as faculty resiliency, adult learning, and the career life cycle.

Contributors (in alphabetical order)

John L. "Jay" Allen Jr., Psy.D.

Dr. Jay Allen received his doctorate in clinical psychology with an emphasis in counseling from Southern California University for Professional Studies. His master's degree was earned at Vermont College of Union Institute & University's Department of Graduate Psychology and Counseling; his BFA is from New York University. He also studied at Warnborough College in Oxford, England, and the Alfred Adler Institute in New York. Dr. Allen is an addictions counselor in a state-sponsored treatment facility in Maryland, where he leads group therapy and has been instrumental in introducing hypnotherapy. He is currently co-leading a study on the effects of buprenorphine.

Warren Corson III, Ph.D., NCC, LPC, ACS

Dr. Warren Corson III who is known as "Doc Warren" by most clients and many colleagues, earned a Certificate in Human Services from Tunxis College, an Associates in Drug & Alcohol Rehabilitation Counseling from Tunxis College, a Bachelor's degree in Psychology from Vermont College of Norwich University, a Master's degree in Counseling Psychology from Vermont College of Norwich University, a Certificate of Advanced Graduate Studies in School Counseling from Vermont College of Norwich University, a Certificate in Advanced Graduate Studies in Counselor Education and Supervision from Vermont College of the Union Institute & University and a Ph.D with a specialization in Counselor Education & Supervision from Union Institute & University. He is a Licensed Professional Counselor, a Nationally Certified Counselor, a certified school counselor and an Approved Clinical Supervisor. Dr. Corson has been a counselor, guest lecturer and trainer in the field of counseling for many years. He is an outspoken advocate for social change and social justice; believing that all people have a right to equal access to health and mental health care regardless of their ability to pay. He is currently the Clinical & Executive Director of Community Counseling Center of Central Connecticut Inc. (www.cccofcentralct.org, www.docwarren.org) which is a not-for- profit organization he founded in 2005 to provide free or low cost counseling to those in need in the central Connecticut area. Dr. Corson was named Counselor of the Year (2007-2008) by the Connecticut Counselor Association for his contributions to the field. He has appeared on many television shows, newspaper and magazine articles; most recently appearing on *Health Care Now* and in *Counseling Today*.

Emily J. Davis, Psy.D.

Dr. Davis holds a B.A. in Psychology from Boston University and a Doctorate in Clinical Psychology from the Massachusetts School of Professional Psychology. She is a Licensed Mental Health Counselor and National Certified Counselor trained in Behavioral Neurology and neuropsychology through Harvard Medical School, and in Cognitive-Developmental Therapy through the Language and Cognitive Development Center of Boston, MA. She holds status as an expert witness in clinical psychology and in child therapy in two Massachusetts court systems.

Dr. Davis has a range of professional interests in the field of psychology. Her past research interests included studies of the frontal lobe, executive functioning, and ADHD. Current research interests relate to outcome studies of adolescent and family interventions in the community mental health sector. She is also interested in psychopharmacology and multidisciplinary integration of services.

Dr. Davis has applied her knowledge of psychology in a range of settings from program development and consultation to direct provision of psychotherapy. She has worked in urban, suburban, and rural public schools delivering psychological assessment and counseling services, and has developed and supervised curricula in therapeutic and residential schools. She designed a federally funded vocational rehabilitation program for urban populations with major mental illness, and founded an educational consulting firm. Dr. Davis has special interests in treating clients with dual diagnoses, and children and adolescents with major mental illness and their families.

Ann-Marie DeGraffenreidt, JD

Ann-Marie DeGraffenreidt earned her JD from New York University School of Law and her undergraduate degree from Yale University. She is admitted to the practice of law in the state of Connecticut. Throughout her legal career, which spans over 20 years, she has concentrated on the intersection of child welfare (including juvenile delinquency), mental health, and education. She has represented the state, local school districts, and children at various points in her career. In addition, she has taught on the college level and currently teaches on the graduate level as an adjunct. She has presented at state and national conferences. She is currently engaged in research concerning diversion programs and recidivism.

Dorothy Firman, Ed.D.

Dr. Firman received her doctorate in Consulting Psychology from The University of Massachusetts, an M.A. in Transpersonal Psychology from Beacon College, and a B.A. from Goddard College. She is a licensed mental health counselor, a board certified hypnotherapist, a practicing psychotherapist, a psychosynthesis coach and a consultant to businesses and organizations, specializing in group dynamics and interpersonal relationships.

Dr. Firman is the director of Psychosynthesis training at the Synthesis Center, in Amherst, Massachusetts, as well as a member of the affiliated counseling staff. She is a workshop leader, presenting nationally and internationally on a variety of topics. She is the editor of *Reflections on Ecopsychosynthesis*, the first journal of the National Psychosynthesis Association. She is the coauthor of *Daughters and Mothers: Making it Work* (2003), coauthor of the New York Times, best selling *Chicken Soup for the Mother and Daughter Soul* (2003) and coauthor of *Brace for Impact: Miracle on the Hudson, Survivors Share Their Stories of Near Death and Hope for New Life.* (2009).

Sharon A. Hoferer, MA

Sharon Hoferer received her MA in psychology/clinical mental health counseling from Union Institute & University. She completed an 18-month internship at an inner city clinic working as the primary counselor for children, adolescents, and their families. Ms. Hoferer is an editorial assistant for the Div 56 (trauma division) newsletter of the American Psychological Association and currently serves as a co-moderator for a professional listserv on dissociation. Her background includes over 20 years as a teacher and program administrator in academic settings (K- Adults), a training coordinator of parenting programs for at-risk parents, and a crisis intervention counselor.

Richard Judah, D.Ed.

Dr. Judah received his BA in Psychology from California State University in Sacramento, an M.A. in Psychology and Counseling from Assumption College, and a D.Ed. in Counselor Education from Pennsylvania State University. He is a licensed Clinical Psychologist and a board certified health services provider and has extensive experience in the mental health field as a clinician and clinical services director. Dr. Judah is an Approved Clinical Supervisor (ACS). He maintained a successful private practice in psychology for over 25 years and taught graduate courses in psychology and special education at Fitchburg State College and Assumption College. Dr. Judah is also a school psychologist with extensive experience in the testing and diagnosis of learning problems and developmental disabilities. He is a Senior Special Education Consultant with Futures Health Corps, a company providing special education and clinical services and management to 25,000 students and individuals. He has training and experience in neuropsychology and forensic psychology, has published articles, and is currently engaged in research in the following areas: Complimentary approaches to the treatment of Attention Deficit Hyperactivity Disorder (ADHD); Learning Disabilities and Executive Functioning Disorder; and Application of computers in the counseling process.

Raven (Karen Weinert) Kim, RN, MA

Raven earned a Master of Arts in Counseling Psychology from Union Institute & University and is a Licensed Professional Registered Nurse. Raven is a Board Eligible National Certified Counselor and holds certifications in Transpersonal Clinical Hypnotherapy and Eye Movement Therapy, earned through the Transpersonal Hypnotherapy Institute in Boulder, Colorado. She has an extensive background in the field of expressive arts and integrating mind-body wellness. Her work in the field of addictions and with trauma survivors shaped her graduate research. Raven currently serves as Team Leader and Trauma Specialist with ACT (Assertive Community Treatment) an evidence-based practice. The multidisciplinary team is consumer driven and works toward assisting severely mentally ill individuals maintain independence within their community. Raven was a co-presenter of a half-day workshop at the International Society for the Study of Trauma and Dissociation Conference in Philadelphia, in Nov. 2007.

Scott Rice, Ph.D.

Dr. Rice received a Bachelor of Science degree from Boston College in Business Management, and a Master's degree, and Certificate of Advanced Graduate Studies from the University of Massachusetts-Boston in School Psychology. He holds a Ph.D. in Counseling Psychology from the University of Massachusetts-Amherst.

Dr. Rice is licensed as a psychologist and health care provider in Massachusetts, with specialization in clinical psychology and school psychology. He is state certified as a school psychologist in Massachusetts and holds national certification in school psychology (NCSP). He is an Approved Clinical Supervisor (ACS).

Dr. Rice's professional experiences include the practice of psychology in public school settings, and providing psychotherapy services to children and families in inpatient and outpatient settings, schools, and in private practice. His interests include psychological assessment and intervention for learning and emotional problems, and individual and group counseling with children and adolescents.

Theresa (Terry) E. Ruby, PT, PhD, GCS, LMHC,

Dr. Ruby is currently affiliated with Morton Hospital and Medical Center Homecare and Community Counseling of Bristol County (CCBC), in Taunton, MA. She is a Board Certified Geriatric Physical Therapist, a Licensed Mental Health Counselor, and holds a doctorate in Gerontology and Counselor Education and Supervision. She is Massachusetts State Court Mediator with specialty training in Elder Mediation. Dr. Ruby is the main visiting mental health clinician for the Elder Mobile Outreach Team (EMOT) through CCBC. She is a member of the American Physical Therapy Association, the American Mental Health Counselor Association, and the Massachusetts Association of Older Americans.

Cynthia Rutledge, Ed.D.

Dr. Cynthia Rutledge earned an Ed.D. in Educational Psychology from American International College in Springfield, MA. She holds several additional graduate degrees in school psychology and education leadership from Southern Connecticut State University and from the University of Hartford. Dr. Rutledge is a state and nationally certified school psychologist and a certified school administrator. Her career has included college level teaching, school psychological services and administration in K-12 public education settings, and private practice. She has extensive experience in the evaluation of learning disabilities and social and emotional disturbances, therapeutic interventions with conduct disordered youth, and the alternative education of delinquent and at-risk youth. She has published articles, presented at various conferences, both state and nationally, and is currently engaged in researching issues surrounding the effects of education and recidivism of delinquent youth.

Jennifer A. Smith, MA, Clinical Mental Health Counseling

Ms. Smith received a BA in English from Tufts University and an MA in Clinical Mental Health Counseling from Union Institute & University. Her seven-year career has included supportive counseling, case management and group facilitation with homeless youth in shelter settings, as well as program design, on call crisis response, mediation, and ongoing support to families with adolescents. Ms. Smith is currently responsible for program outcomes evaluation and research-based program development at a non-profit youth service bureau in northeastern Vermont. In addition, she is a research assistant for the New England Network for Child, Youth and Family Services, and runs Calmposition, her small writing consultation business. Ms. Smith's interests include adolescent development, neuropsychology, and narrative and art therapy.

Walter Stephaniv, Ph.D.

Dr. Stephaniv received his BA in Honors Psychology from McMaster University, Magna Cum Laude. He obtained his Master's Degree in Pre-Clinical Psychology and a Ph.D. in School Psychology, both from Ball State University. He obtained two postdoctoral programs, one in Clinical Respecialization and the second in Clinical Psychopharmacology. His internships were at the Hines Veterans Administration and the Federal Bureau of Prisons, respectively.

Dr. Stephaniv was in the first iteration of the Postdoctoral Program in Clinical Psychopharmacology, and was also it's co-director at the Illinois School of Professional Psychology (ISPP). In addition Dr. Stephaniv was the Director of the Clinical School Psychology Program at ISPP. Dr. Stephaniv has also been on faculty at Loyola University and has been an active member of several leading hospital allied health staff.

Dr. Stephaniv has had extensive experience in training interns, having been Chief Psychologist and Director of Clinical Training at University Hospital and was responsible for leading their faculty into APA accreditation. He is an Approved Clinical Supervisor (ACS). Dr. Stephaniv is dually licensed as a clinical psychologist-health service provider and school psychologist. Dr. Stephaniv's interests are in neuropsychology, psychopharmacology, cross cultural issues, and Epicureanism.

Elizabeth Strazar, MA

Ms.Strazar is a licensed professional counselor in the state of Connecticut with 22 years of counseling experience. She also holds a certification in humanistic-transpersonal psychotherapy and extensive training in expressive arts modalities. Elizabeth has utilized expressive arts therapy with adolescents at risk, women at midlife, and in her work with individuals experiencing the symptoms of prolonged and severe psychological disorders. She currently specializes in helping clients access and utilize creative self-expression in addressing experiences of crisis and transition

Sandra Valente, Ph.D., LADC, LPC

Dr. Valente is Professor of Psychology at Naugatuck Valley Community College in Waterbury, Connecticut, where she coordinates the Drug and Alcohol Recovery Counselor Program. She also works as a psychotherapist in private practice. She has over 20 years of experience working with individuals with mental illness, co-occurring disorders, and 12 years experience in the addictions field. She has presented at local and national conferences on topics which include addiction issues, abandonment, ethics in counseling, and grief and loss.

Frank Vargo, Ed.D.

Dr. Vargo is a professor of Graduate Studies in the Department of Graduate Psychology and Counseling at Union Institute and University. He holds a Doctor of Education in Educational Psychology, and formal post-doctoral clinical training in clinical psychology and pediatric/developmental neuropsychology. Dr. Vargo also holds graduate degrees in clinical psychology/child clinical development, school neuropsychology, school psychology, counseling, education, and a bachelor's degree in music education. He is also pursuing current graduate/doctoral studies in teaching and learning, curriculum, and educational administration and leadership. In addition to his teaching responsibilities at Union Institute & University, Dr. Vargo is also the director of *The Fireside Center for Psychological and Educational Services* in Leominster, Massachusetts, and he is a practicing school psychologist. Dr. Vargo has published widely in the areas of clinical and educational psychology, education practice and policy, learning disabilities, special education, and counseling.

Dr. Vargo is a licensed psychologist and health care provider, a nationally certified school psychologist, a licensed educational psychologist, a licensed/certified guidance counselor, a licensed/certified school adjustment counselor and social worker, a licensed/certified special education director, and a licensed/certified music educator.

Dr. Vargo's specializations include clinical/pediatric/developmental neuropsychology, diagnosis and treatment of children and adults with learning disabilities and neurodevelopmental disorders, differential diagnosis in special education, and curriculum development for specific clinical and special education populations.

Dr. Vargo is also a highly regarded adult, child, and family therapist.

Andy Vengrove, Ed.D.

Dr. Vengrove holds his B.A. from Evergreen State College and a M.A. in Counseling Psychology from Tufts University with a focus in School Psychology, and a Doctor of Education in Educational Psychology from American International College. Dr. Vengrove is a Licensed Educational Psychologist and is a certified by the Commonwealth of Massachusetts as a school psychologist and school social worker/school adjustment counselor.

Dr. Vengrove has extensive experience working in the public schools completing psychological evaluations, working with at-risk children and adolescents in regular and special education programs, providing individual and group counseling and teacher/program consultation, and coordinating building-based and system wide crisis intervention programs.

Dr. Vengrove has taught undergraduate and graduate courses and has been a Field Faculty Advisor at Vermont College. He specializes in crisis intervention within the schools and communities and has presented workshops and taught graduate courses on this topic. His other areas of interest include the assessment of social and emotional difficulties in children and adolescents, alternative approaches to working with at-risk students, and issues related to cultural diversity both within the field of counseling and in the public schools.

Robert F. Wubbenhorst, MA

Mr. Wubbenhorst earned a BA from Norwich University and a MA in Psychology from Vermont College of Union Institute & University. He is psychotherapist in Vermont as well as the Assistant Director of the Master of Arts program in Psychology and Counseling for Union Institute & University in Brattleboro, VT. His career includes experience with criminal offenders, severely mentally ill adults in a day treatment setting, as well as school-based clinical work in secondary education. He has extensive experience in crisis intervention as well as critical incident stress counseling.

www.ingramcontent.com/pod-product-compliance
Lightning Source LLC
Chambersburg PA
CBHW070555270326
41926CB00013B/2325